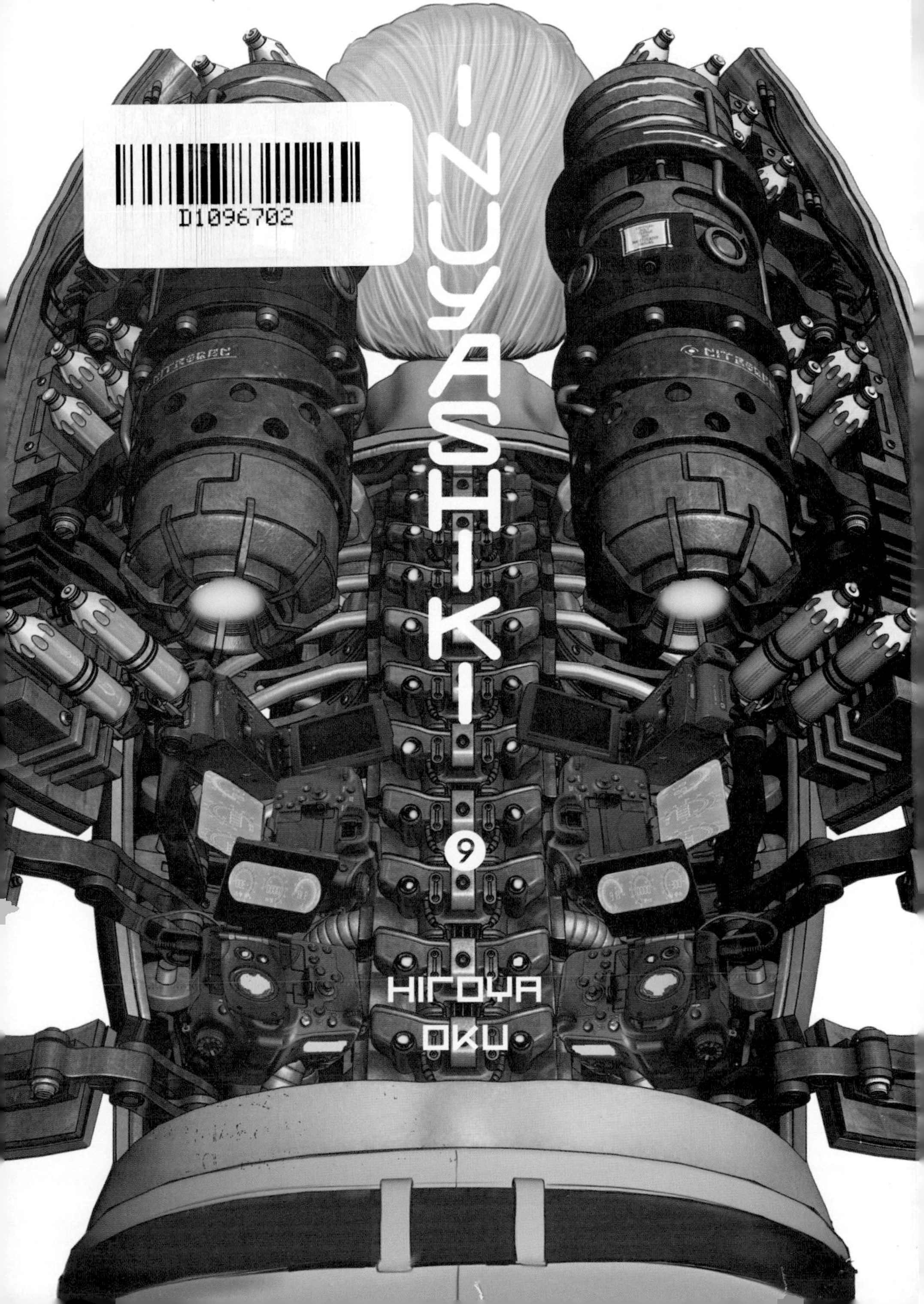
INUYASHIKI
9
HIROYA
OKU

INUYASHIKI 9 CONTENTS

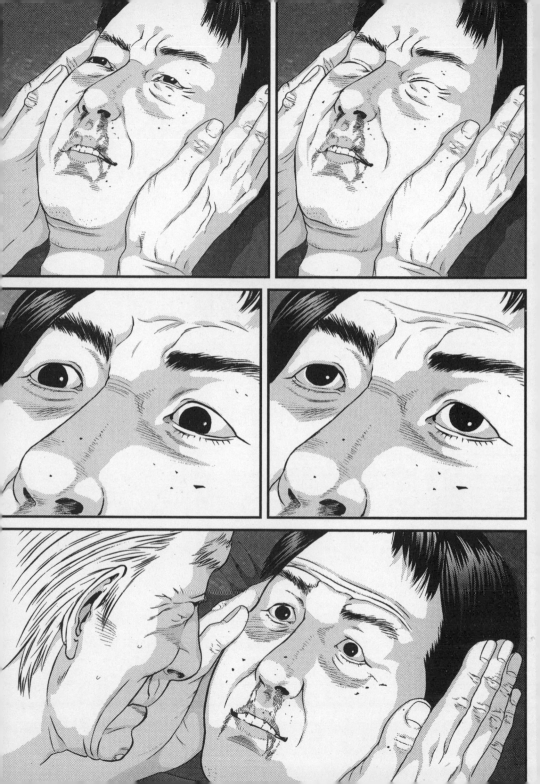

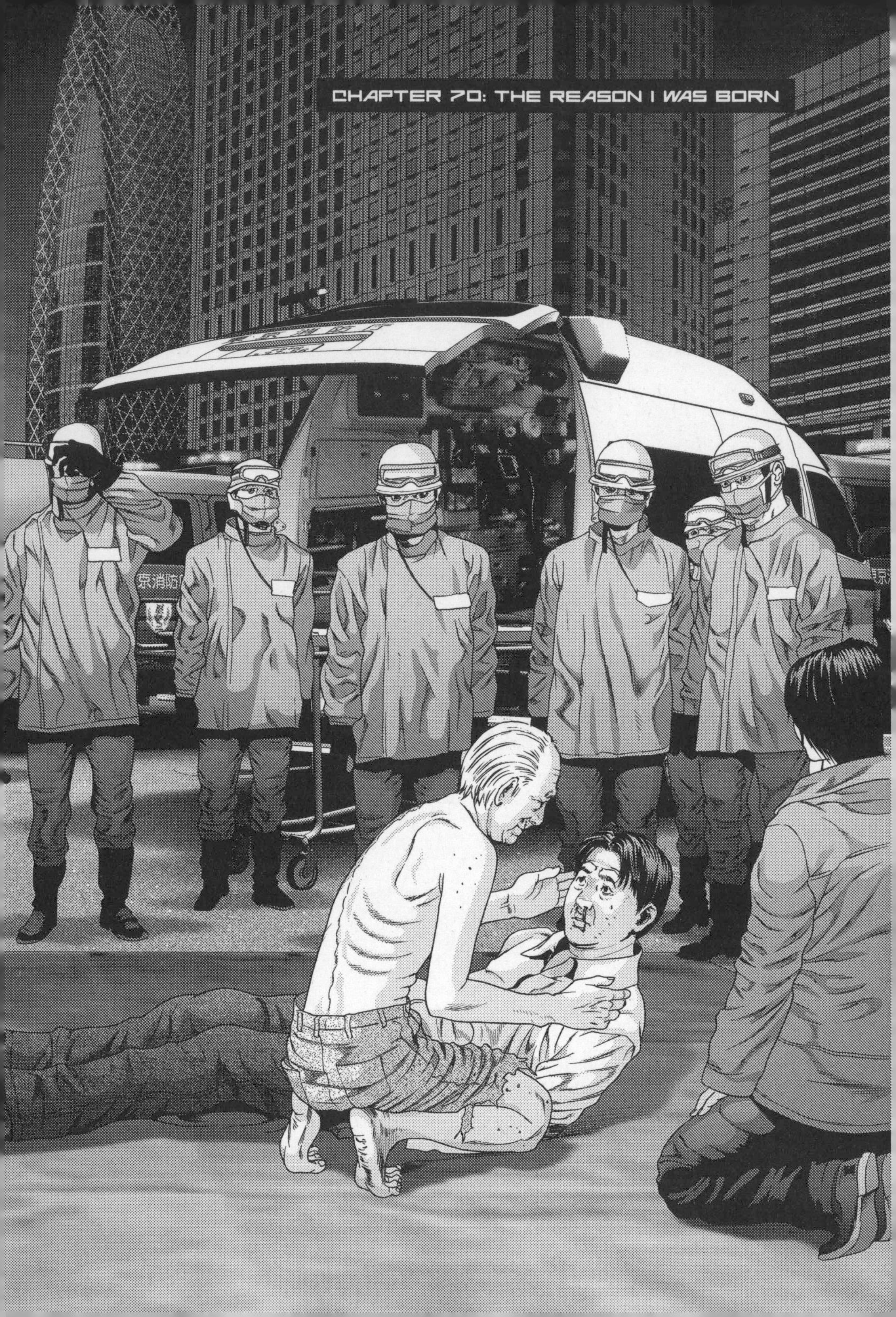
CHAPTER 70: THE REASON I WAS BORN

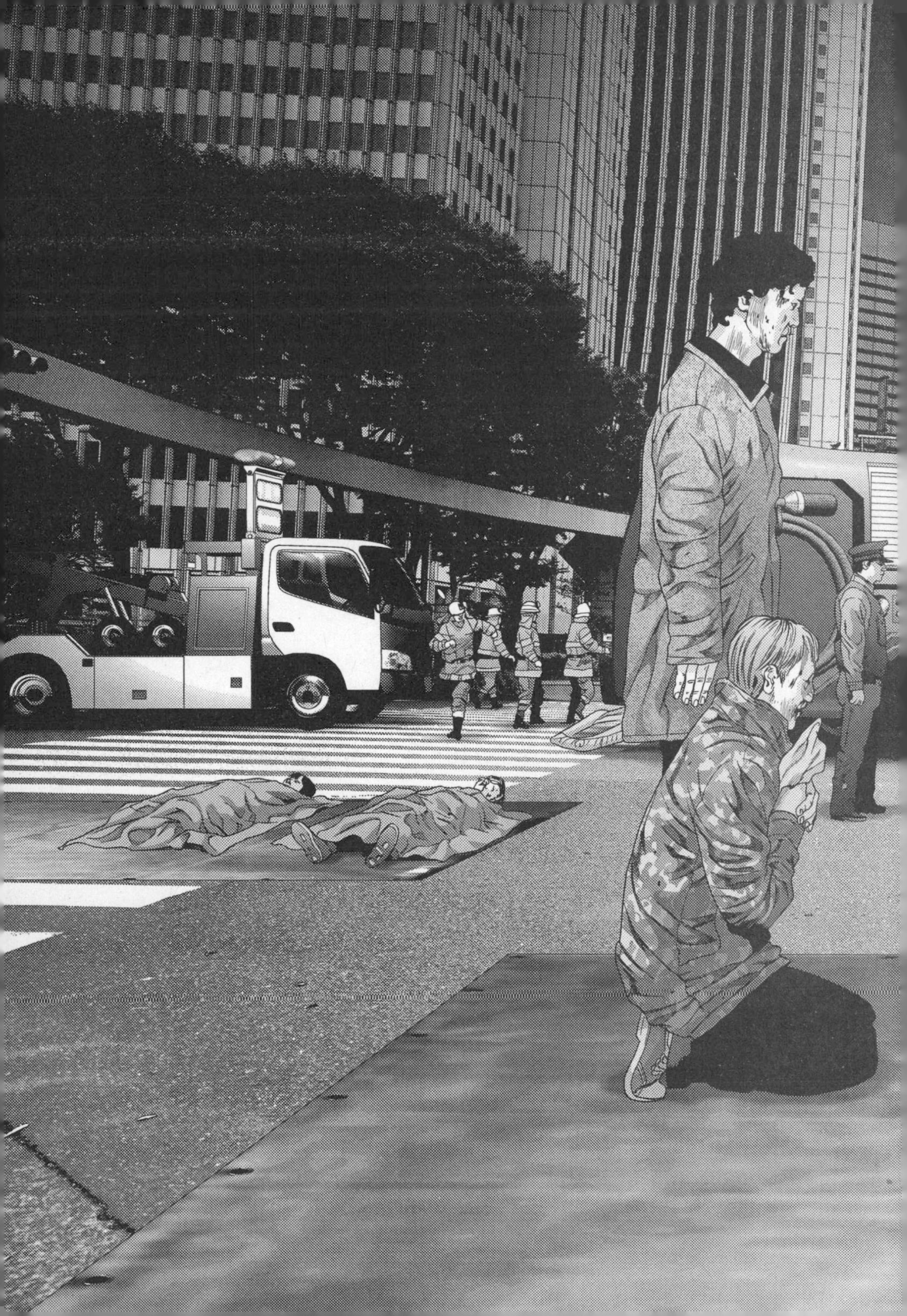

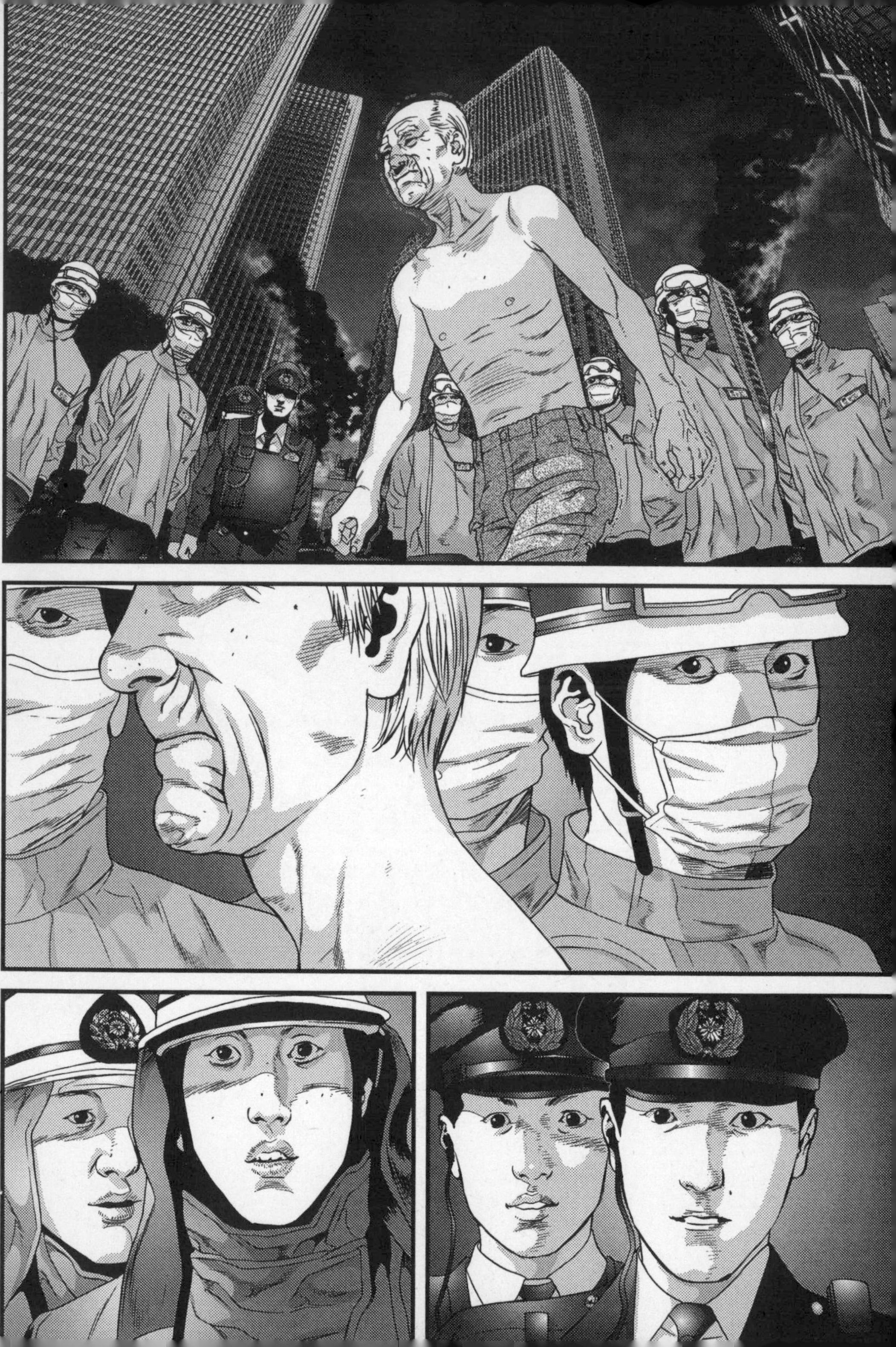

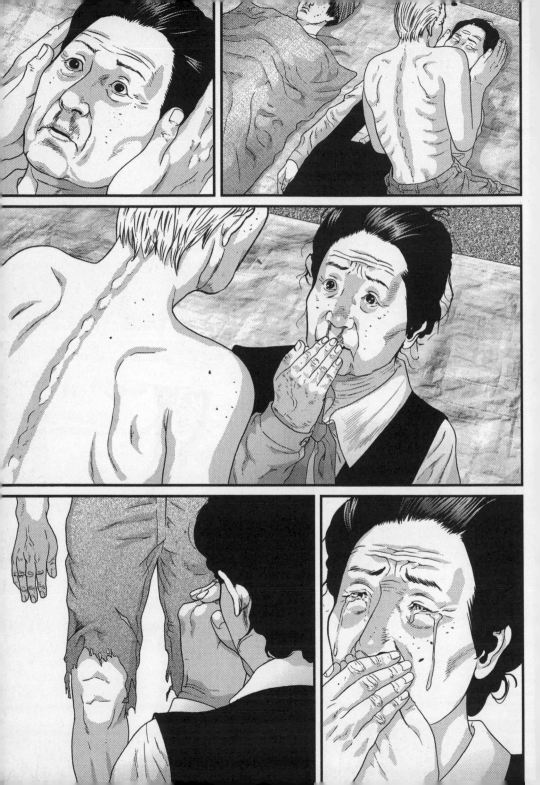

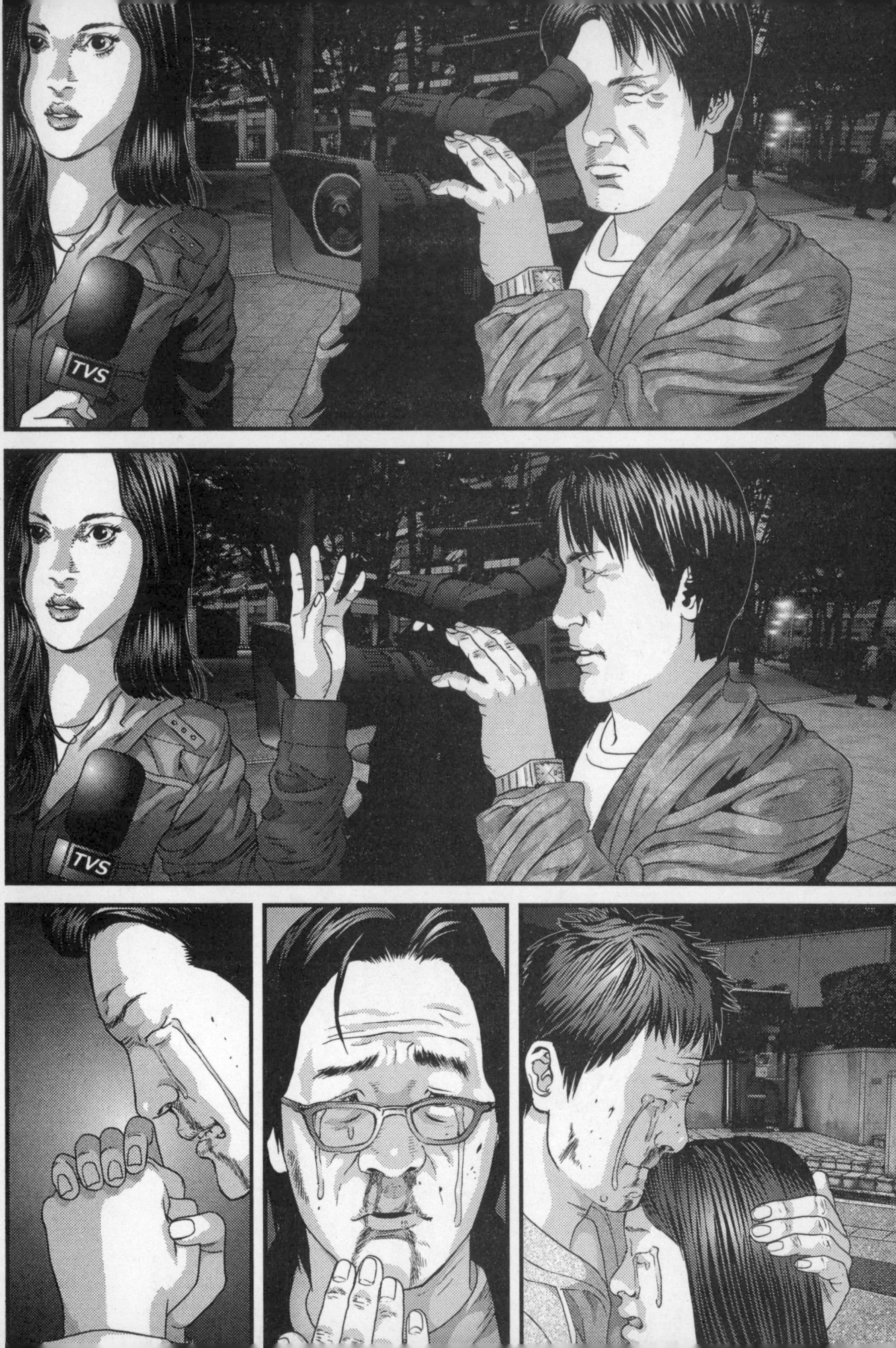
TVS
TVS

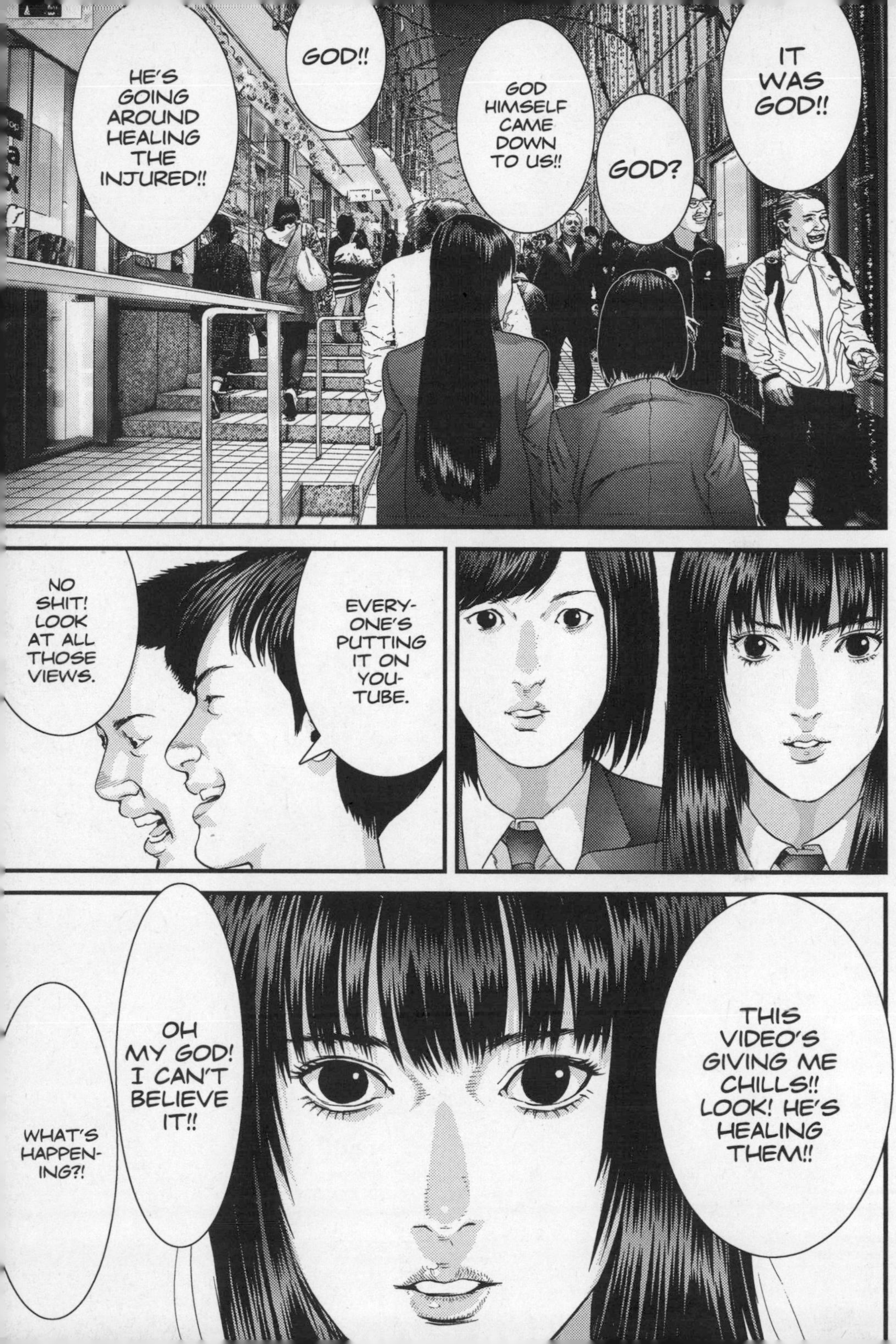
IT WAS GOD!!
GOD?
GOD HIMSELF CAME DOWN TO US!!
GOD!!
HE'S GOING AROUND HEALING THE INJURED!!
EVERY-ONE'S PUTTING IT ON YOU-TUBE.
NO SHIT! LOOK AT ALL THOSE VIEWS.
THIS VIDEO'S GIVING ME CHILLS!! LOOK! HE'S HEALING THEM!!
OH MY GOD! I CAN'T BELIEVE IT!!
WHAT'S HAPPEN-ING?!

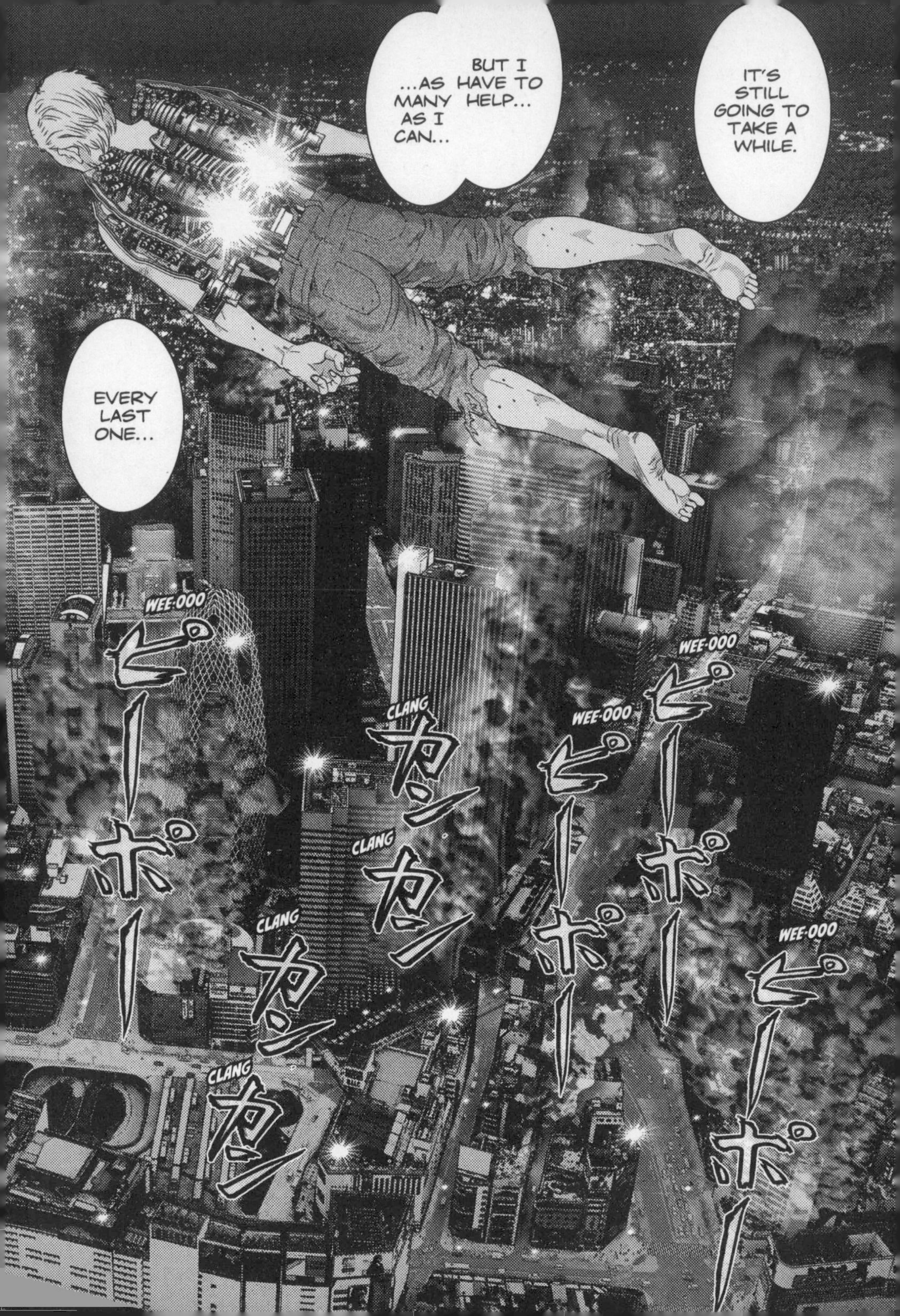
IT'S STILL GOING TO TAKE A WHILE.
BUT I HAVE TO HELP... ...AS MANY AS I CAN...
EVERY LAST ONE...
WEE-OOO
ピーポー
WEE-OOO
ピーポー
WEE-OOO
ピーポー
CLANG
カン
CLANG
カン
CLANG
カン
CLANG
カン
WEE-OOO
ピーポー

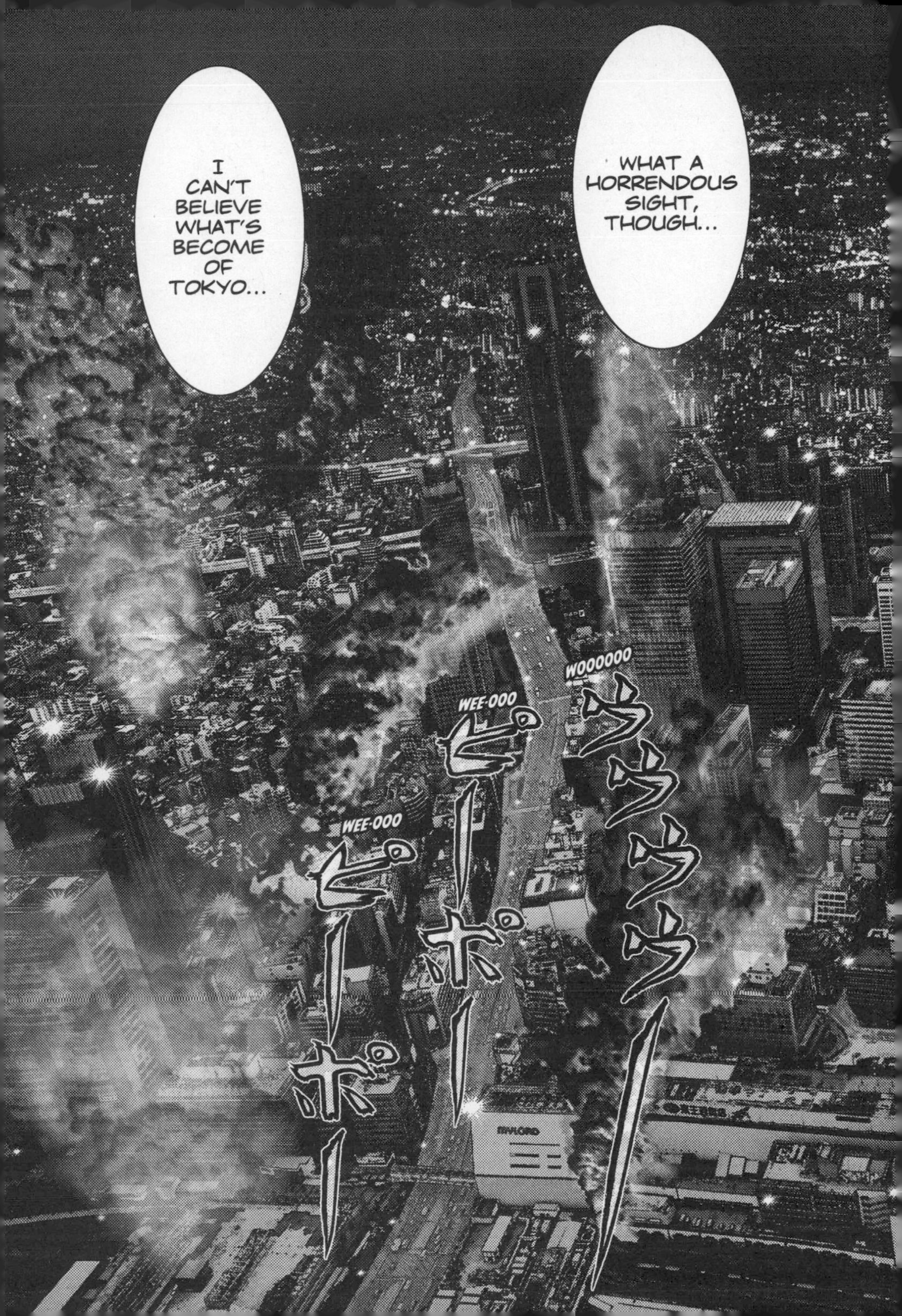
WHAT A HORRENDOUS SIGHT, THOUGH...
I CAN'T BELIEVE WHAT'S BECOME OF TOKYO...
WOOOOOO
ウウウー
WEE-OOO
ピーポー
WEE-OOO
ピーポー

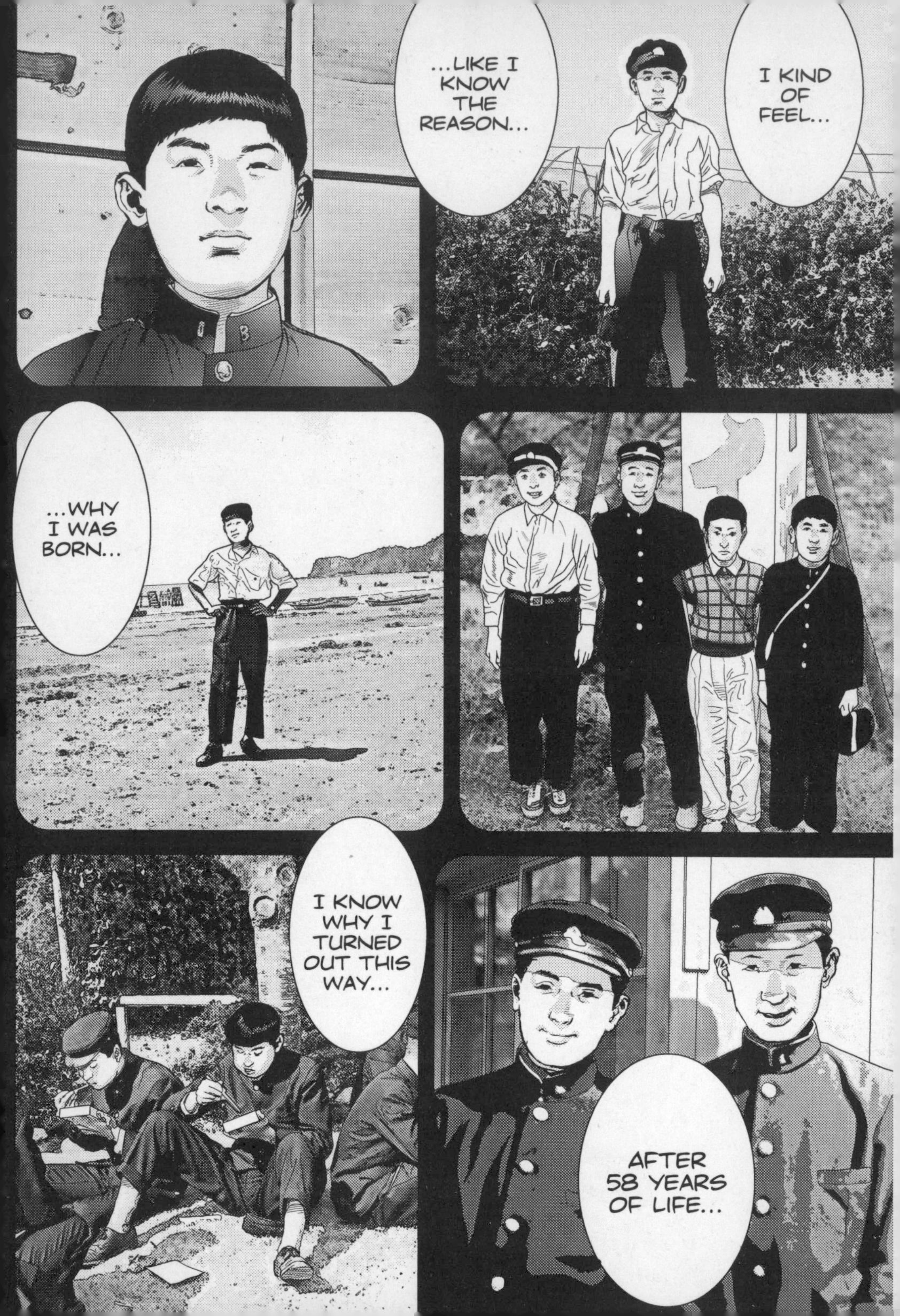
I KIND OF FEEL...
...LIKE I KNOW THE REASON...
...WHY I WAS BORN...
AFTER 58 YEARS OF LIFE...
I KNOW WHY I TURNED OUT THIS WAY...

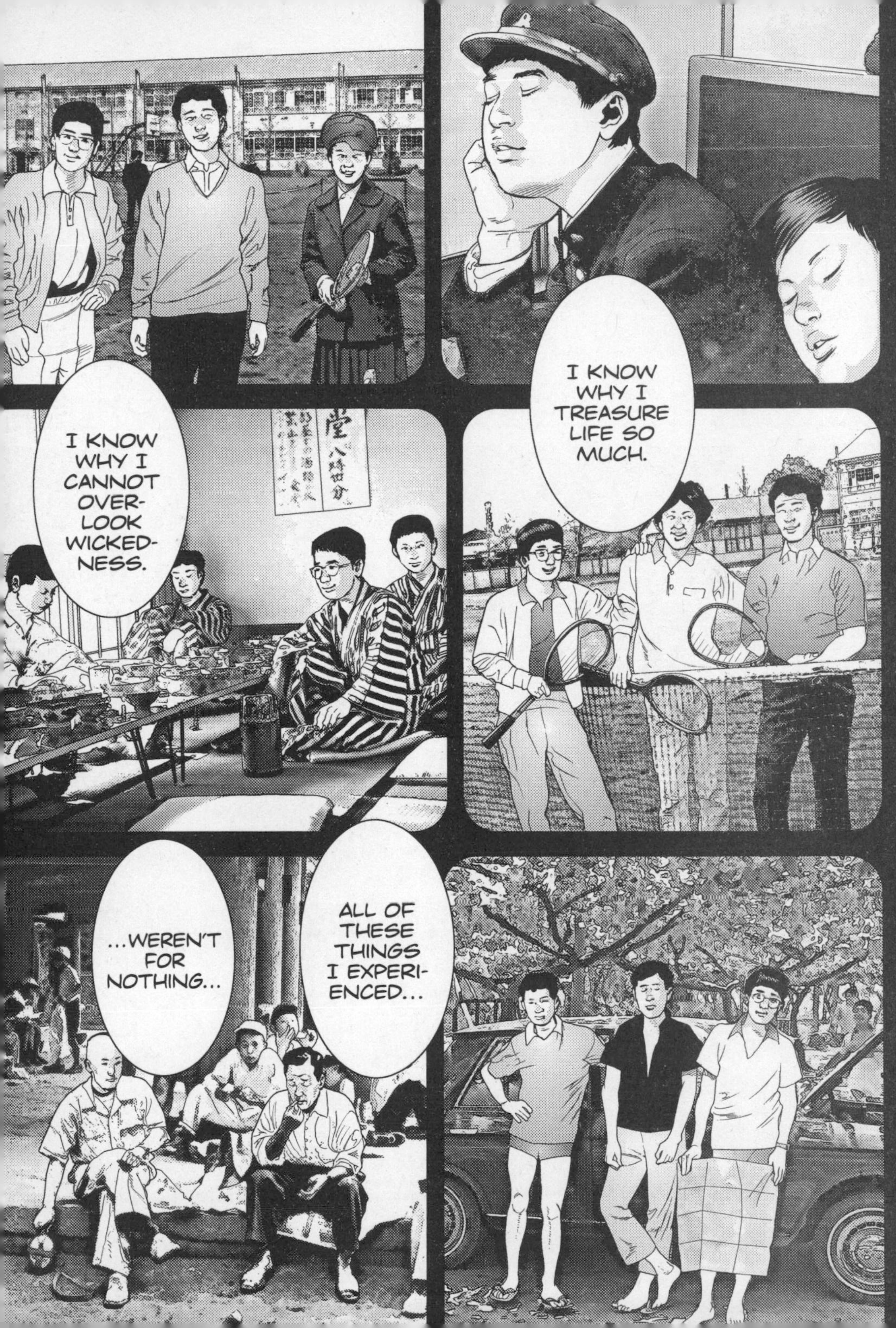
I KNOW WHY I TREASURE LIFE SO MUCH.
I KNOW WHY I CANNOT OVER-LOOK WICKED-NESS.
ALL OF THESE THINGS I EXPERI-ENCED...
...WEREN'T FOR NOTHING...

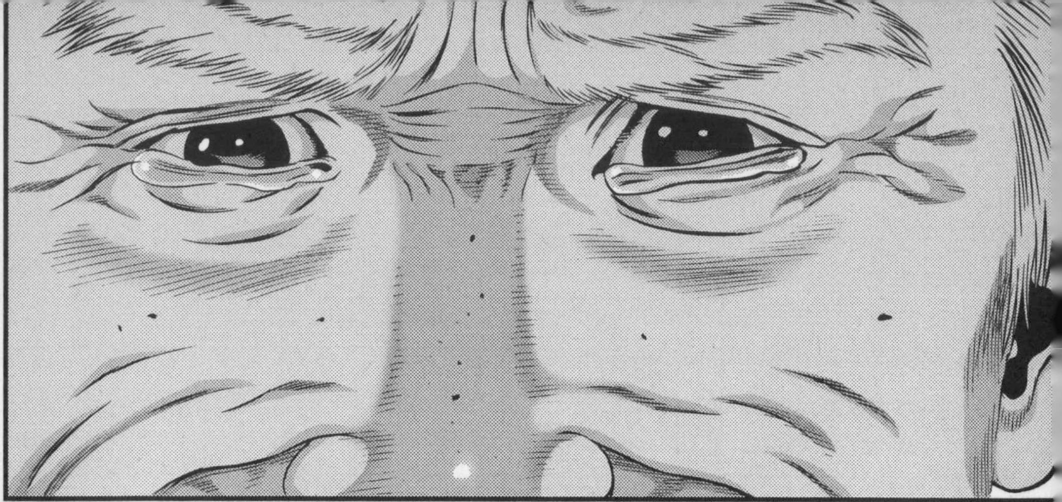

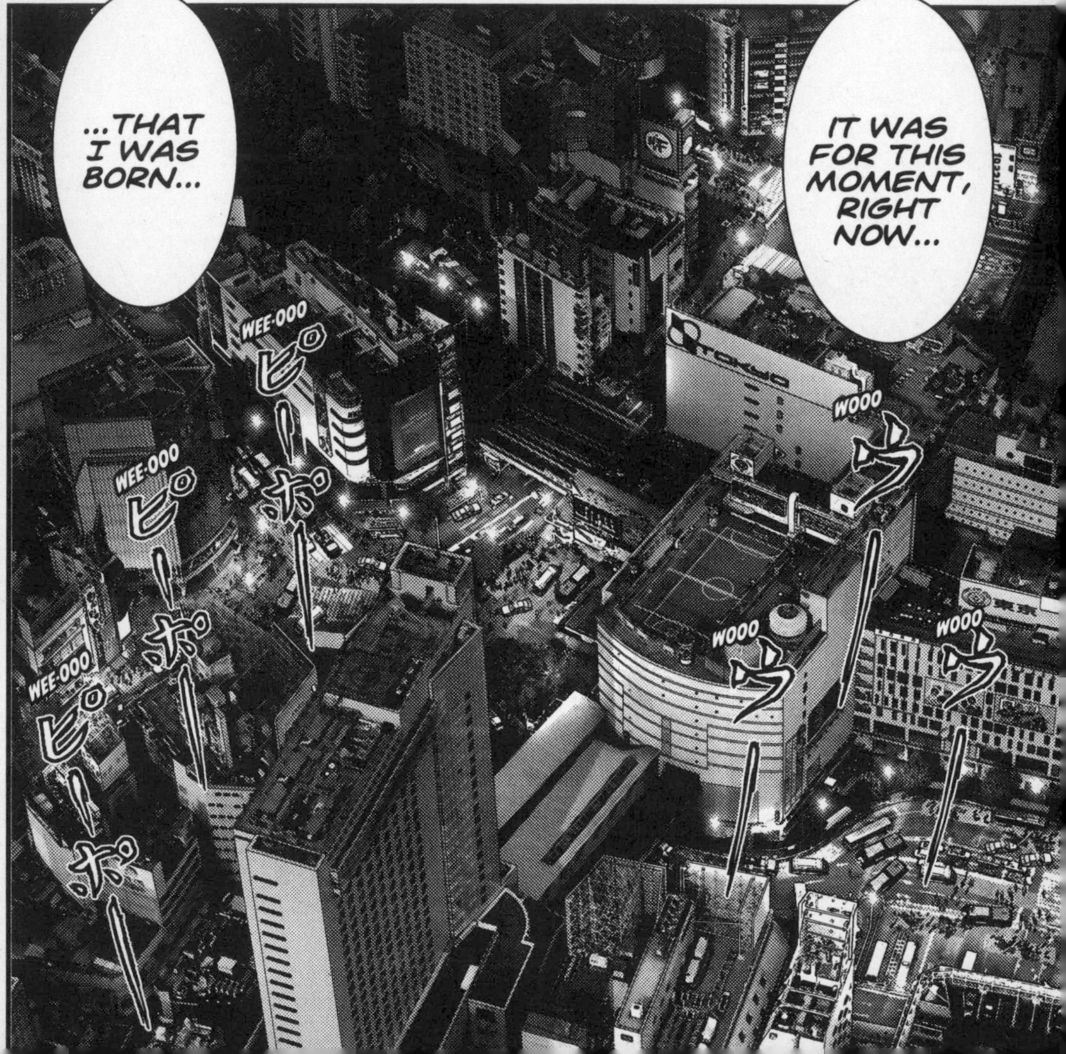
IT WAS FOR THIS MOMENT, RIGHT NOW...
...THAT I WAS BORN...
WOOO
ウー
WOOO
ウー
WOOO
ウー
WEE-OOO
ピーポー
WEE-OOO
ピーポー
WEE-OOO
ピーポー

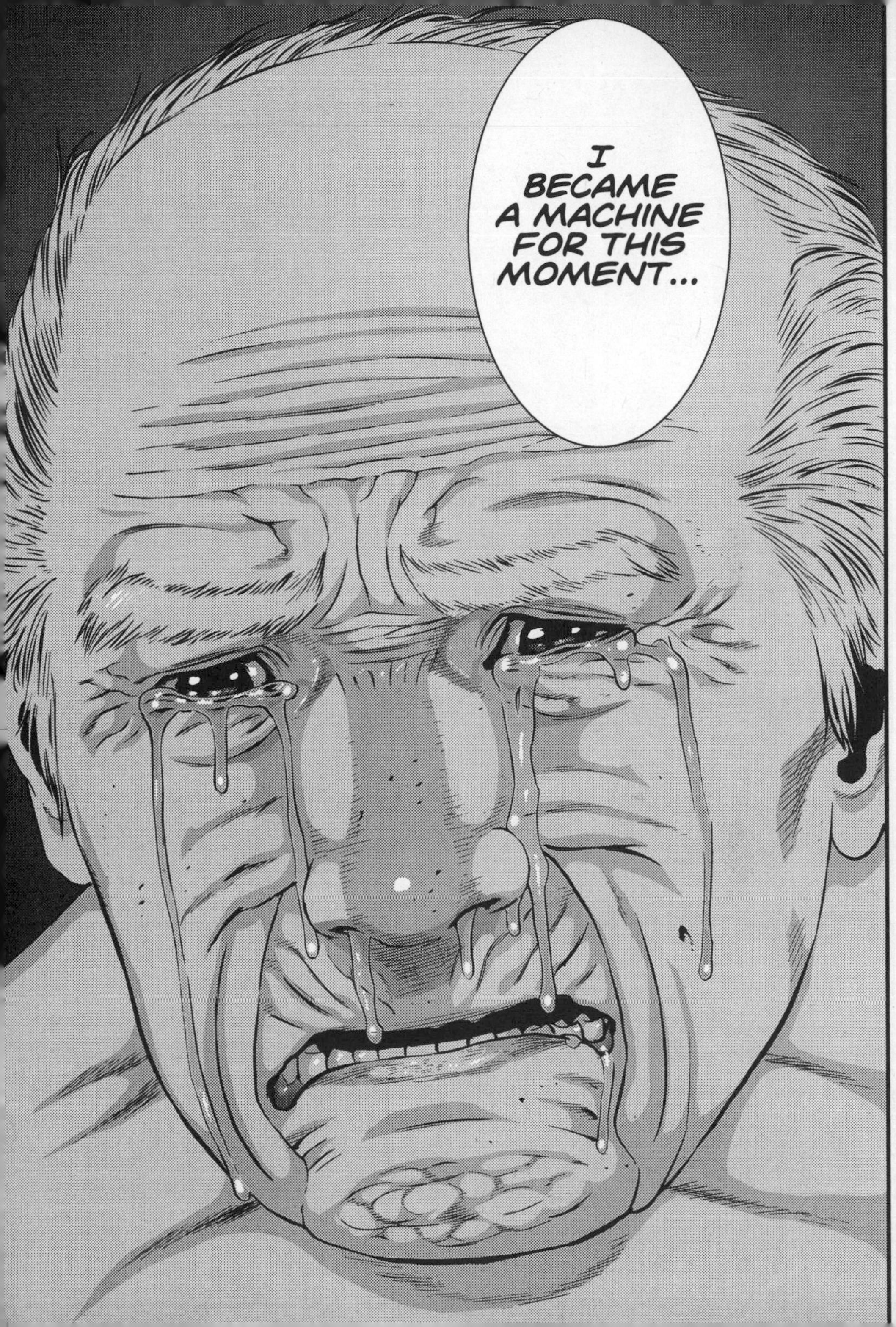
I BECAME A MACHINE FOR THIS MOMENT...

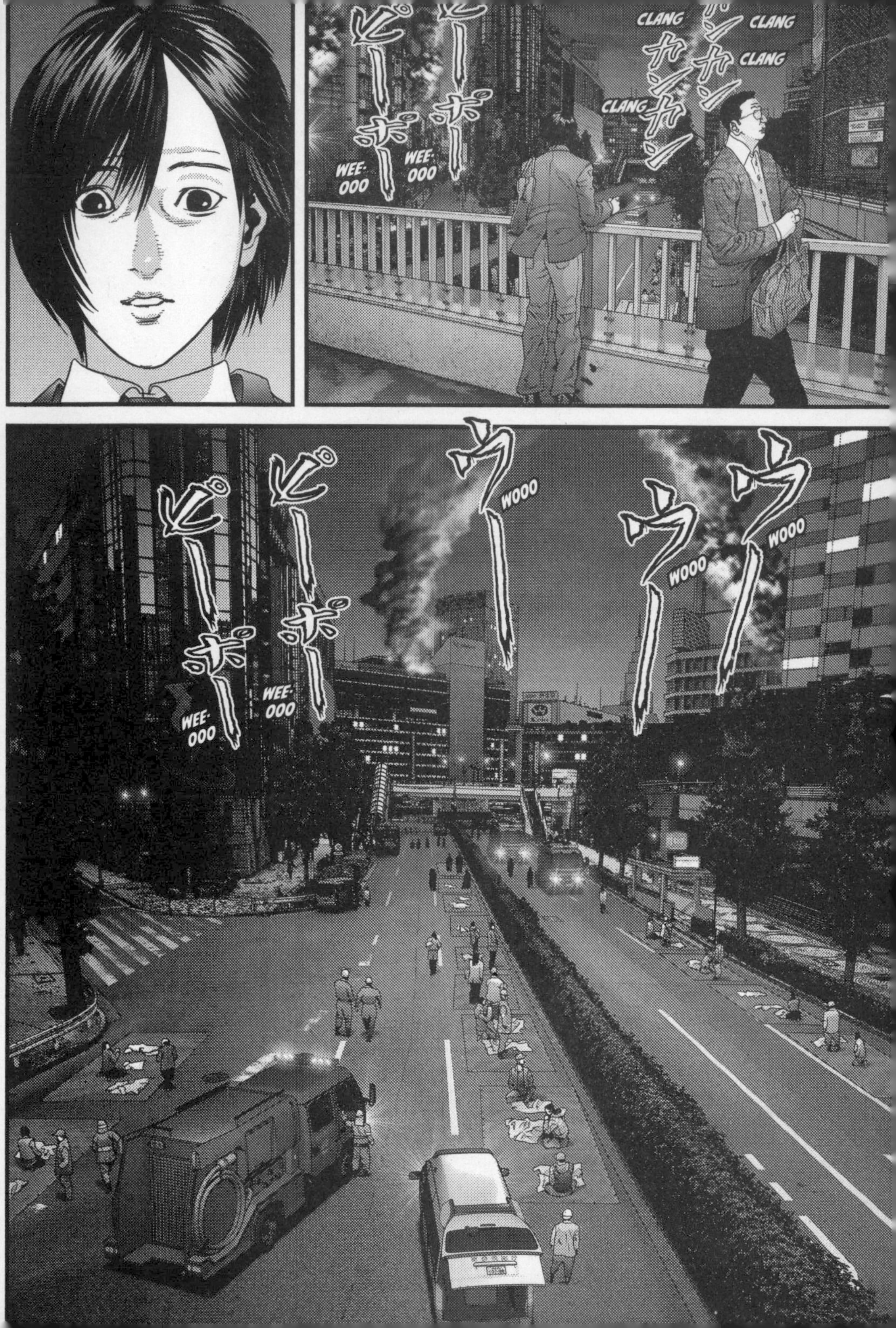
CLANG
CLANG
CLANG
CLANG
WEE-OOO
WEE-OOO
WOOO
WOOO
WOOO
WEE-OOO
WEE-OOO

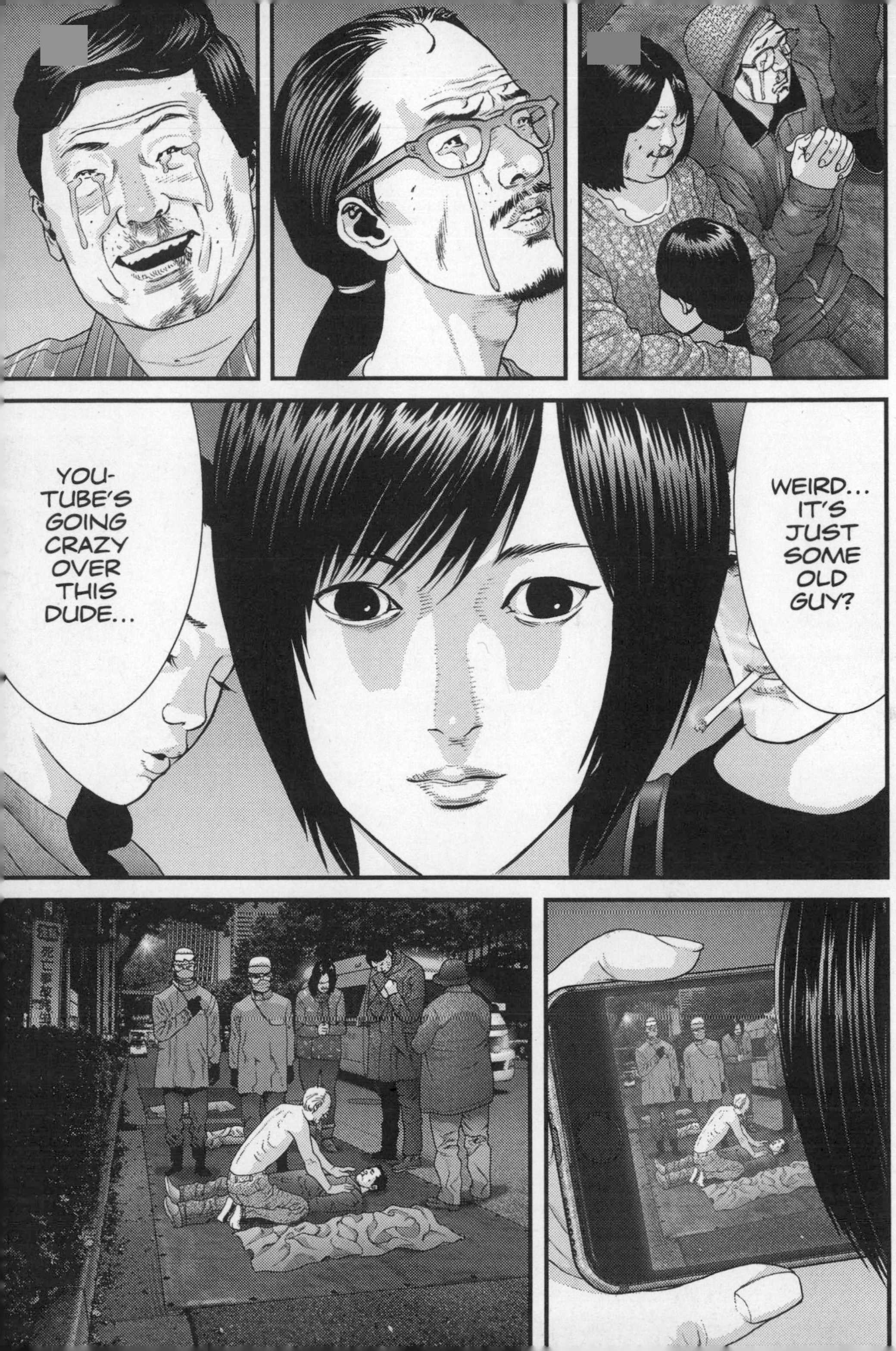
WEIRD... IT'S JUST SOME OLD GUY?
YOU-TUBE'S GOING CRAZY OVER THIS DUDE...

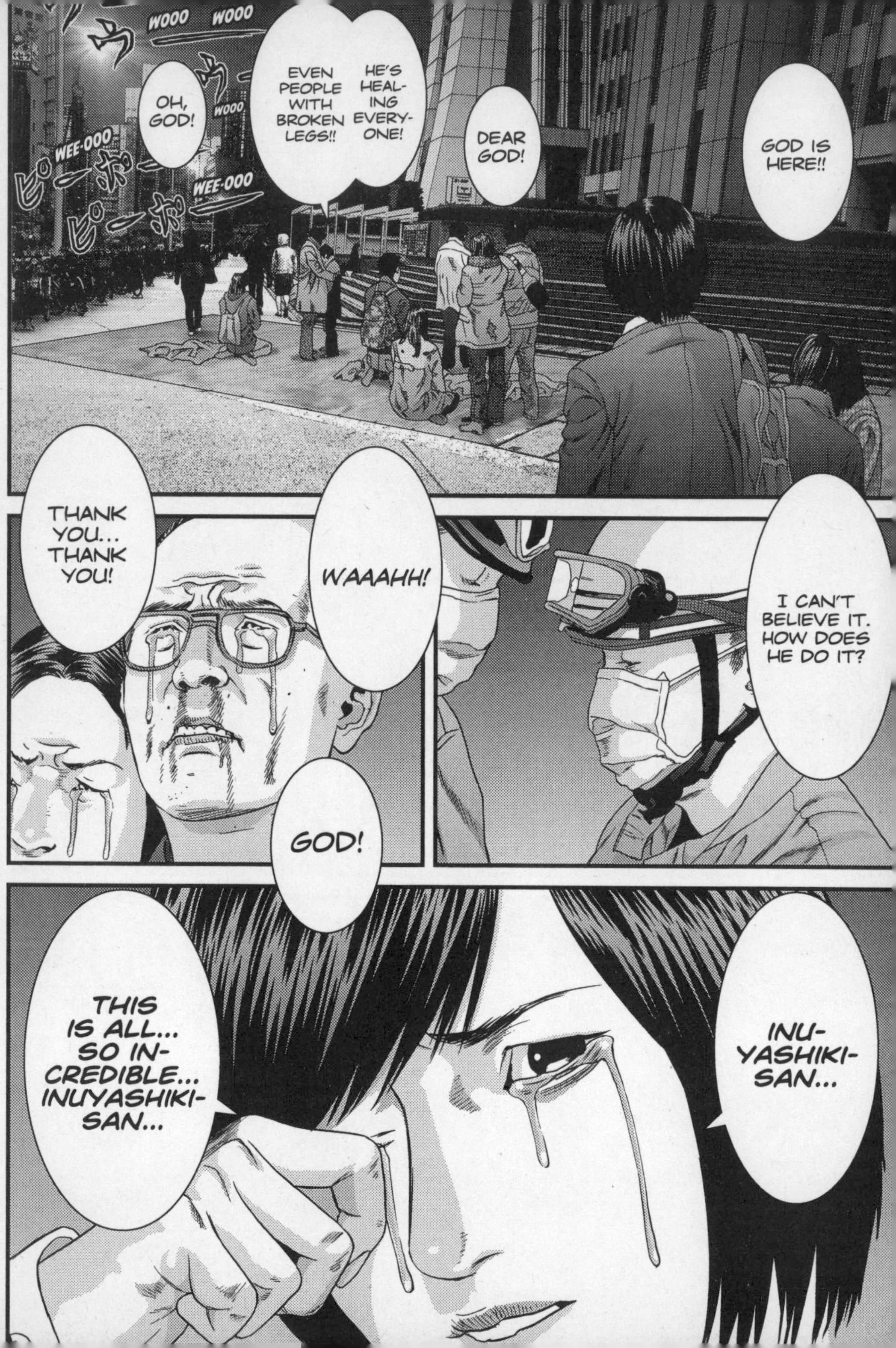
GOD IS HERE!!
DEAR GOD!
HE'S HEAL-ING EVERY-ONE!
EVEN PEOPLE WITH BROKEN LEGS!!
OH, GOD!
WOOO WOOO
WOOO
WEE-OOO
WEE-OOO
I CAN'T BELIEVE IT. HOW DOES HE DO IT?
WAAAHH!
THANK YOU... THANK YOU!
GOD!
INU-YASHIKI-SAN...
THIS IS ALL... SO IN-CREDIBLE... INUYASHIKI-SAN...

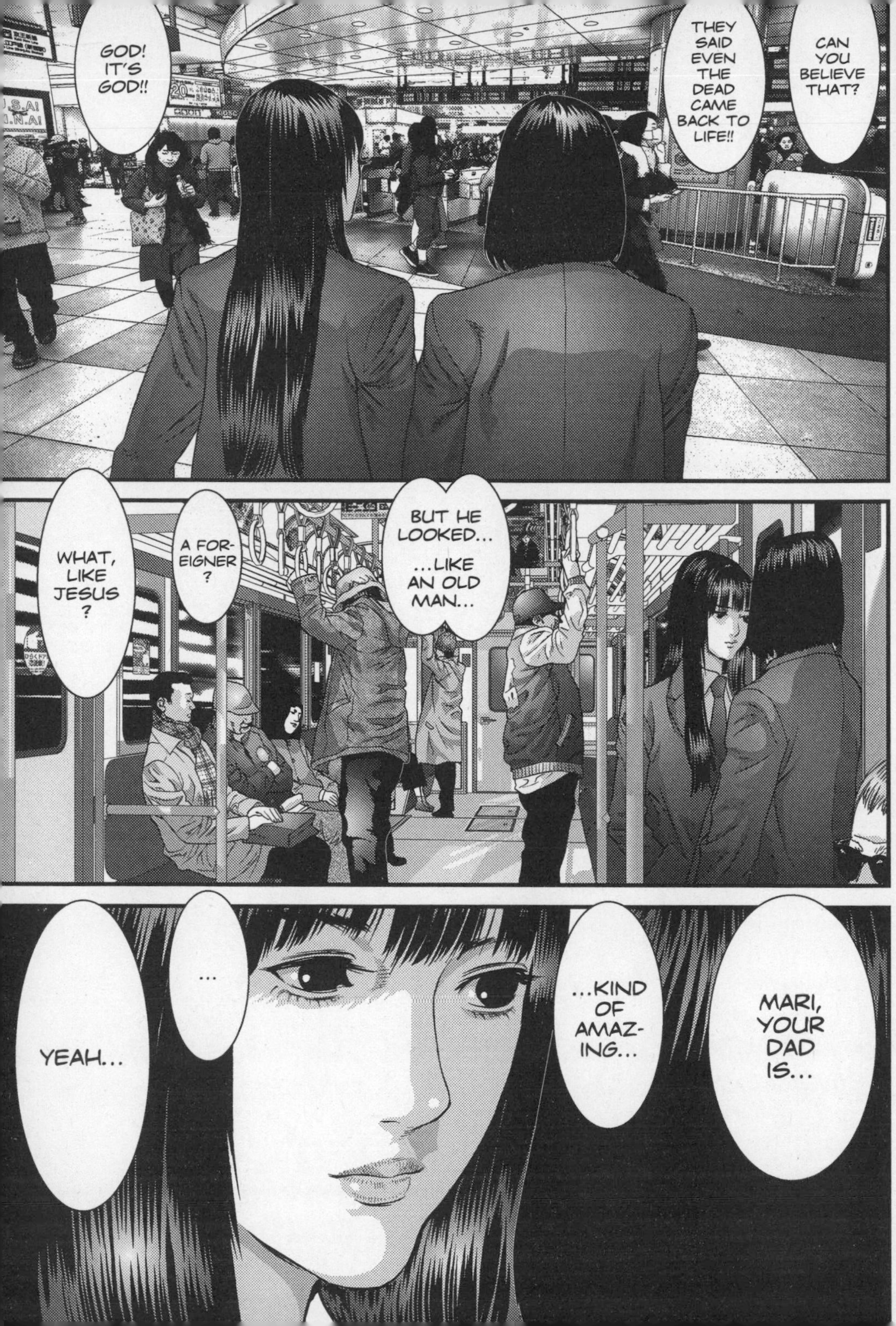
CAN YOU BELIEVE THAT?
THEY SAID EVEN THE DEAD CAME BACK TO LIFE!!
GOD! IT'S GOD!!
BUT HE LOOKED... ...LIKE AN OLD MAN...
A FOR-EIGNER?
WHAT, LIKE JESUS?
MARI, YOUR DAD IS...
...KIND OF AMAZ-ING...
...
YEAH...

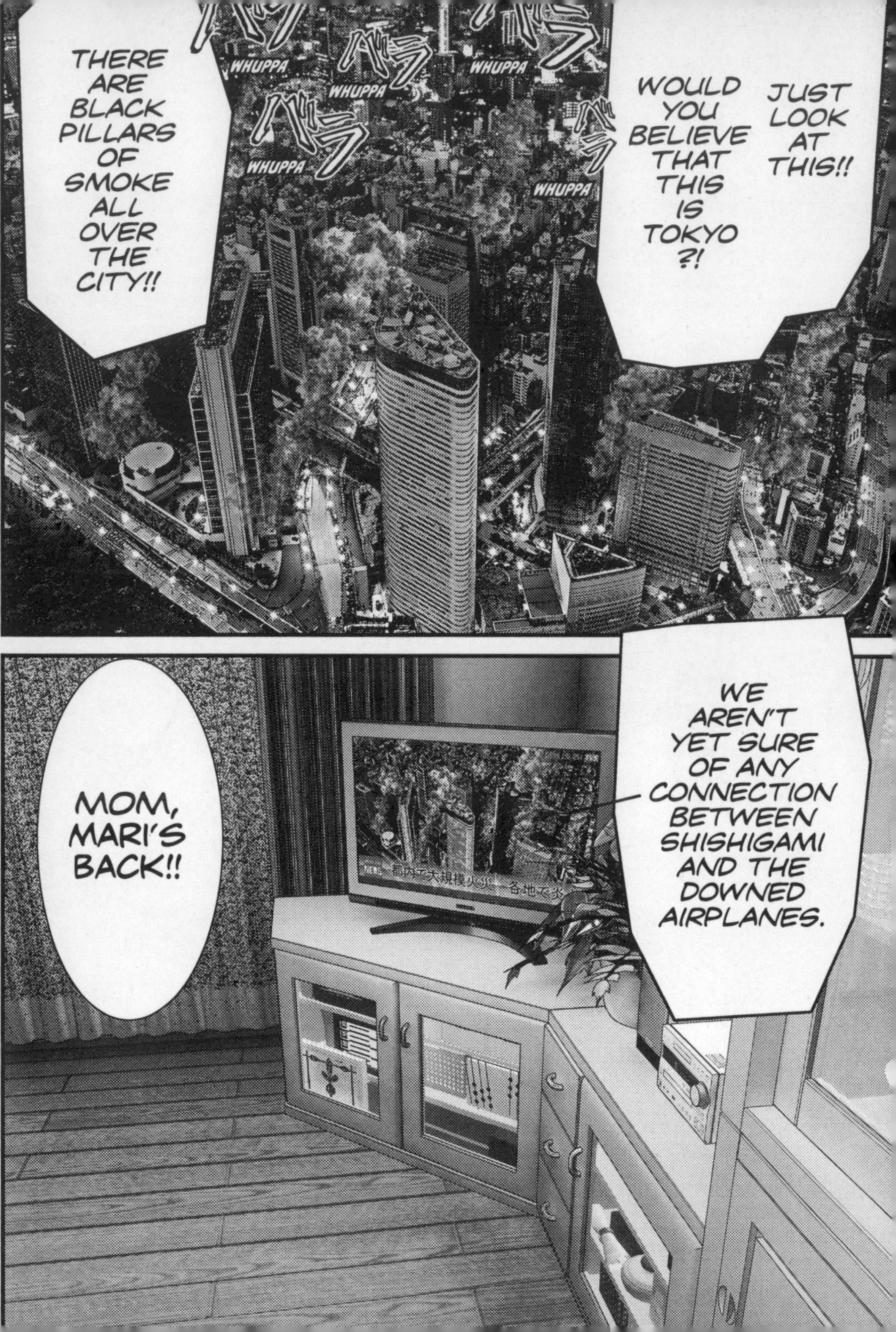
WHUPPA
WHUPPA
WHUPPA
WHUPPA
WHUPPA
JUST LOOK AT THIS!!
WOULD YOU BELIEVE THAT THIS IS TOKYO?!
THERE ARE BLACK PILLARS OF SMOKE ALL OVER THE CITY!!
WE AREN'T YET SURE OF ANY CONNECTION BETWEEN SHISHIGAMI AND THE DOWNED AIRPLANES.
MOM, MARI'S BACK!!

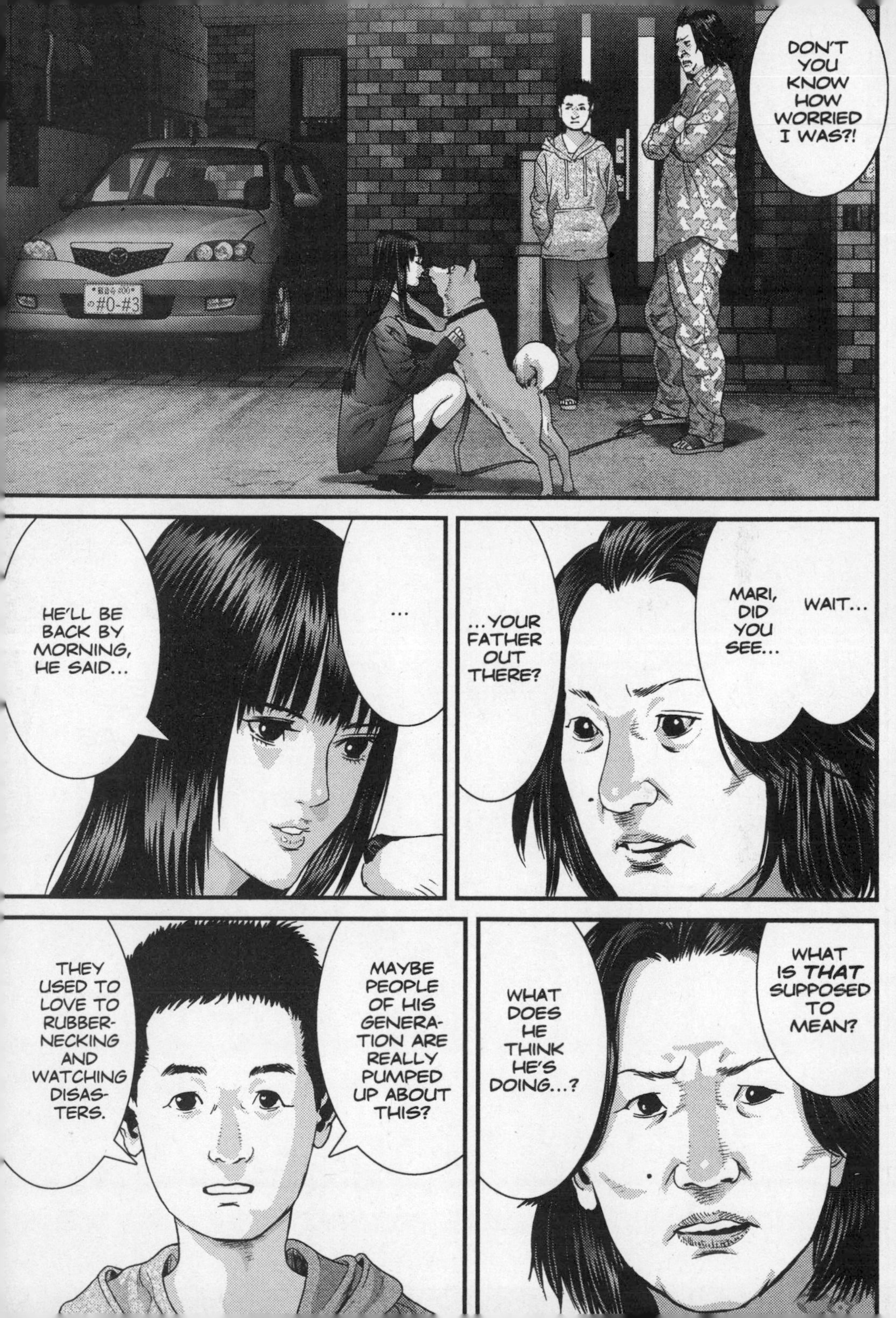
DON'T YOU KNOW HOW WORRIED I WAS?!
WAIT...
MARI, DID YOU SEE...
...YOUR FATHER OUT THERE?
...
HE'LL BE BACK BY MORNING, HE SAID...
WHAT IS *THAT* SUPPOSED TO MEAN?
WHAT DOES HE THINK HE'S DOING...?
MAYBE PEOPLE OF HIS GENERATION ARE REALLY PUMPED UP ABOUT THIS?
THEY USED TO LOVE TO RUBBER-NECKING AND WATCHING DISAS-TERS.

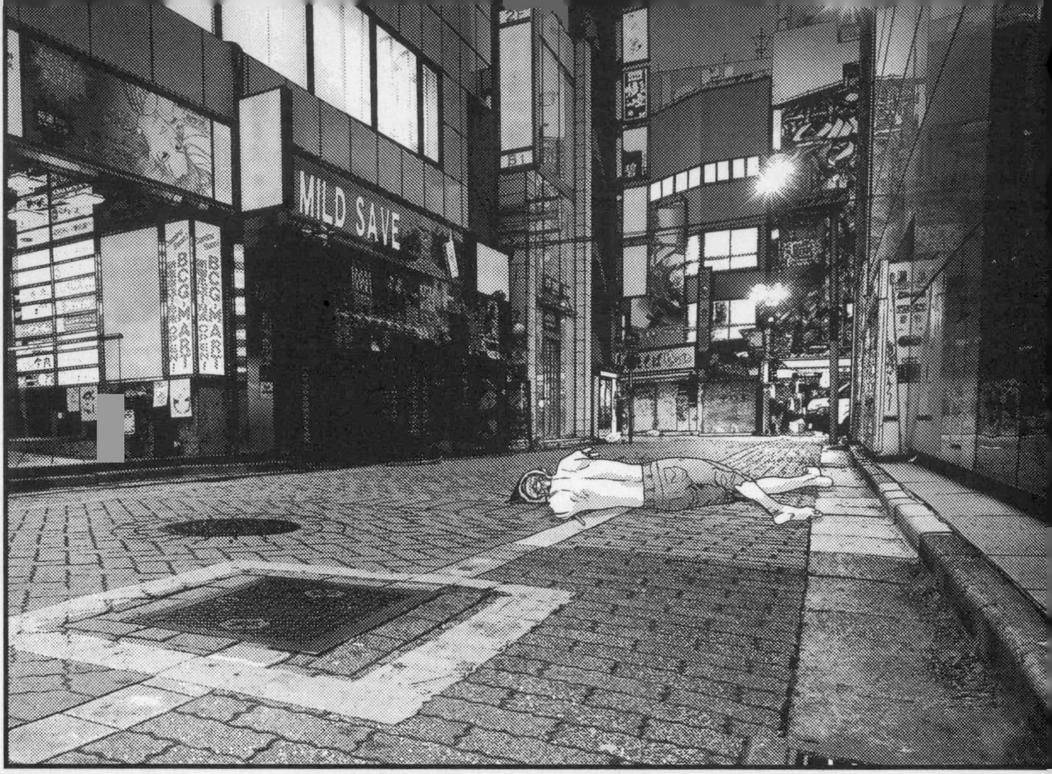
MILD SAVE
BCG MART
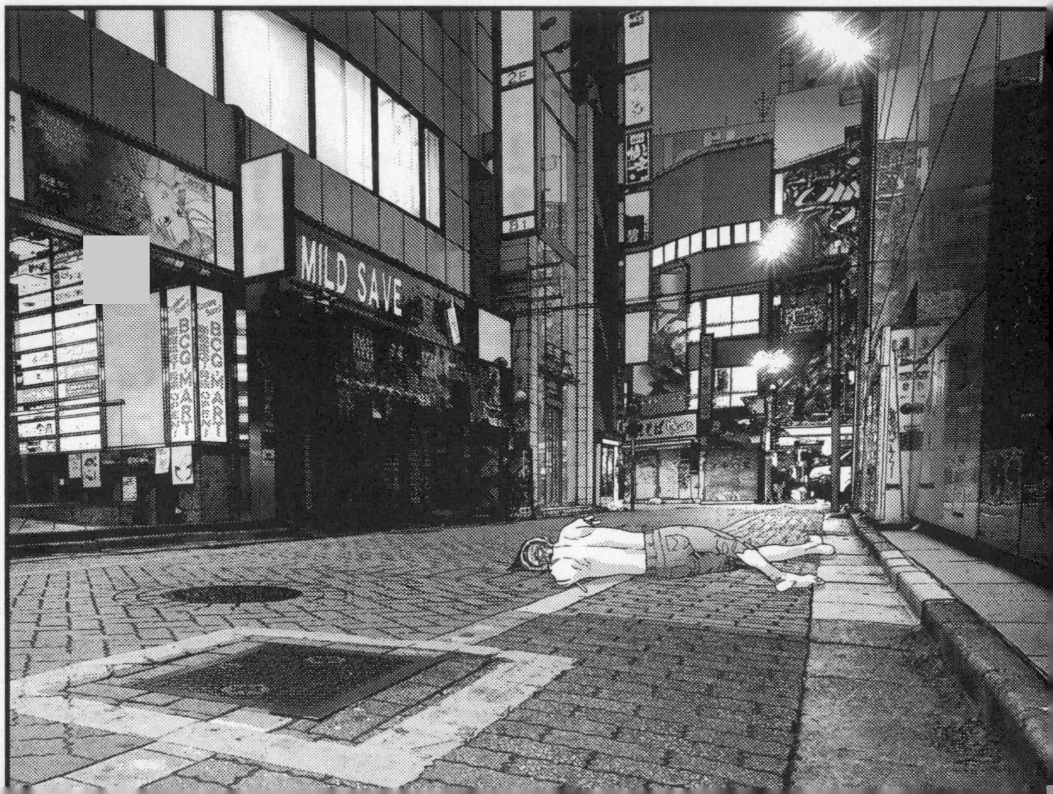
MILD SAVE
BCG MART

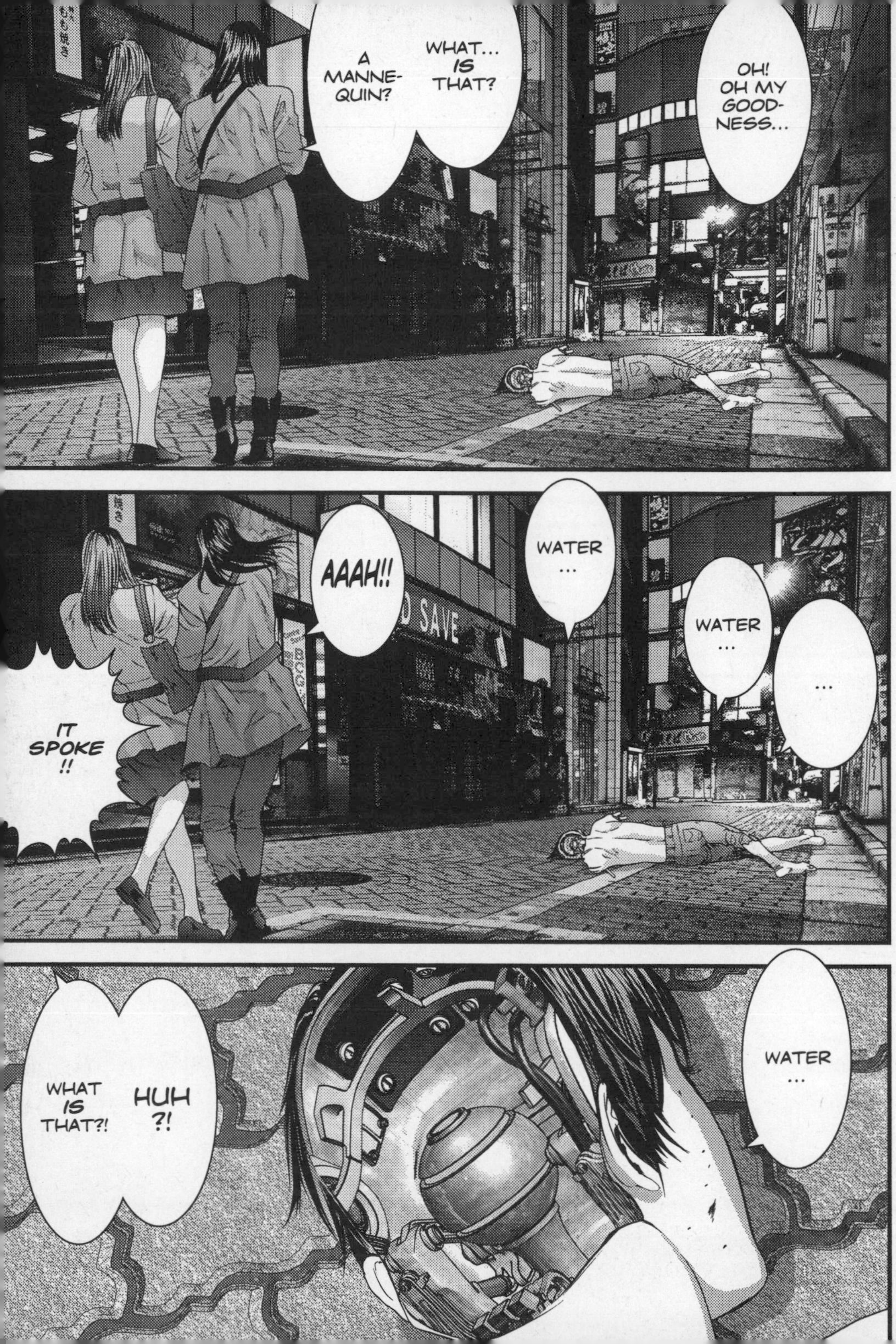
OH! OH MY GOOD-NESS...
WHAT... IS THAT?
A MANNE-QUIN?
...
WATER ...
WATER ...
AAAH!!
IT SPOKE !!
WATER ...
HUH ?!
WHAT IS THAT?!

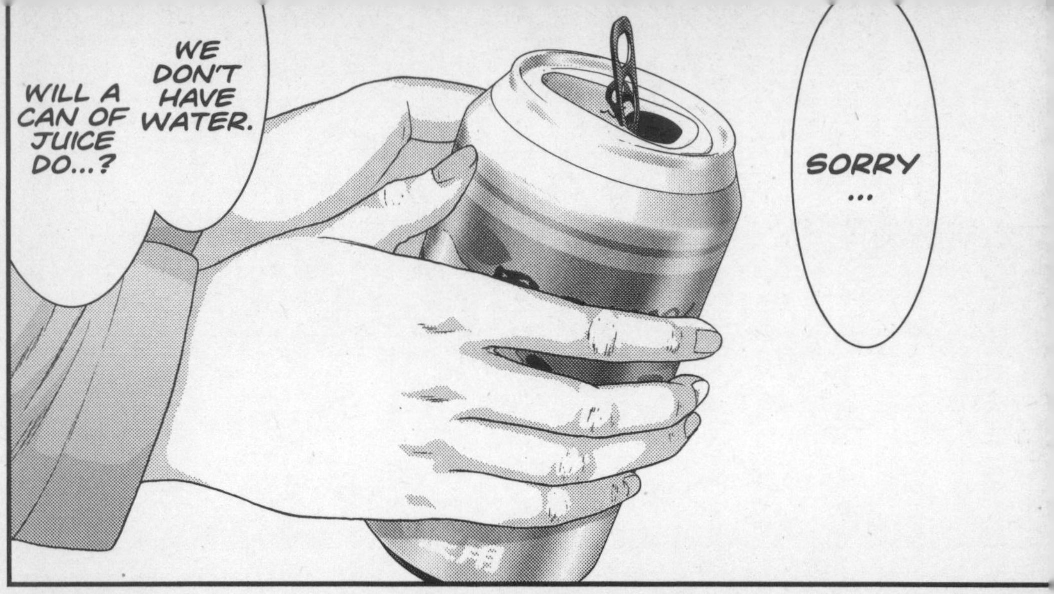
SORRY ...
WE DON'T HAVE WATER.
WILL A CAN OF JUICE DO...?

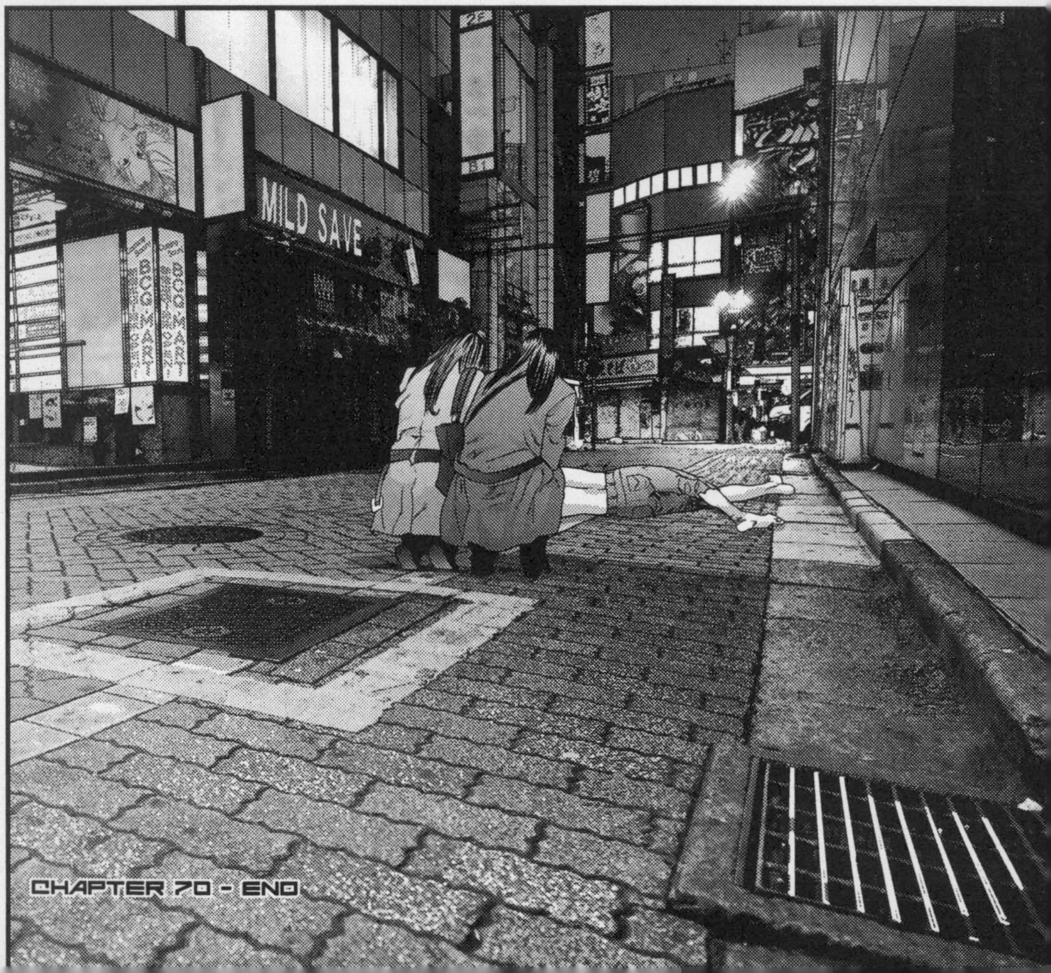
MILD SAVE
CHAPTER 70 - END

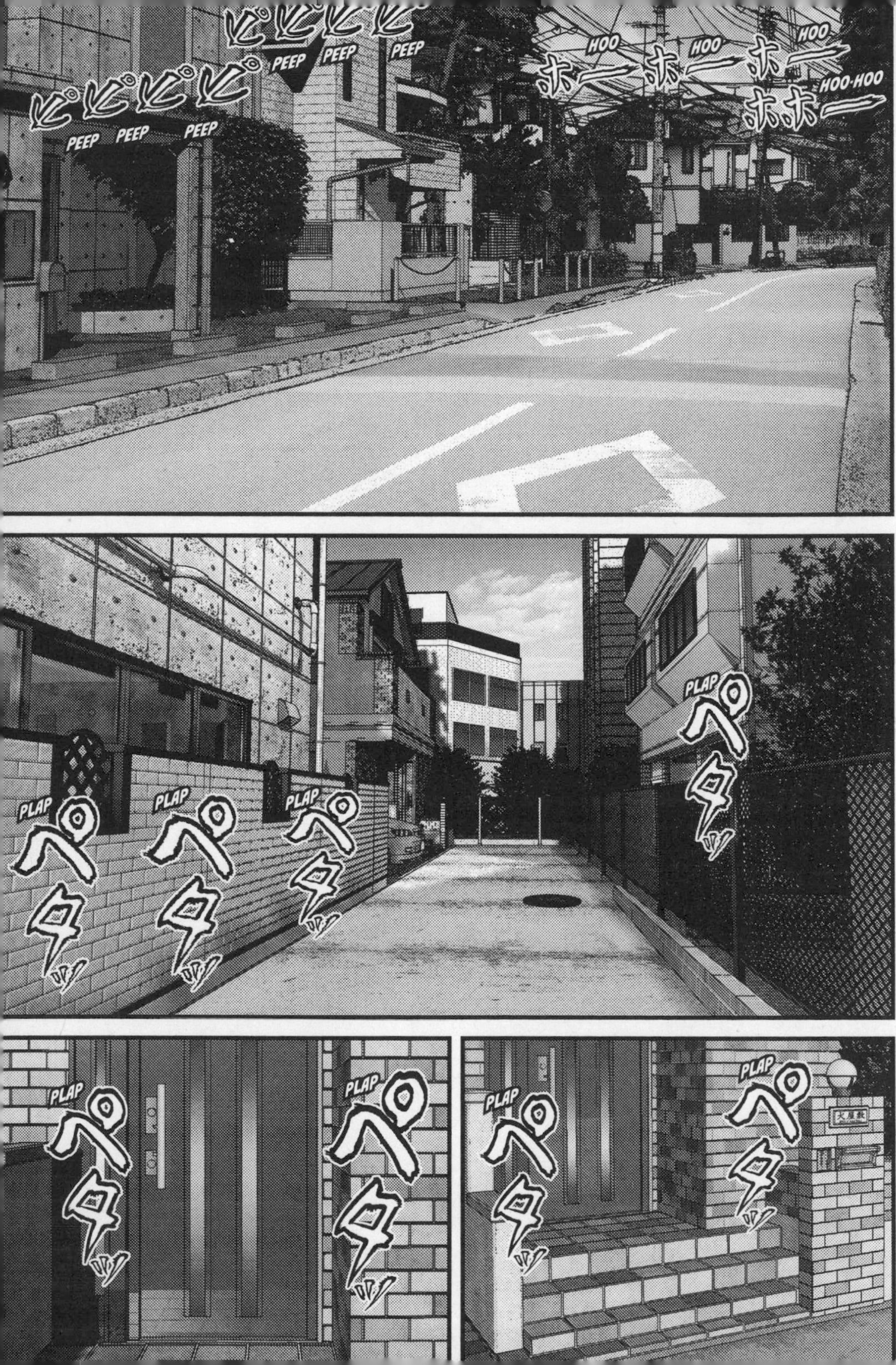
ホーホーホー
HOO HOO HOO
ホホー
HOO-HOO
ピピピピ
PEEP PEEP PEEP
ピピピピ
PEEP PEEP PEEP
ペタ
PLAP
ペタ
PLAP
ペタ
PLAP
ペタ
PLAP
ペタ
PLAP
ペタ
PLAP
犬屋敷
ペタ
PLAP
ペタ
PLAP
SIGN: INUYASHIKI

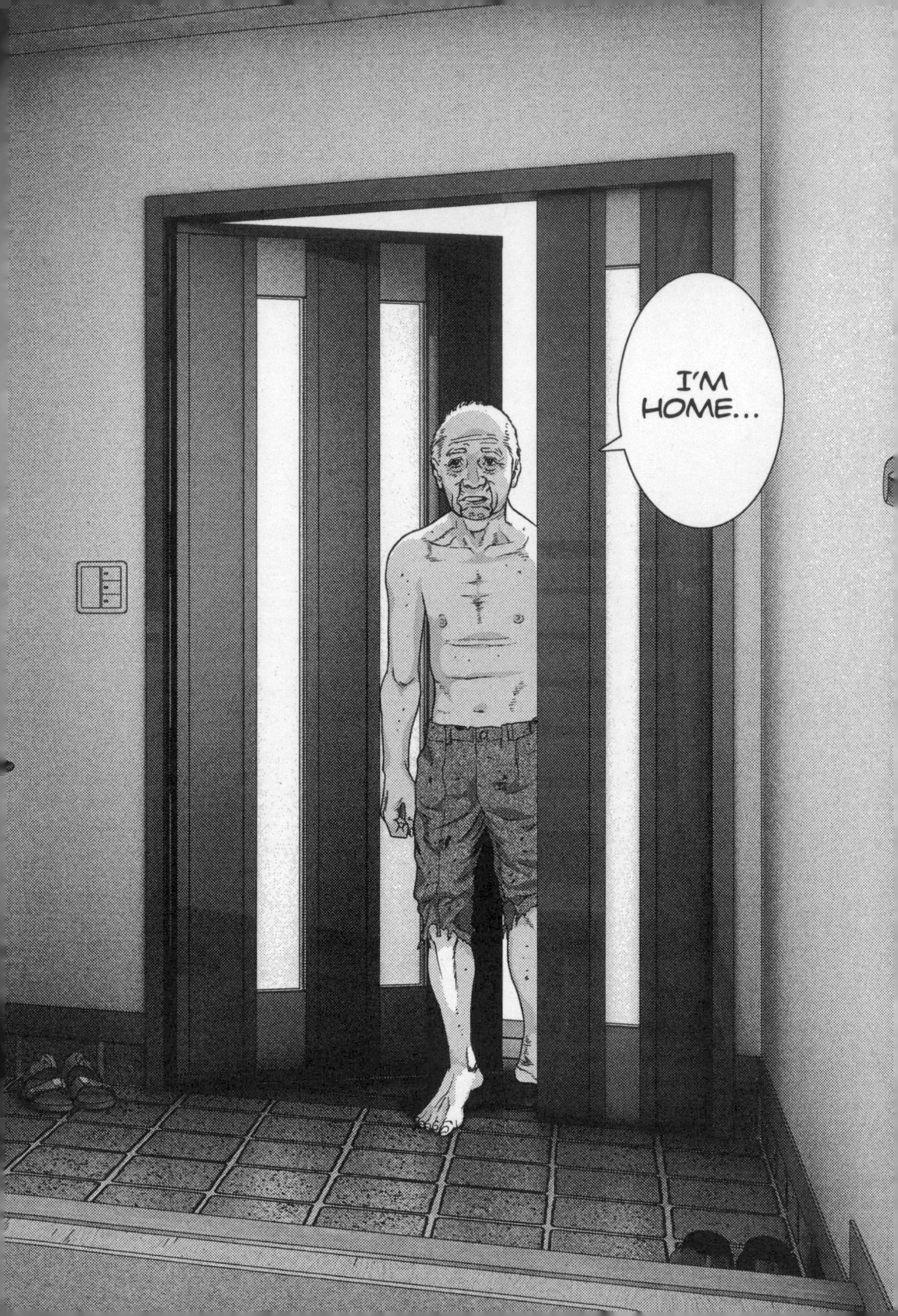
I'M HOME...

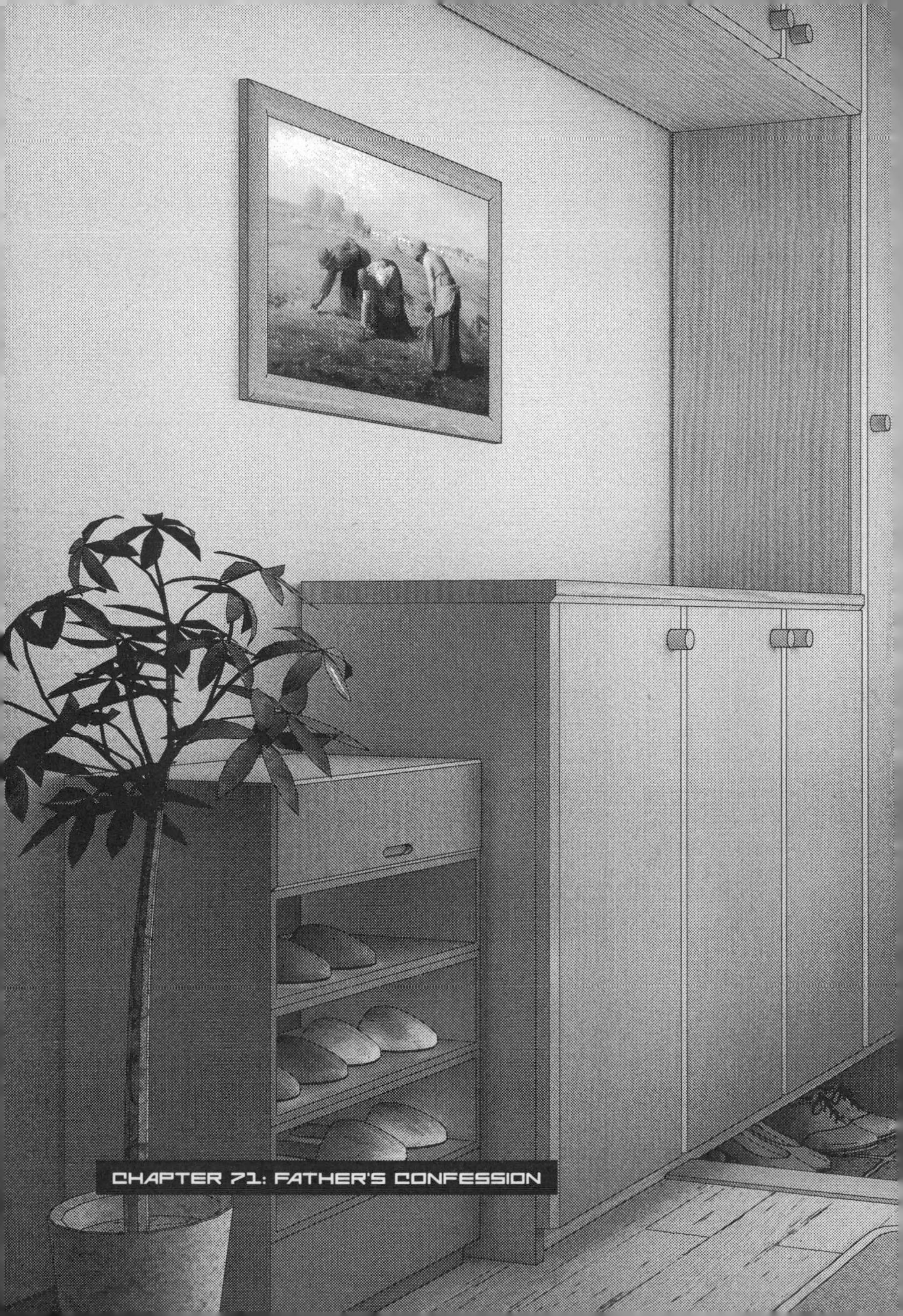
CHAPTER 71: FATHER'S CONFESSION

SILENCE
?!
ギッ
CRRK
CRK
ギッ
ギッ
CRK
ギッ
CRK
ギッ
CRK
キイッ
CREAK

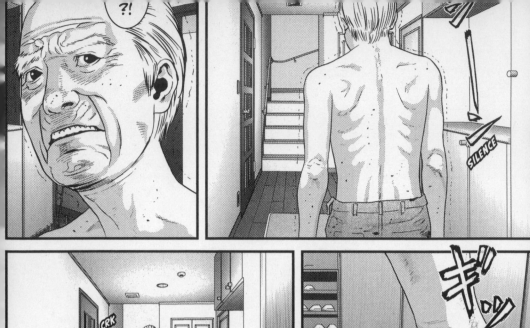

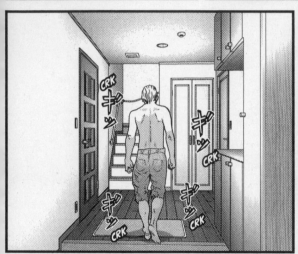

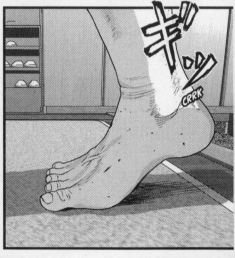

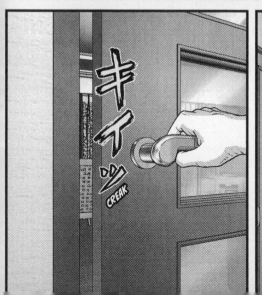

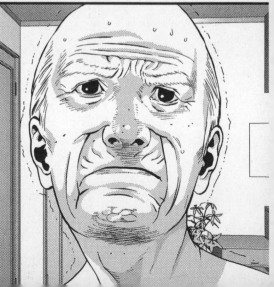

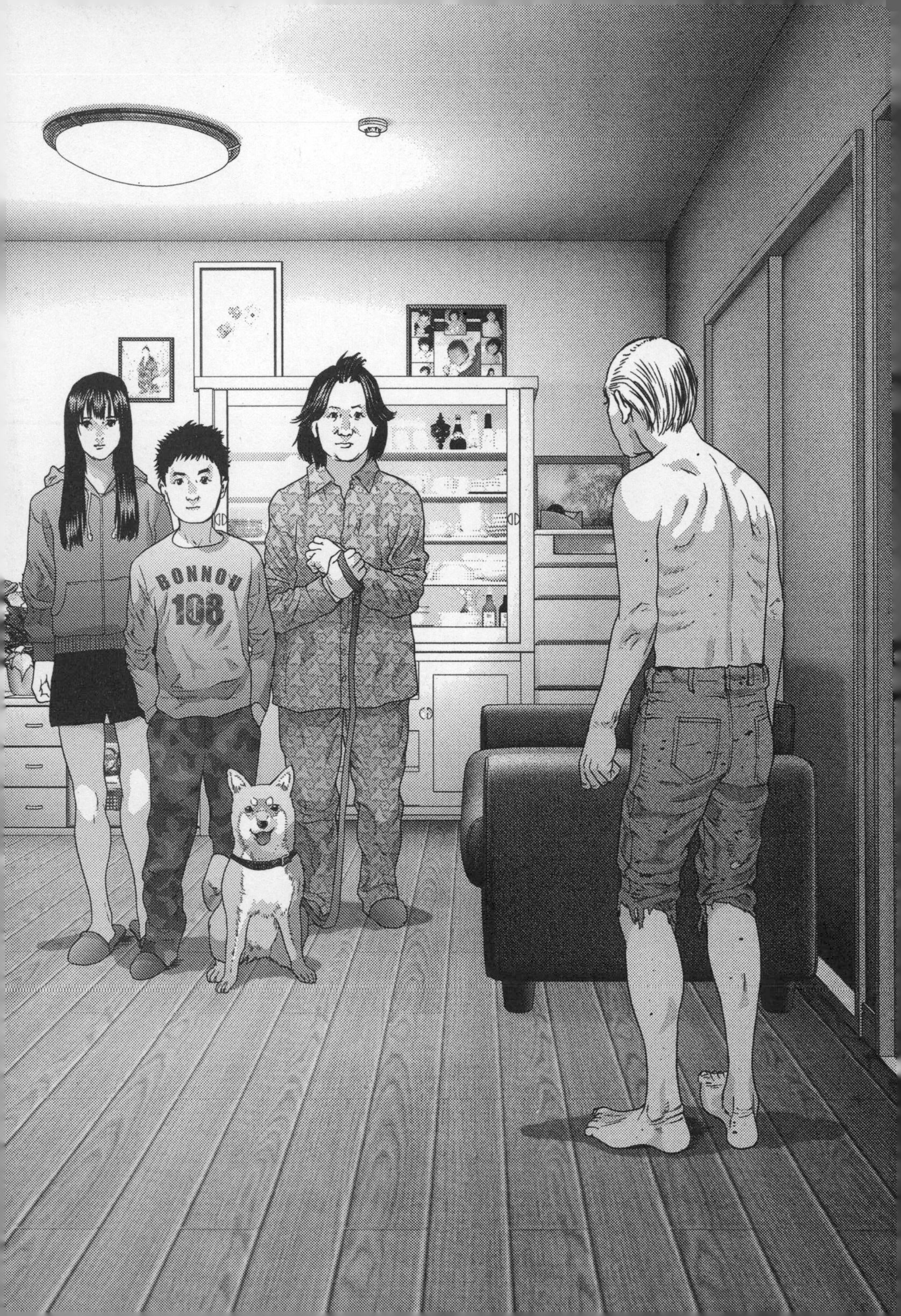
BONNOU
108

WHAT ?!
WHAT'S... GOING ON?

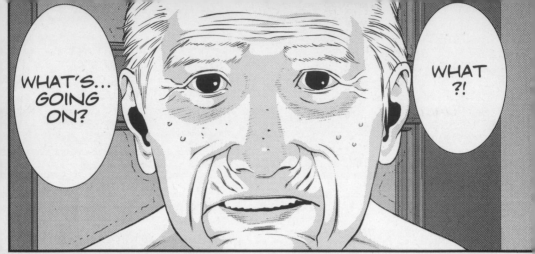

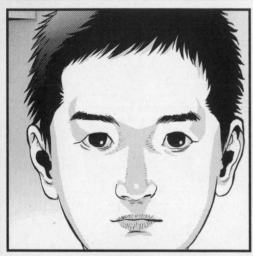

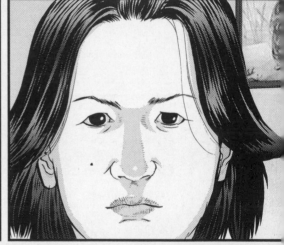

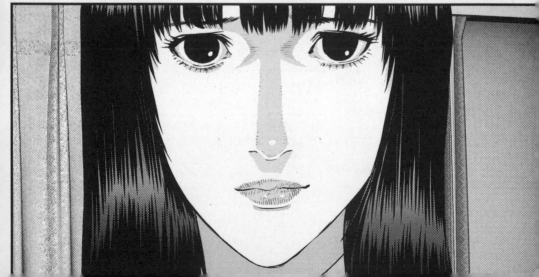

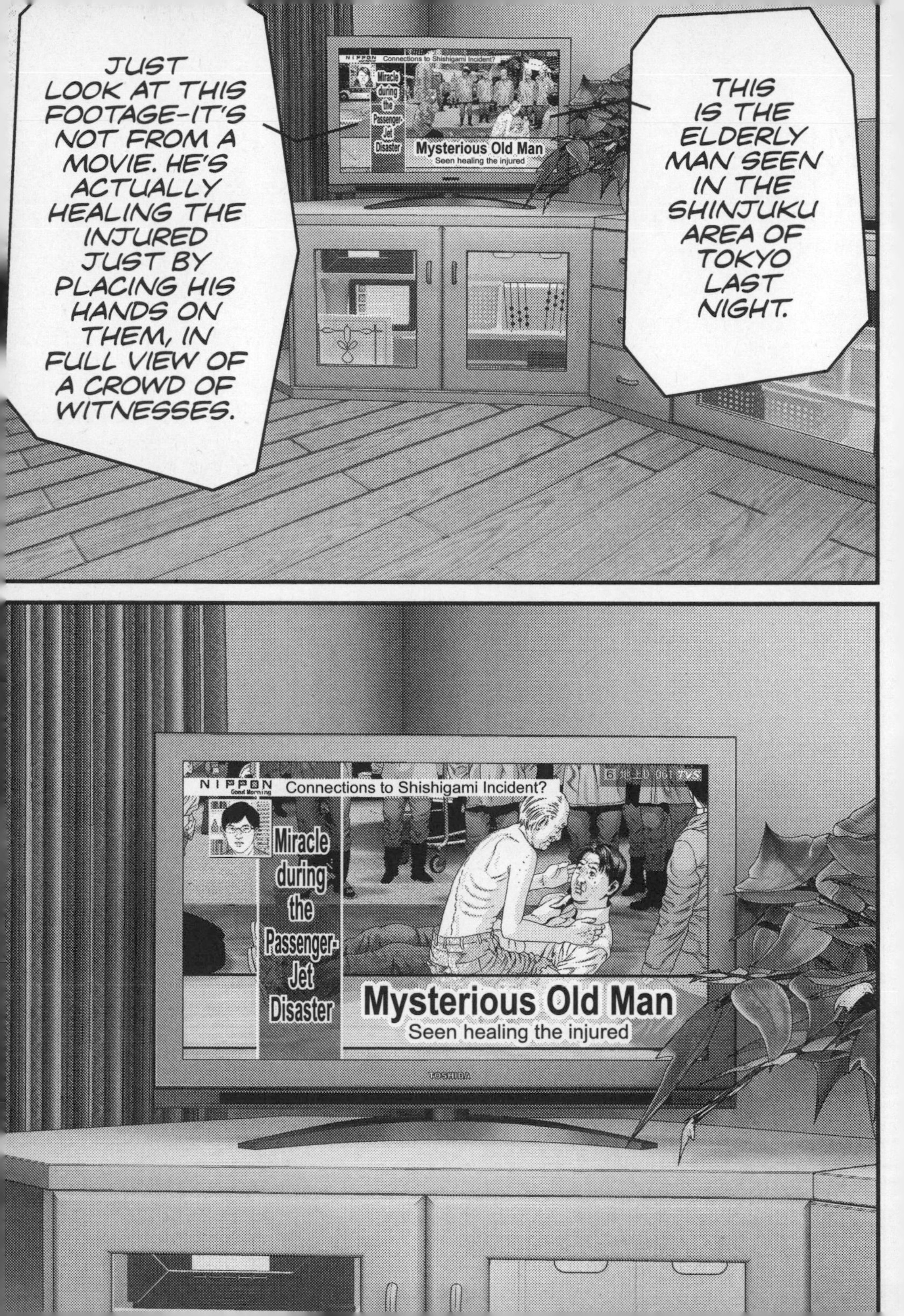
THIS IS THE ELDERLY MAN SEEN IN THE SHINJUKU AREA OF TOKYO LAST NIGHT.
JUST LOOK AT THIS FOOTAGE–IT'S NOT FROM A MOVIE. HE'S ACTUALLY HEALING THE INJURED JUST BY PLACING HIS HANDS ON THEM, IN FULL VIEW OF A CROWD OF WITNESSES.
NIPPON
Connections to Shishigami Incident?
Miracle during the Passenger-Jet Disaster
Mysterious Old Man
Seen healing the injured
NIPPON Good Morning
Connections to Shishigami Incident?
Miracle during the Passenger-Jet Disaster
Mysterious Old Man
Seen healing the injured
TOSHIBA

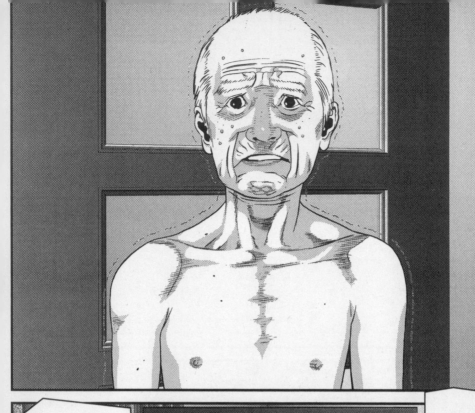

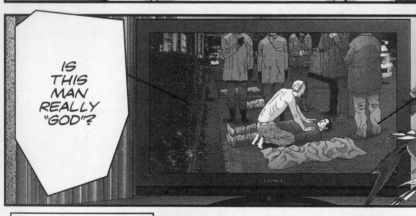

COULD THE COMMENTS ON THE INTERNET BE TRUE?
IS THIS MAN REALLY "GOD"?
ARE SUCH MIRACLES TRULY POSSIBLE IN REALITY?
WE INTER-VIEWED THE PEOPLE HE SAVED...

DEAR ...
...IS THAT... REALLY YOU?
...

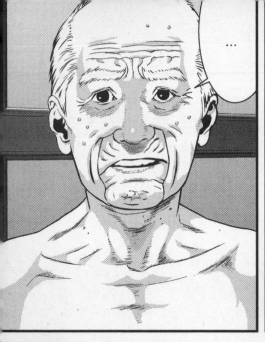

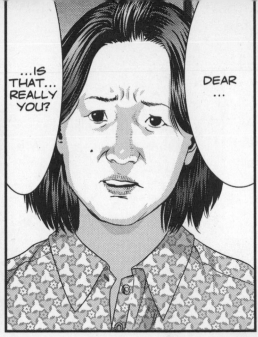

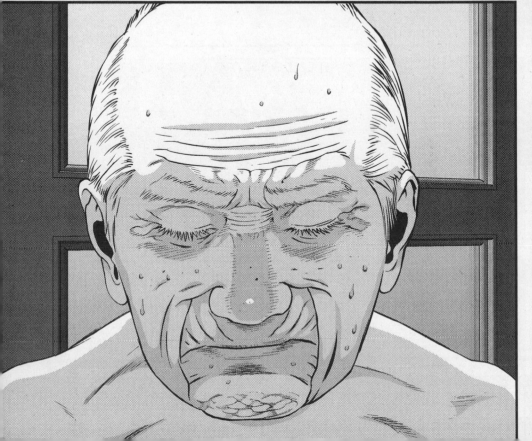

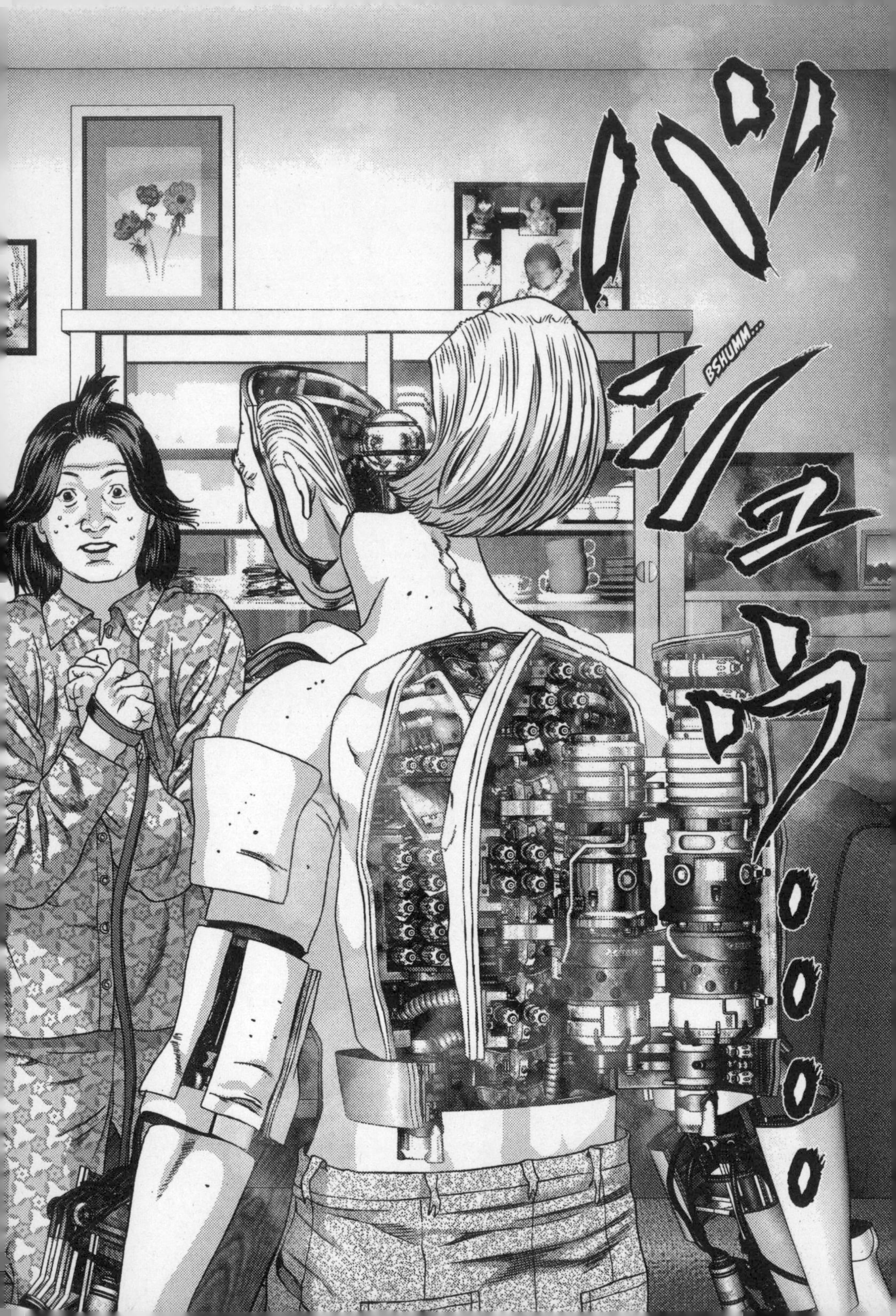
バシュウ
BSHUMM...

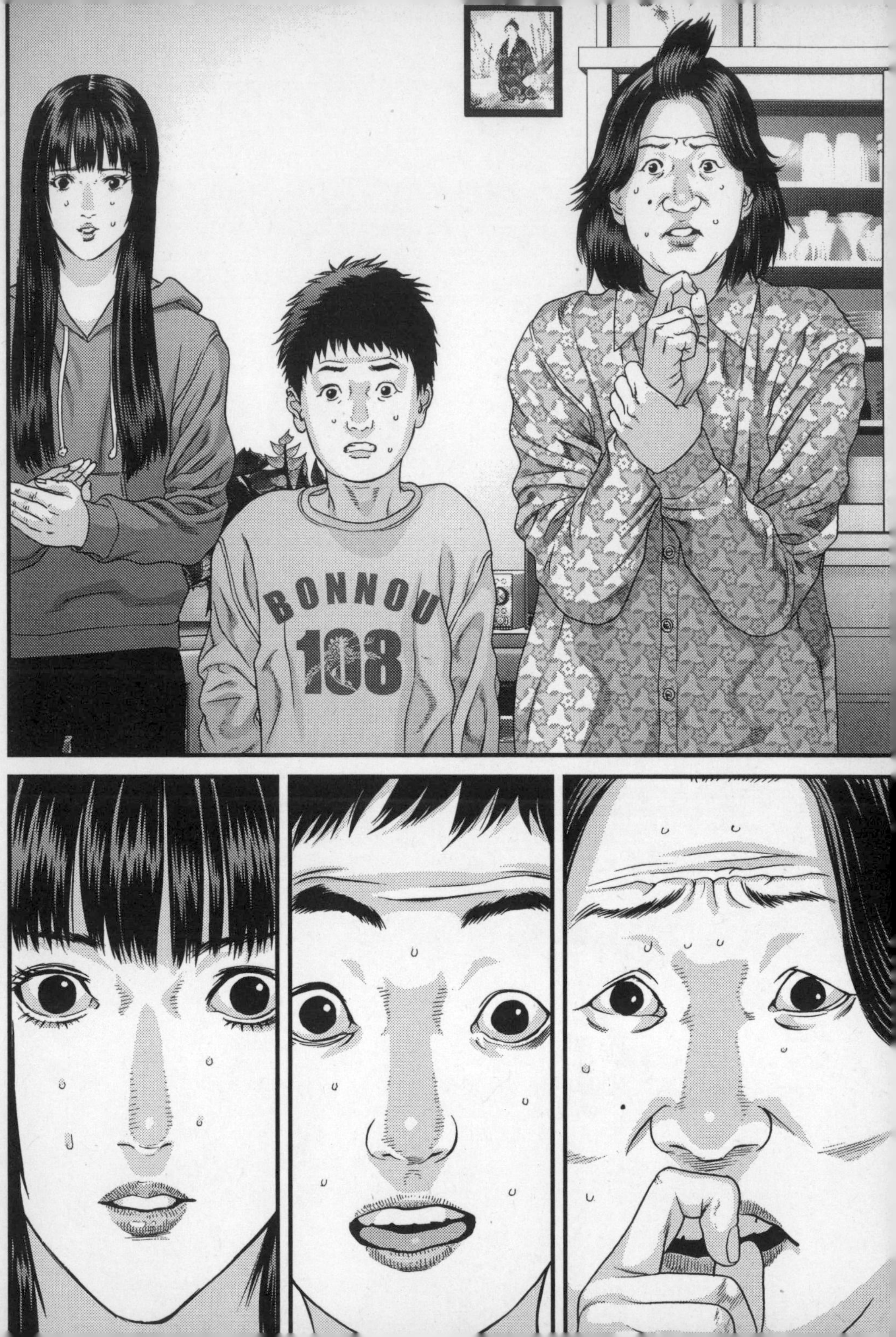
BONNOU
108

THUD
I'M SORRY...
I'M SO... ...SORRY...

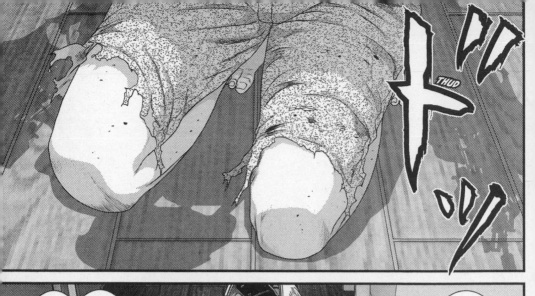

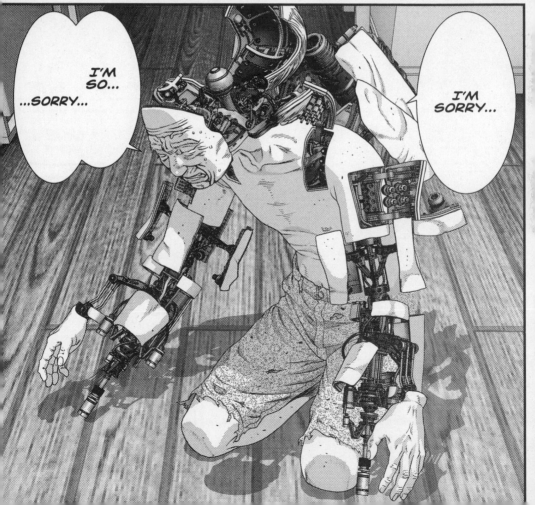

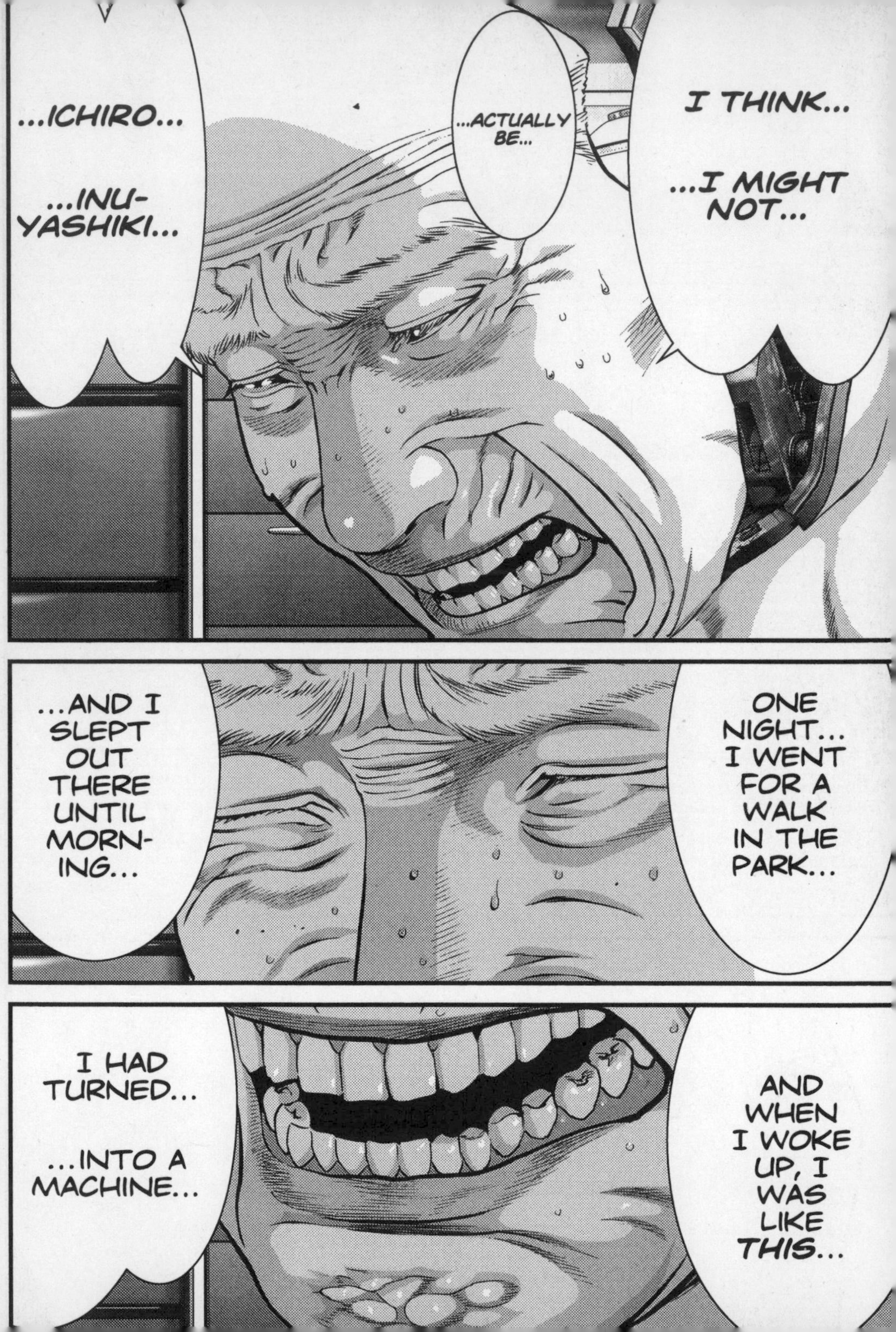
I THINK...
...I MIGHT NOT...
...ACTUALLY BE...
...ICHIRO...
...INU-YASHIKI...
ONE NIGHT... I WENT FOR A WALK IN THE PARK...
...AND I SLEPT OUT THERE UNTIL MORNING...
AND WHEN I WOKE UP, I WAS LIKE THIS...
I HAD TURNED...
...INTO A MACHINE...

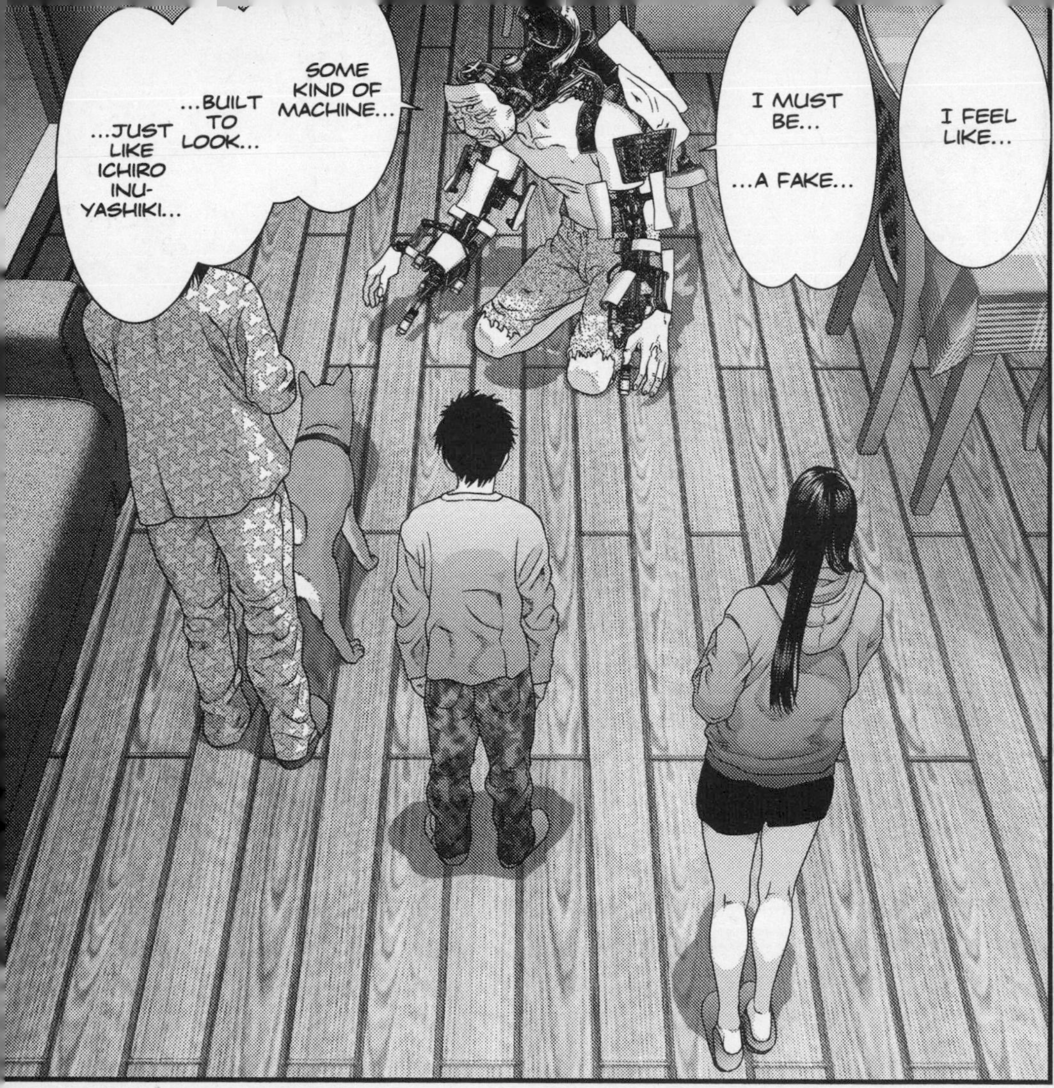
I FEEL LIKE...
I MUST BE... ...A FAKE...
SOME KIND OF MACHINE... ...BUILT TO LOOK... ...JUST LIKE ICHIRO INU-YASHIKI...
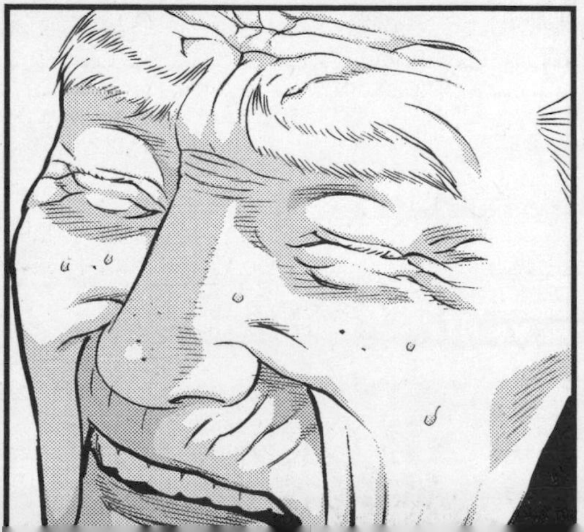
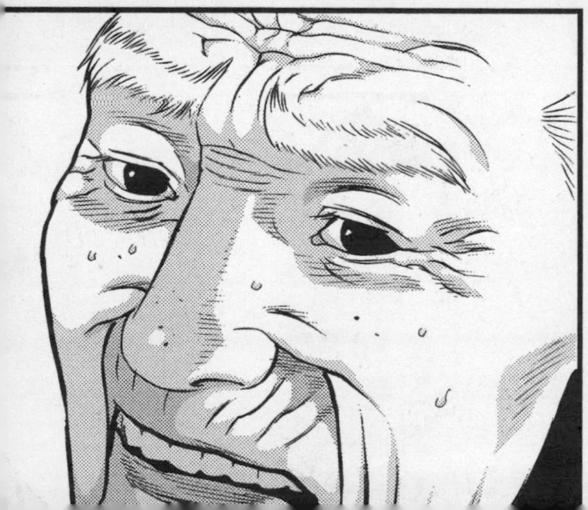

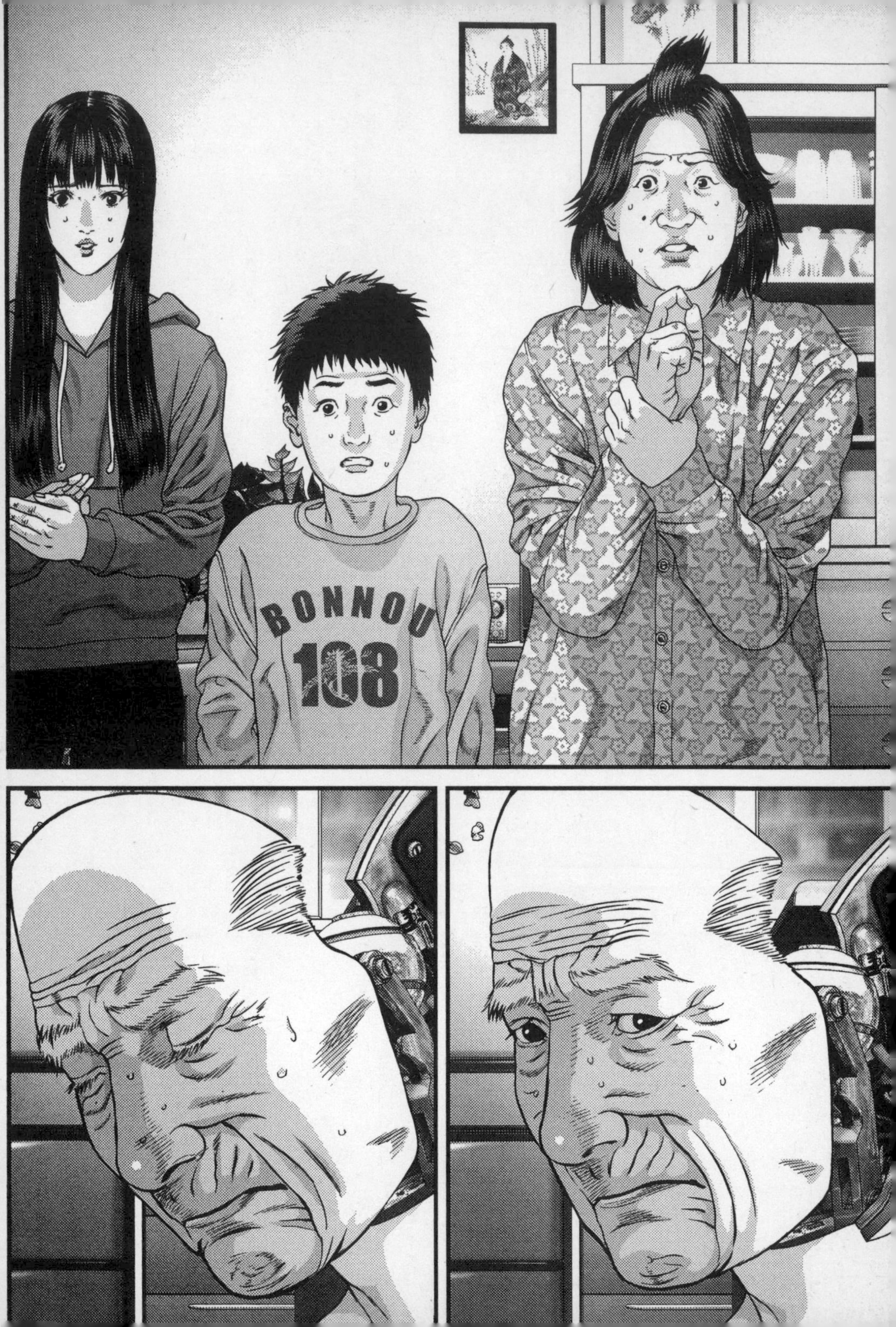
BONNOU
108

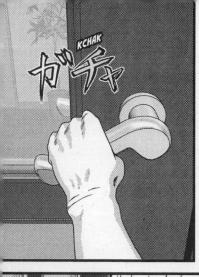

KCHAK

I'M SORRY...

...FOR NOT SAYING ANYTHING EARLIER...

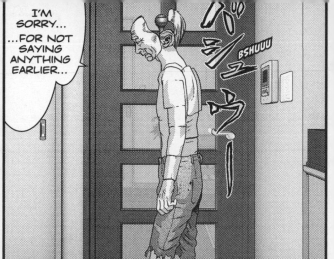

BSHUUU

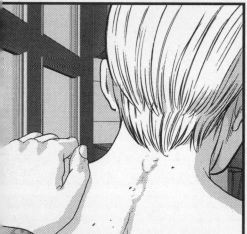

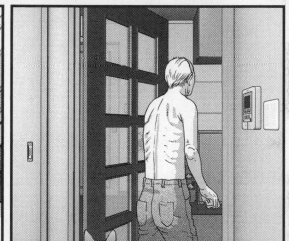

UH...

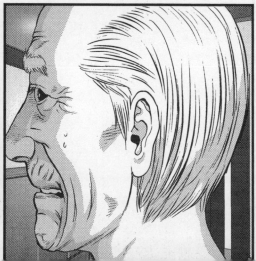

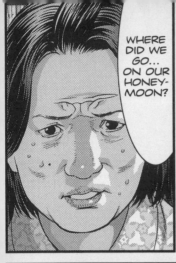

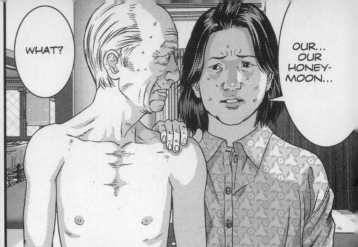

OUR... OUR HONEY-MOON...
WHAT?
WHERE DID WE GO... ON OUR HONEY-MOON?
TO... ATAMI...
...AND?!
WHAT HAP-PENED THERE?
YOU SAID... YOU WANTED TO VISIT THE ADULT MUSEUM...
SO... WE RODE ON THE ROPEWAY THERE...
AND I SLIPPED ON THE STEPS OF ATAMI CASTLE...
...AND LANDED HARD ON MY BACK-SIDE.
SO WE WERE LATE TO HAVE LUNCH...
...AND NONE OF THE PLACES WERE OPEN...

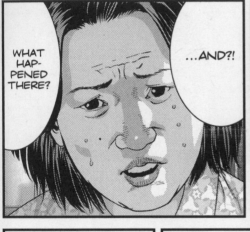

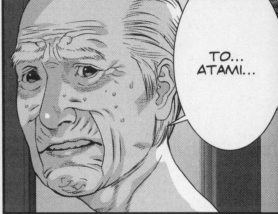

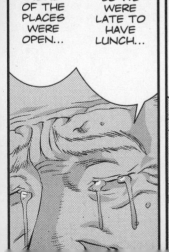

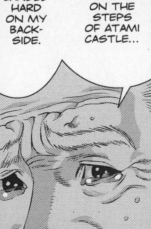

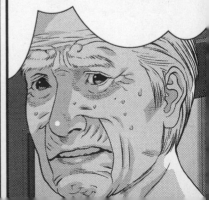

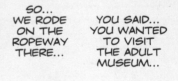

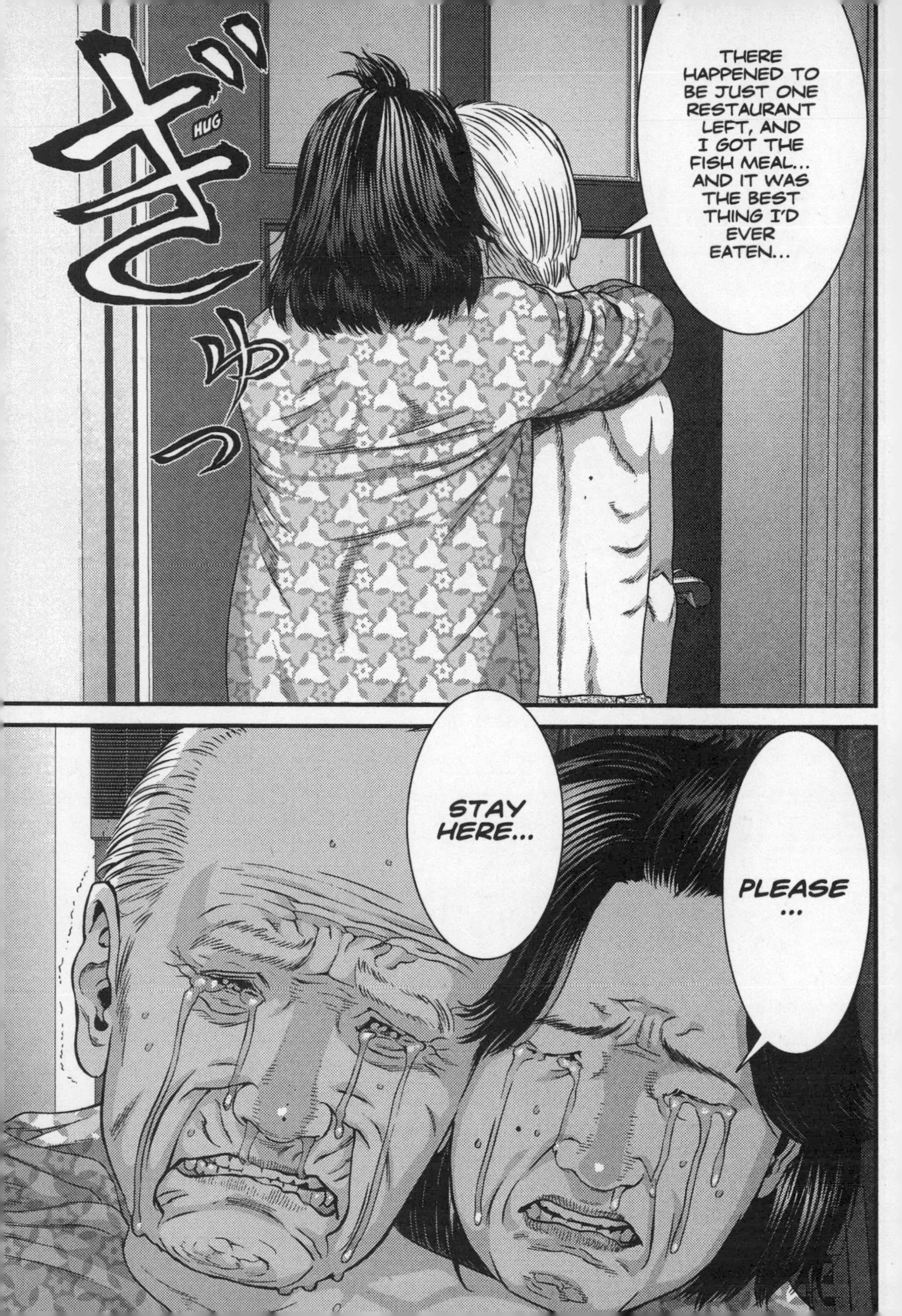
THERE HAPPENED TO BE JUST ONE RESTAURANT LEFT, AND I GOT THE FISH MEAL... AND IT WAS THE BEST THING I'D EVER EATEN...
ぎゅっ
HUG
PLEASE ...
STAY HERE...

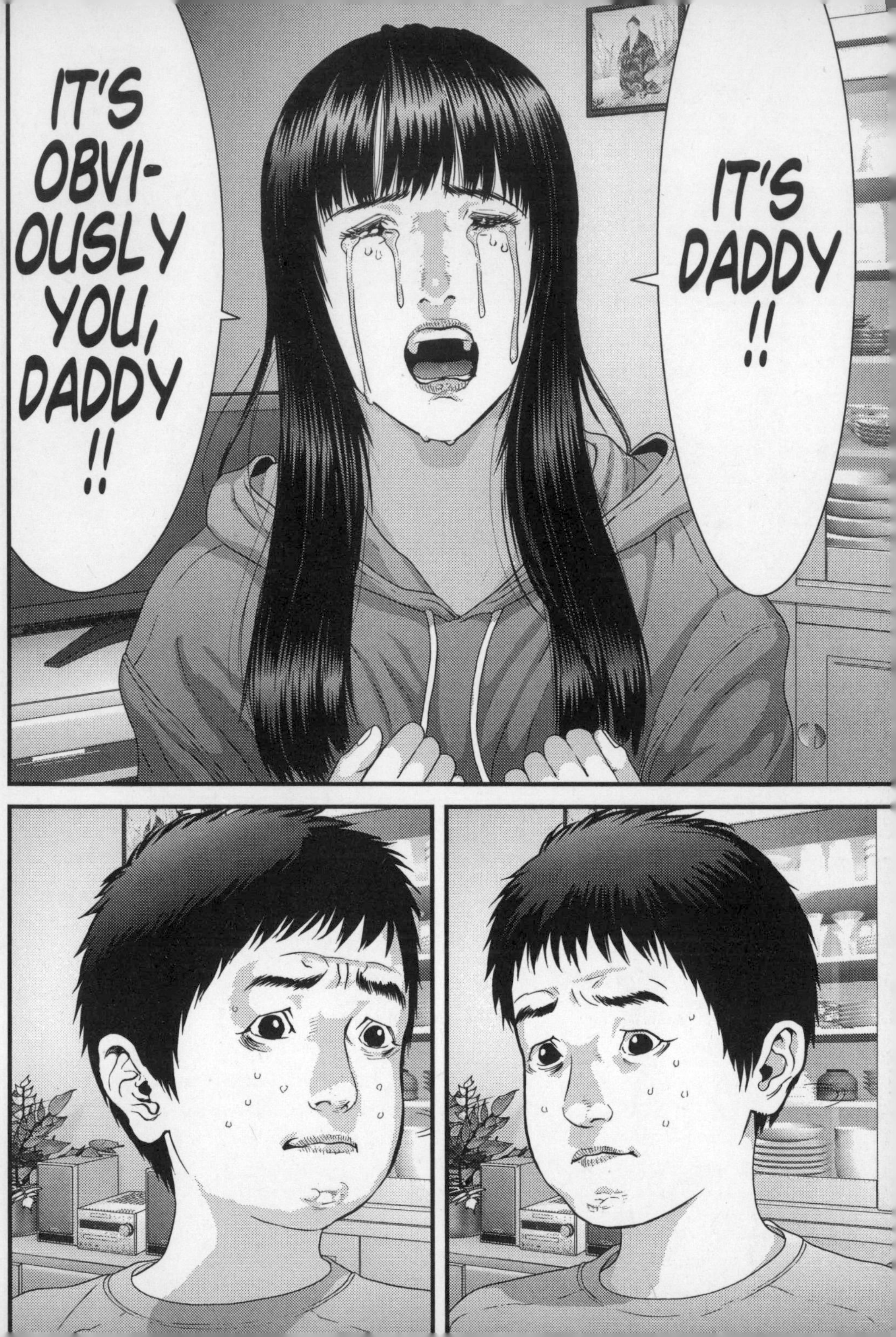
IT'S DADDY !!
IT'S OBVIOUSLY YOU, DADDY !!

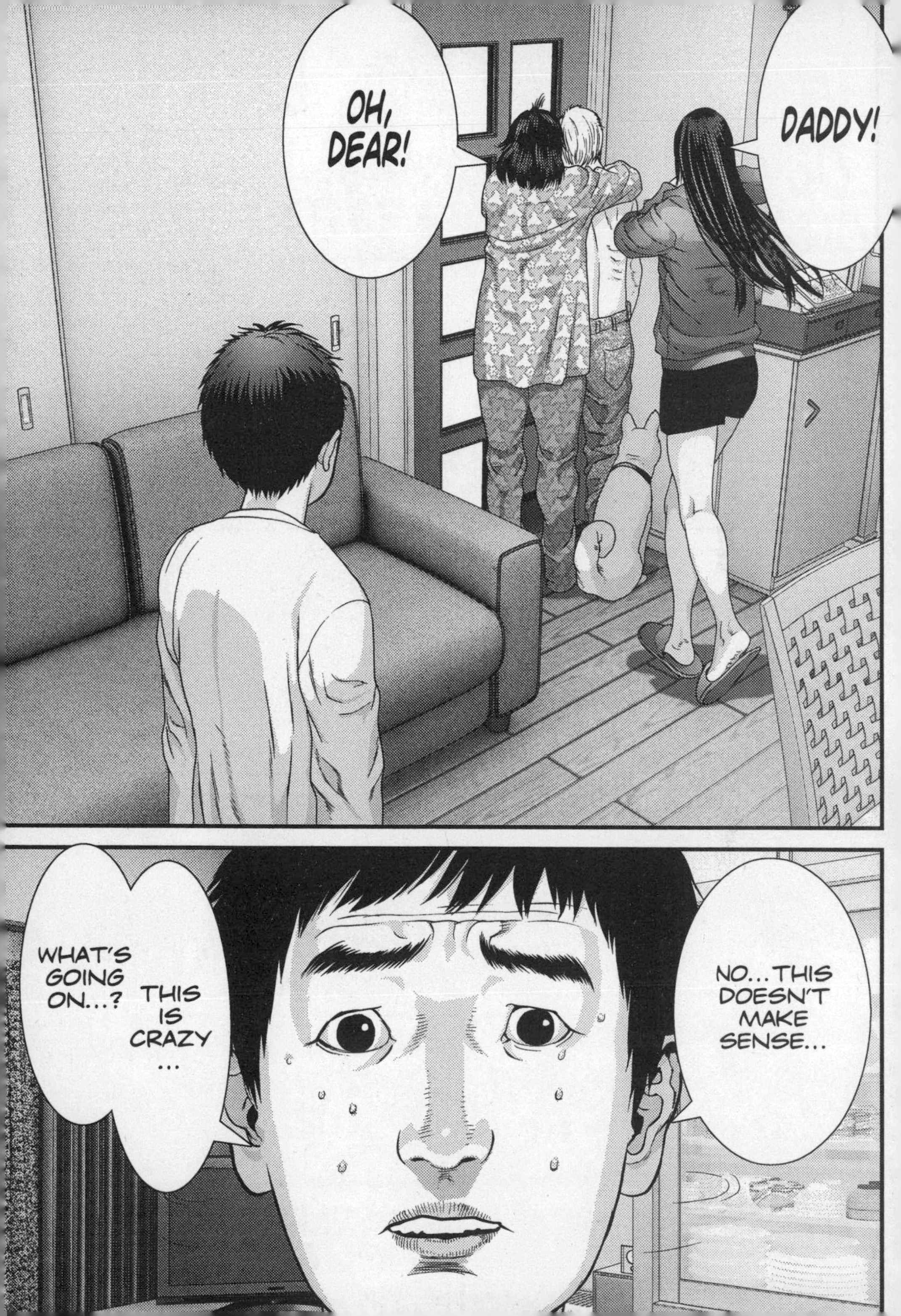
DADDY!
OH, DEAR!
NO... THIS DOESN'T MAKE SENSE...
WHAT'S GOING ON...?
THIS IS CRAZY ...

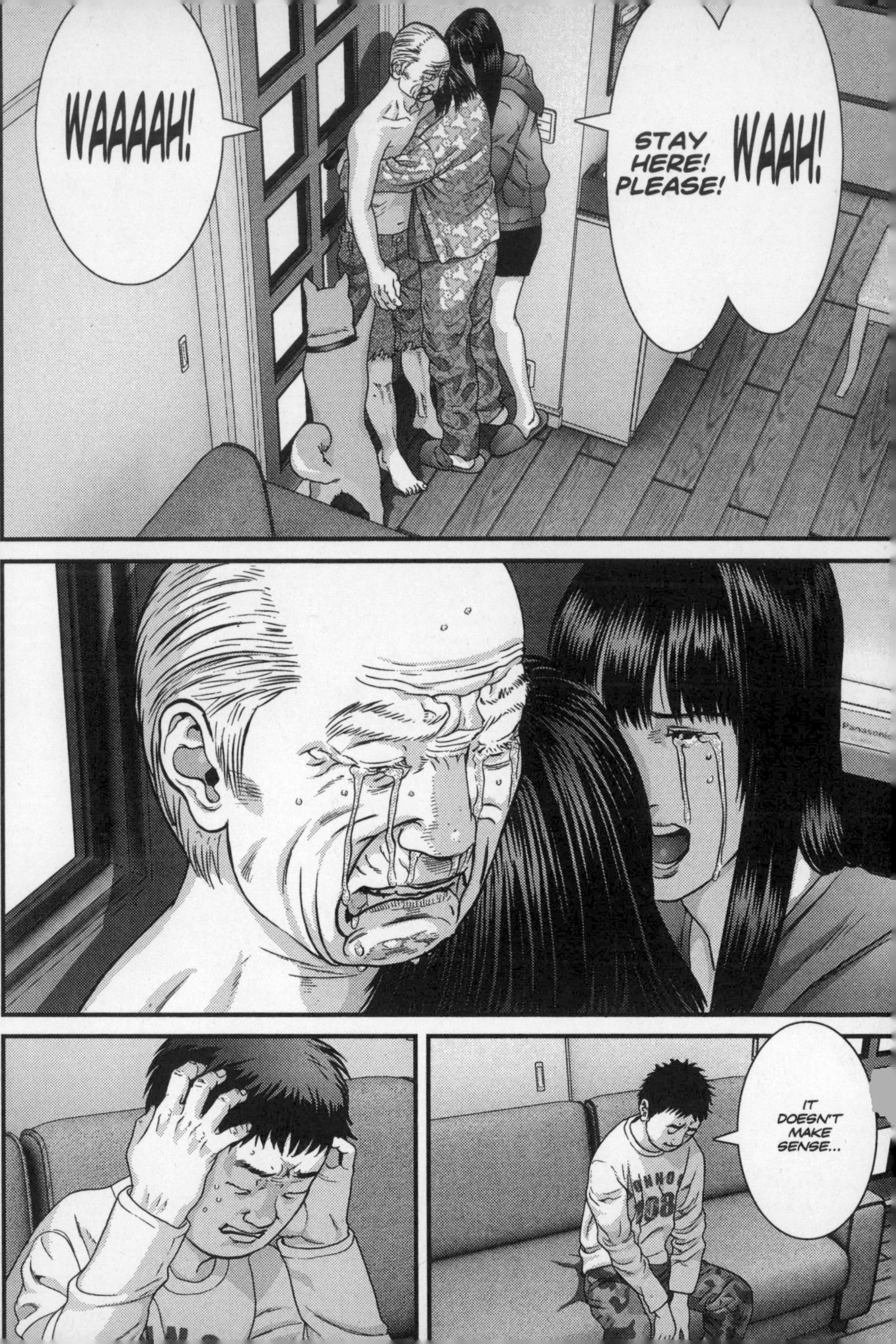
STAY HERE! PLEASE!
WAAH!
WAAAAH!
IT DOESN'T MAKE SENSE...

CHAPTER [illegible] - END

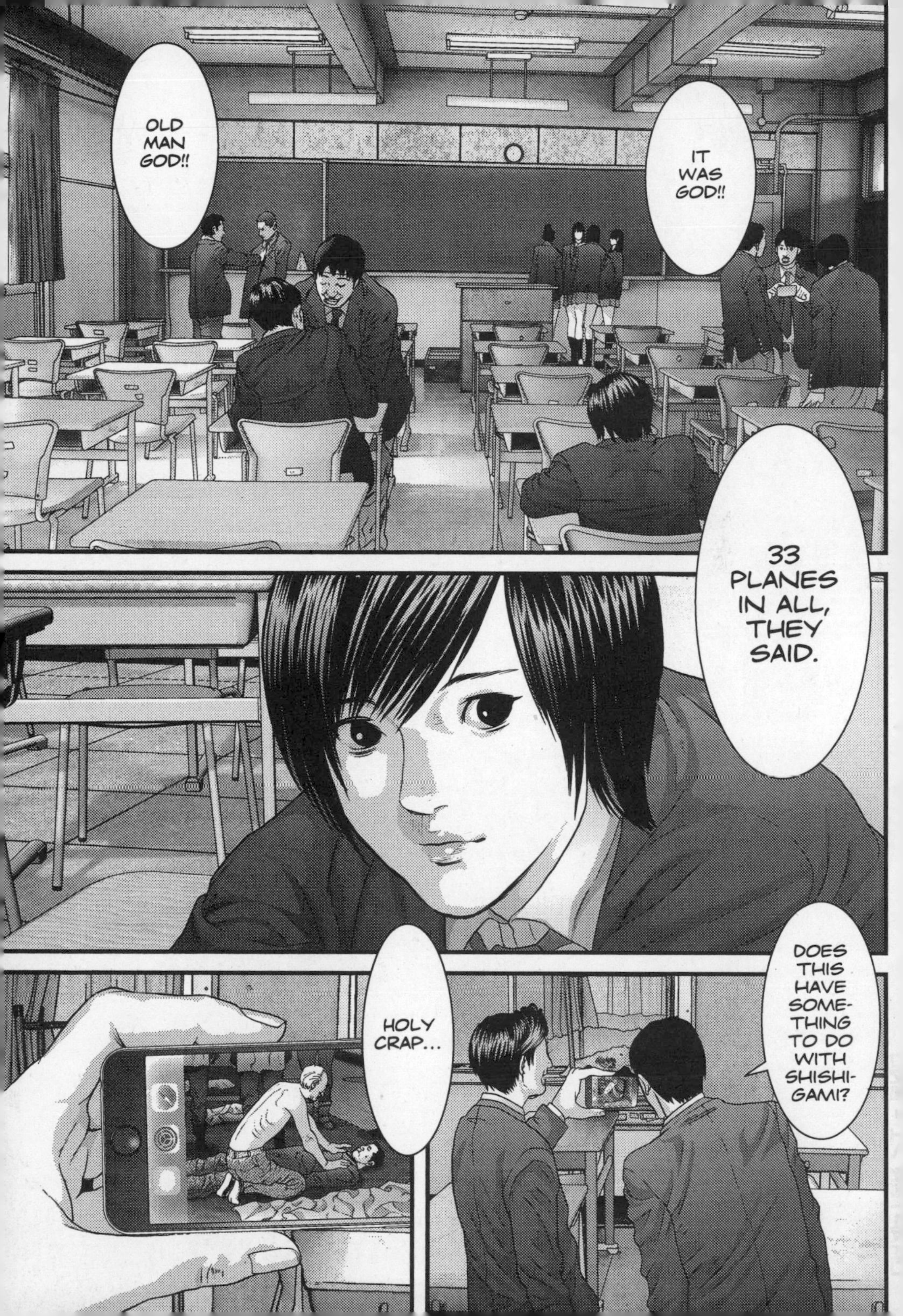
IT WAS GOD!!
OLD MAN GOD!!
33 PLANES IN ALL, THEY SAID.
DOES THIS HAVE SOME-THING TO DO WITH SHISHI-GAMI?
HOLY CRAP...

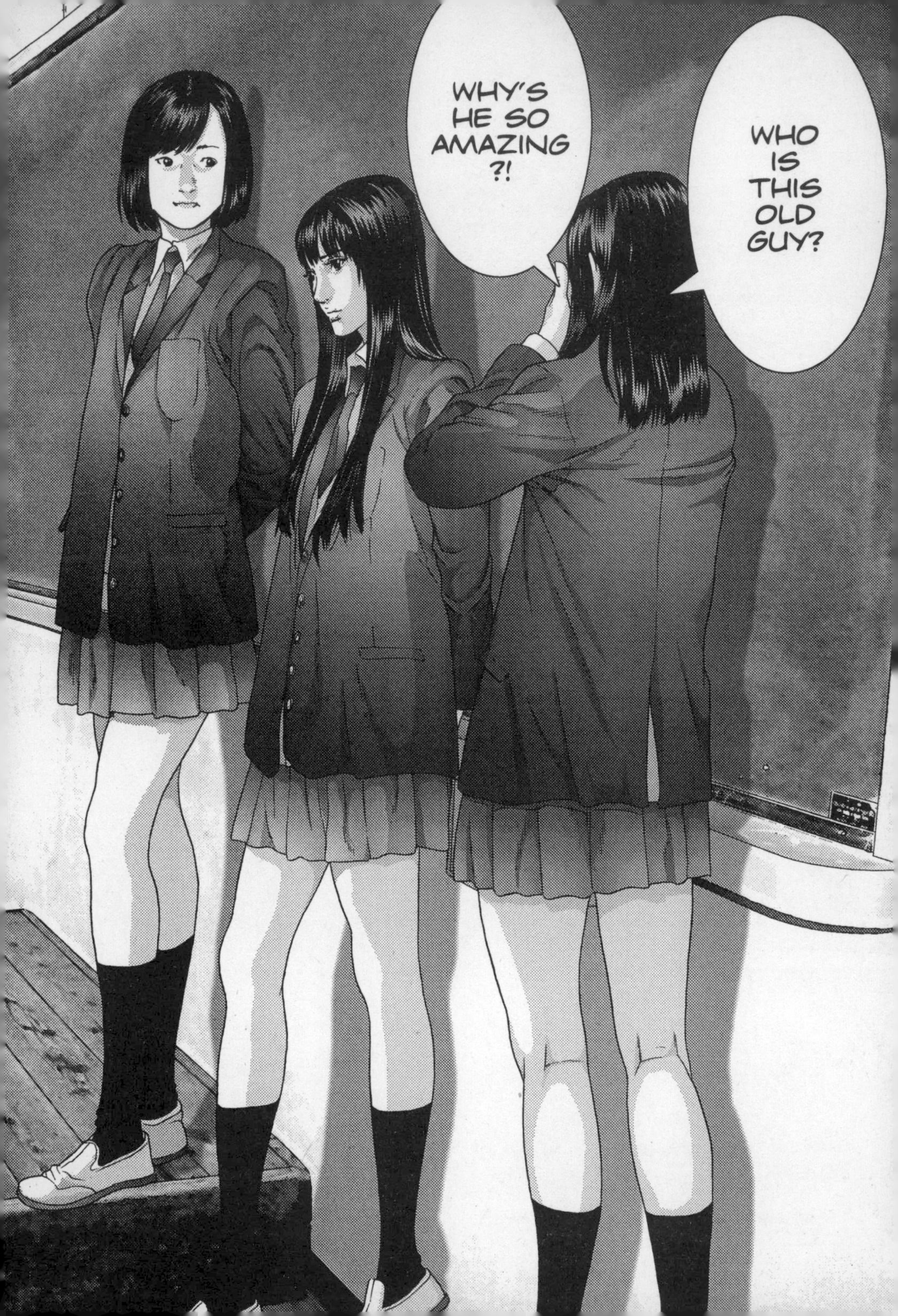
WHO IS THIS OLD GUY?
WHY'S HE SO AMAZING ?!

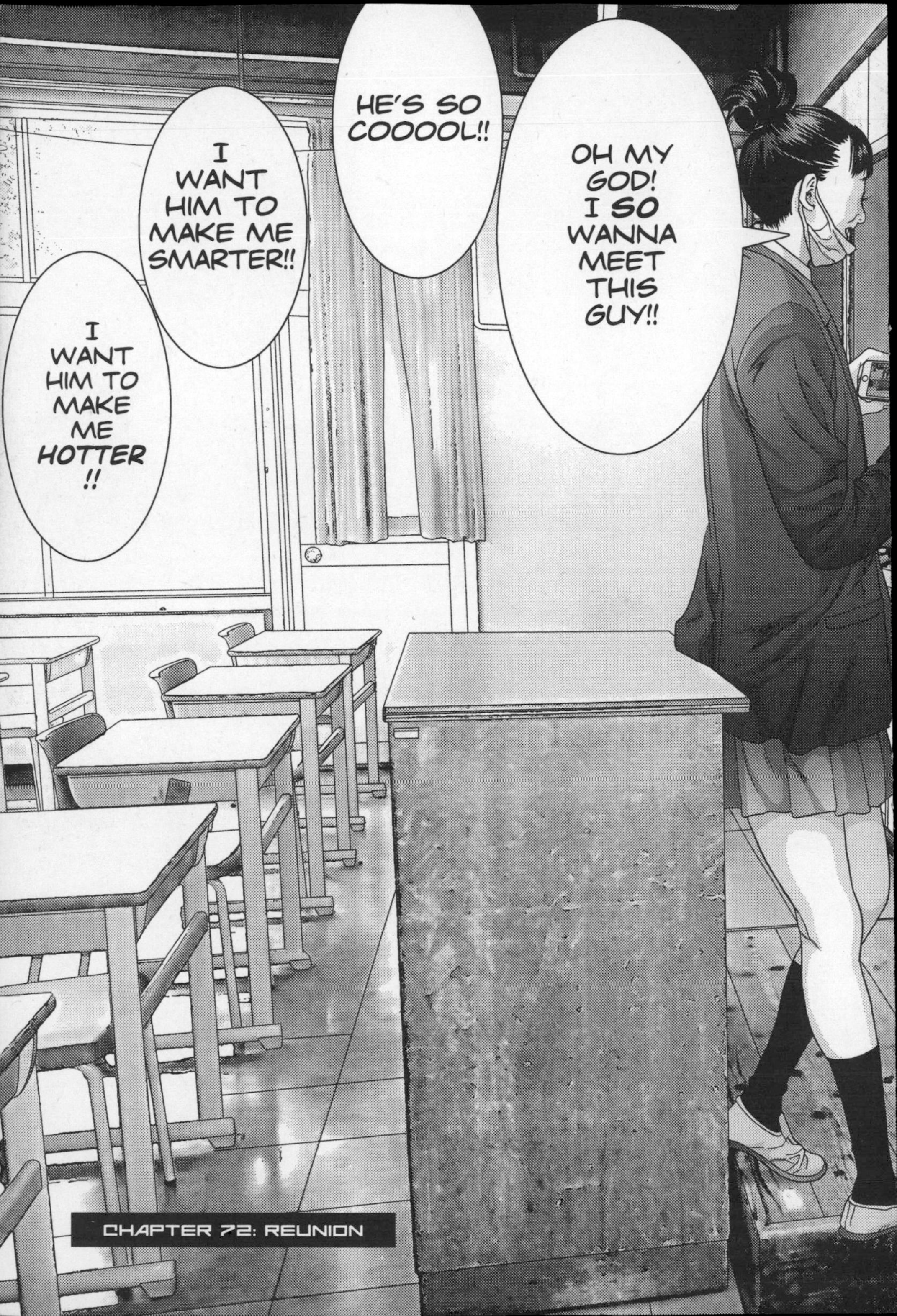
OH MY GOD! I SO WANNA MEET THIS GUY!!
HE'S SO COOOOOL!!
I WANT HIM TO MAKE ME SMARTER!!
I WANT HIM TO MAKE ME HOTTER !!
CHAPTER 72: REUNION

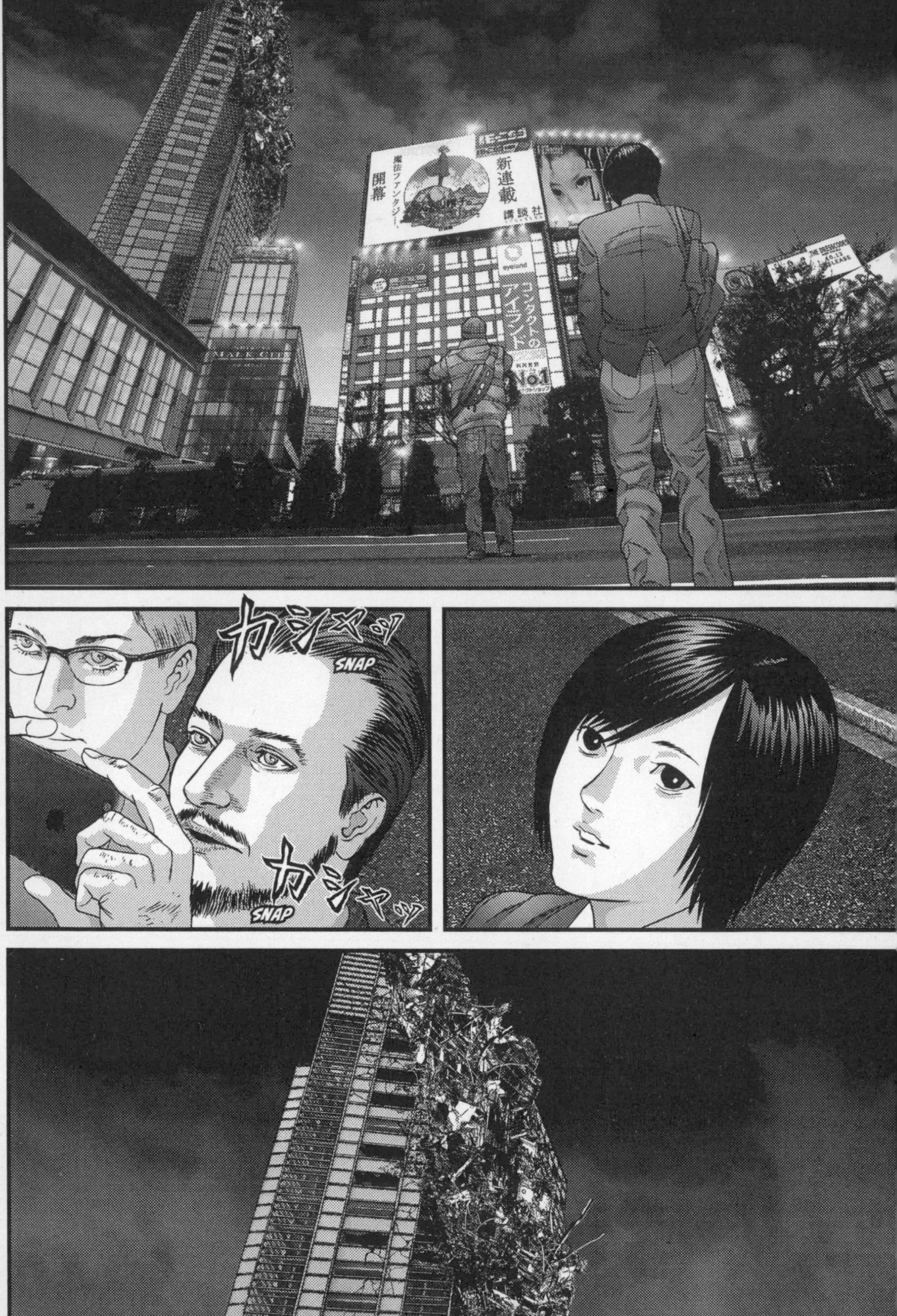

新連載
魔法ファンタジー、開幕
講談社
eyeland
コンタクトのアイランド
No.1
カシャッ
SNAP
カシャッ
SNAP

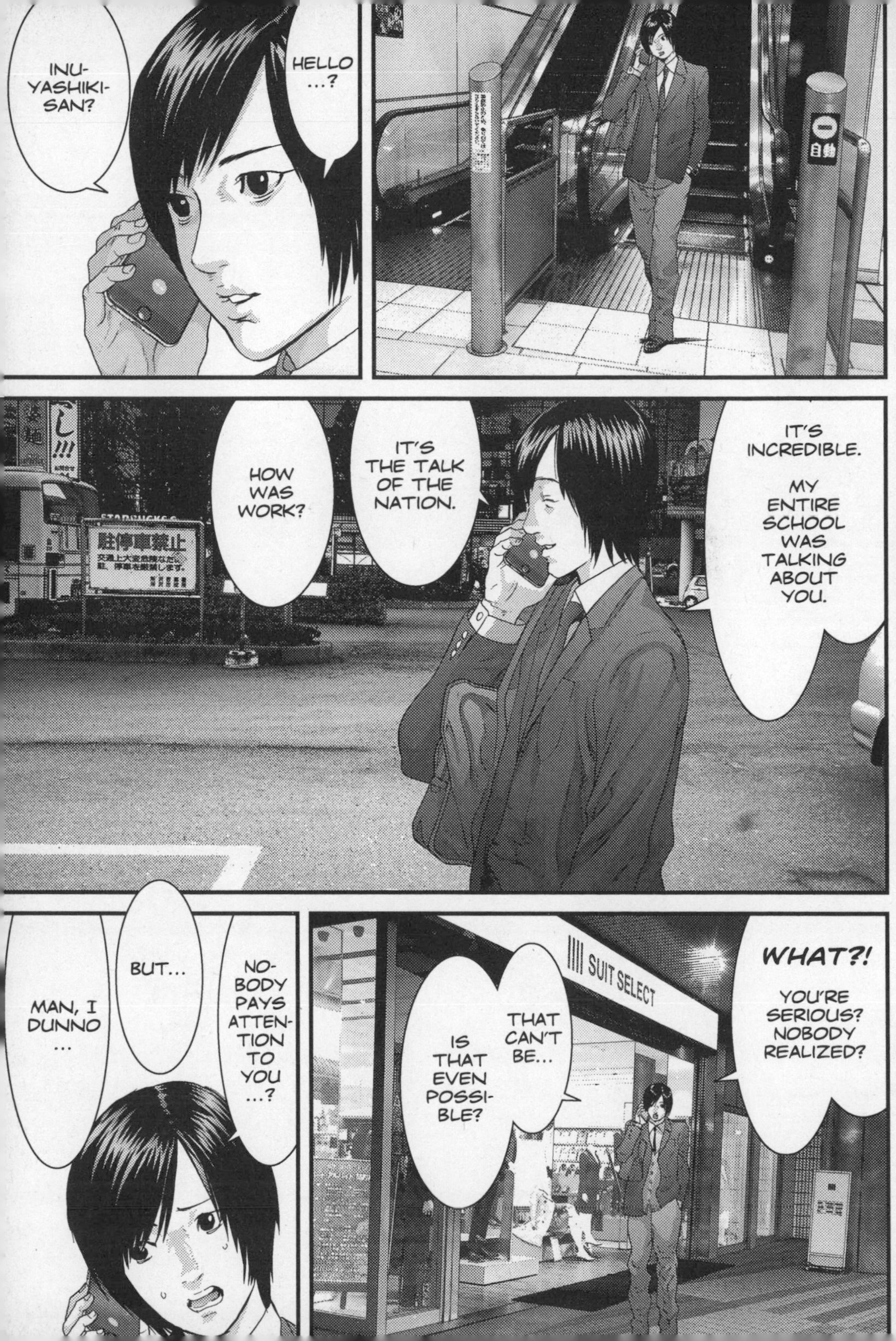
HELLO ...?
INU-YASHIKI-SAN?
IT'S INCREDIBLE.
MY ENTIRE SCHOOL WAS TALKING ABOUT YOU.
IT'S THE TALK OF THE NATION.
HOW WAS WORK?
駐停車禁止
WHAT?!
YOU'RE SERIOUS? NOBODY REALIZED?
SUIT SELECT
THAT CAN'T BE...
IS THAT EVEN POSSIBLE?
NO-BODY PAYS ATTENTION TO YOU ...?
BUT...
MAN, I DUNNO ...

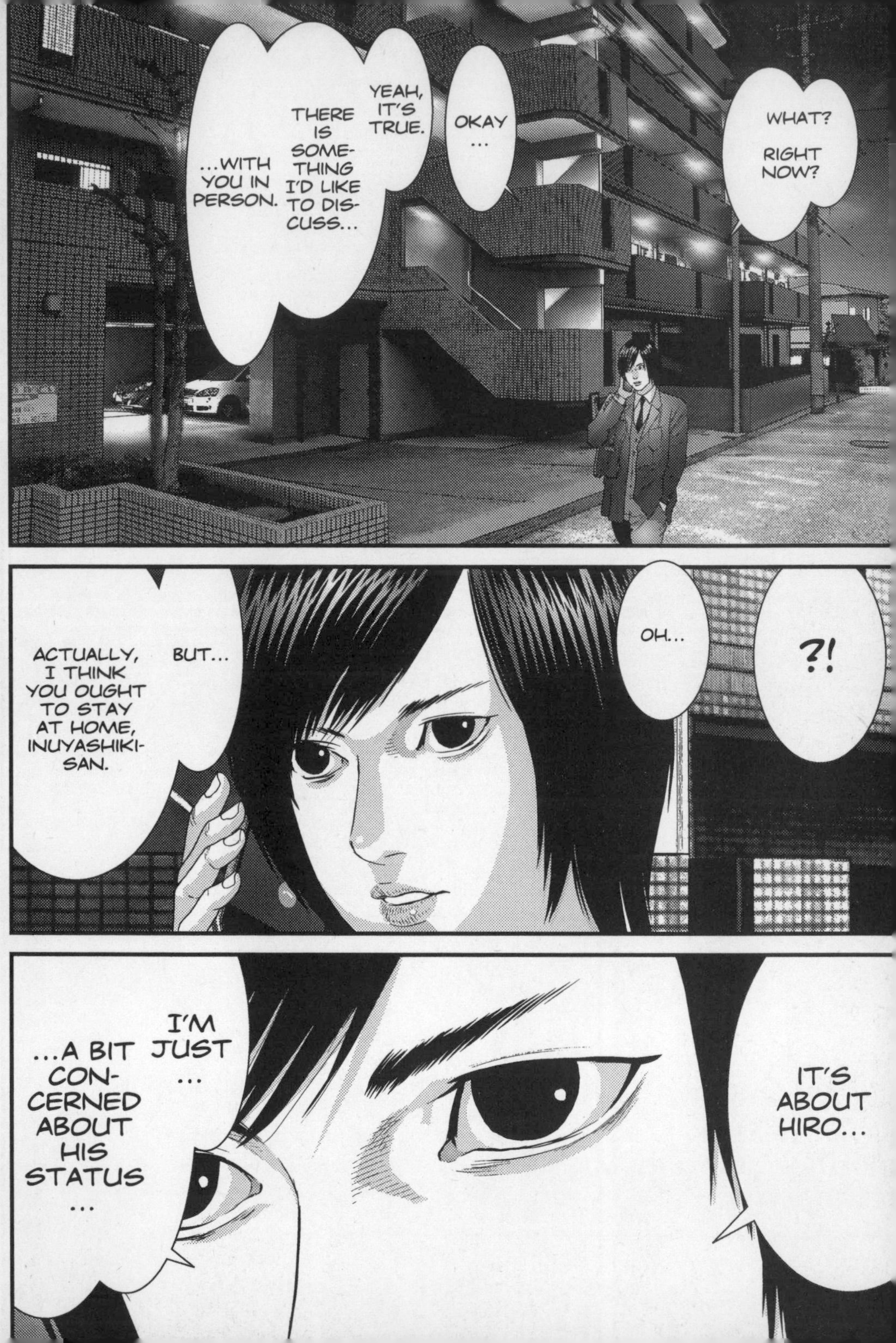
WHAT? RIGHT NOW?
OKAY ...
YEAH, IT'S TRUE.
THERE IS SOMETHING I'D LIKE TO DISCUSS...
...WITH YOU IN PERSON.
?!
OH...
BUT...
ACTUALLY, I THINK YOU OUGHT TO STAY AT HOME, INUYASHIKI-SAN.
IT'S ABOUT HIRO...
I'M JUST ...
...A BIT CONCERNED ABOUT HIS STATUS ...

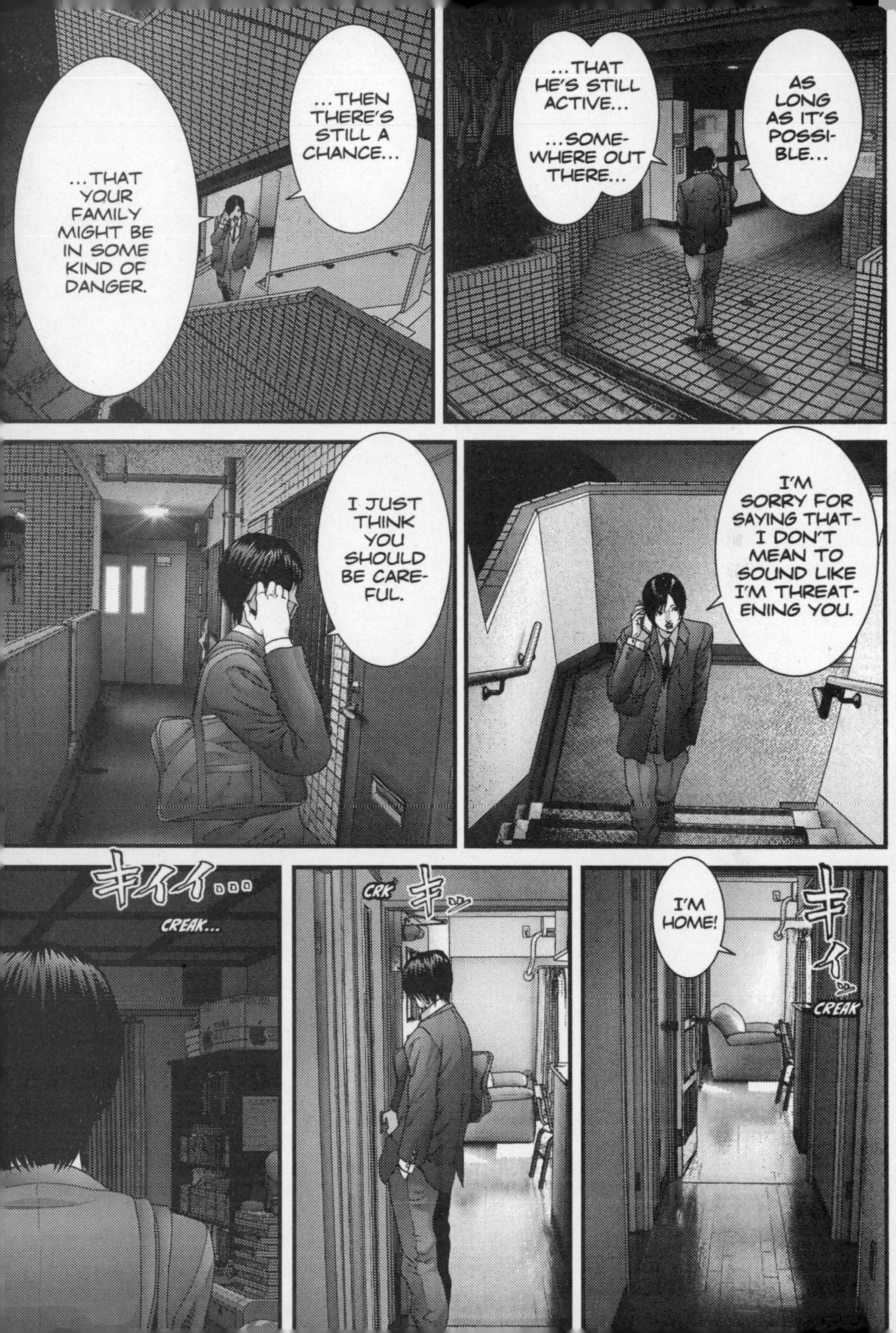
AS LONG AS IT'S POSSIBLE...
...THAT HE'S STILL ACTIVE...
...SOMEWHERE OUT THERE...
...THEN THERE'S STILL A CHANCE...
...THAT YOUR FAMILY MIGHT BE IN SOME KIND OF DANGER.
I'M SORRY FOR SAYING THAT- I DON'T MEAN TO SOUND LIKE I'M THREATENING YOU.
I JUST THINK YOU SHOULD BE CAREFUL.
I'M HOME!
キイ
CREAK
CRK
キッ
キイイ...
CREAK...

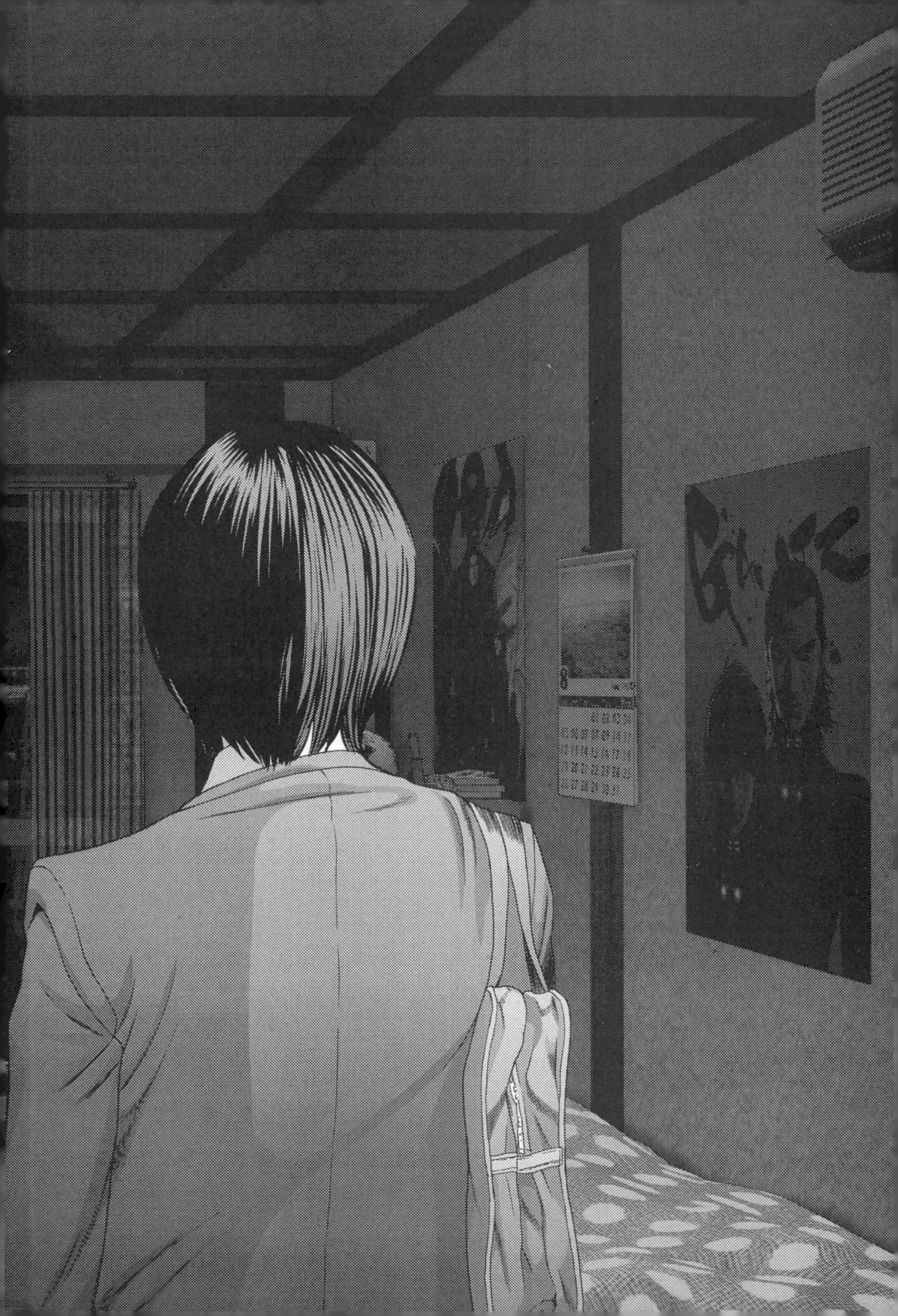

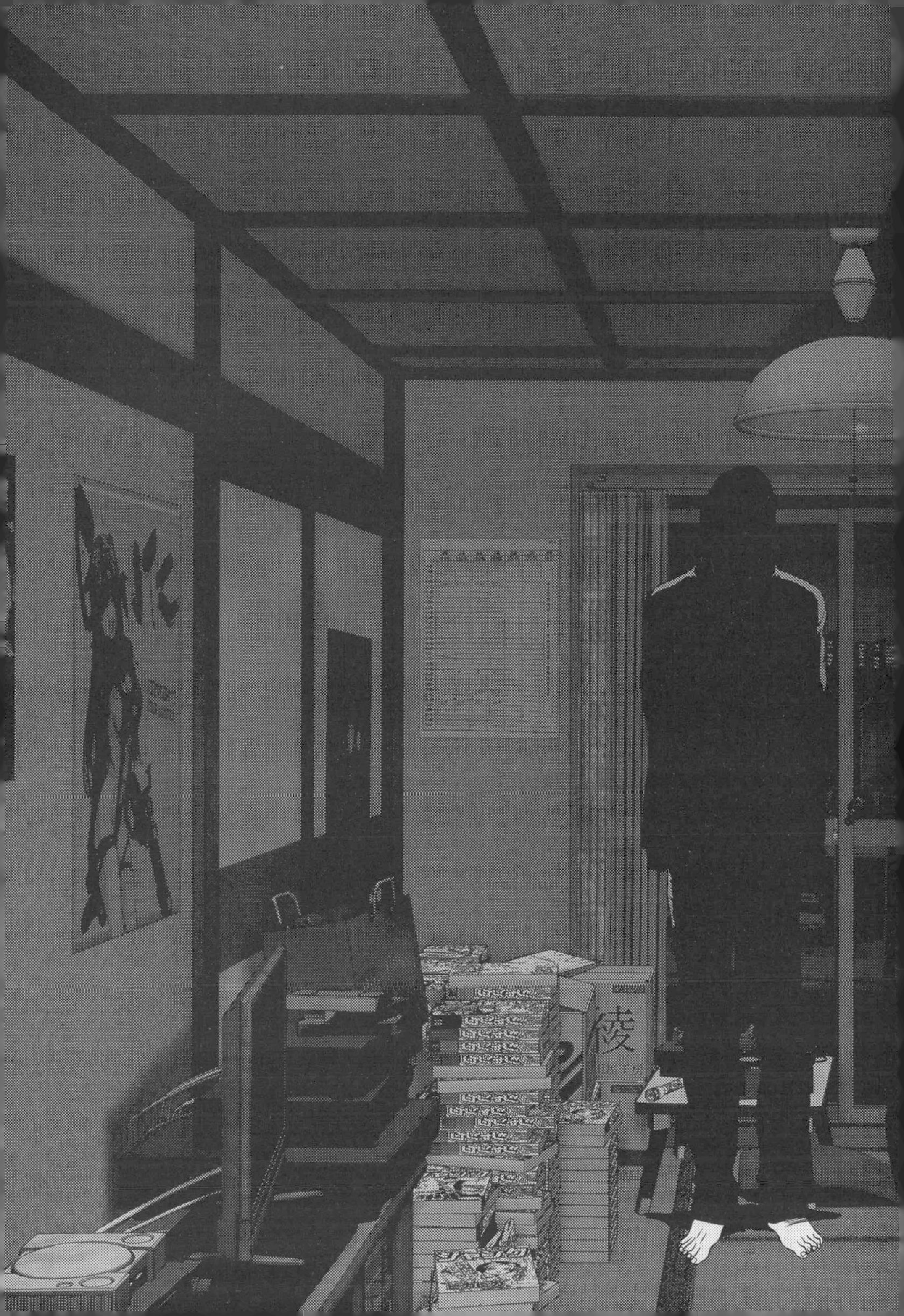
綾

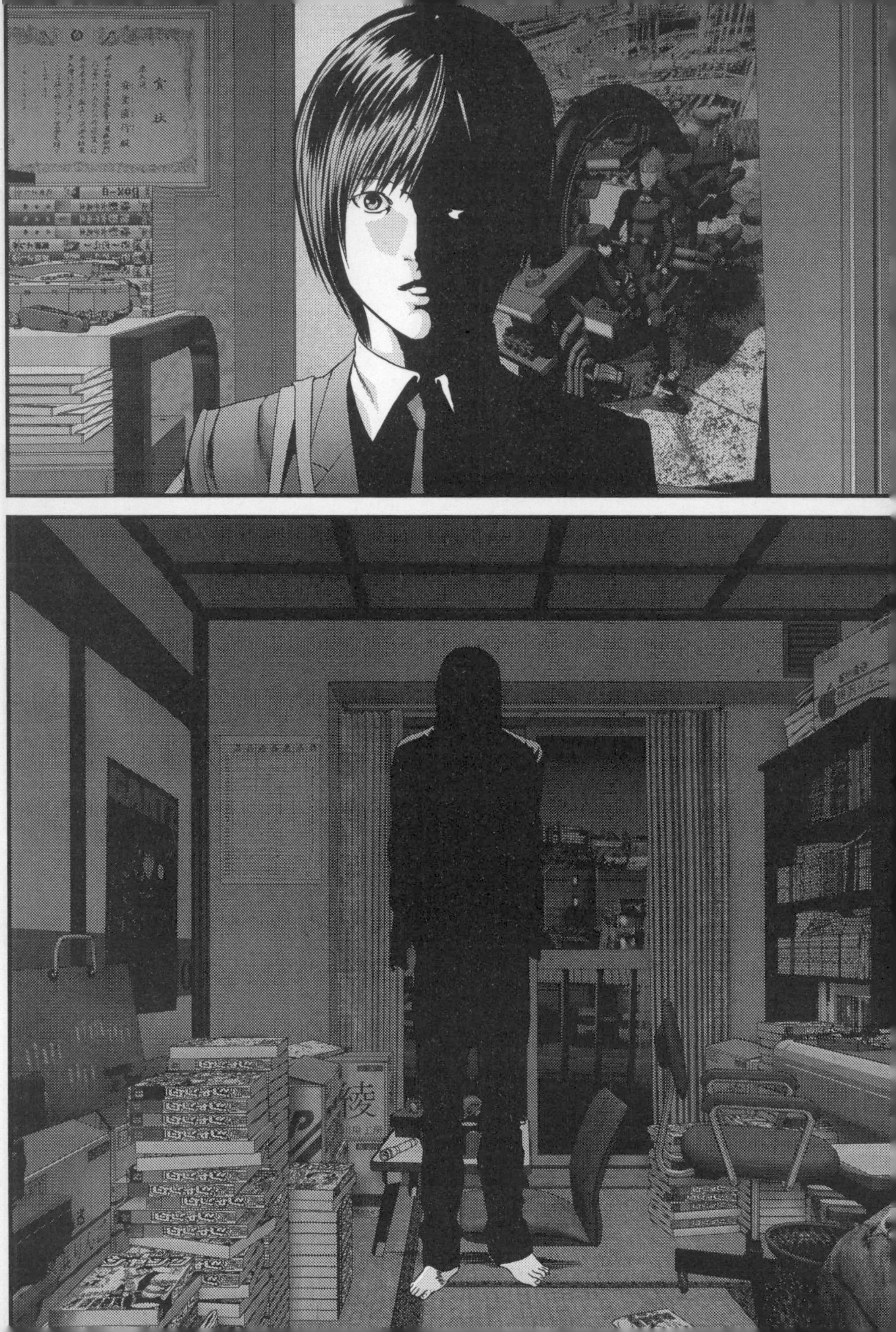
綾

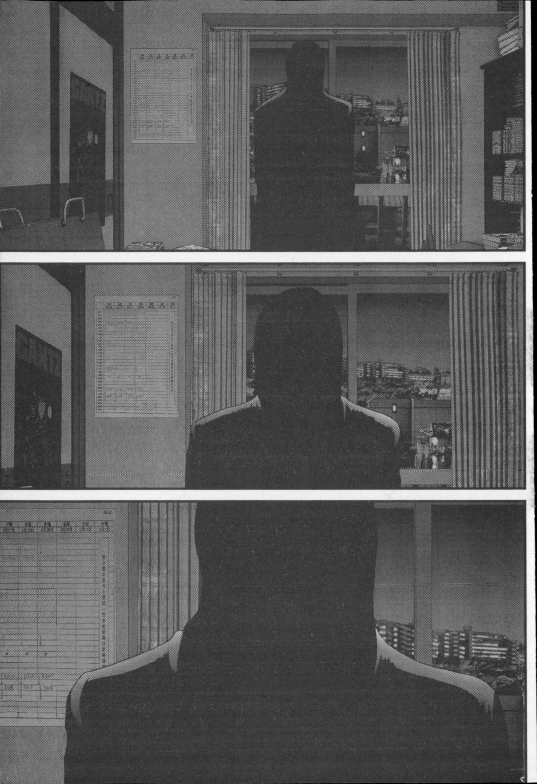

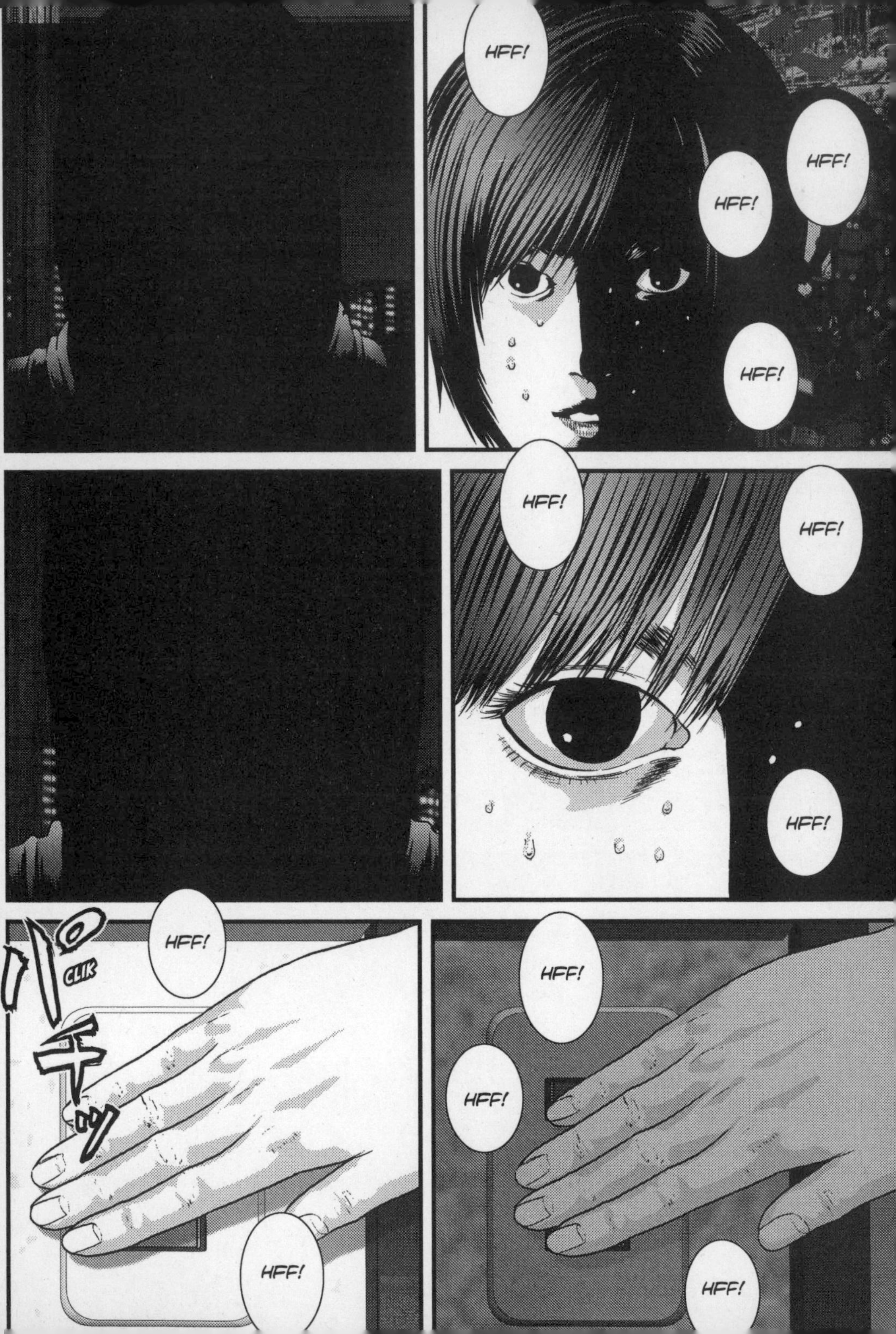
HFF!
HFF!
HFF!
HFF!
HFF!
HFF!
HFF!
HFF!
HFF!
HFF!
パチッ
CLIK
HFF!
HFF!

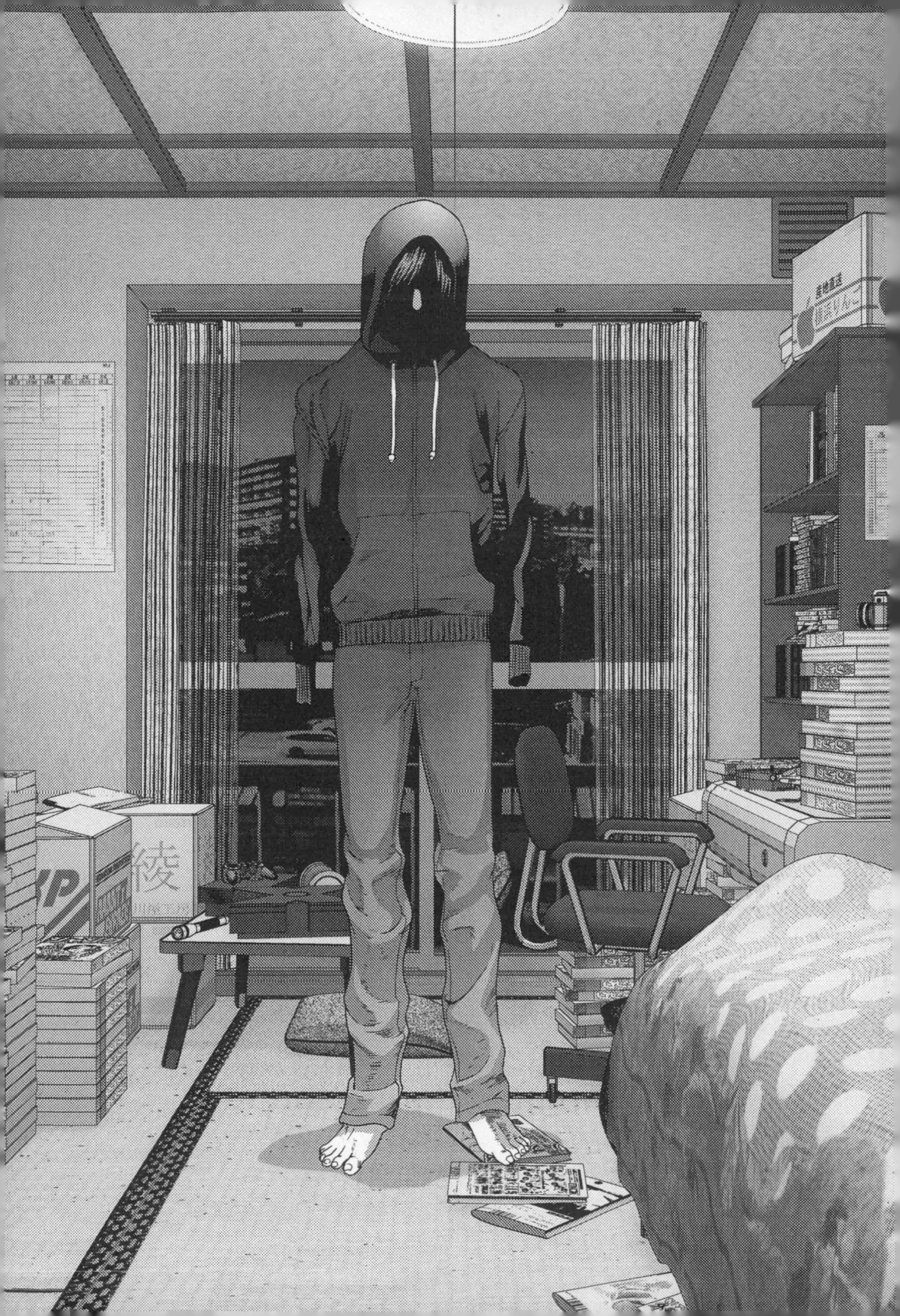
綾

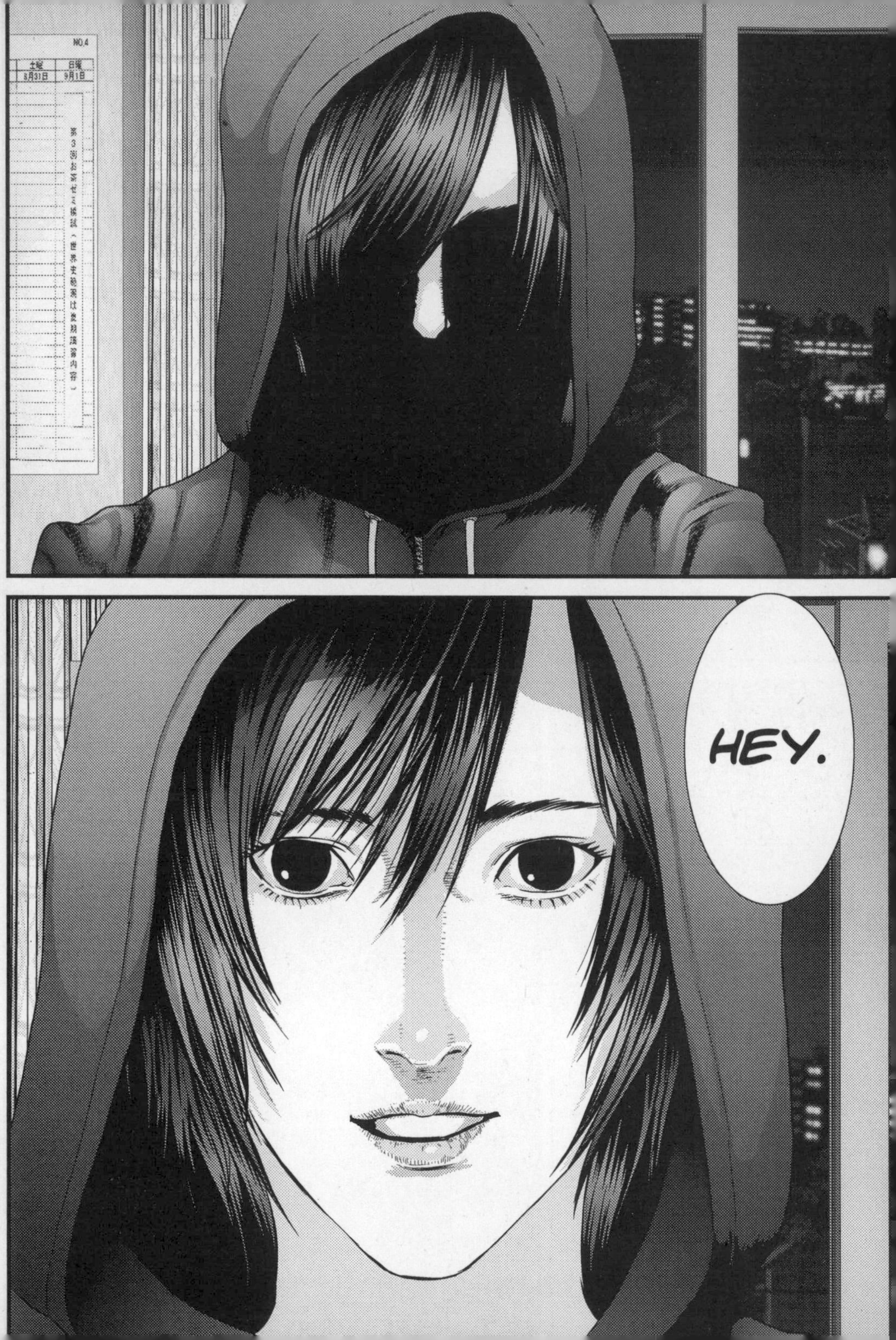
NO.4
8月31日
9月1日
HEY.

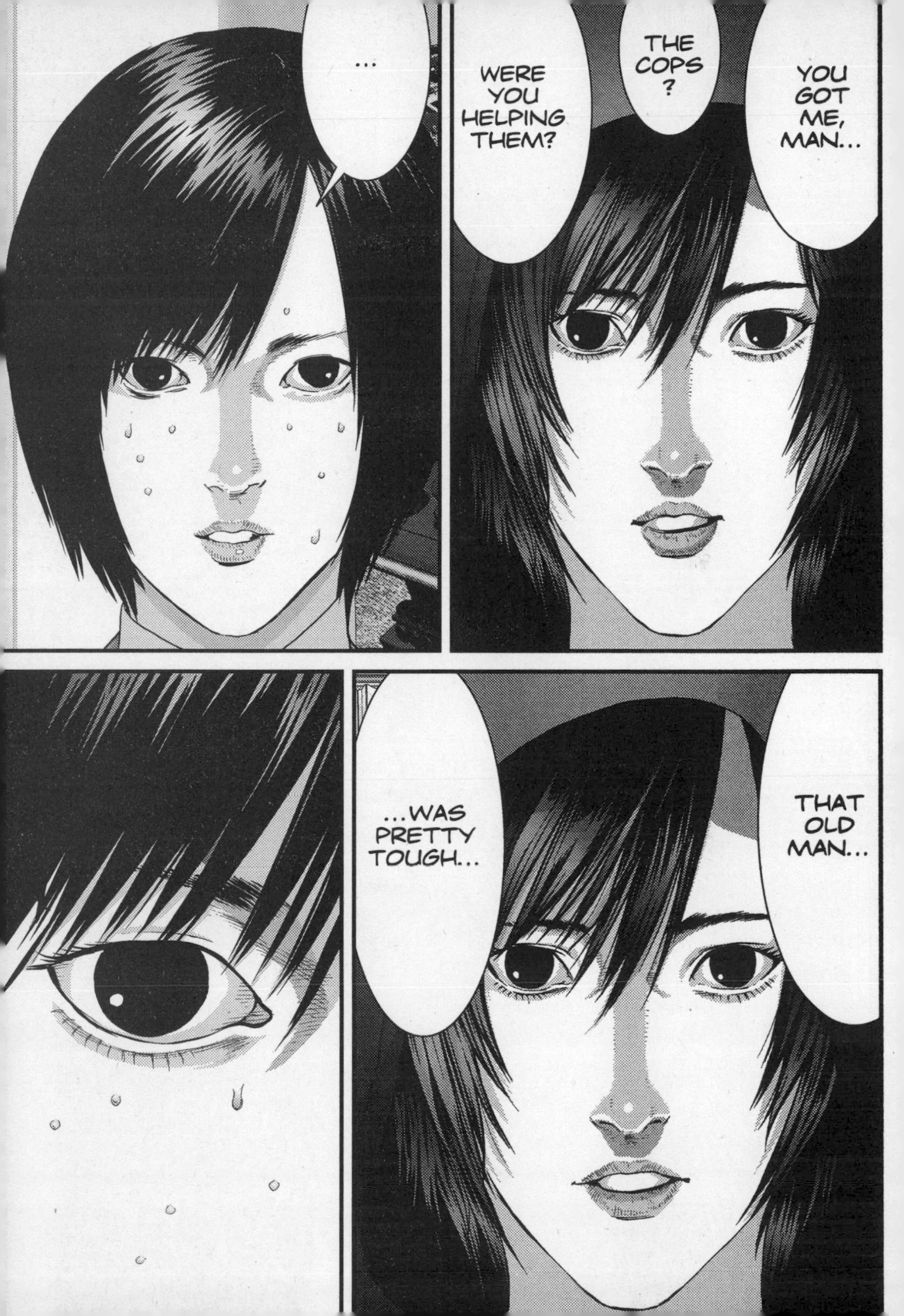
YOU GOT ME, MAN...
THE COPS?
WERE YOU HELPING THEM?
...
THAT OLD MAN...
...WAS PRETTY TOUGH...

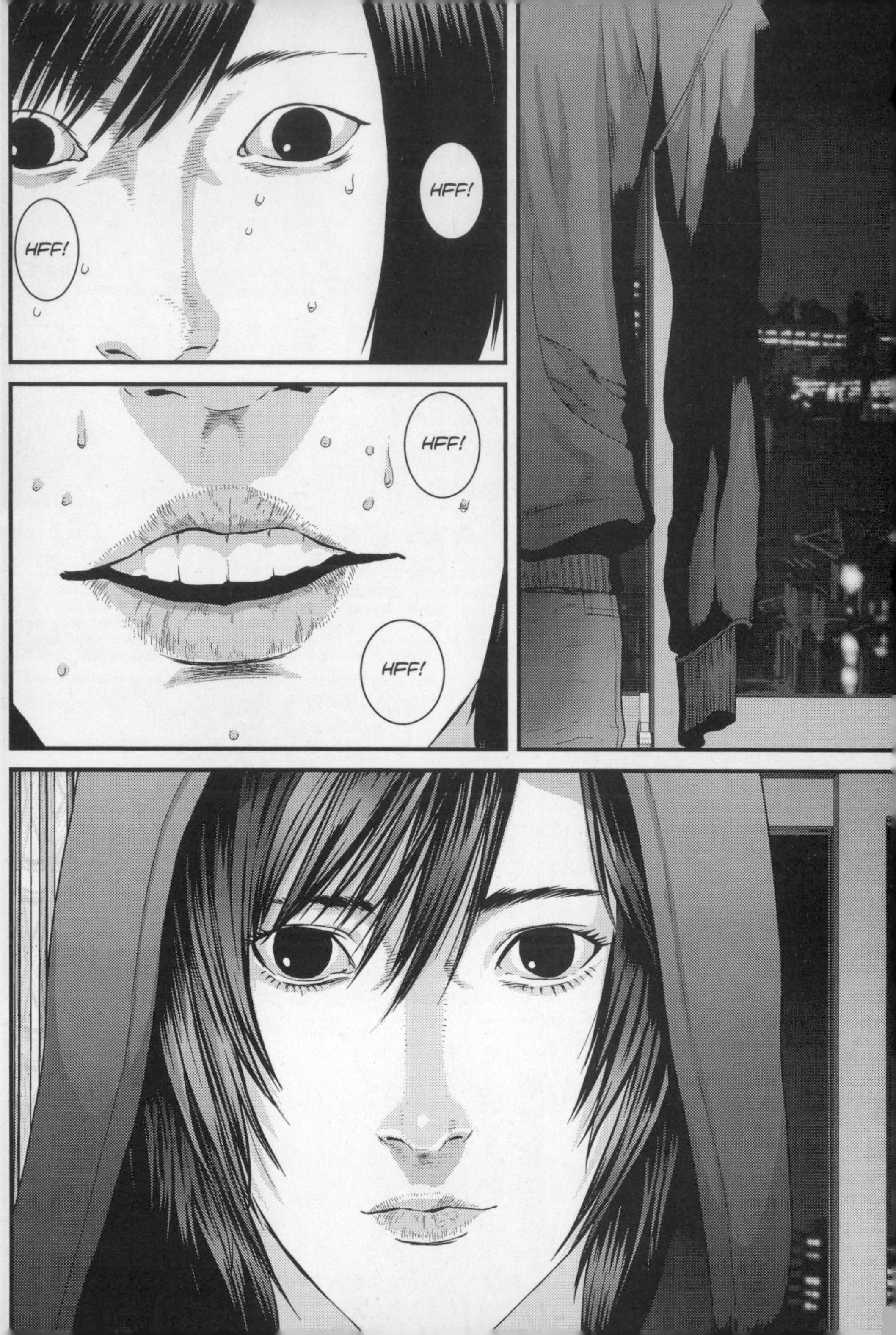
HFF!
HFF!
HFF!
HFF!

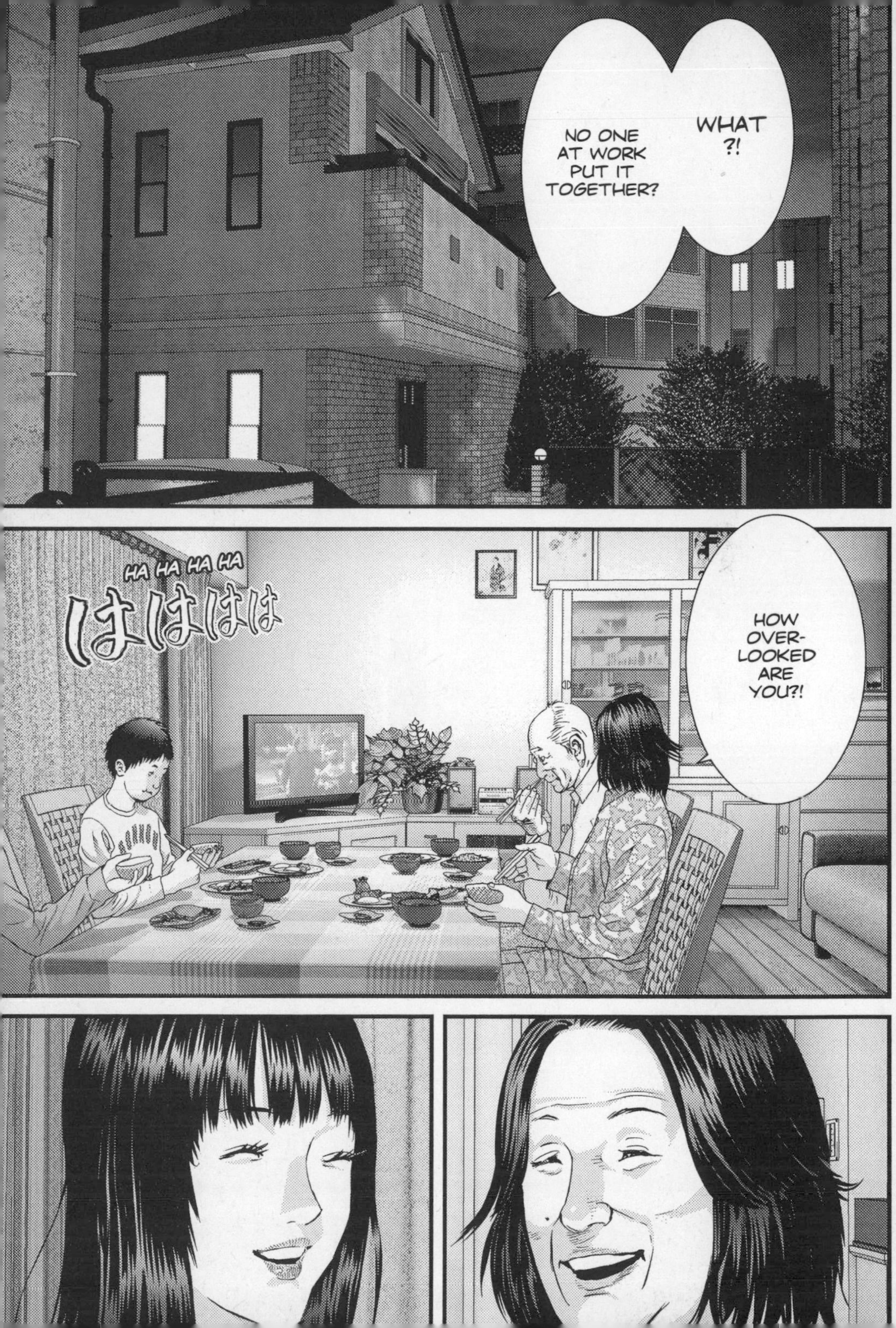
WHAT ?!
NO ONE AT WORK PUT IT TOGETHER?
HOW OVER-LOOKED ARE YOU?!
HA HA HA HA
はははは

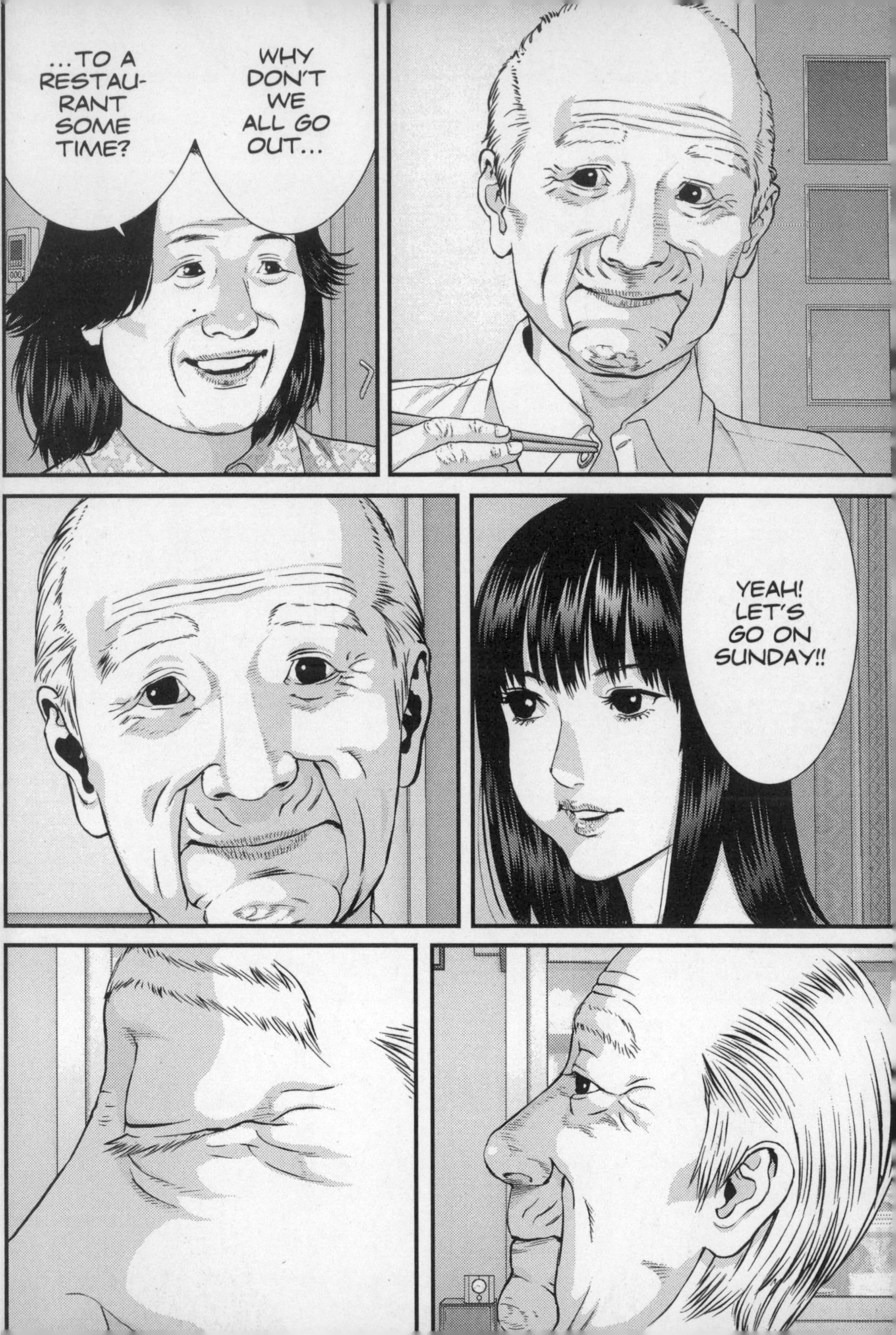
WHY DON'T WE ALL GO OUT...
...TO A RESTAU-RANT SOME TIME?
YEAH! LET'S GO ON SUNDAY!!

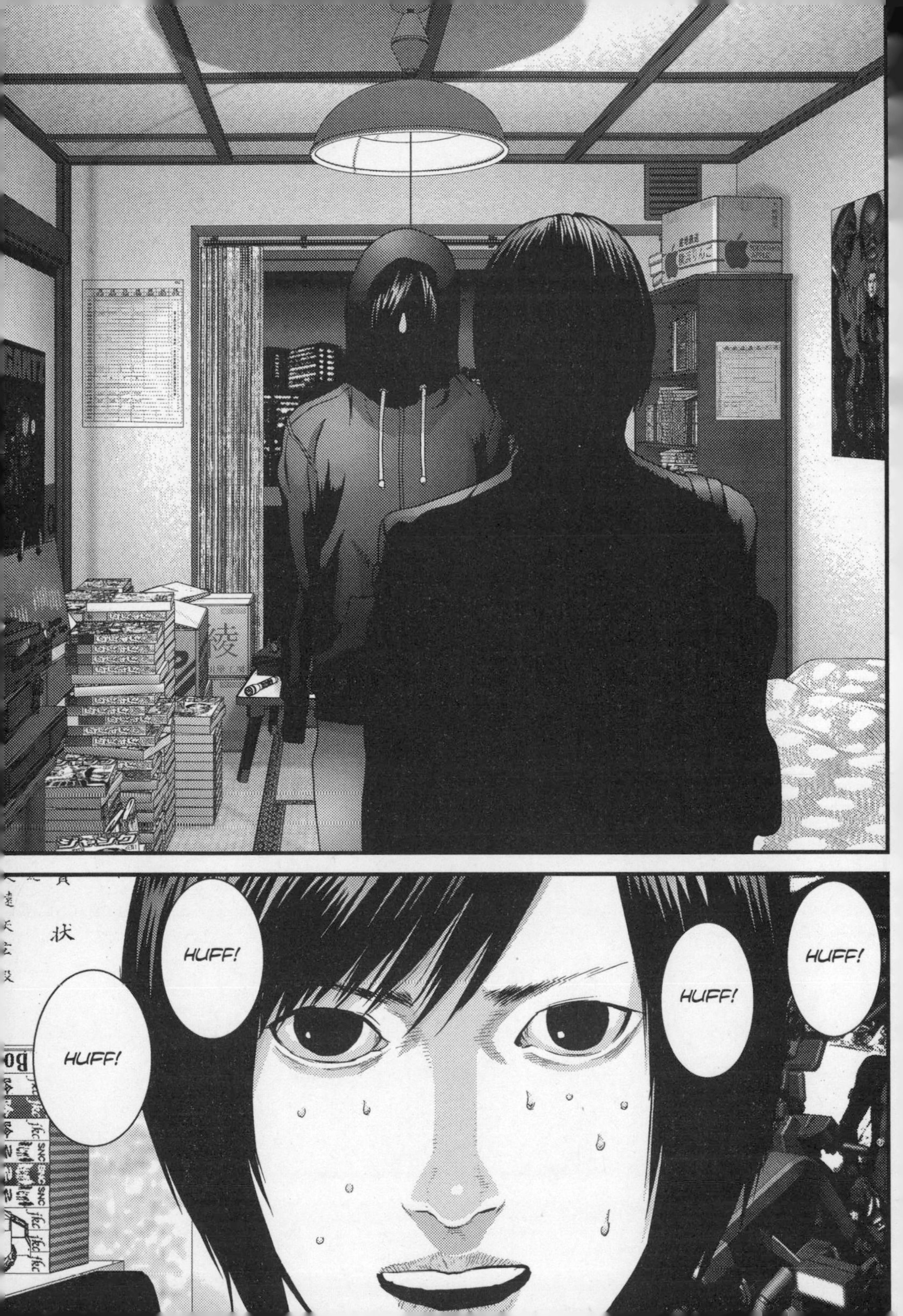
HUFF!
HUFF!
HUFF!
HUFF!

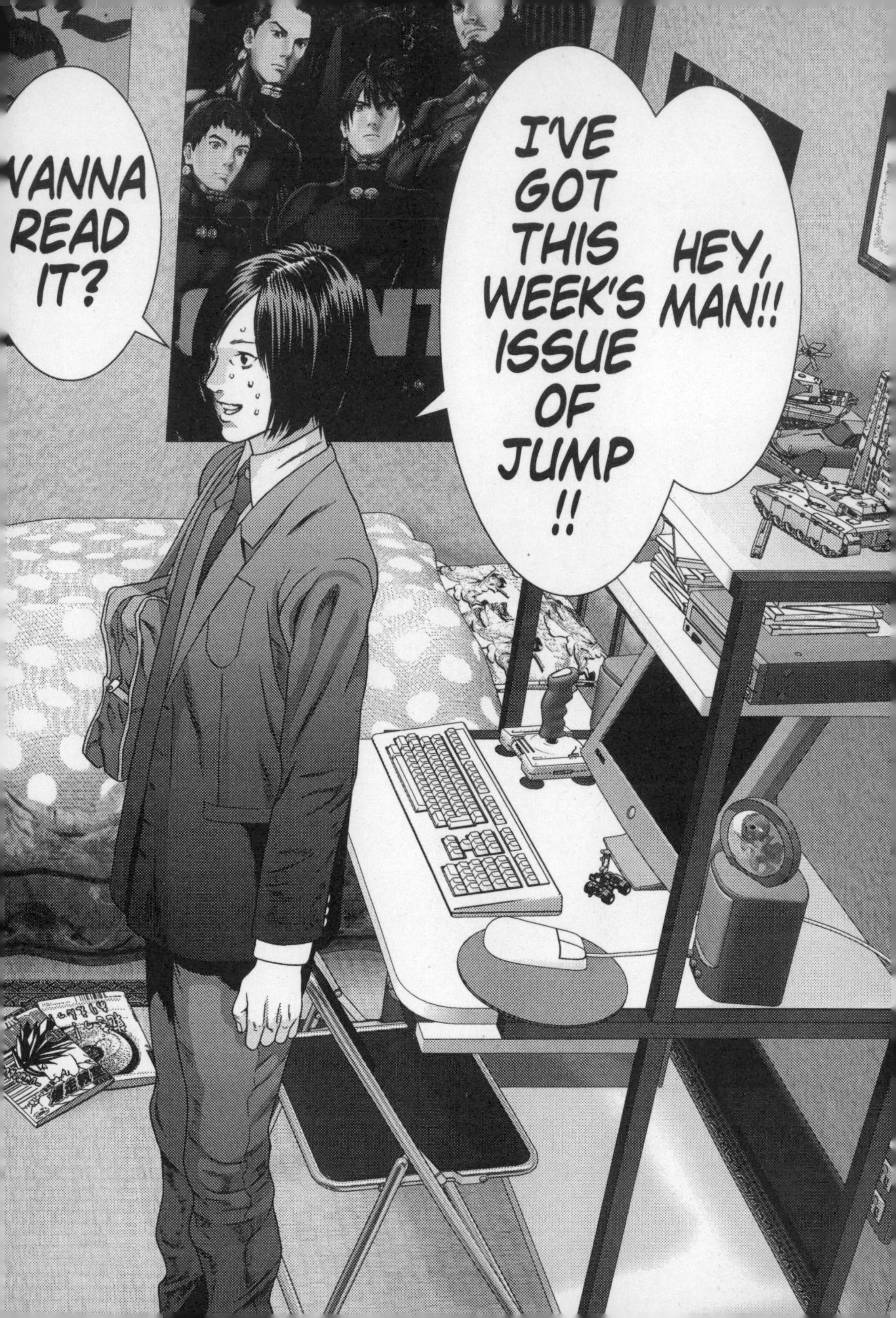
HEY, MAN!!
I'VE GOT THIS WEEK'S ISSUE OF JUMP!!
VANNA READ IT?

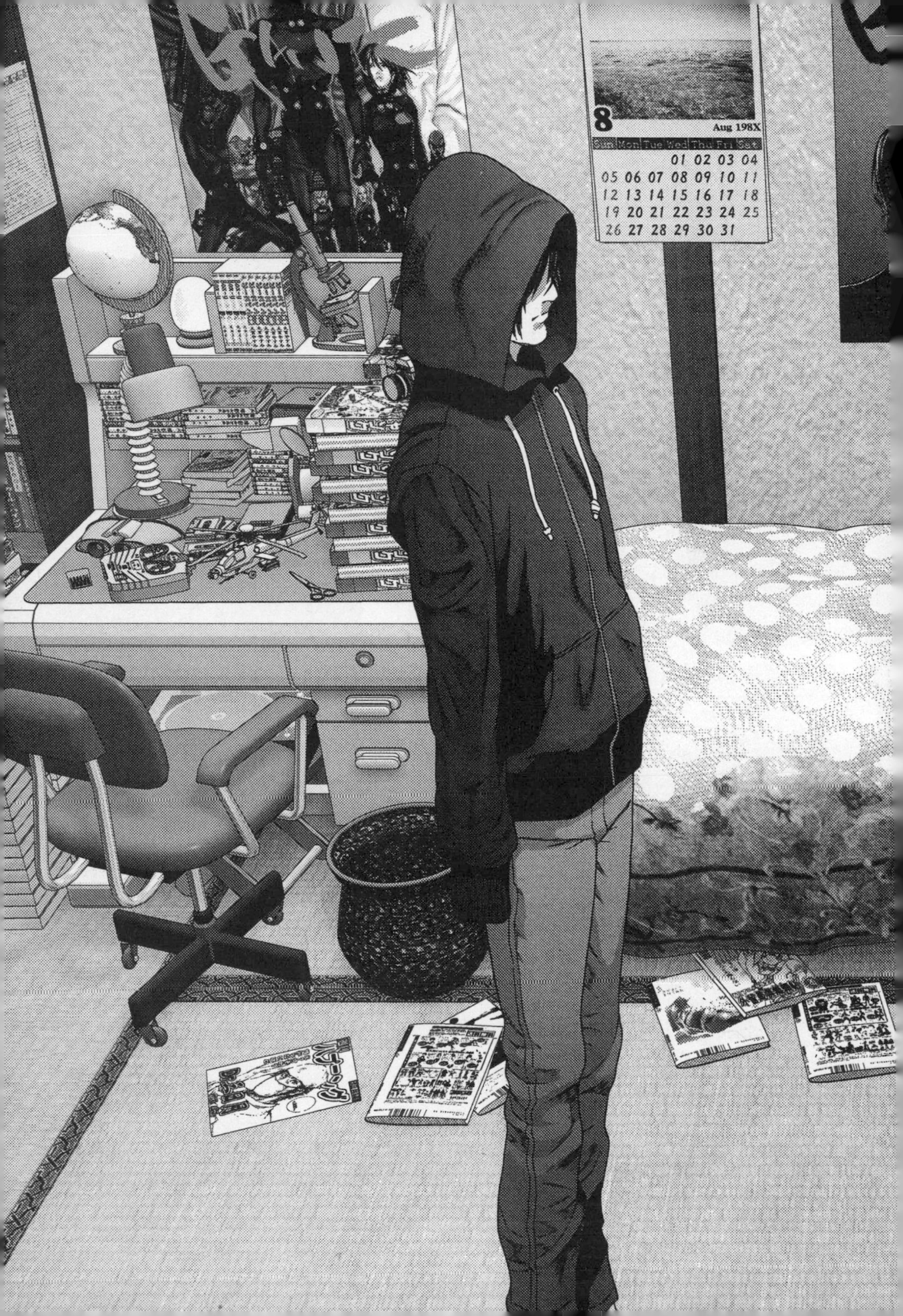
8
Aug 198X
Sun Mon Tue Wed Thu Fri Sat
01 02 03 04
05 06 07 08 09 10 11
12 13 14 15 16 17 18
19 20 21 22 23 24 25
26 27 28 29 30 31

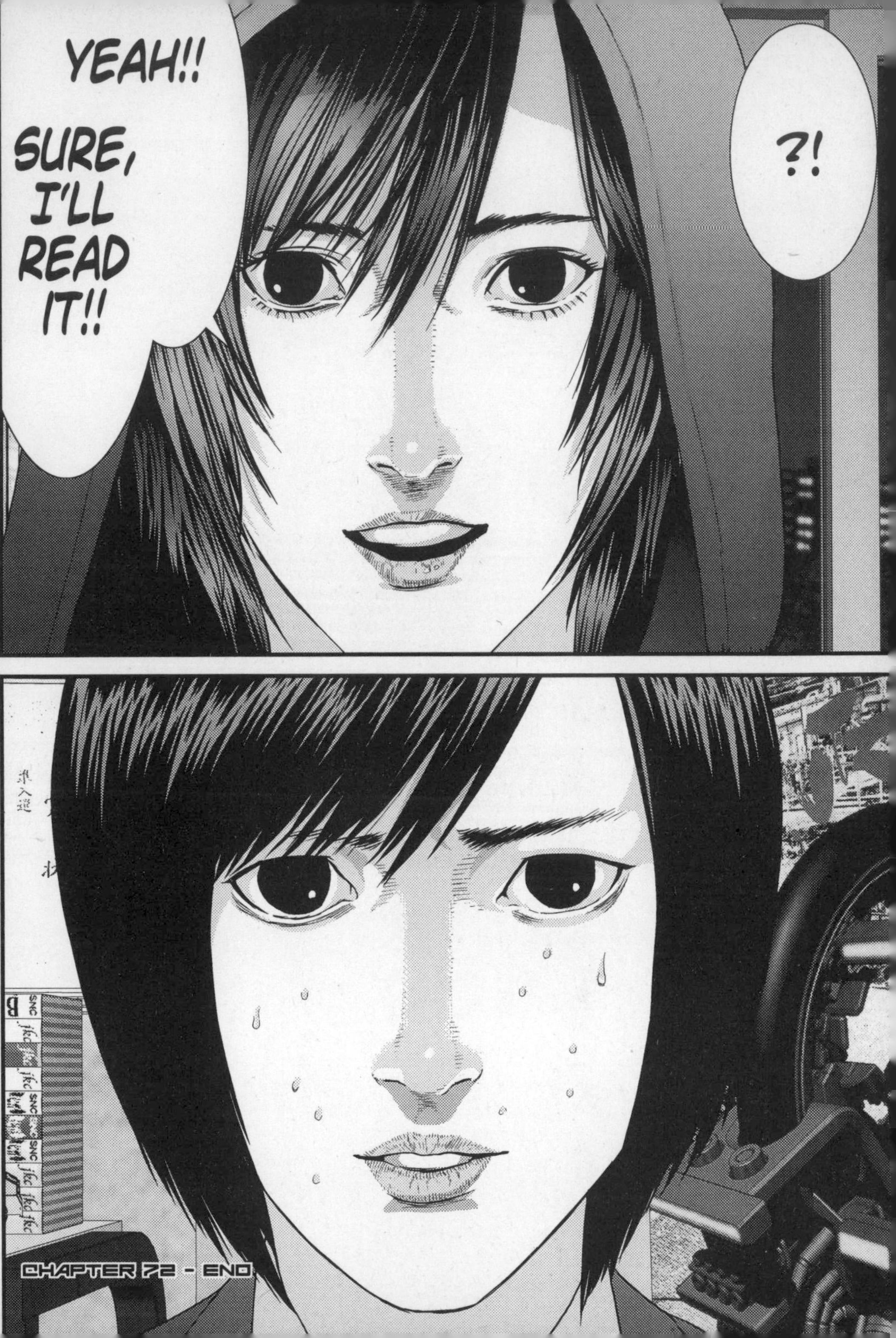
?!
YEAH!!
SURE, I'LL READ IT!!
CHAPTER 72 - END

I N U Y A S H I K I

I N U Y A S H I K I

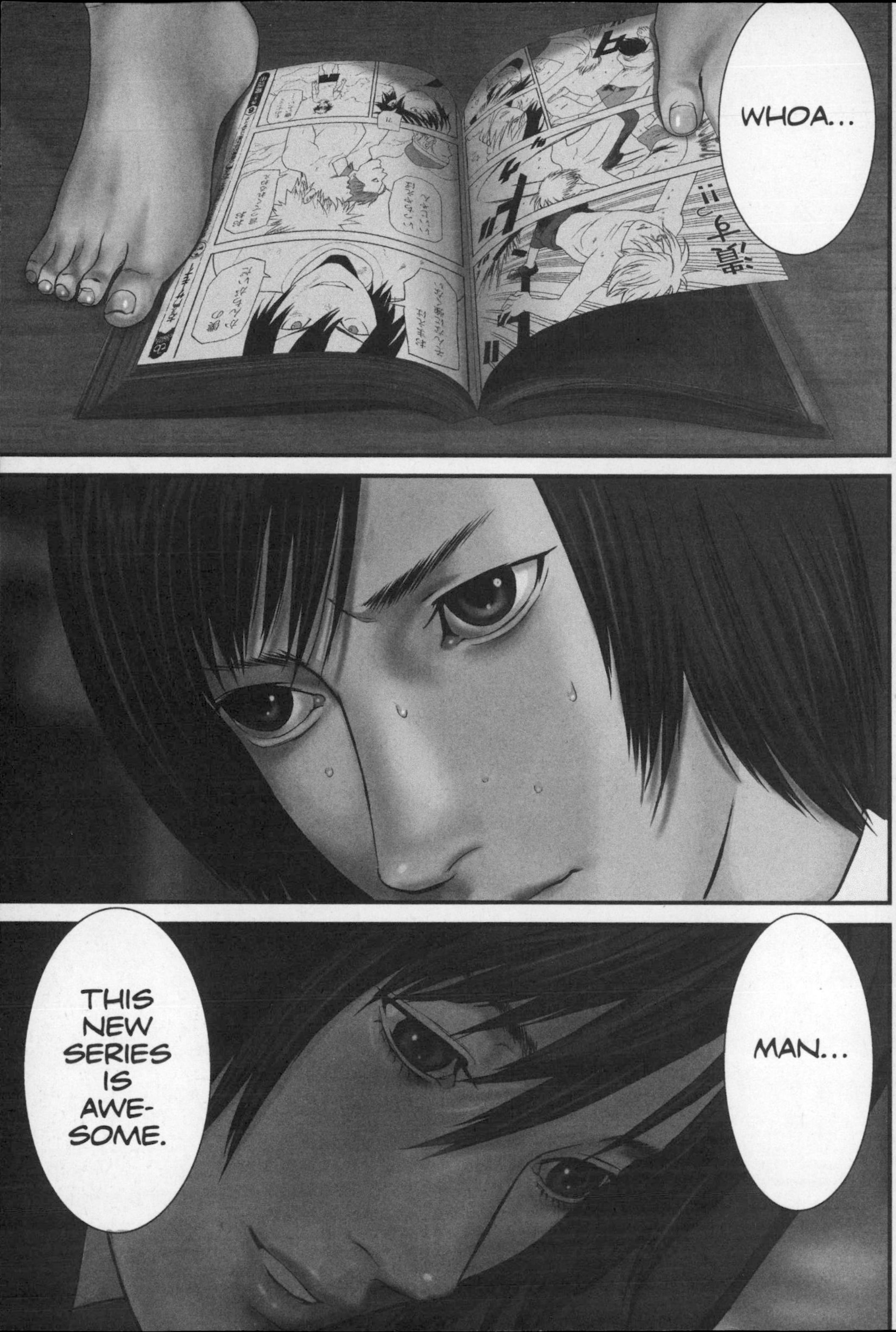
WHOA...
MAN...
THIS NEW SERIES IS AWESOME.

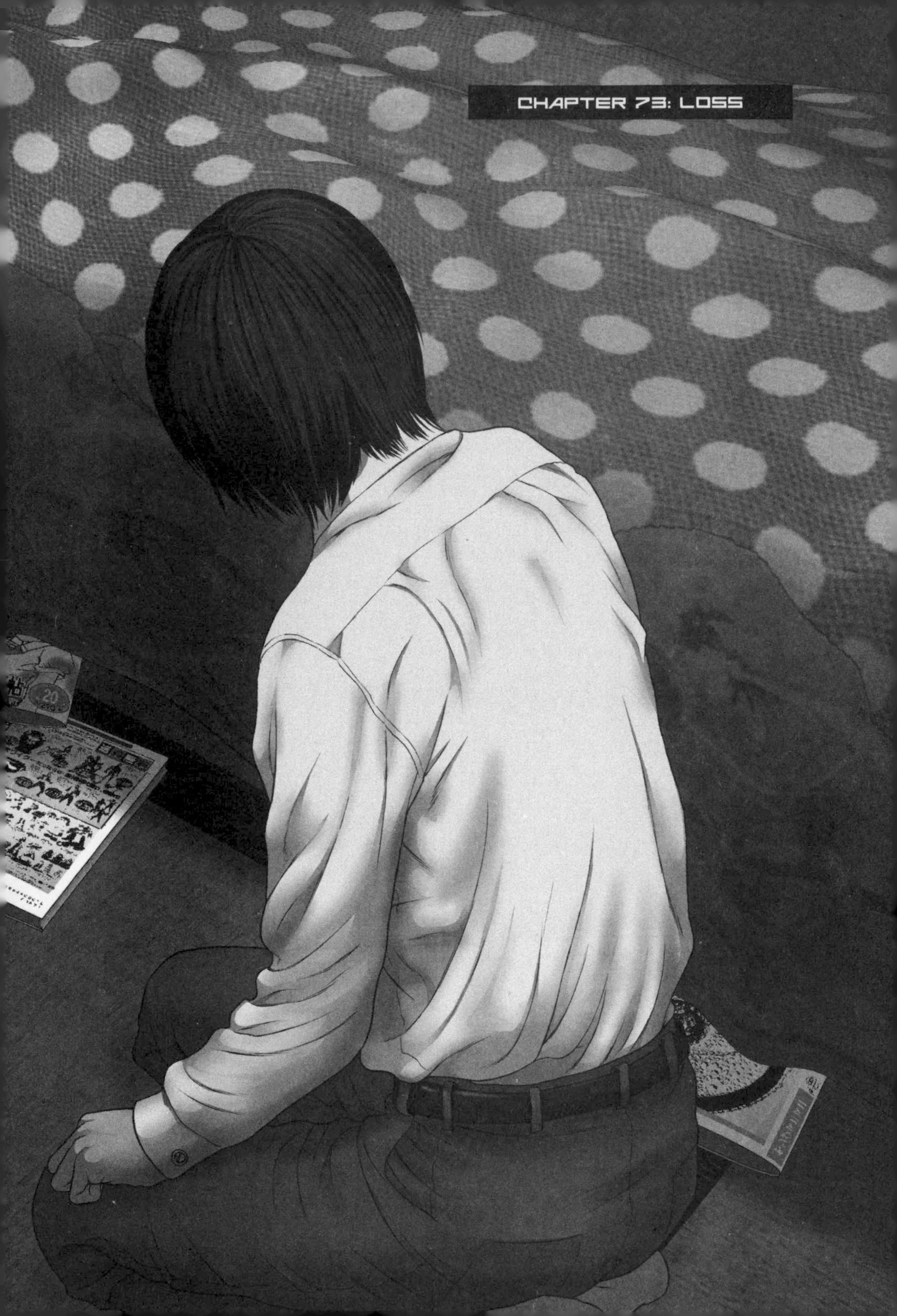
CHAPTER 73: LOSS

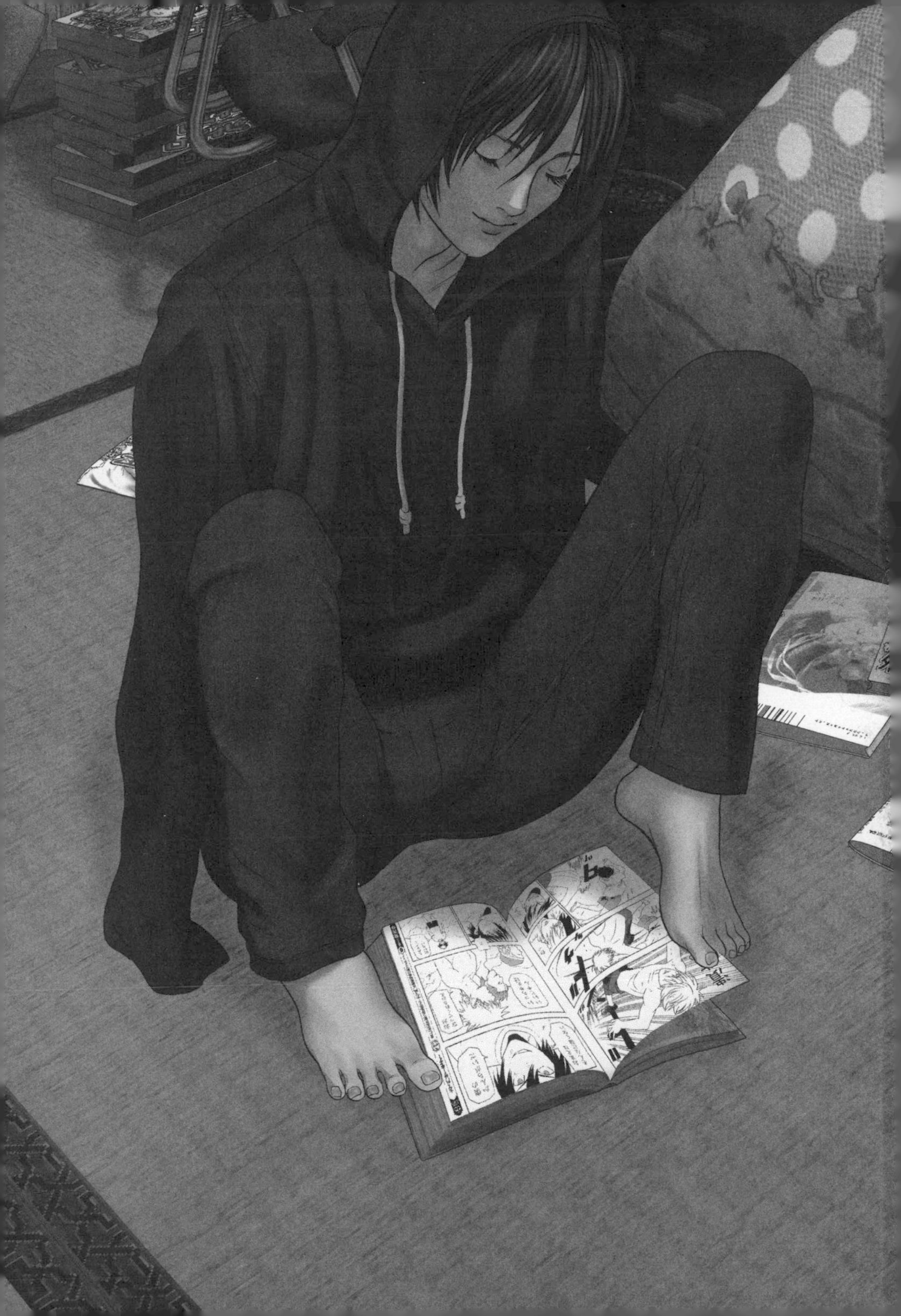

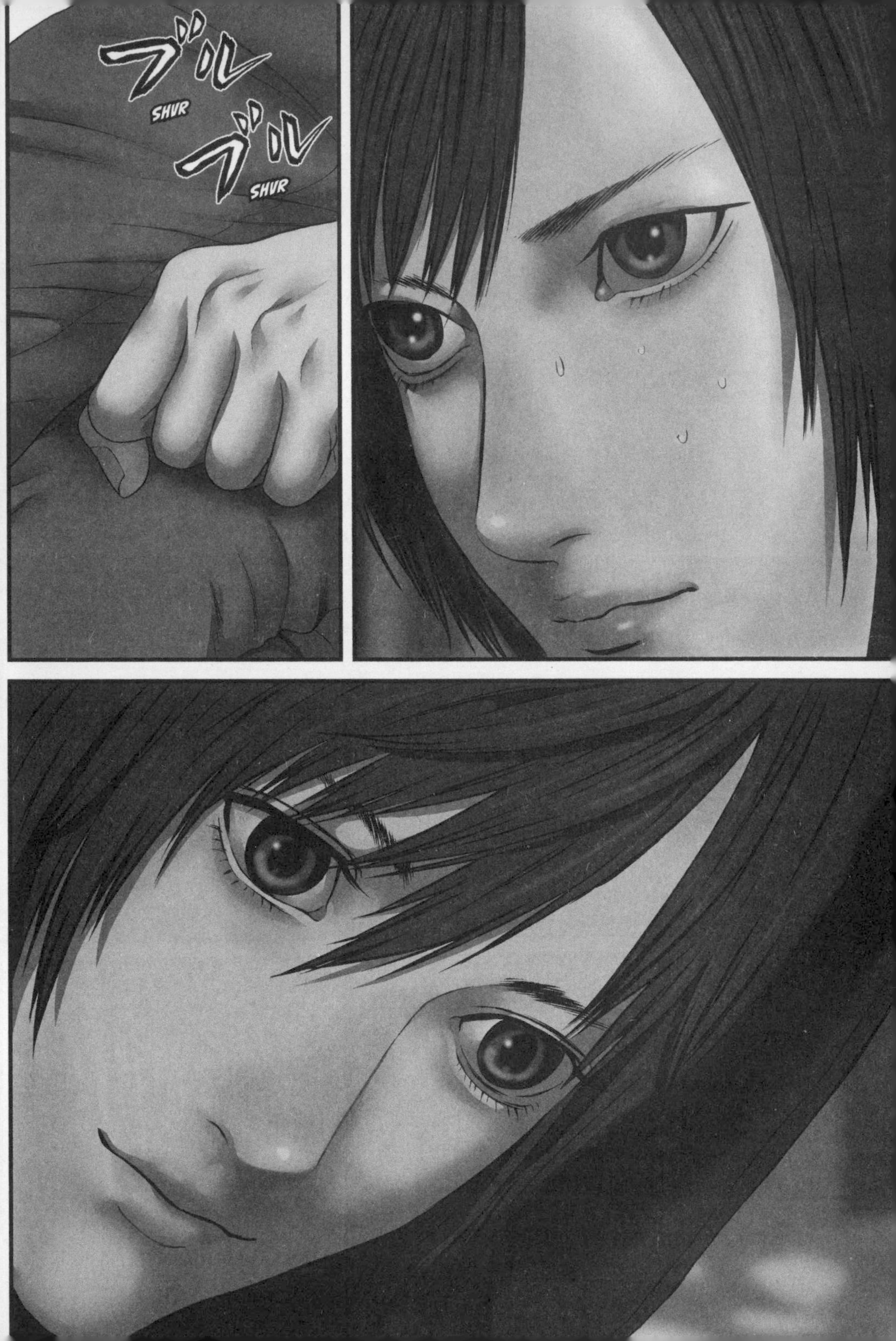
ブル
SHVR
ブル
SHVR

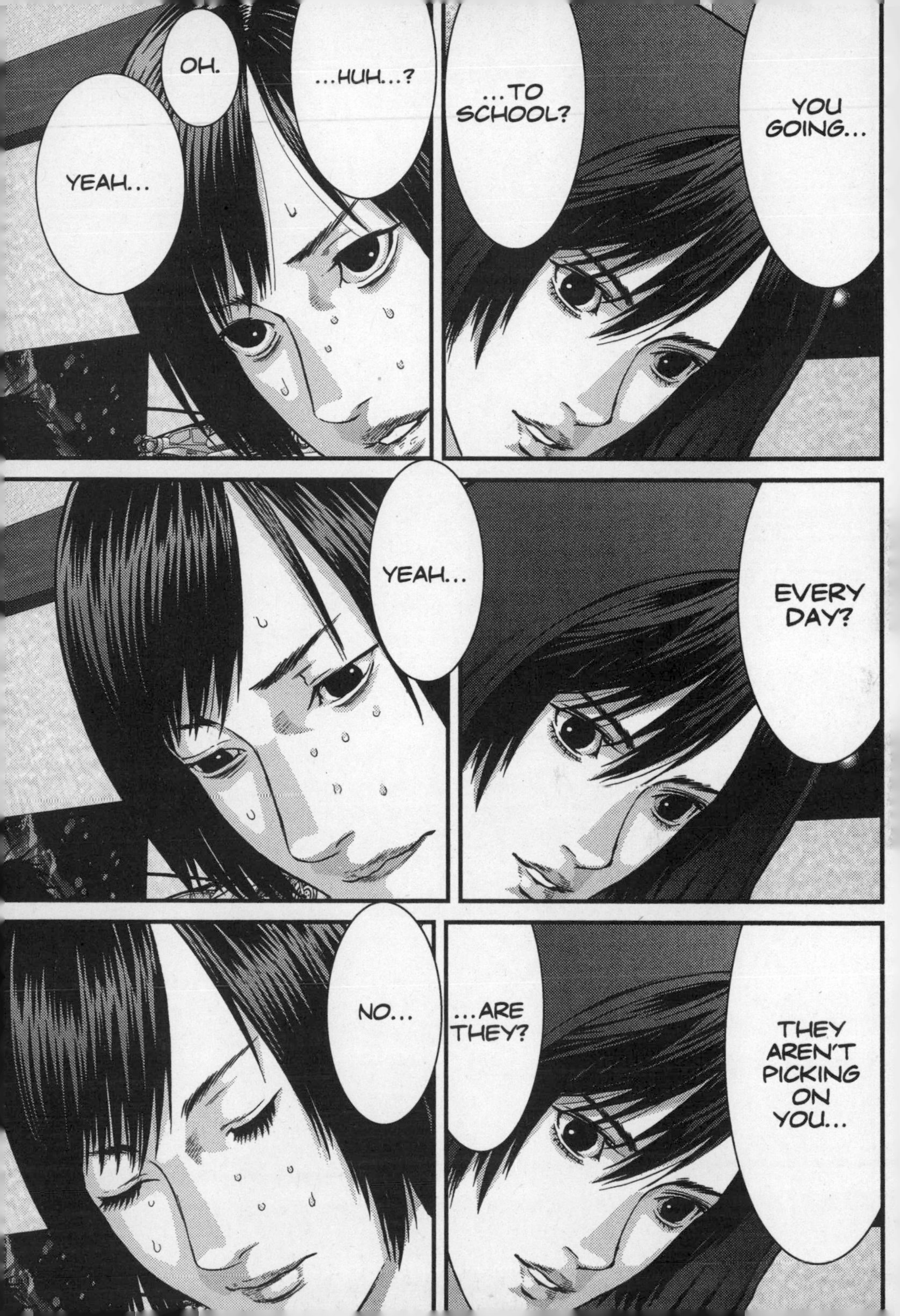

YOU GOING...
...TO SCHOOL?
...HUH...?
OH.
YEAH...
EVERY DAY?
YEAH...
THEY AREN'T PICKING ON YOU...
...ARE THEY?
NO...

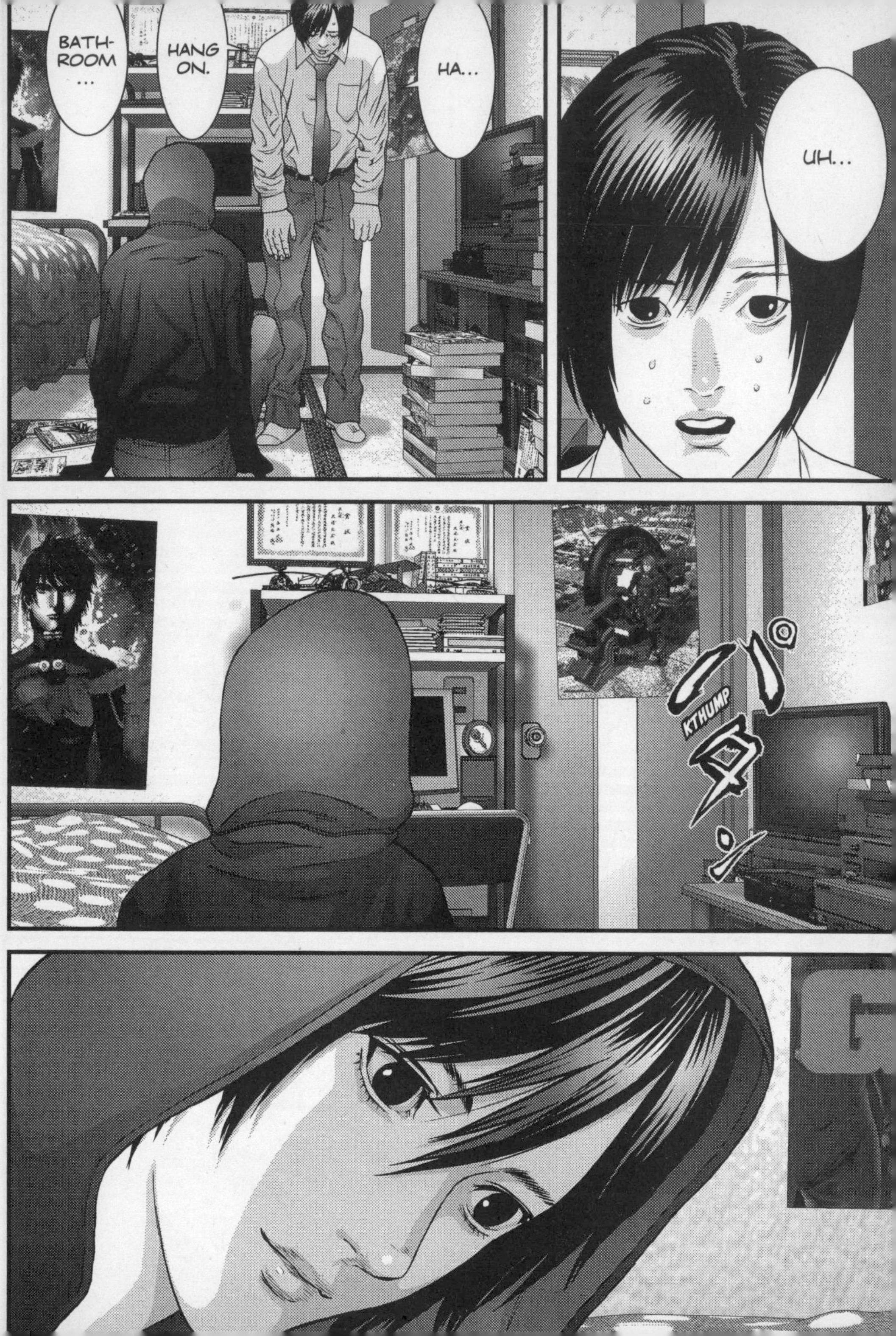
UH...
HA...
HANG ON.
BATH-ROOM ...
パタン
KTHUMP

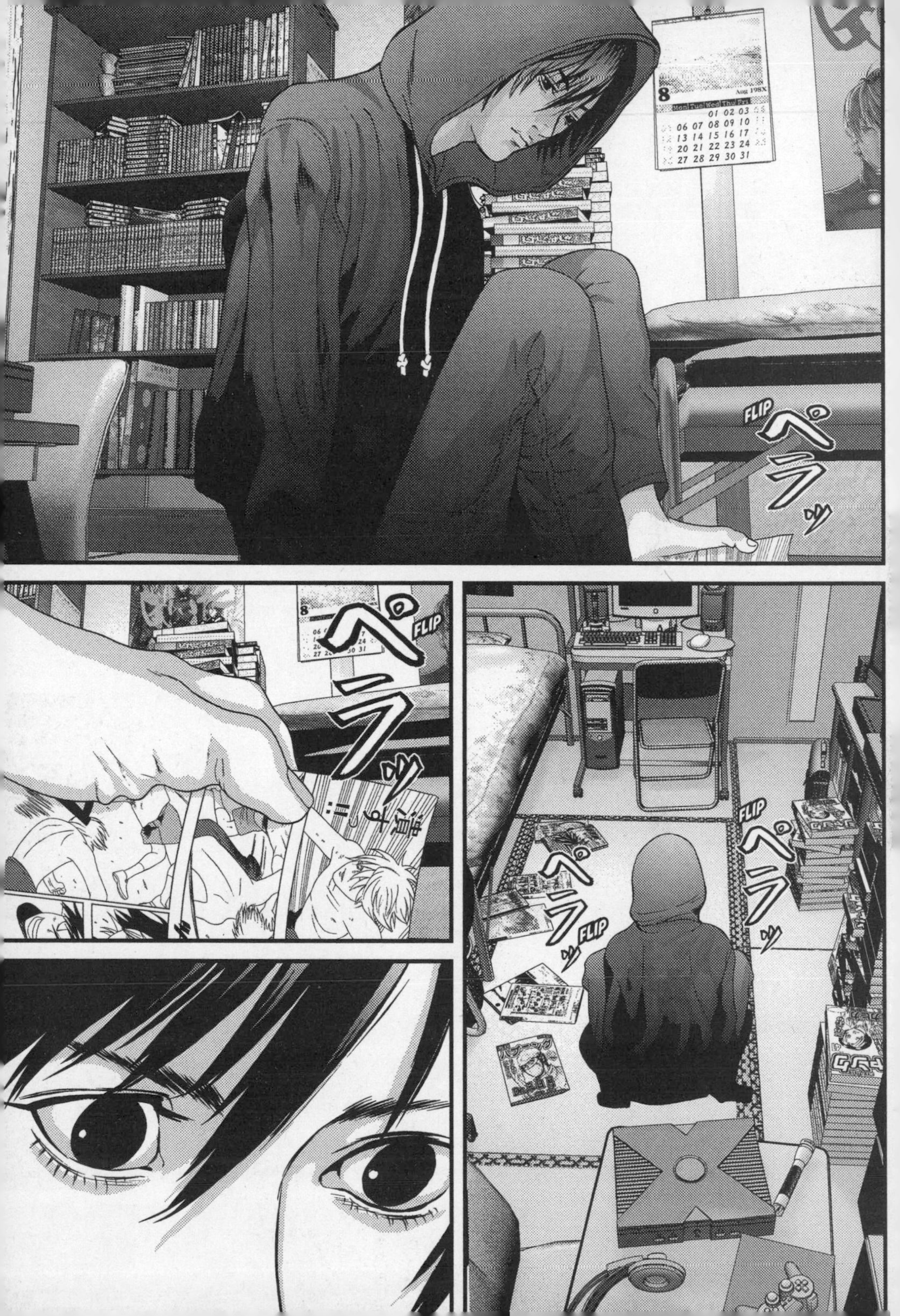
8
Aug 198X
FLIP
ペラッ
FLIP
ペラッ
FLIP
ペラッ
ペラッ
FLIP

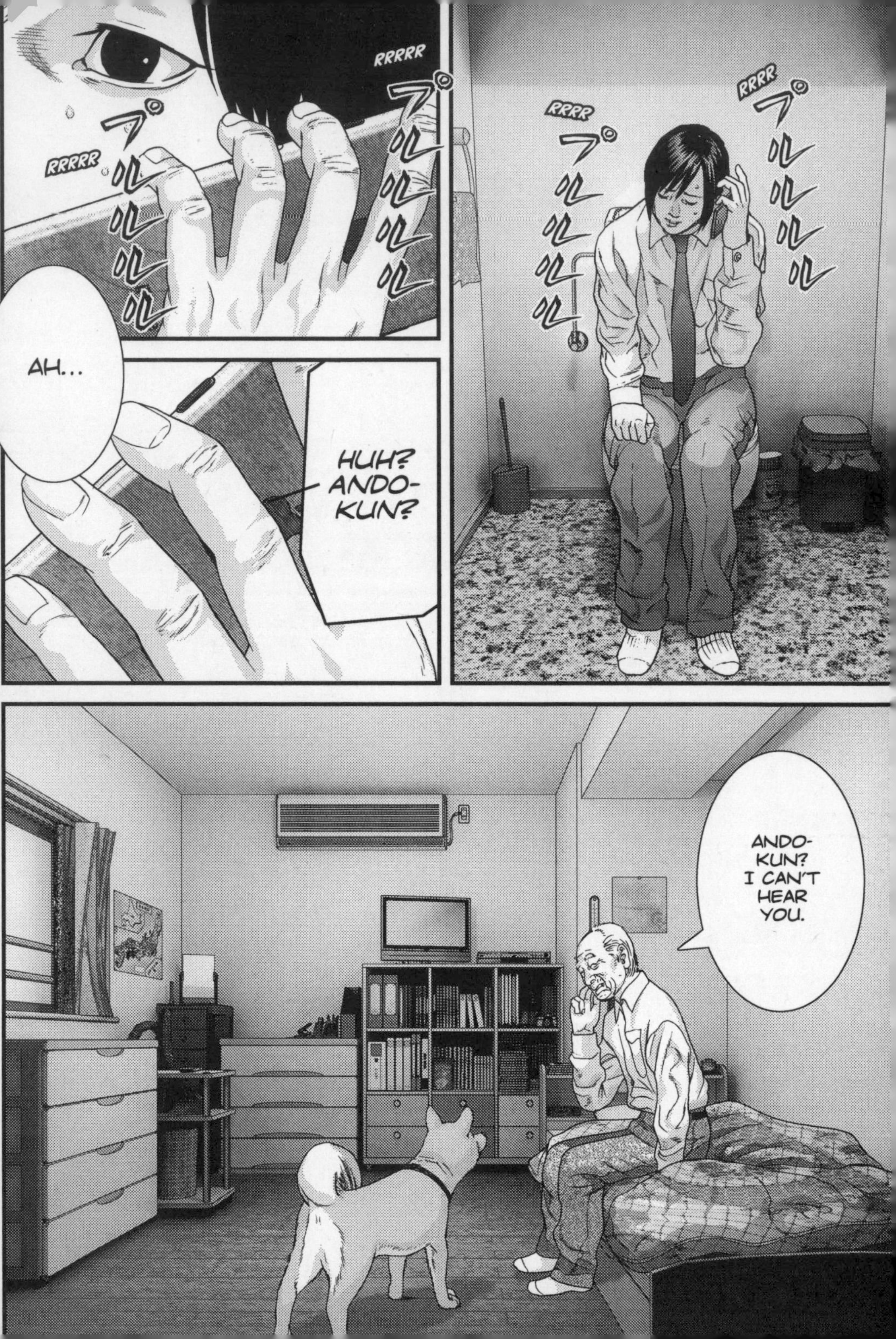
RRRR
プルルルル
RRRR
プルルルル
RRRRR
プルルルル
RRRRR
プルルルルル
AH...
HUH? ANDO-KUN?
ANDO-KUN? I CAN'T HEAR YOU.

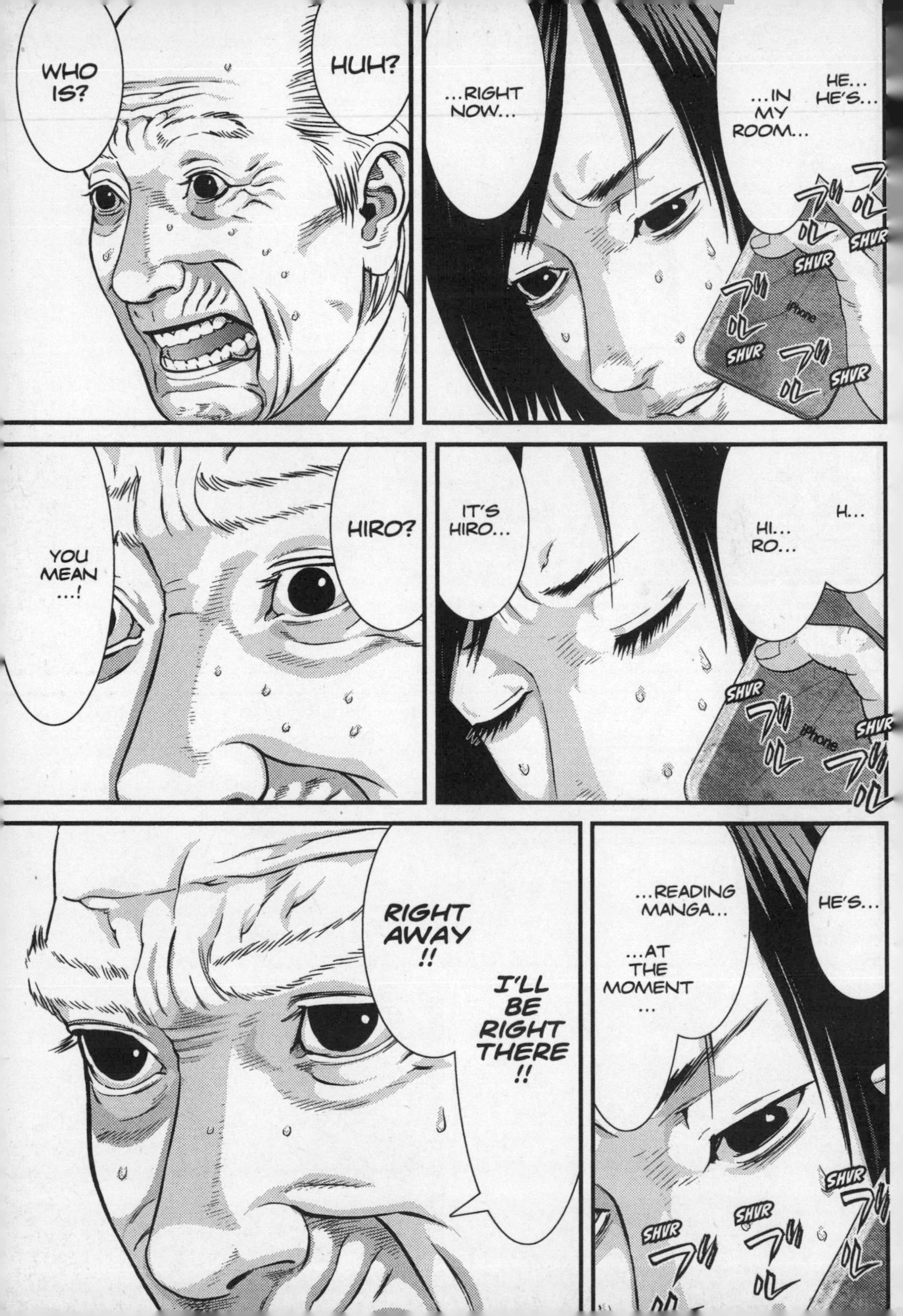
HE... HE'S...
...IN MY ROOM...
...RIGHT NOW...
SHVR
SHVR
SHVR
SHVR
HUH?
WHO IS?
H...
HI... RO...
IT'S HIRO...
SHVR
SHVR
HIRO?
YOU MEAN ...!
HE'S...
...READING MANGA...
...AT THE MOMENT ...
SHVR
SHVR
SHVR
RIGHT AWAY!!
I'LL BE RIGHT THERE!!

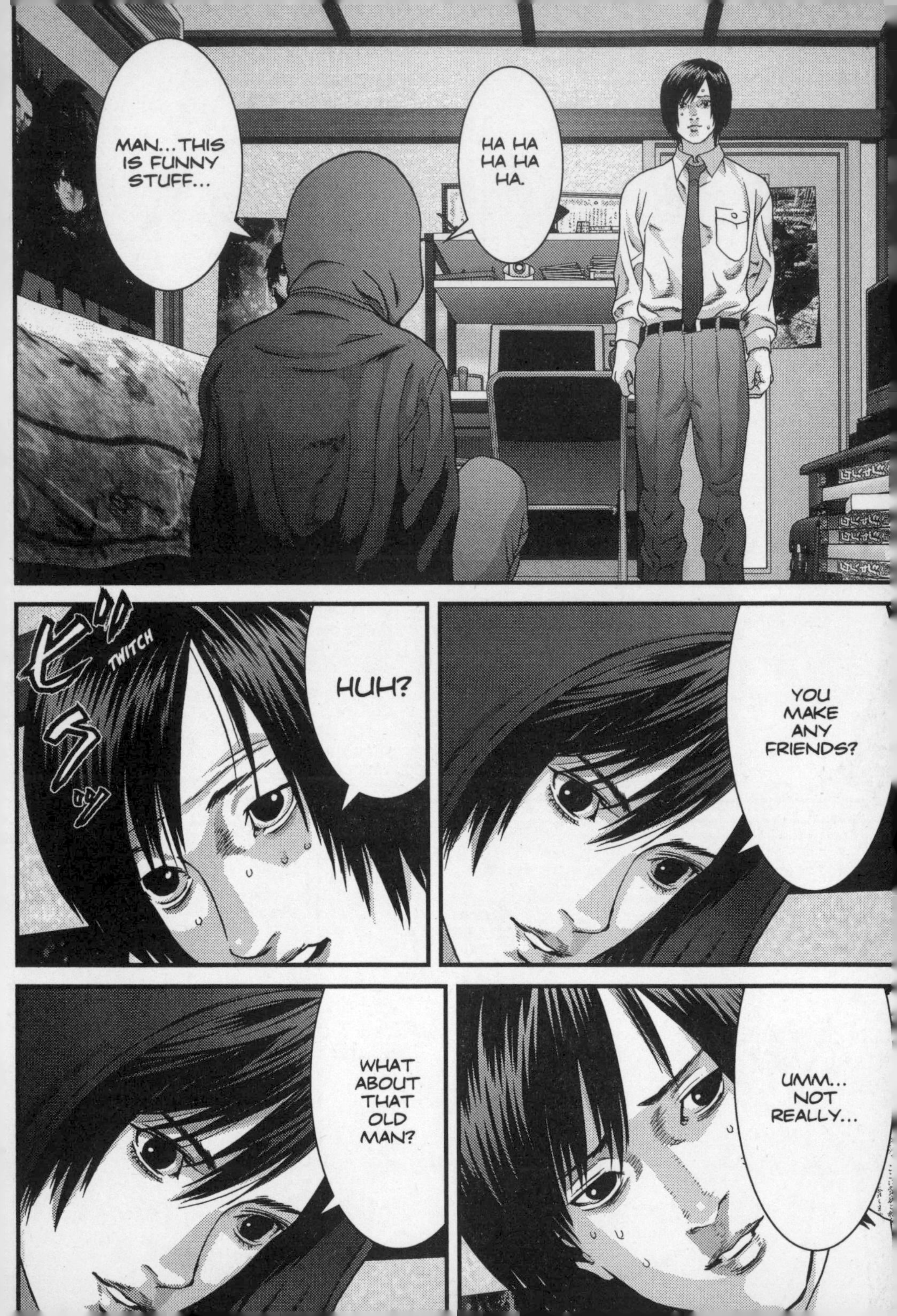
HA HA HA HA HA.
MAN...THIS IS FUNNY STUFF...
YOU MAKE ANY FRIENDS?
HUH?
TWITCH
UMM... NOT REALLY...
WHAT ABOUT THAT OLD MAN?

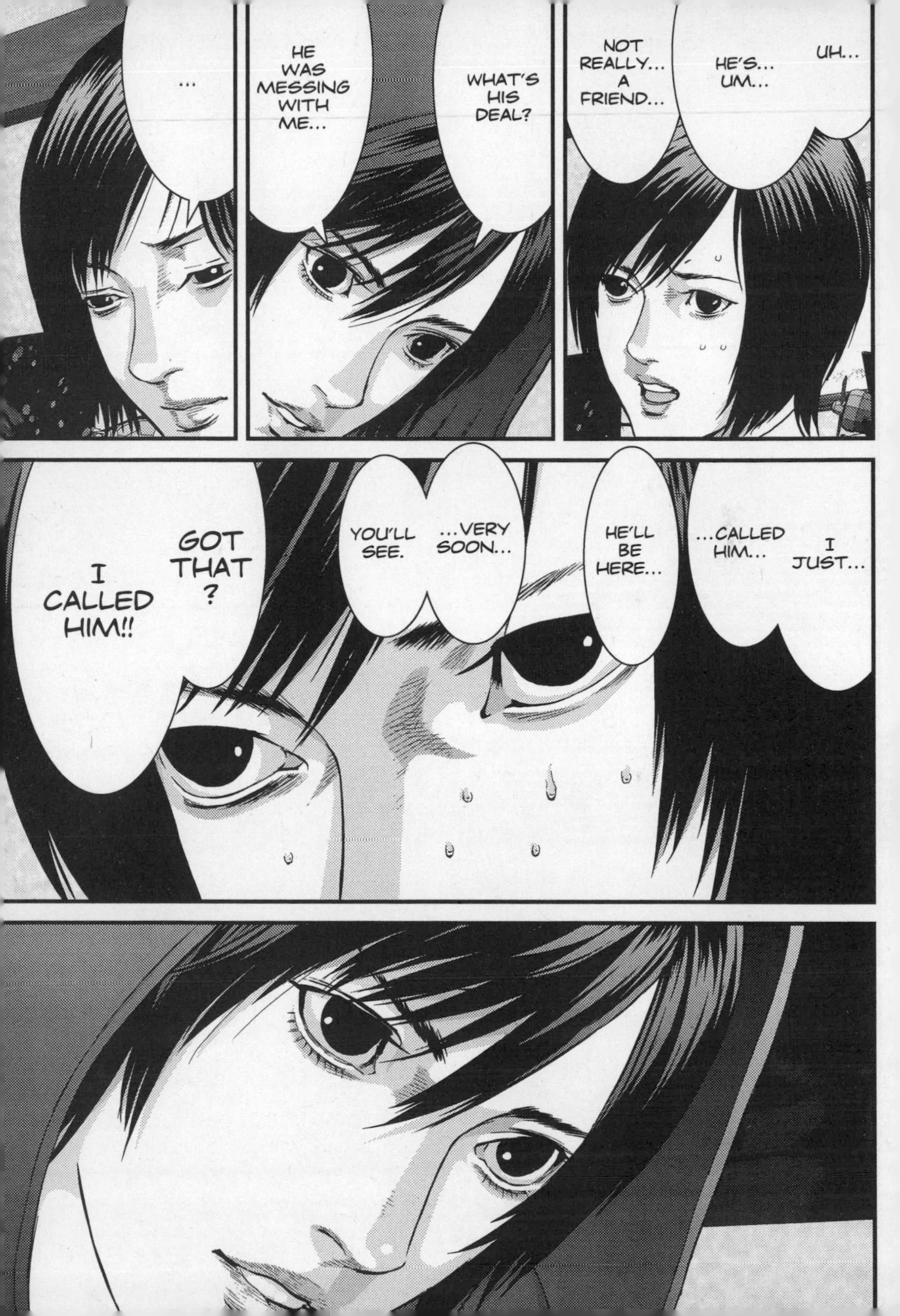
UH...
HE'S... UM...
NOT REALLY... A FRIEND...
WHAT'S HIS DEAL?
HE WAS MESSING WITH ME...
...
I JUST...
...CALLED HIM...
HE'LL BE HERE...
...VERY SOON...
YOU'LL SEE.
GOT THAT?
I CALLED HIM!!

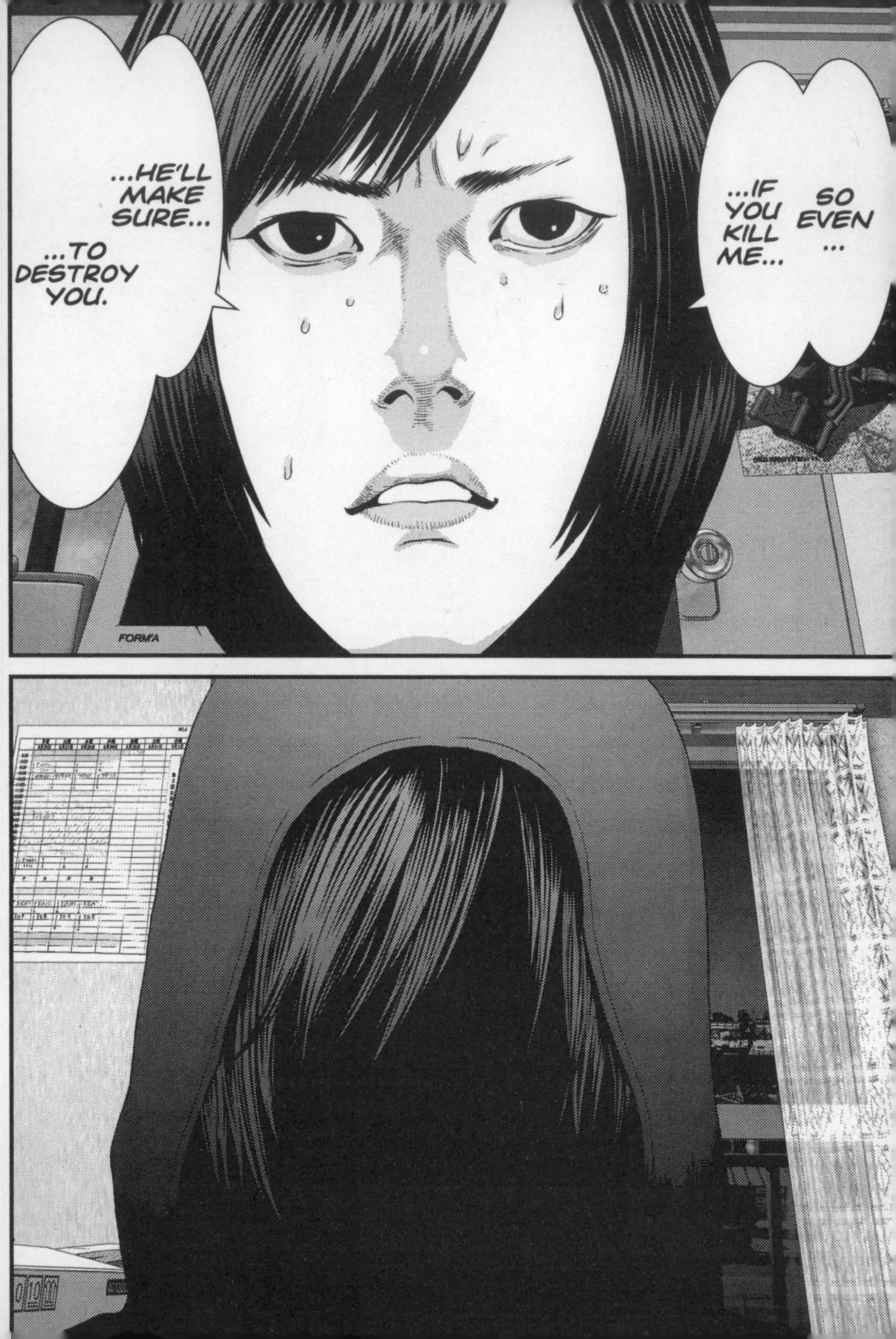
SO EVEN ...
...IF YOU KILL ME...
...HE'LL MAKE SURE...
...TO DESTROY YOU.
FORM'A

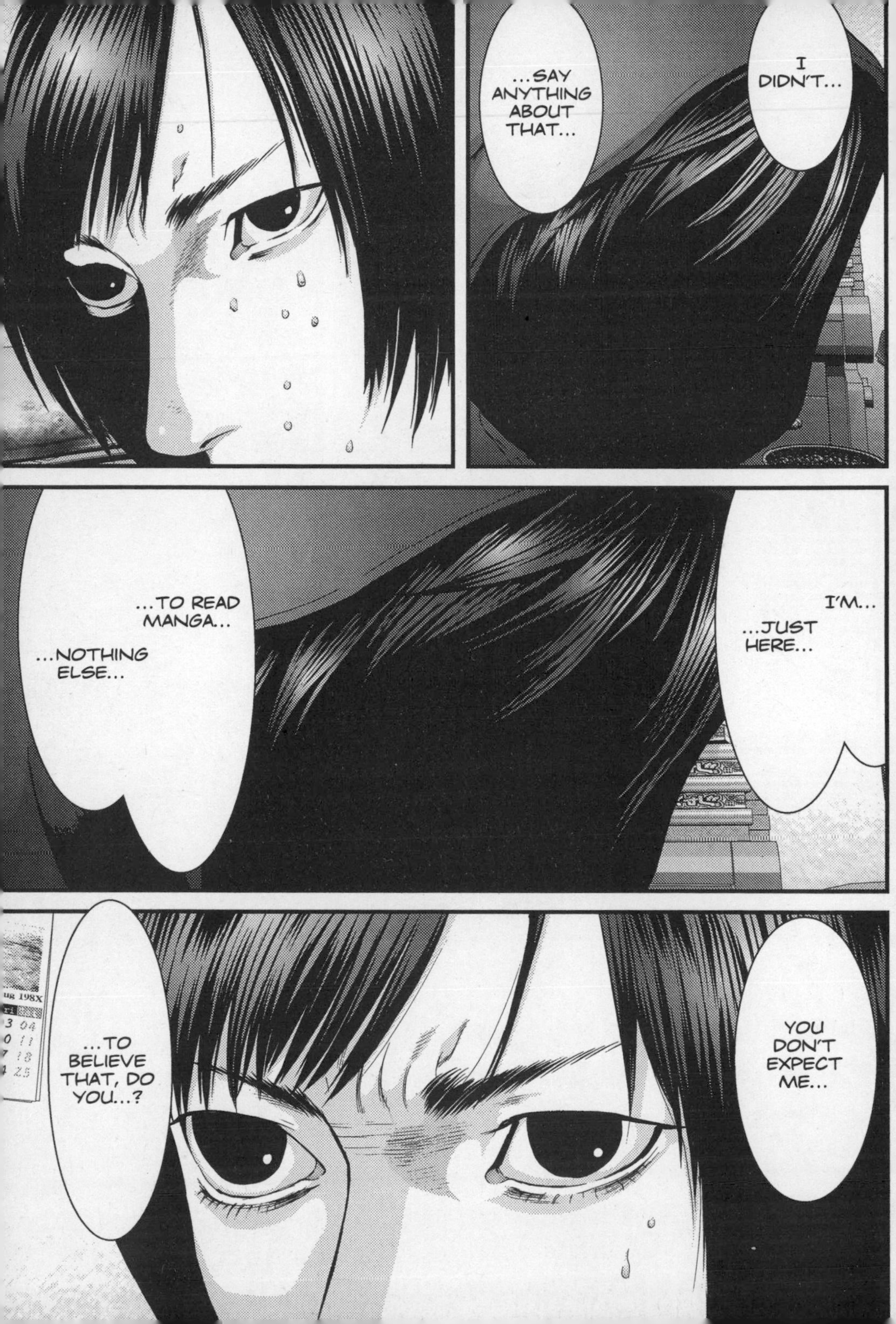
I DIDN'T...
...SAY ANYTHING ABOUT THAT...
I'M...
...JUST HERE...
...TO READ MANGA...
...NOTHING ELSE...
YOU DON'T EXPECT ME...
...TO BELIEVE THAT, DO YOU...?

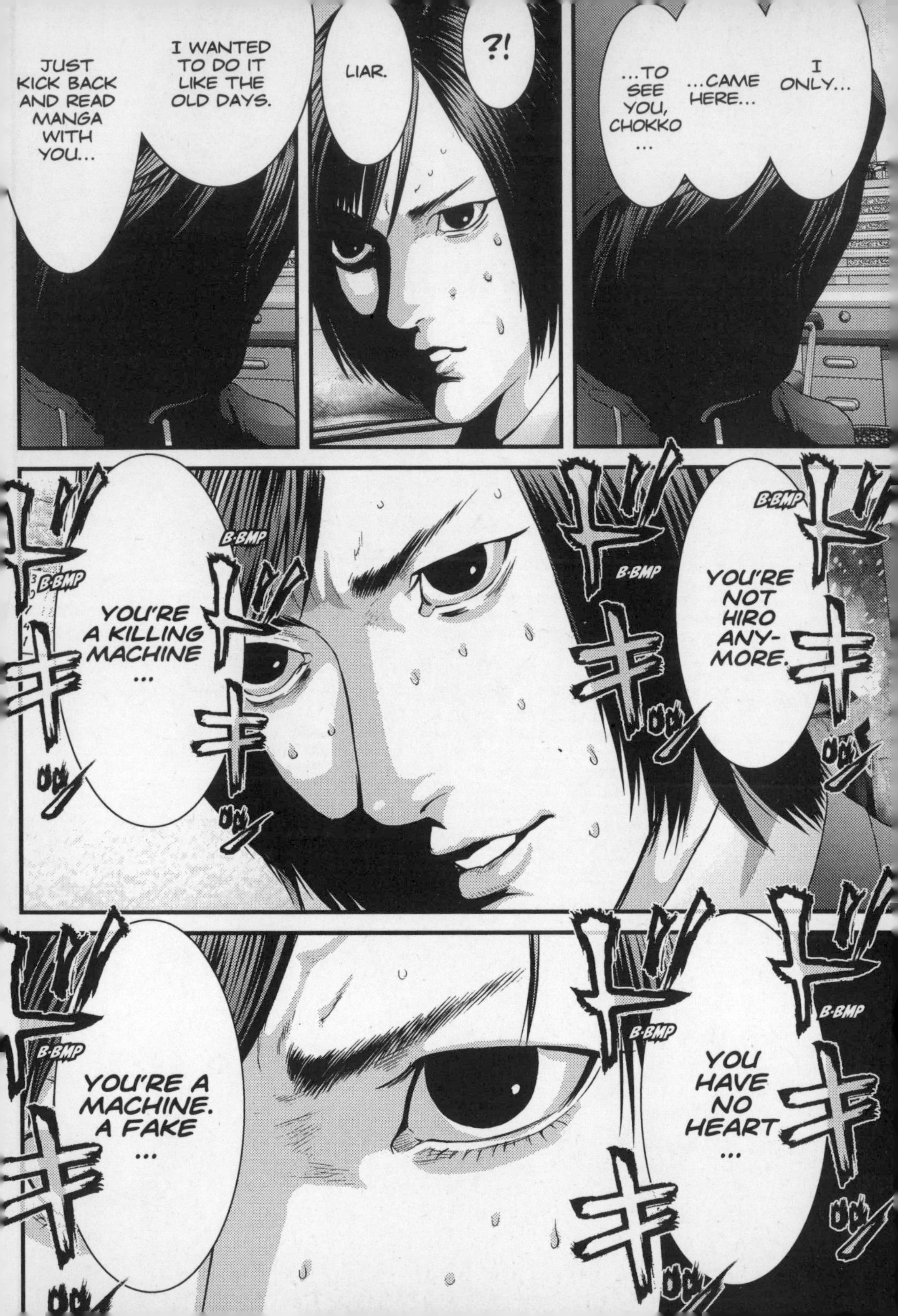
I ONLY...
...CAME HERE...
...TO SEE YOU, CHOKKO ...
?!
LIAR.
I WANTED TO DO IT LIKE THE OLD DAYS.
JUST KICK BACK AND READ MANGA WITH YOU...
B-BMP
B-BMP
YOU'RE NOT HIRO ANYMORE.
B-BMP
B-BMP
YOU'RE A KILLING MACHINE ...
B-BMP
B-BMP
YOU HAVE NO HEART ...
B-BMP
YOU'RE A MACHINE. A FAKE ...

HOW MANY PEOPLE HAVE YOU KILLED?
B-BMP
B-BMP
HOW MANY ?!

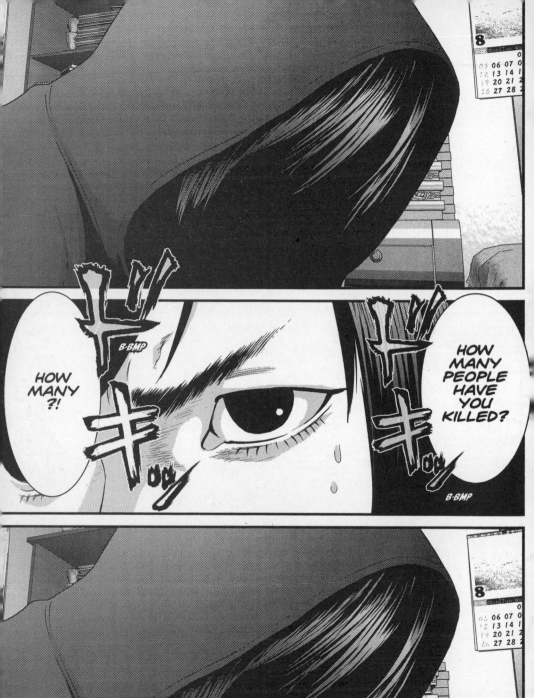

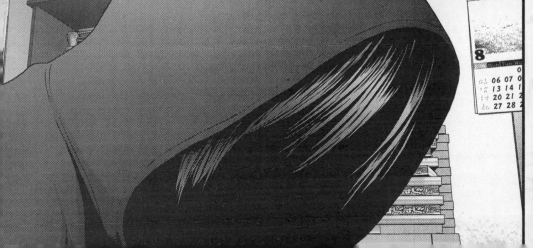

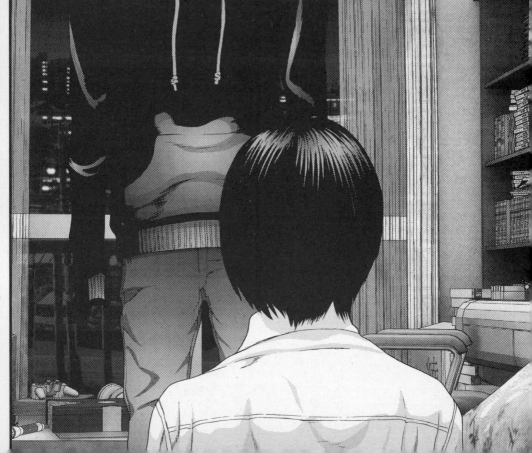

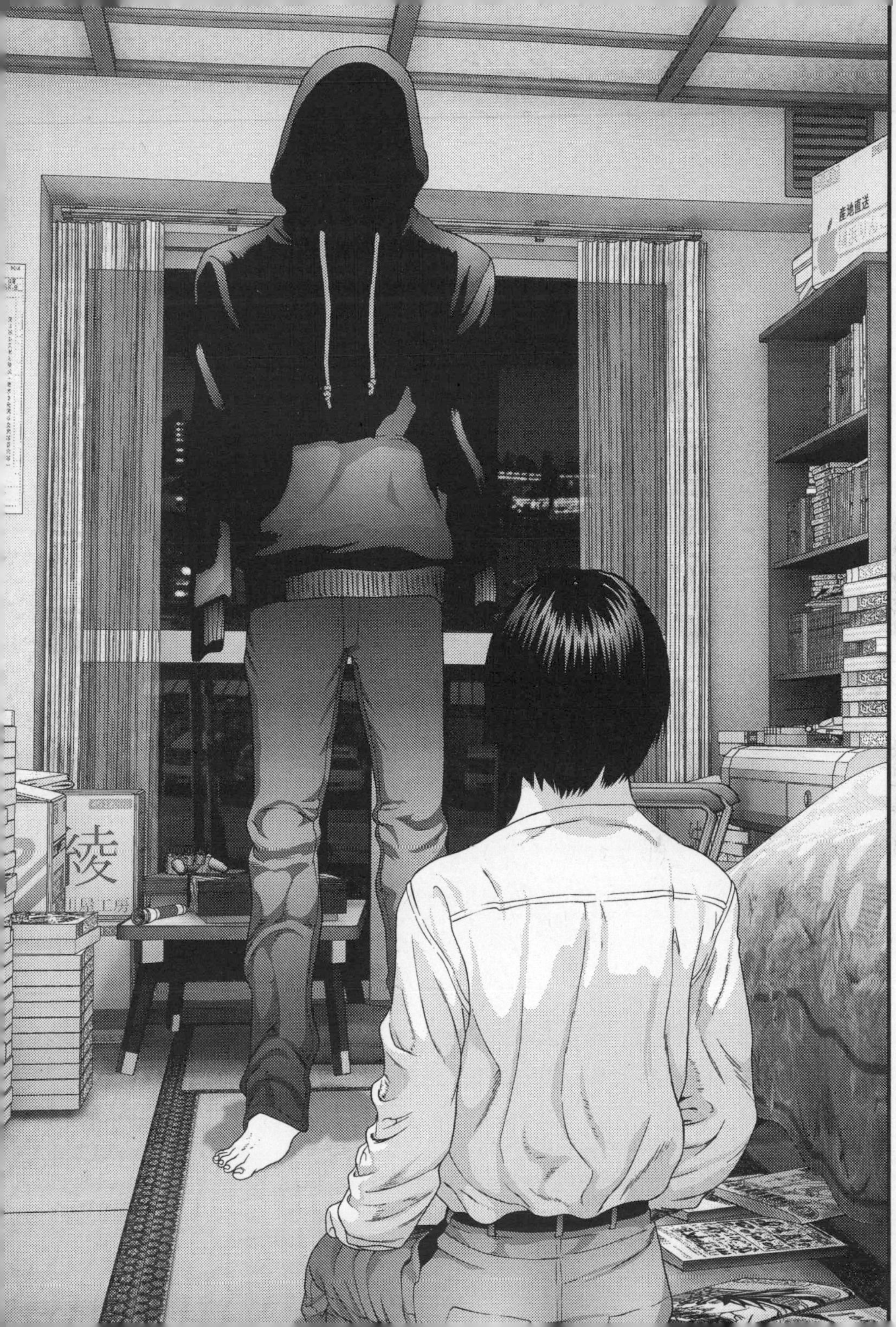
産地直送
綾

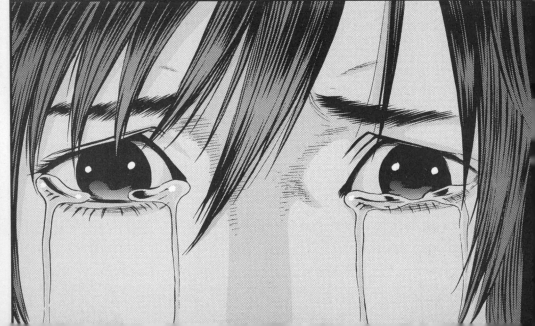

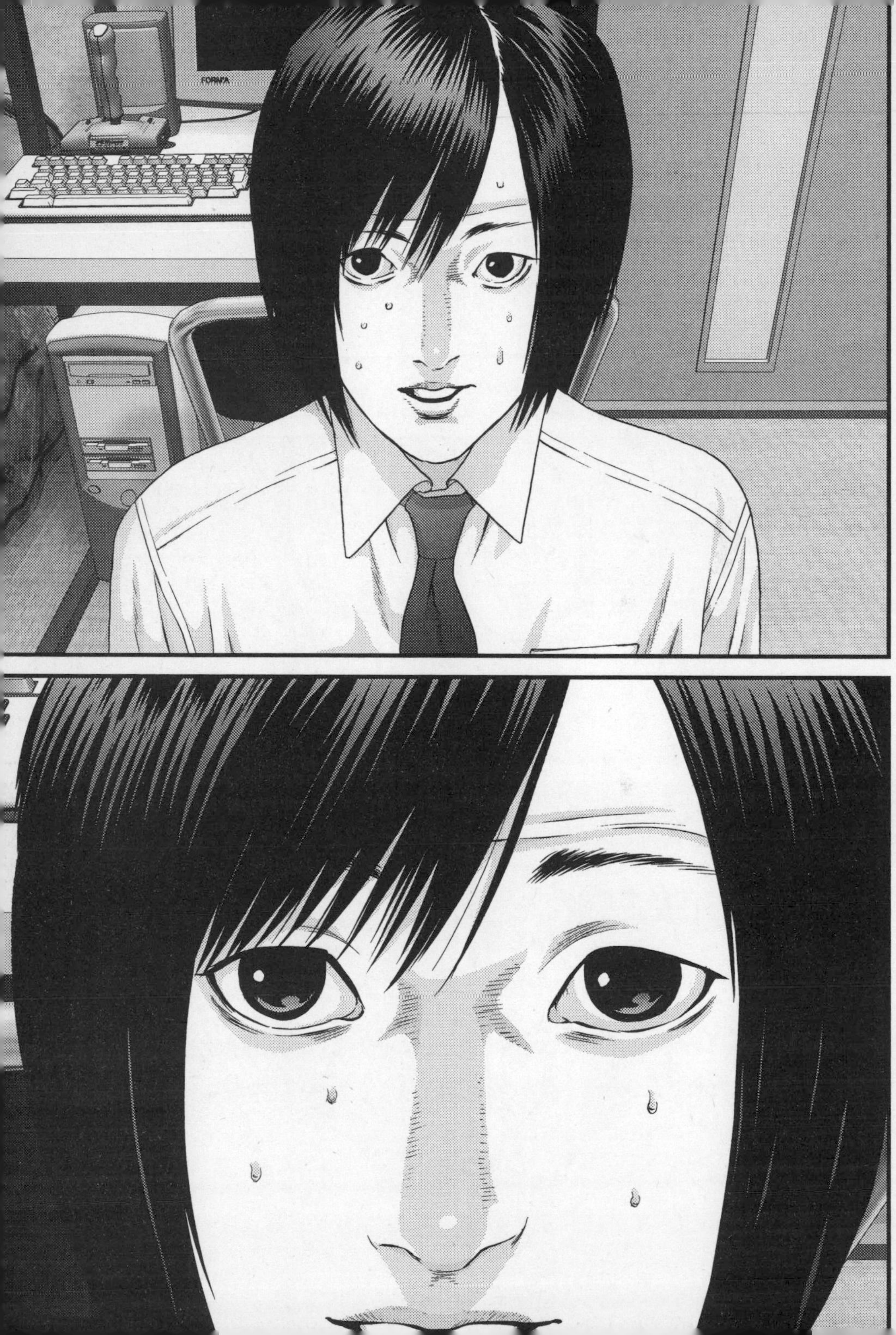
FORMA

DING-DONG

NAO-YUKIII!

OH!

INU-YA-SHIKI-SAN.

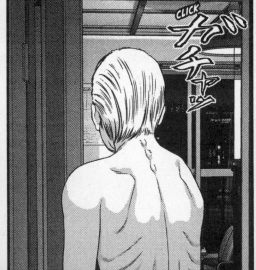

CLICK

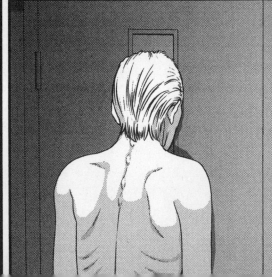

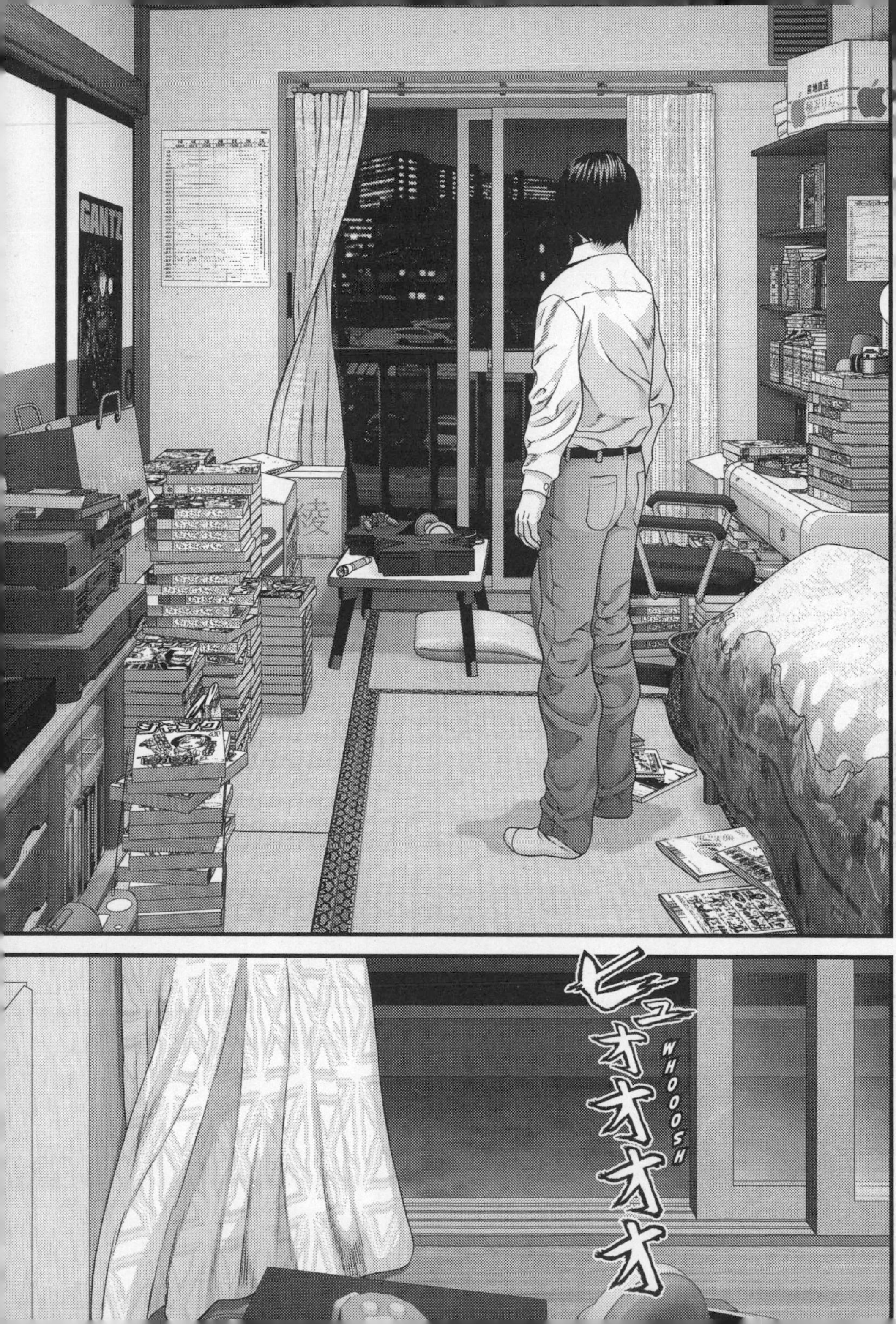
GANTZ
ヒュオオオオ
WHOOOSH

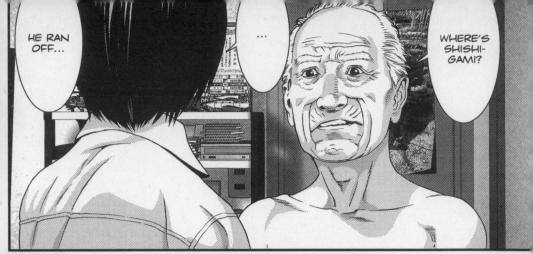

HE RAN OFF...

...

WHERE'S SHISHI-GAMI?

N... NO...

ME ...?

ARE YOU... CRY-ING?

HUH?

CHAPTER 73 · END

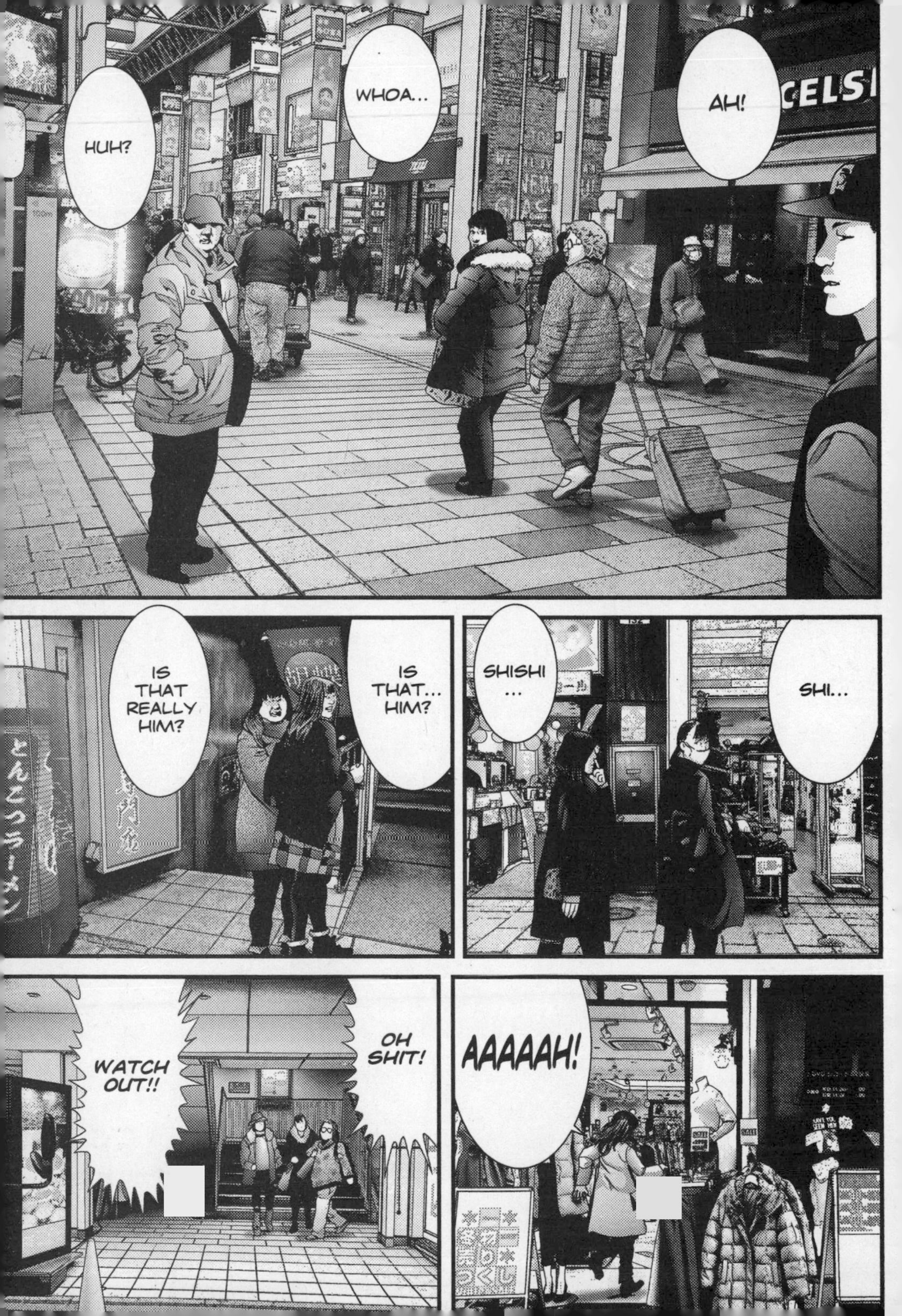
AH!
WHOA...
HUH?
SHI...
SHISHI ...
IS THAT... HIM?
IS THAT REALLY HIM?
とんこつラーメン
AAAAAH!
OH SHIT!
WATCH OUT!!

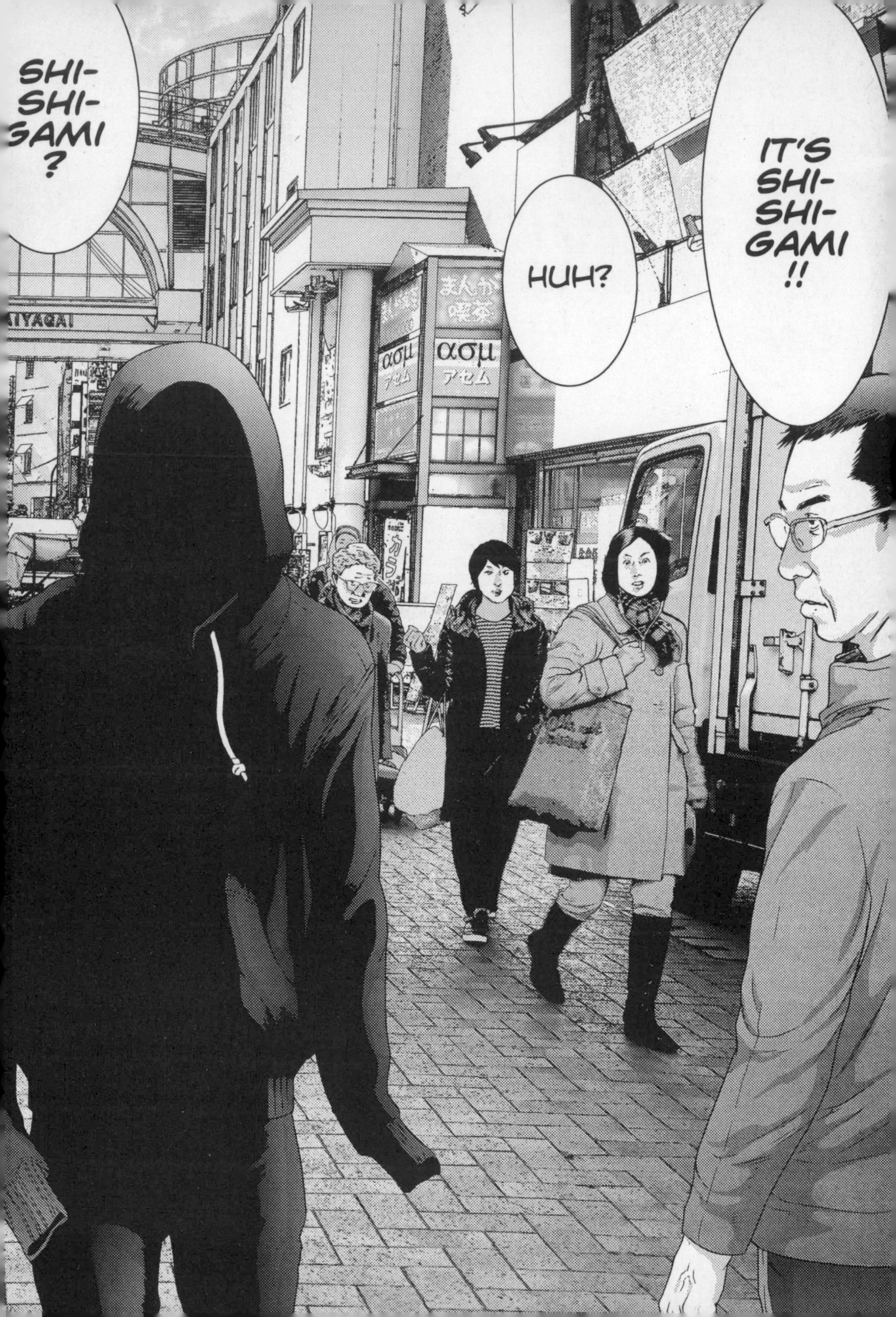
IT'S SHI-SHI-GAMI!!
HUH?
SHI-SHI-GAMI?

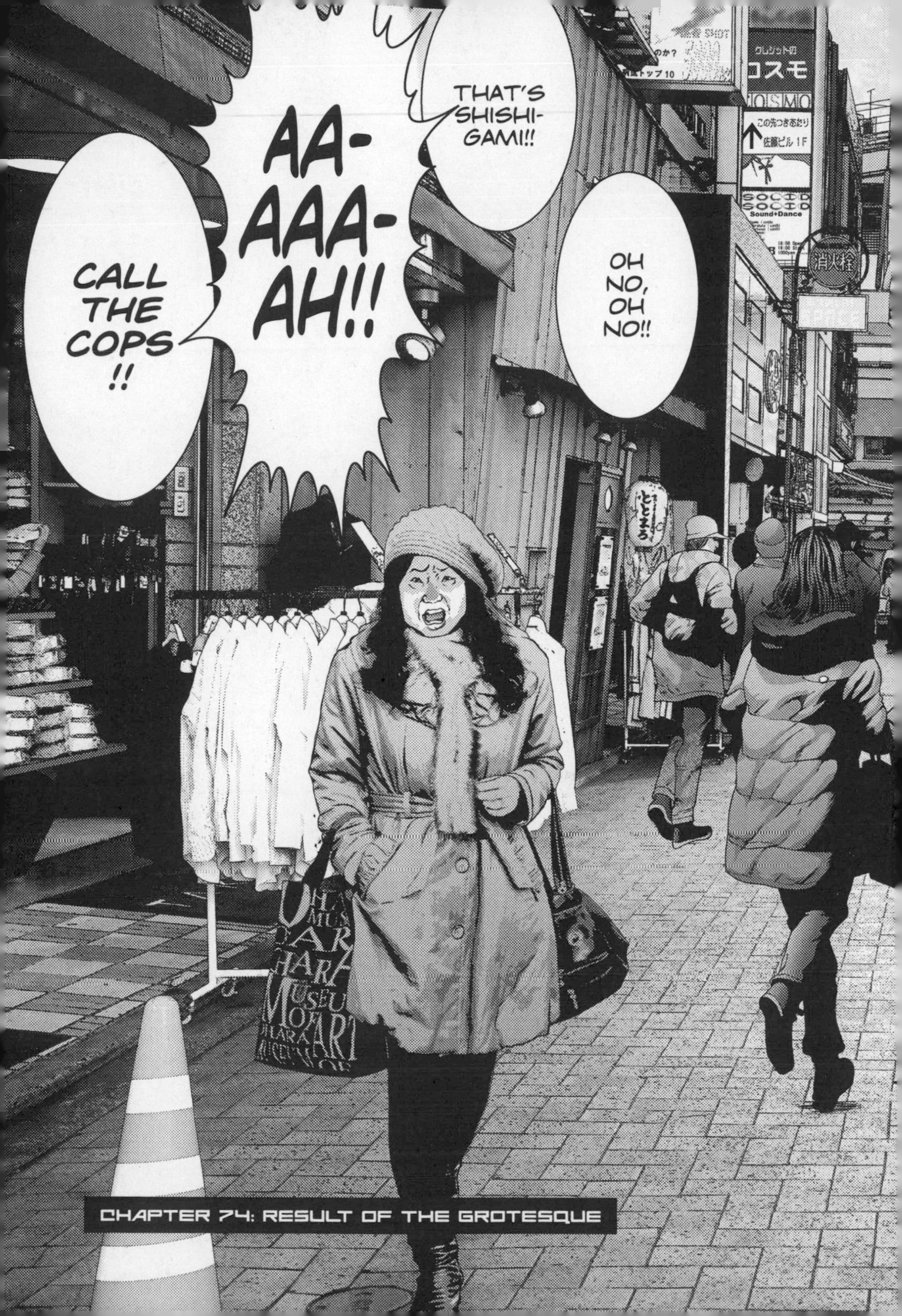
THAT'S SHISHI-GAMI!!
OH NO, OH NO!!
AA-AAA-AH!!
CALL THE COPS!!
CHAPTER 74: RESULT OF THE GROTESQUE

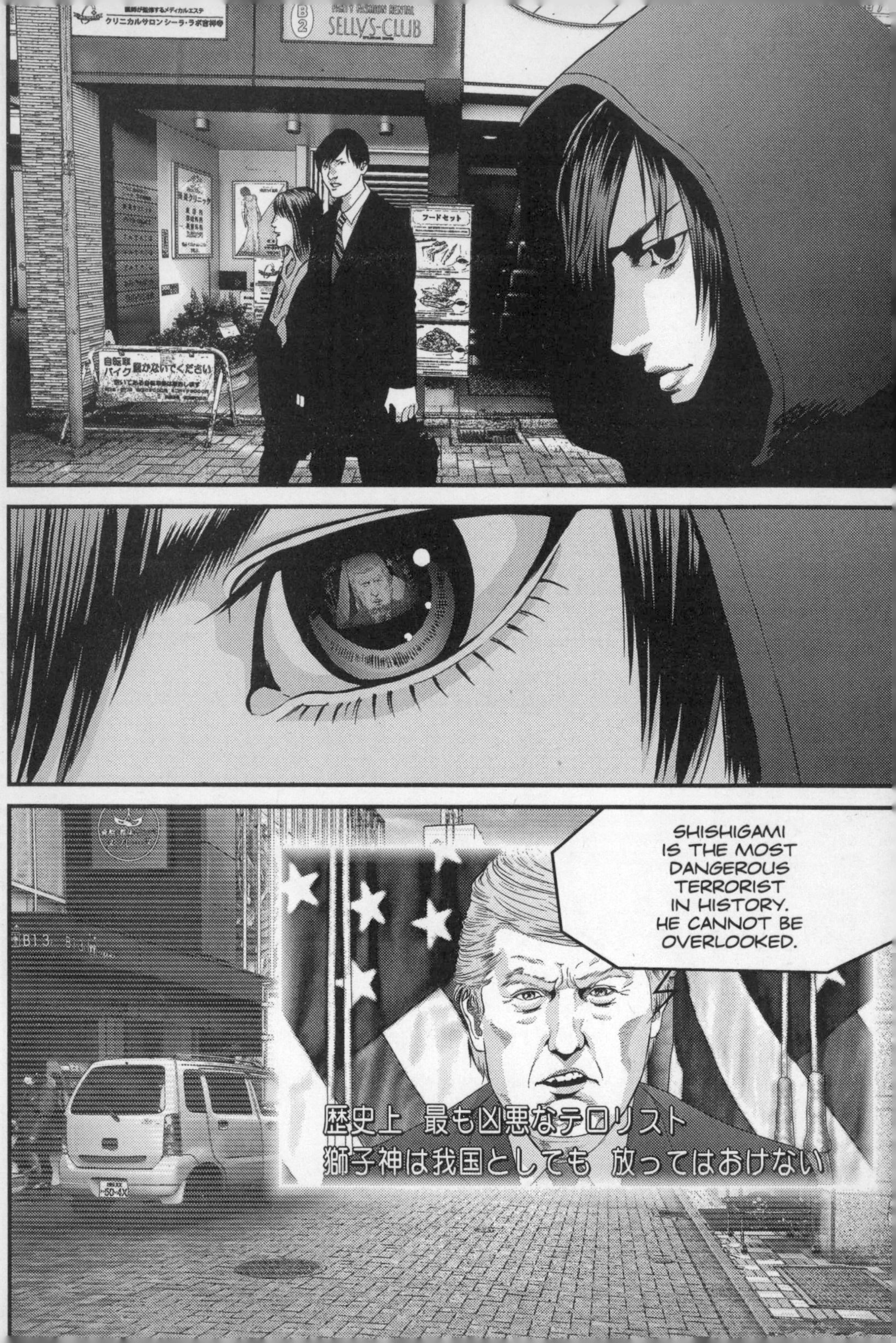
医師が監修するメディカルエステ
クリニカルサロン シーラ・ラボ吉祥寺
SELLY'S-CLUB
フードセット
自転車 バイク 置かないでください
SHISHIGAMI IS THE MOST DANGEROUS TERRORIST IN HISTORY. HE CANNOT BE OVERLOOKED.
歴史上　最も凶悪なテロリスト
獅子神は我国としても　放ってはおけない

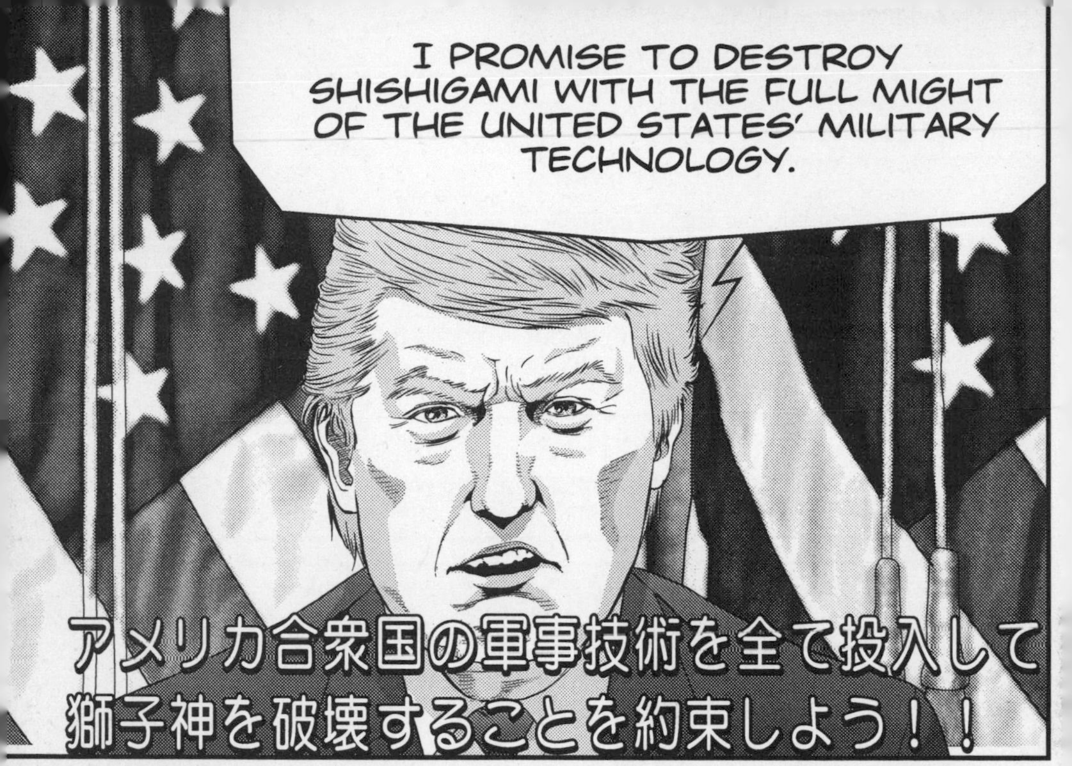
I PROMISE TO DESTROY SHISHIGAMI WITH THE FULL MIGHT OF THE UNITED STATES' MILITARY TECHNOLOGY.
アメリカ合衆国の軍事技術を全て投入して
獅子神を破壊することを約束しよう！！
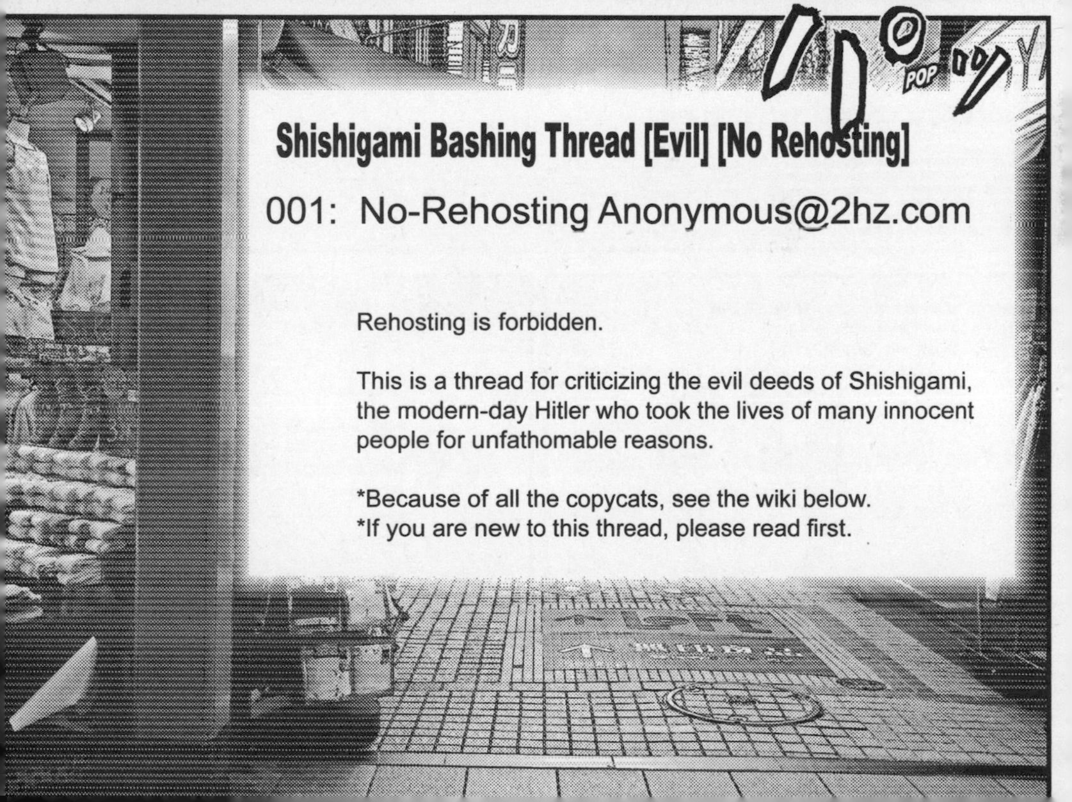
POP
Shishigami Bashing Thread [Evil] [No Rehosting]
001: No-Rehosting Anonymous@2hz.com
Rehosting is forbidden.
This is a thread for criticizing the evil deeds of Shishigami, the modern-day Hitler who took the lives of many innocent people for unfathomable reasons.
*Because of all the copycats, see the wiki below.
*If you are new to this thread, please read first.

highest when it comes to serial killers?

066: No-Rehosting Anonymous (Gaff-STcS): 2017/0X/13(W) 14:08:56.006 ID:a5s
In terms of killers who did it personally,
that'd be Anders Breivik in Norway, with 77.
Shishigami's easily got him beat.

067: No-Rehosting Anonymous (8fd9-iEnf): 2017/0X/13 (W) 14:09:06.100 ID:0jE+w
Shishigami is the enemy of humanity
We should use the combined intelligence of mankind to destroy him

068: No-Rehosting Anonymous (7f26-YL1f): 2017/0X/13 (W) 14:10:14.855 ID:0wqB
All of Shisshy's fanbase cult should be put to death
along with my Dad, for divorcing Mom.
That's what I think.

069: No-Rehosting Anonymous (wf1a-kkJf): 2017/0X/13 (W) 14:10:23.841 ID:0Hy

He's like an android or robot or something so wouldn't laws for humans not apply to him?

981: No-Rehosting Anonymous (uf09-0Plf): 2017/0X/14 (Th) 01:32:00.156 ID:0pyf
Do these Shishigami-robot theorists have a source or any evidence or anything?
You guys watch too much anime

982: No-Rehosting Anonymous (Laf3-lyrS): 2017/0X/14 (Th) 01:32:27.172 ID:a+9u
Is Hiro NASA-made?

983: No-Rehosting Anonymous (wf1a-kkJf): 2017/0X/14 (Th) 01:32:35.370 ID:0Hy
It's the new model of the Forerunner

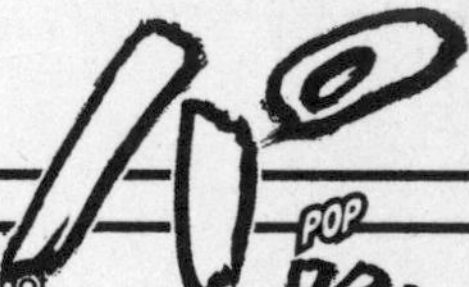
POP

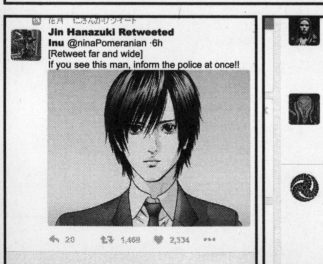

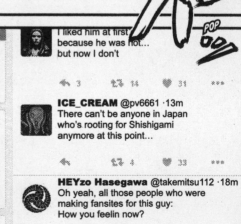

I liked him at first
because he was hot...
but now I don't

3 14 31

ICE_CREAM @pv6661 ·13m
There can't be anyone in Japan
who's rooting for Shishigami
anymore at this point...

4 33

HEYzo Hasegawa @takemitsu112 ·18m
Oh yeah, all those people who were
making fansites for this guy:
How you feelin now?

ハッ ハッ

Jin Hanazuki Retweeted
Inu @ninaPomeranian ·6h
[Retweet far and wide]
If you see this man, inform the police at once!!

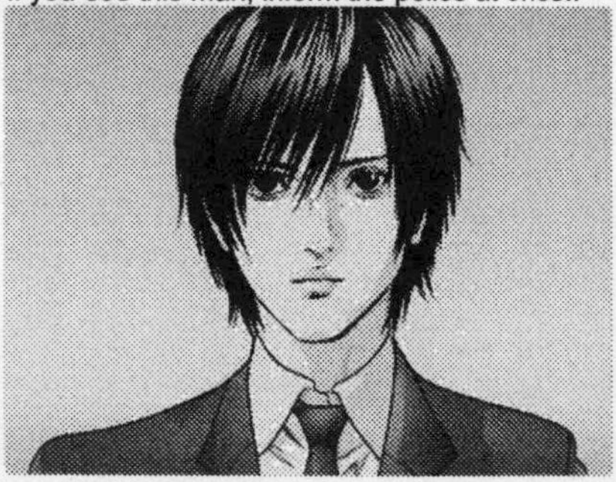

20 1,468 2,334

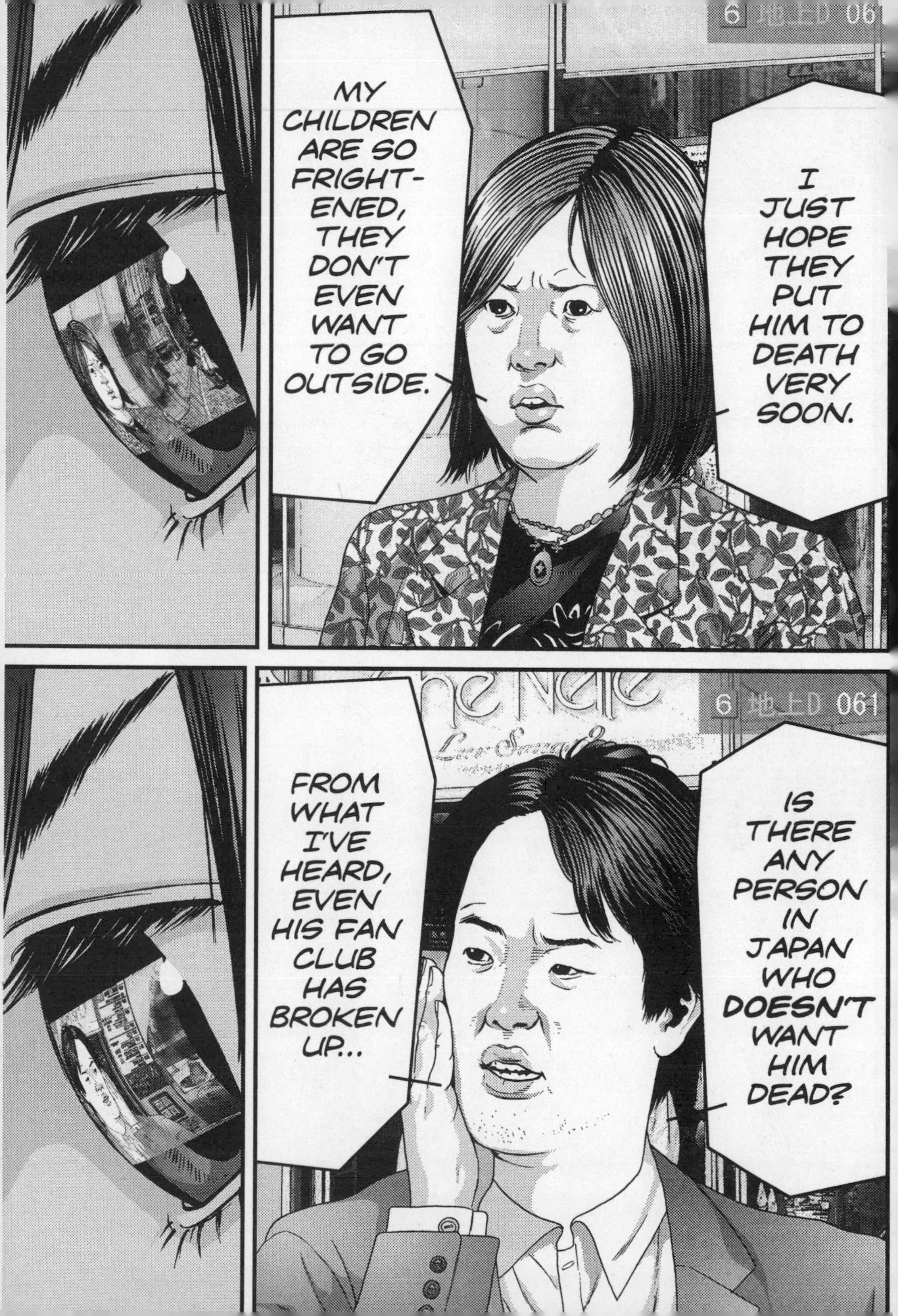
6 地上D 06
MY CHILDREN ARE SO FRIGHT-ENED, THEY DON'T EVEN WANT TO GO OUTSIDE.
I JUST HOPE THEY PUT HIM TO DEATH VERY SOON.
6 地上D 061
FROM WHAT I'VE HEARD, EVEN HIS FAN CLUB HAS BROKEN UP...
IS THERE ANY PERSON IN JAPAN WHO DOESN'T WANT HIM DEAD?

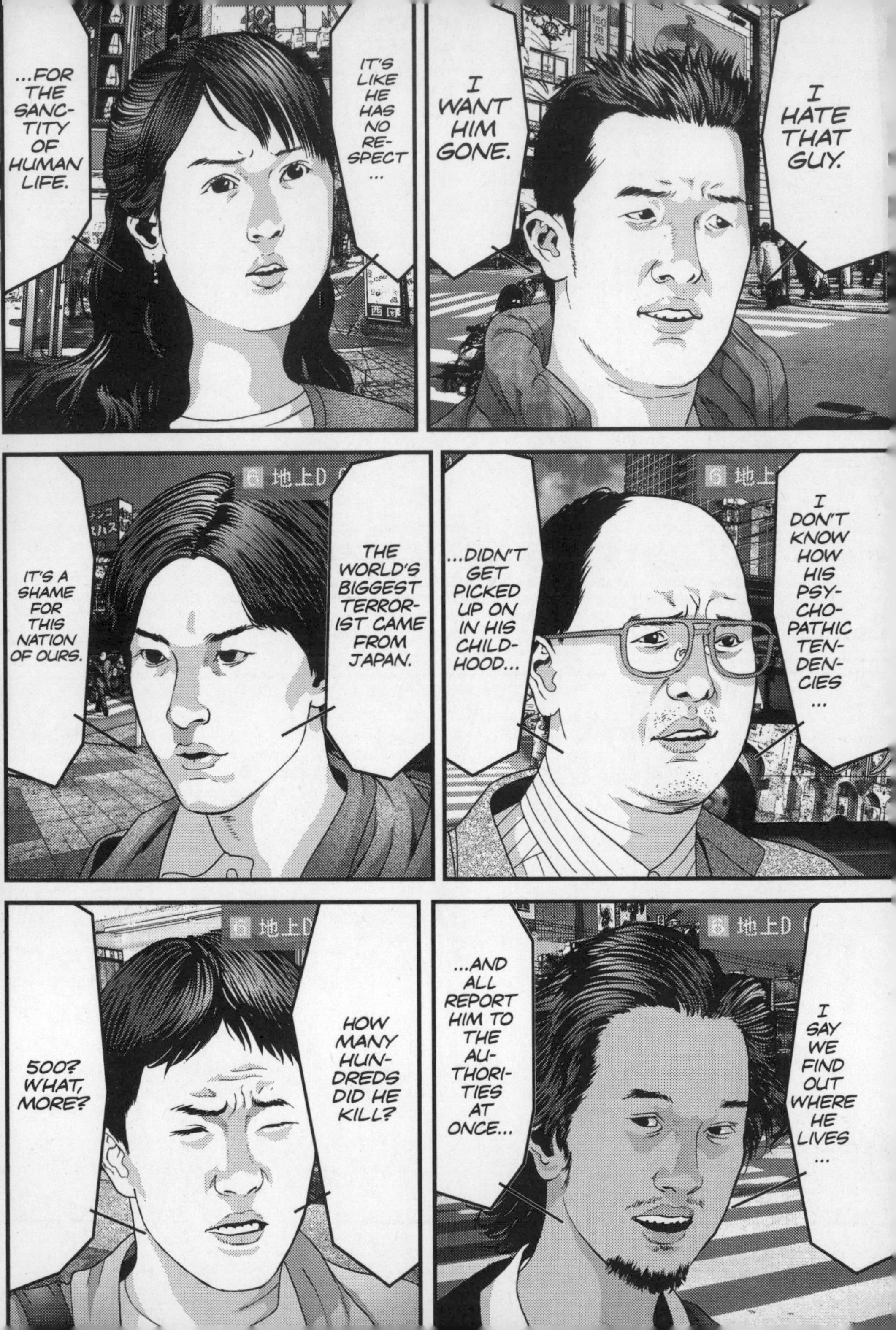
I HATE THAT GUY.
I WANT HIM GONE.
IT'S LIKE HE HAS NO RESPECT ...
...FOR THE SANCTITY OF HUMAN LIFE.
I DON'T KNOW HOW HIS PSYCHOPATHIC TENDENCIES ...
...DIDN'T GET PICKED UP ON IN HIS CHILDHOOD...
THE WORLD'S BIGGEST TERRORIST CAME FROM JAPAN.
IT'S A SHAME FOR THIS NATION OF OURS.
I SAY WE FIND OUT WHERE HE LIVES ...
...AND ALL REPORT HIM TO THE AUTHORITIES AT ONCE...
HOW MANY HUNDREDS DID HE KILL?
500? WHAT, MORE?

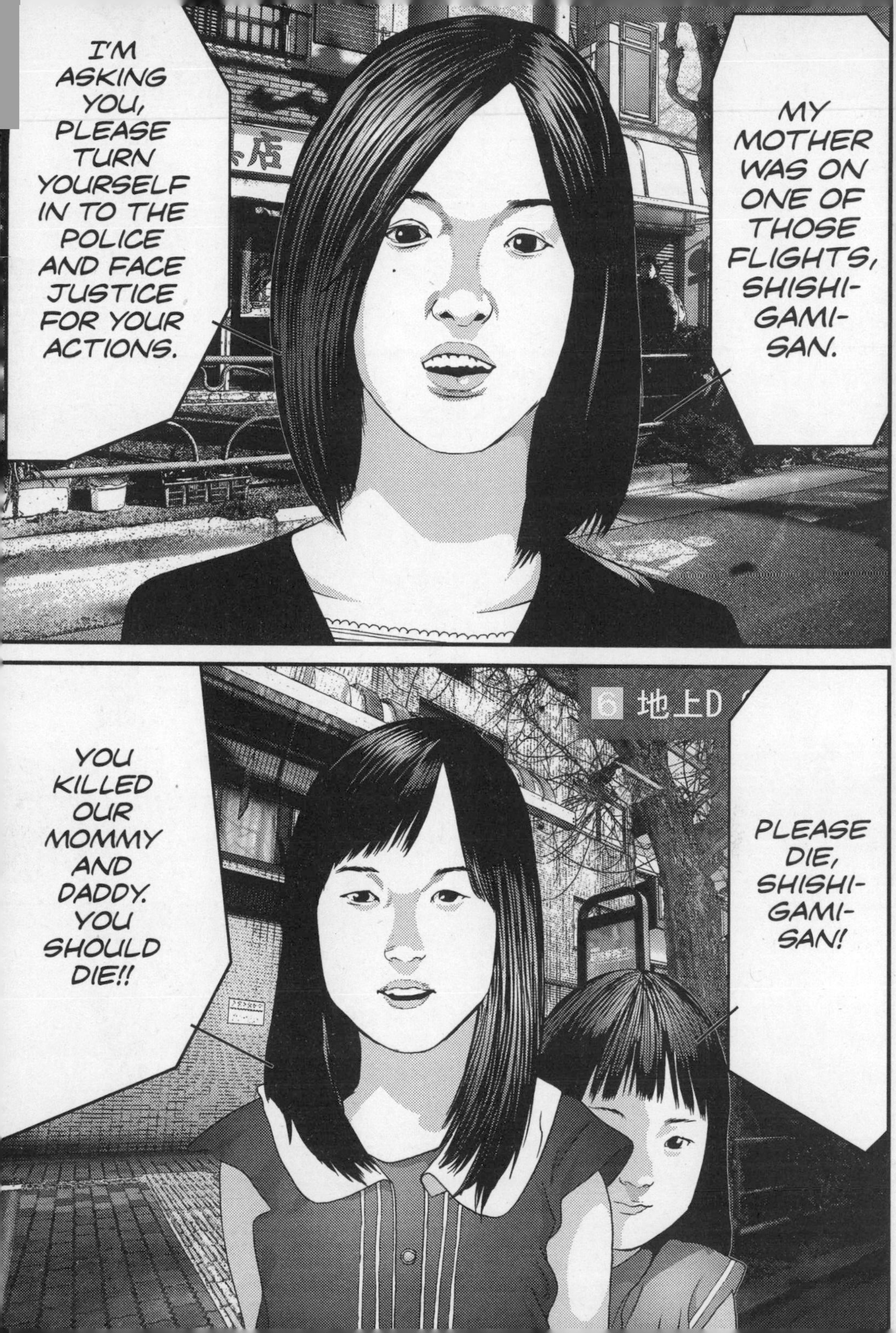
MY MOTHER WAS ON ONE OF THOSE FLIGHTS, SHISHI-GAMI-SAN.
I'M ASKING YOU, PLEASE TURN YOURSELF IN TO THE POLICE AND FACE JUSTICE FOR YOUR ACTIONS.
6 地上D
PLEASE DIE, SHISHI-GAMI-SAN!
YOU KILLED OUR MOMMY AND DADDY. YOU SHOULD DIE!!

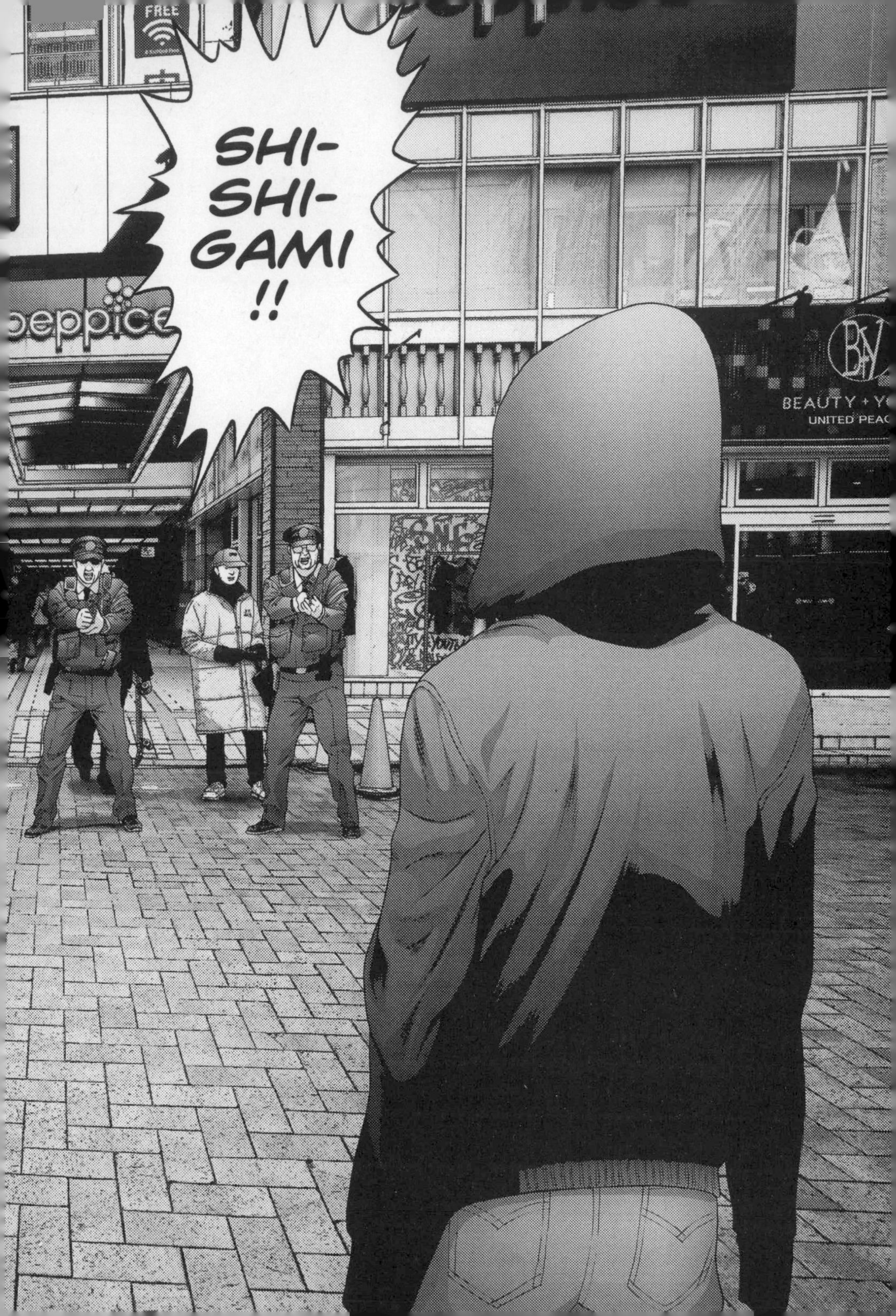
SHI-SHI-GAMI !!
FREE

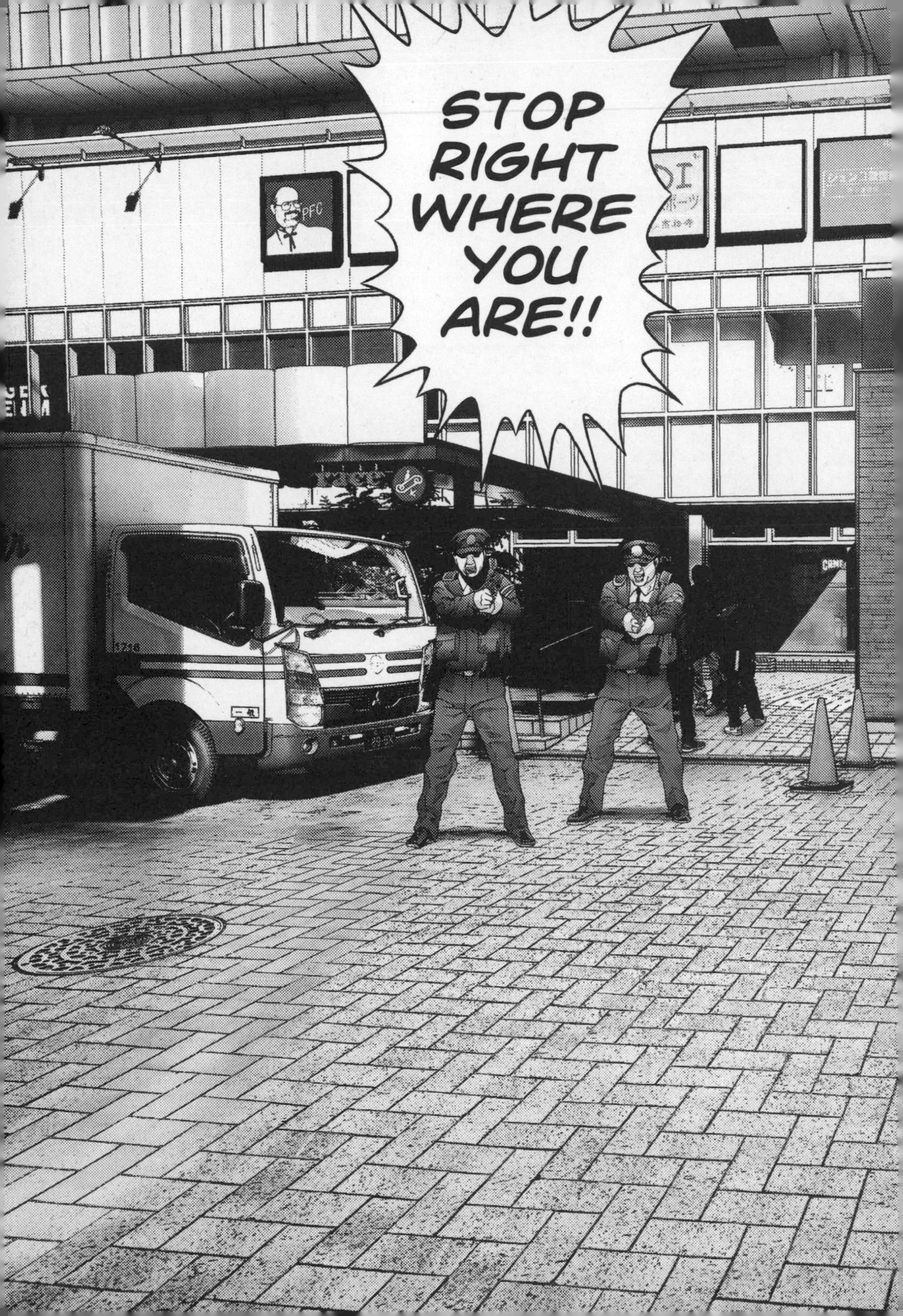
STOP RIGHT WHERE YOU ARE!!
PFC

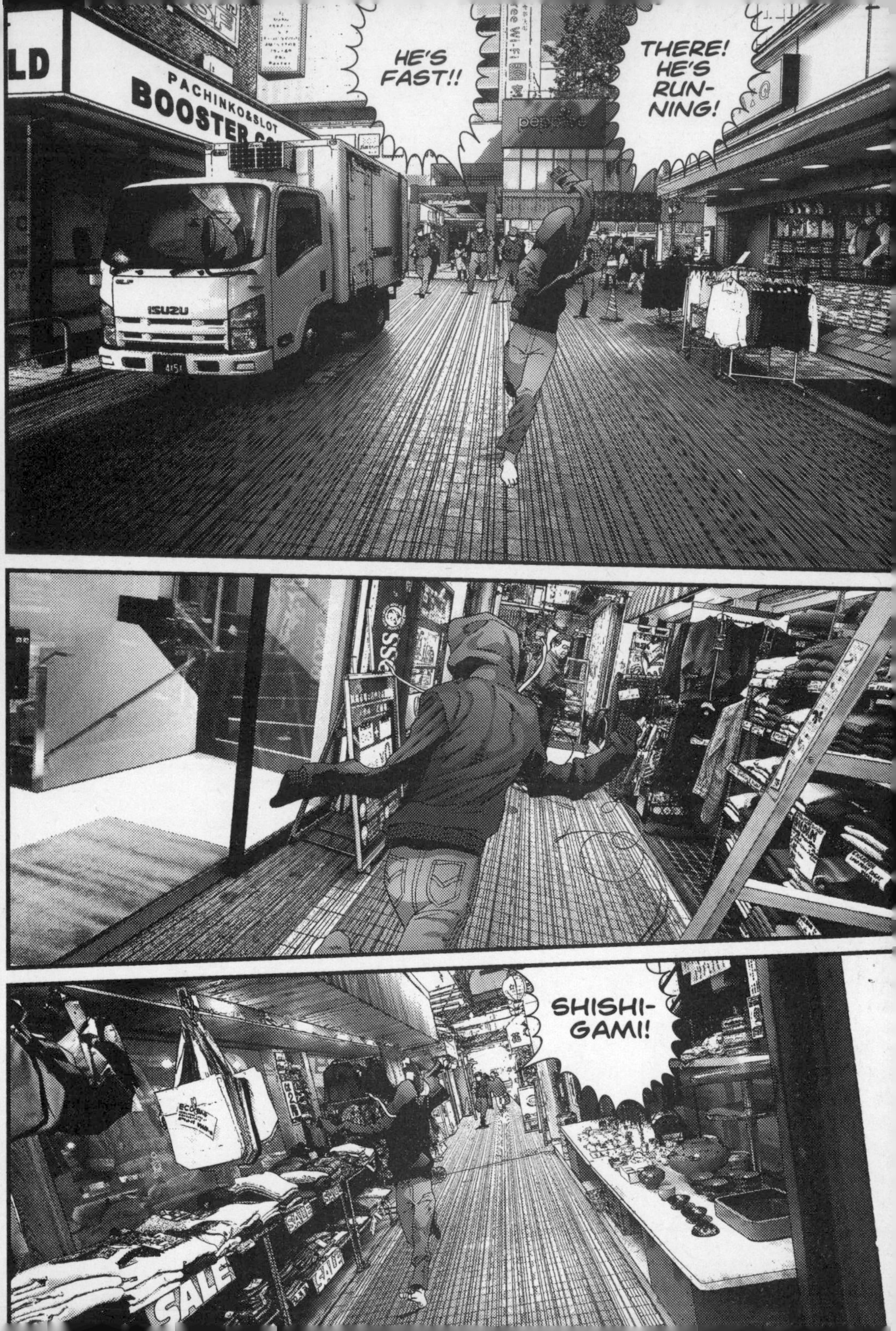
THERE! HE'S RUN-NING!
HE'S FAST!!
PACHINKO&SLOT
ISUZU
SHISHI-GAMI!
SALE

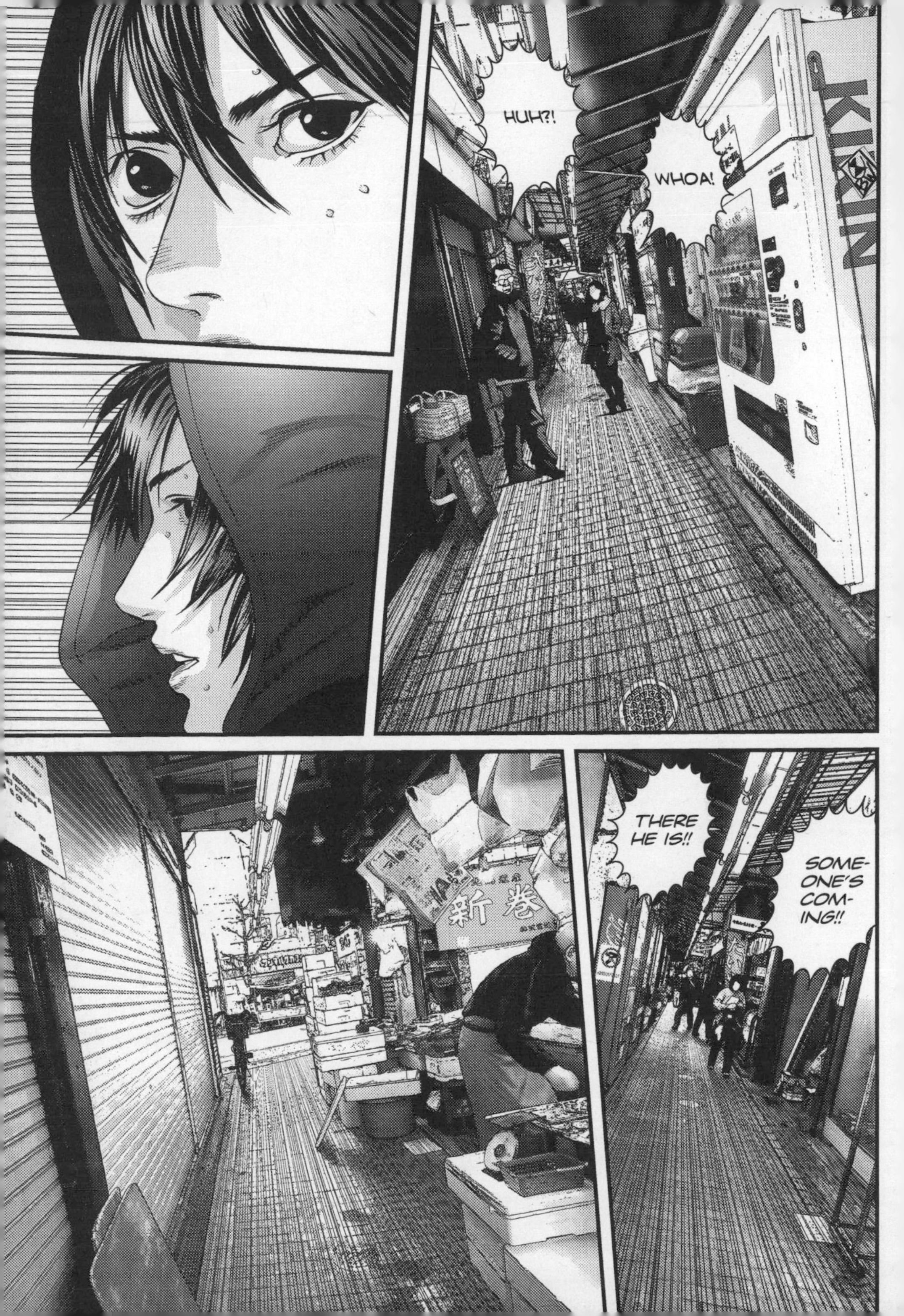
HUH?!
WHOA!
KIRIN
THERE HE IS!!
SOME-ONE'S COMING!!
新巻

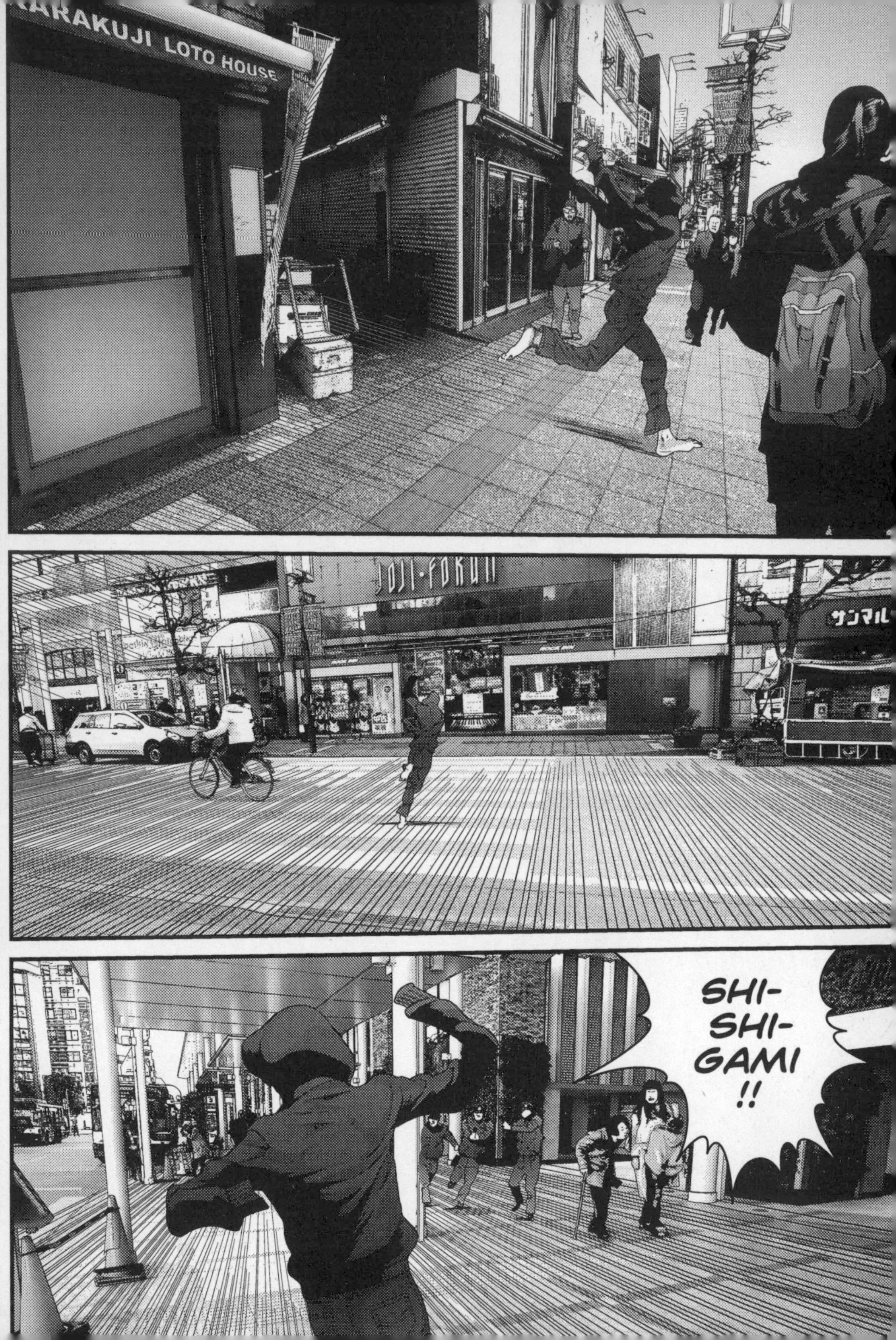
ARAKUJI LOTO HOUSE
サンマル
SHI-
SHI-
GAMI
!!

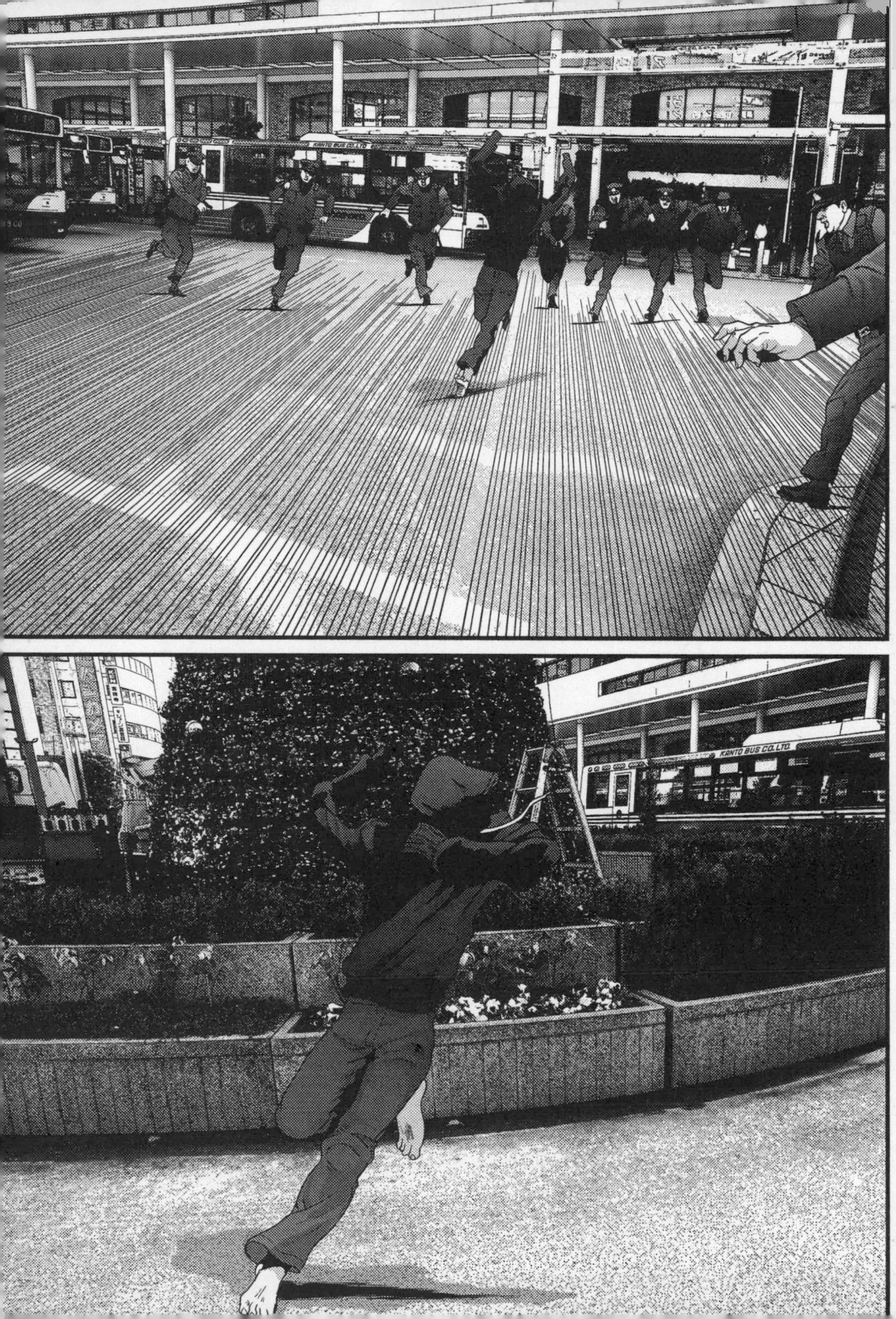
KANTO BUS CO.LTD

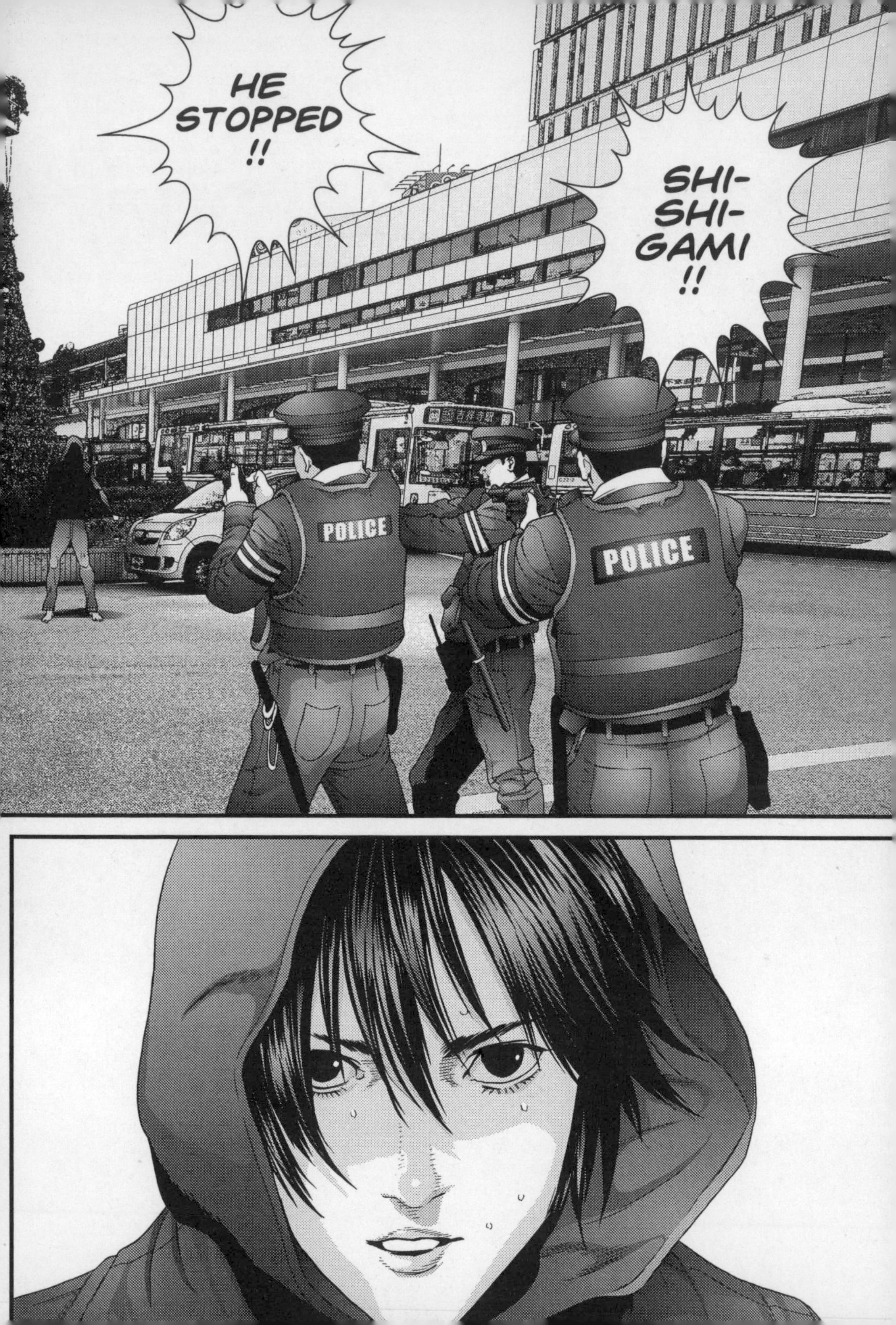
SHI-SHI-GAMI!!
HE STOPPED!!
POLICE
POLICE

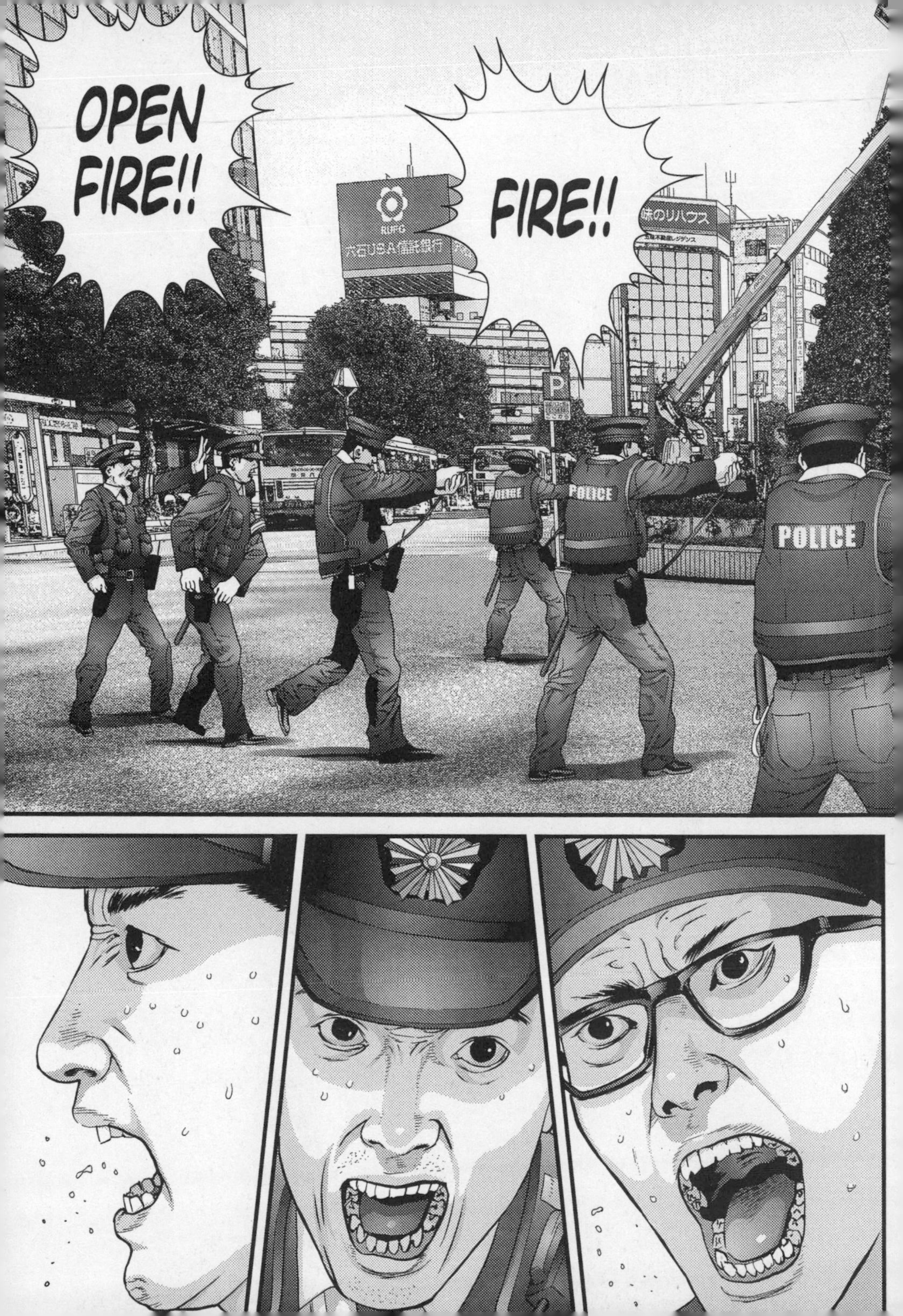
FIRE!!
OPEN FIRE!!
RUFG
六石USA信託銀行
味のリハウス
POLICE
POLICE
POLICE

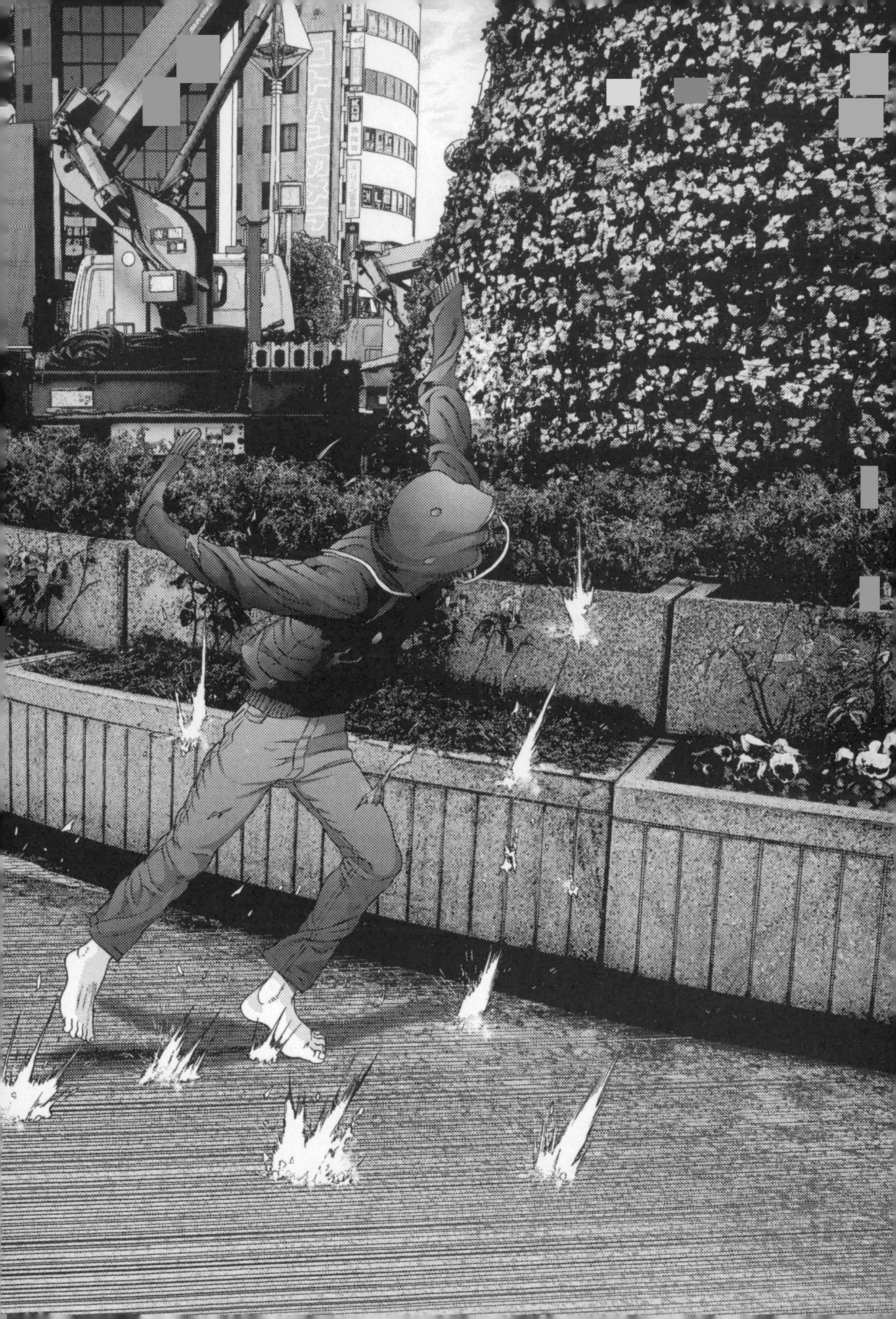

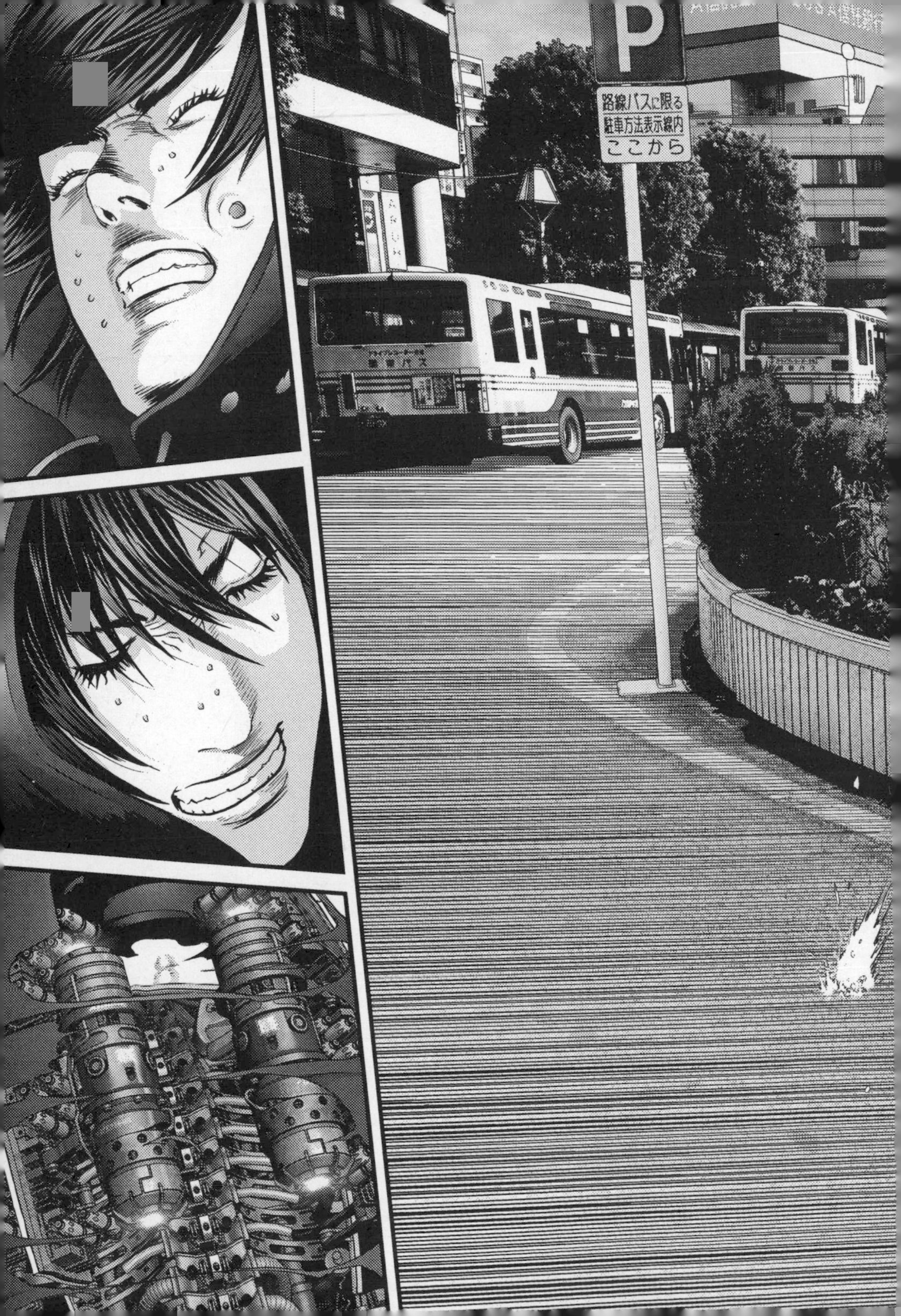
P
路線バスに限る
駐車方法表示線内
ここから

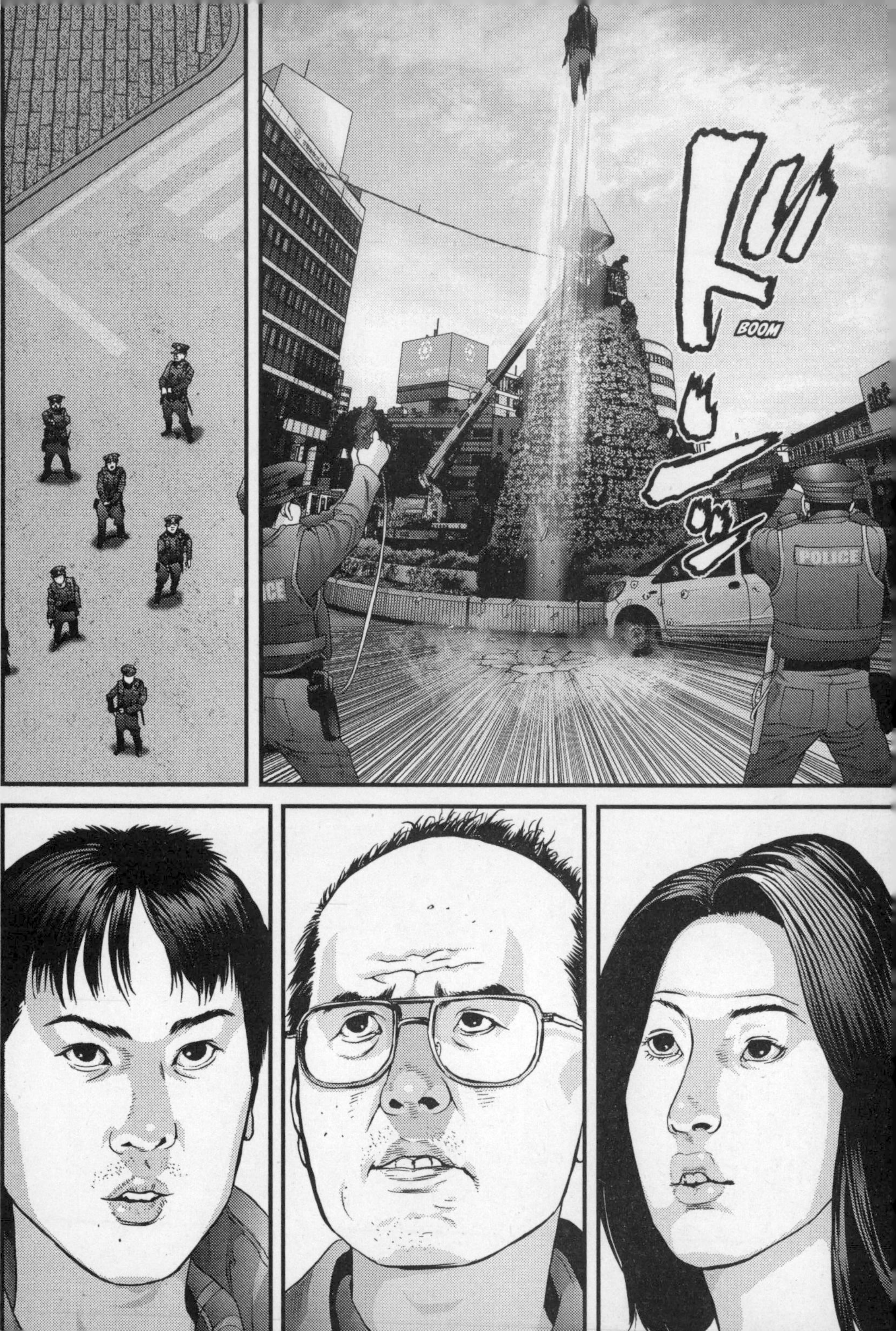
BOOM
POLICE

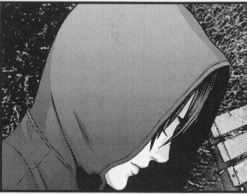

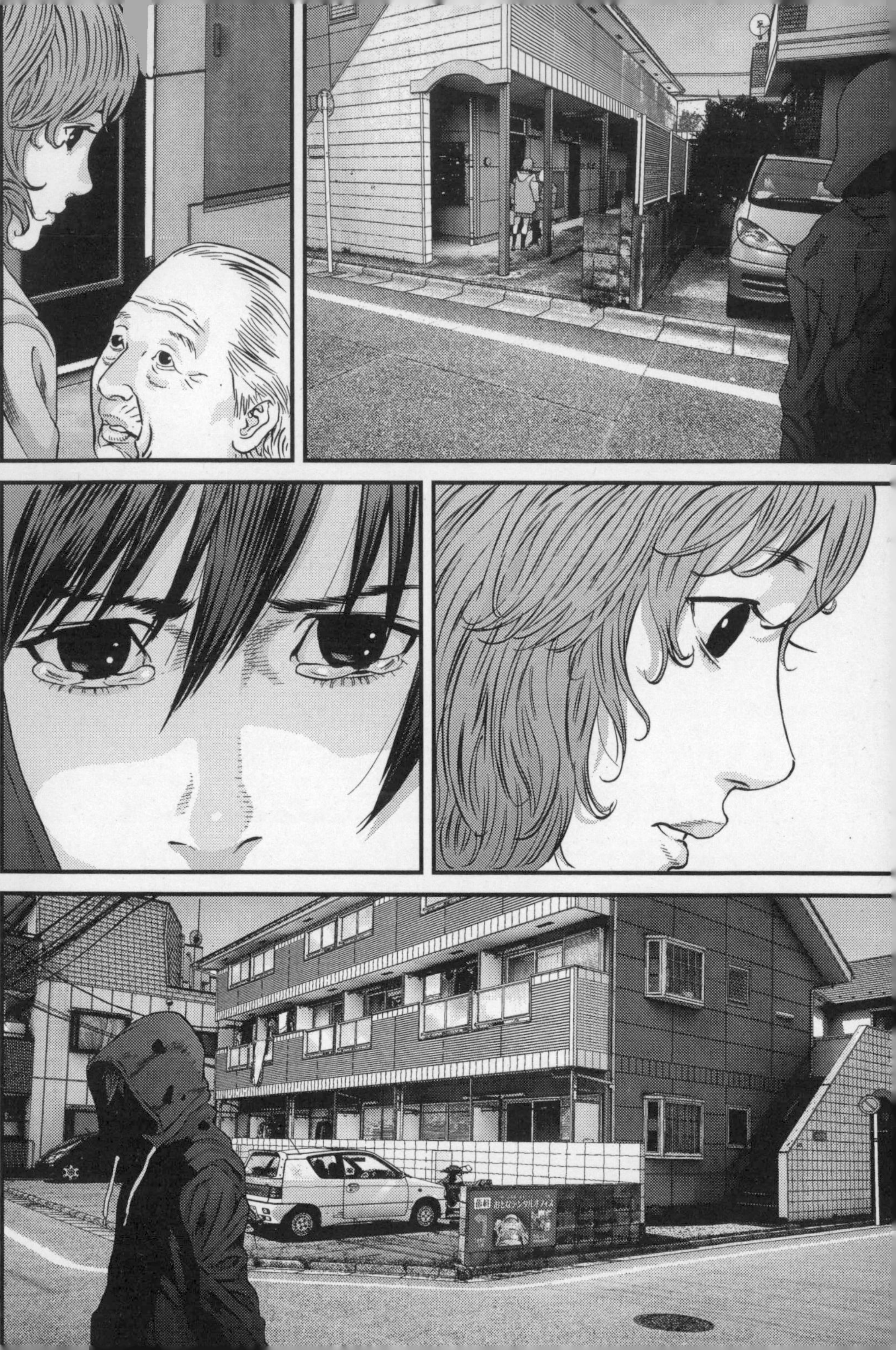

CHAPTER 74 - END

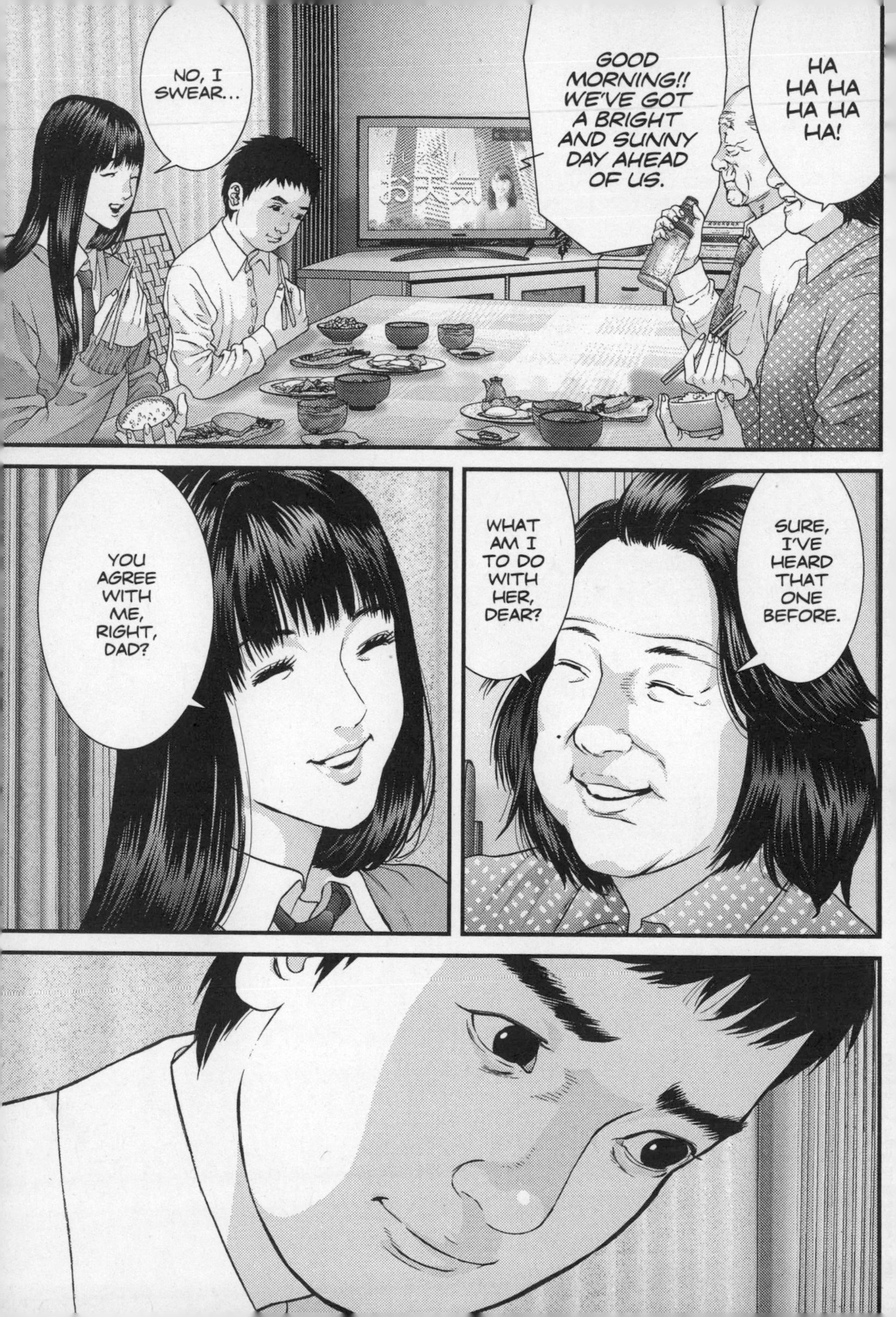
HA HA HA HA HA HA!
GOOD MORNING!! WE'VE GOT A BRIGHT AND SUNNY DAY AHEAD OF US.
お天気
NO, I SWEAR...
SURE, I'VE HEARD THAT ONE BEFORE.
WHAT AM I TO DO WITH HER, DEAR?
YOU AGREE WITH ME, RIGHT, DAD?

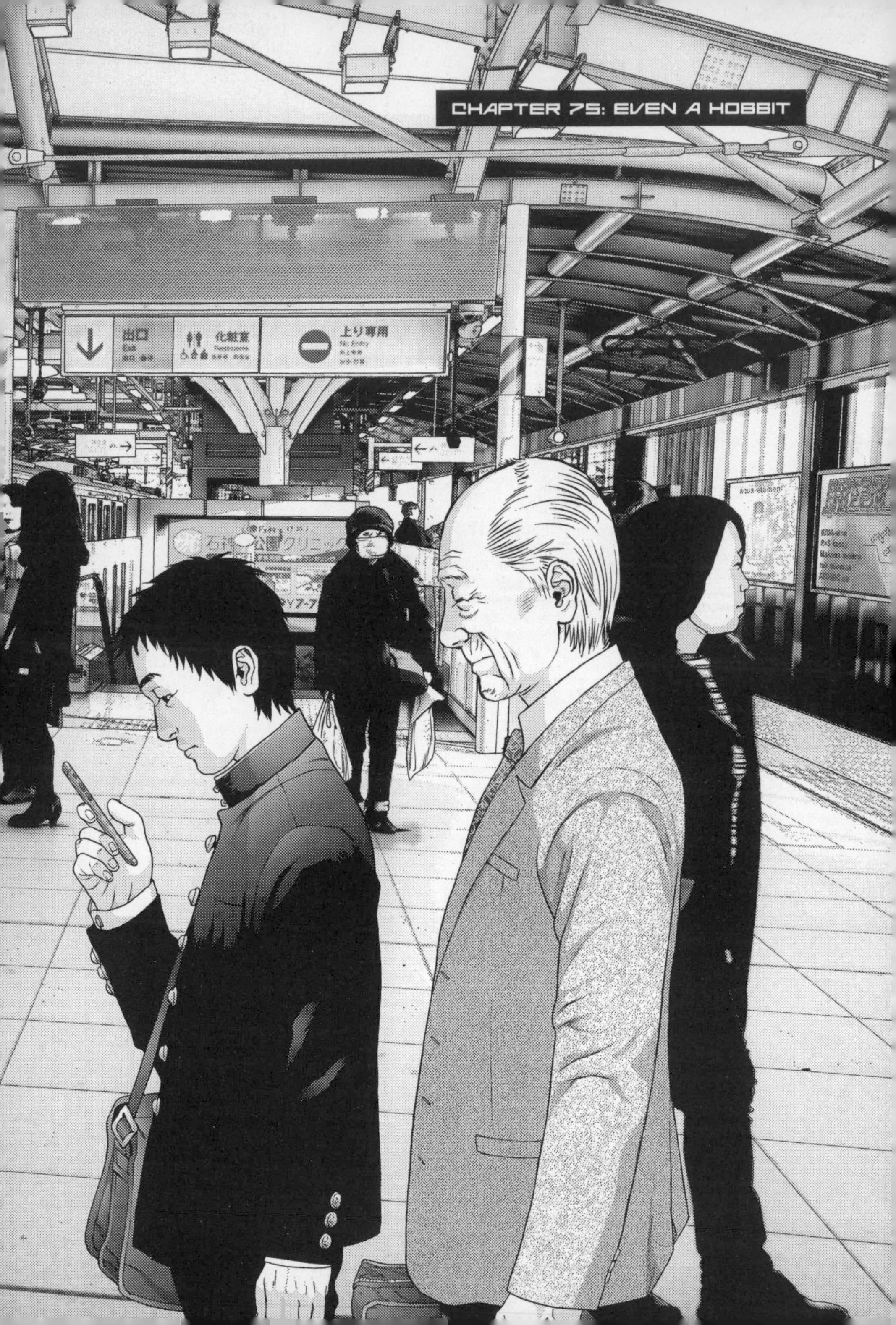
CHAPTER 75: EVEN A HOBBIT
出口
化粧室
上り専用

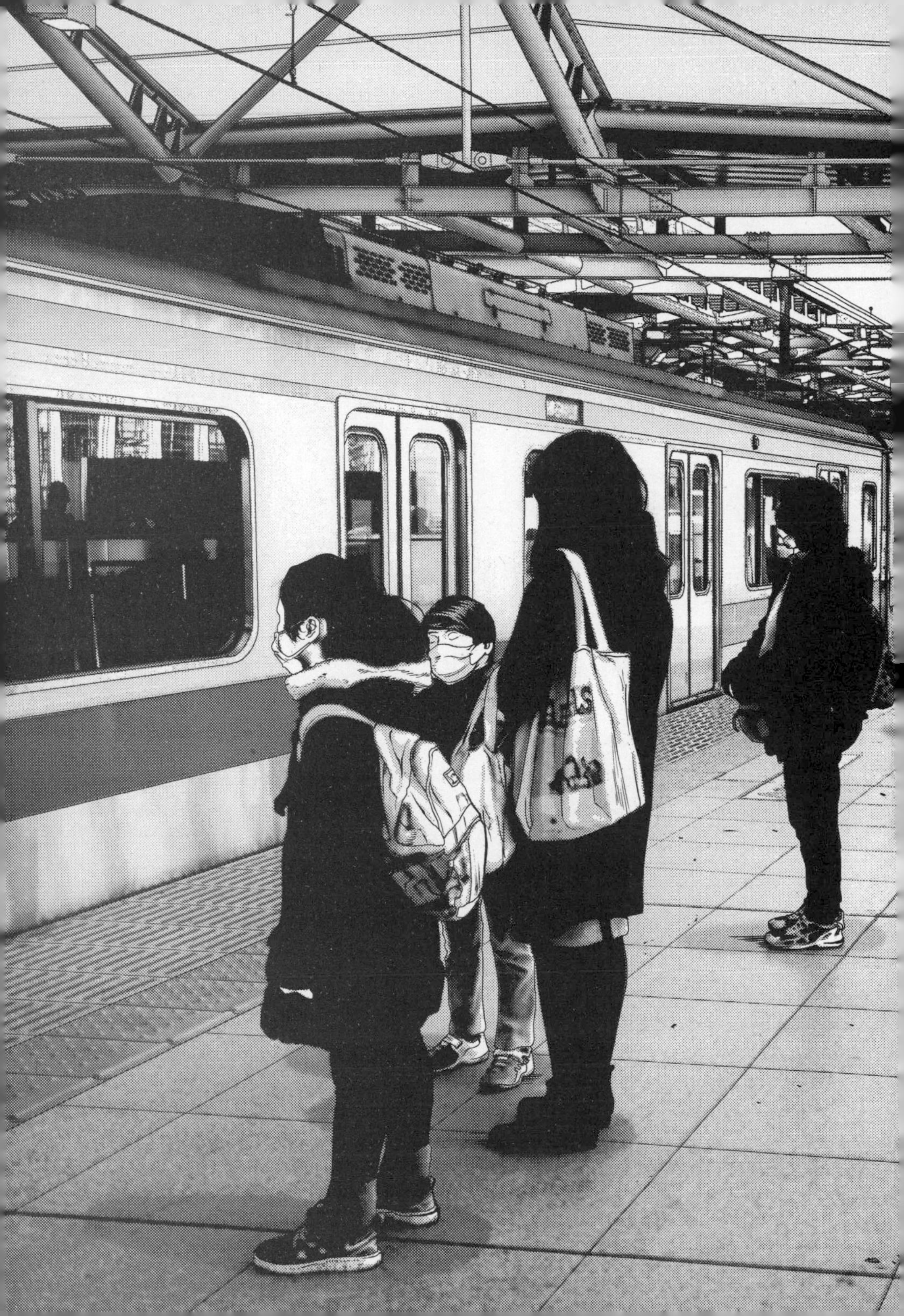

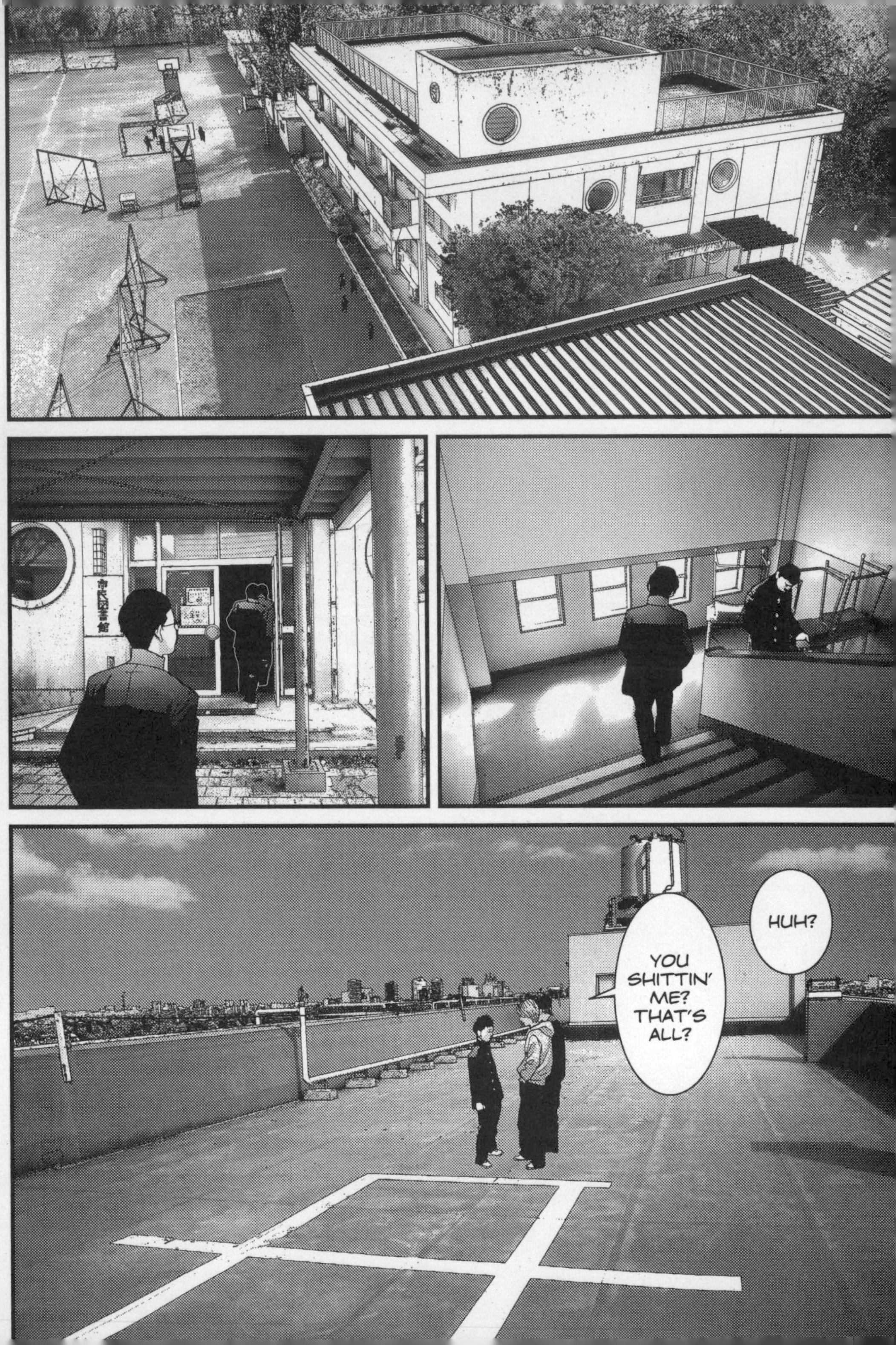
市民図書館
HUH?
YOU SHITTIN' ME? THAT'S ALL?

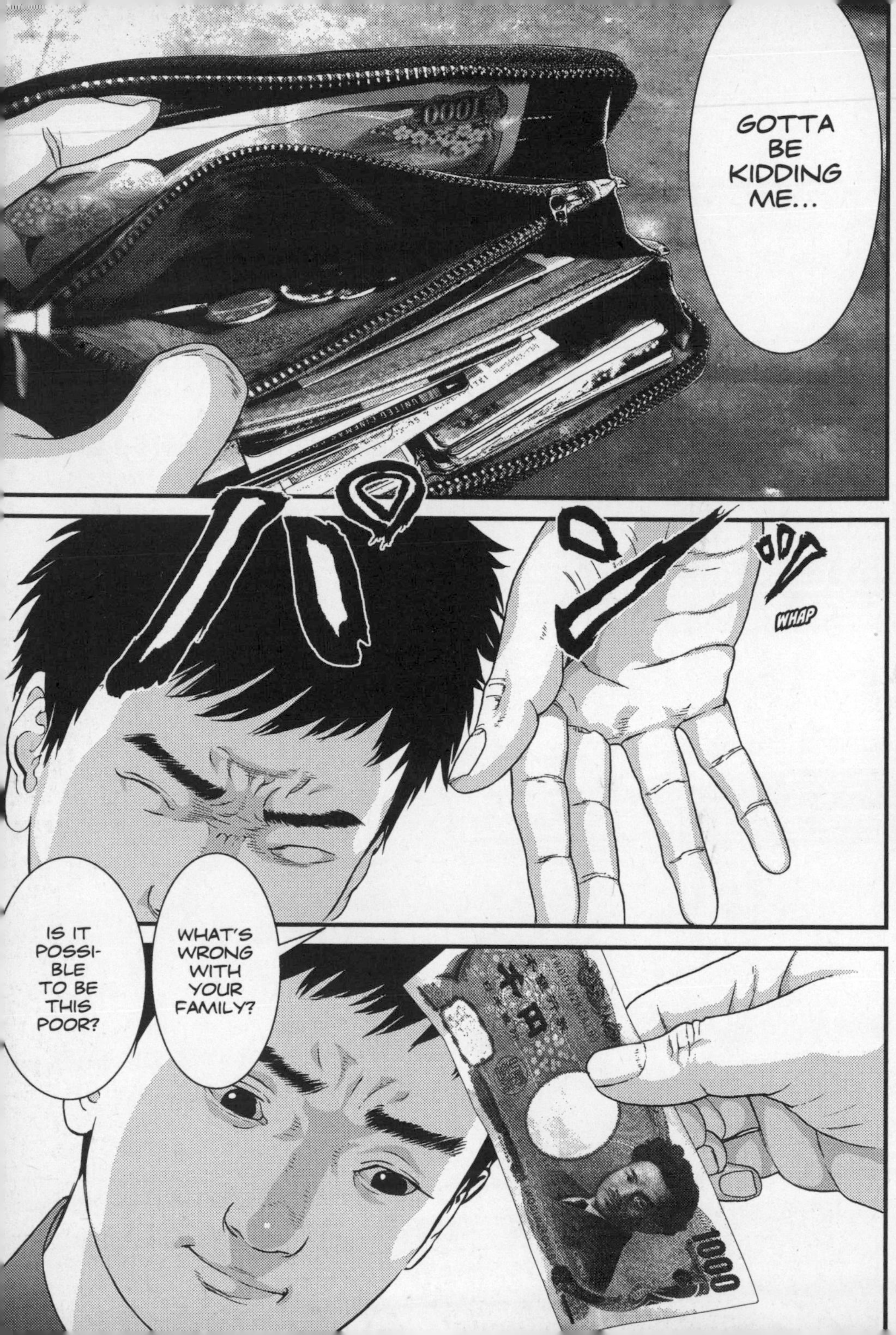
GOTTA BE KIDDING ME...
WHAP
WHAT'S WRONG WITH YOUR FAMILY?
IS IT POSSI-BLE TO BE THIS POOR?

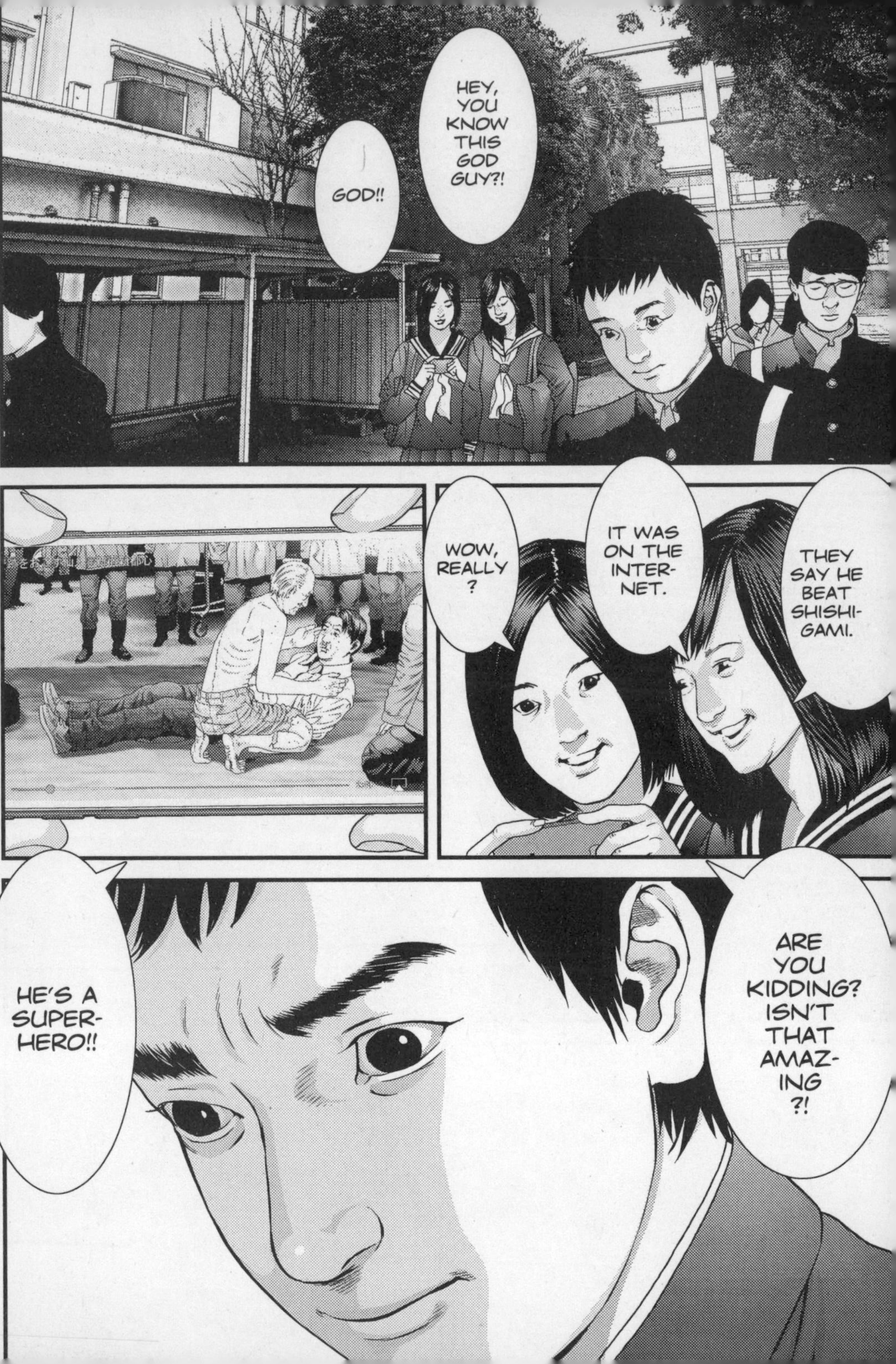
HEY, YOU KNOW THIS GOD GUY?!
GOD!!
THEY SAY HE BEAT SHISHIGAMI.
IT WAS ON THE INTERNET.
WOW, REALLY?
ARE YOU KIDDING? ISN'T THAT AMAZING?!
HE'S A SUPERHERO!!

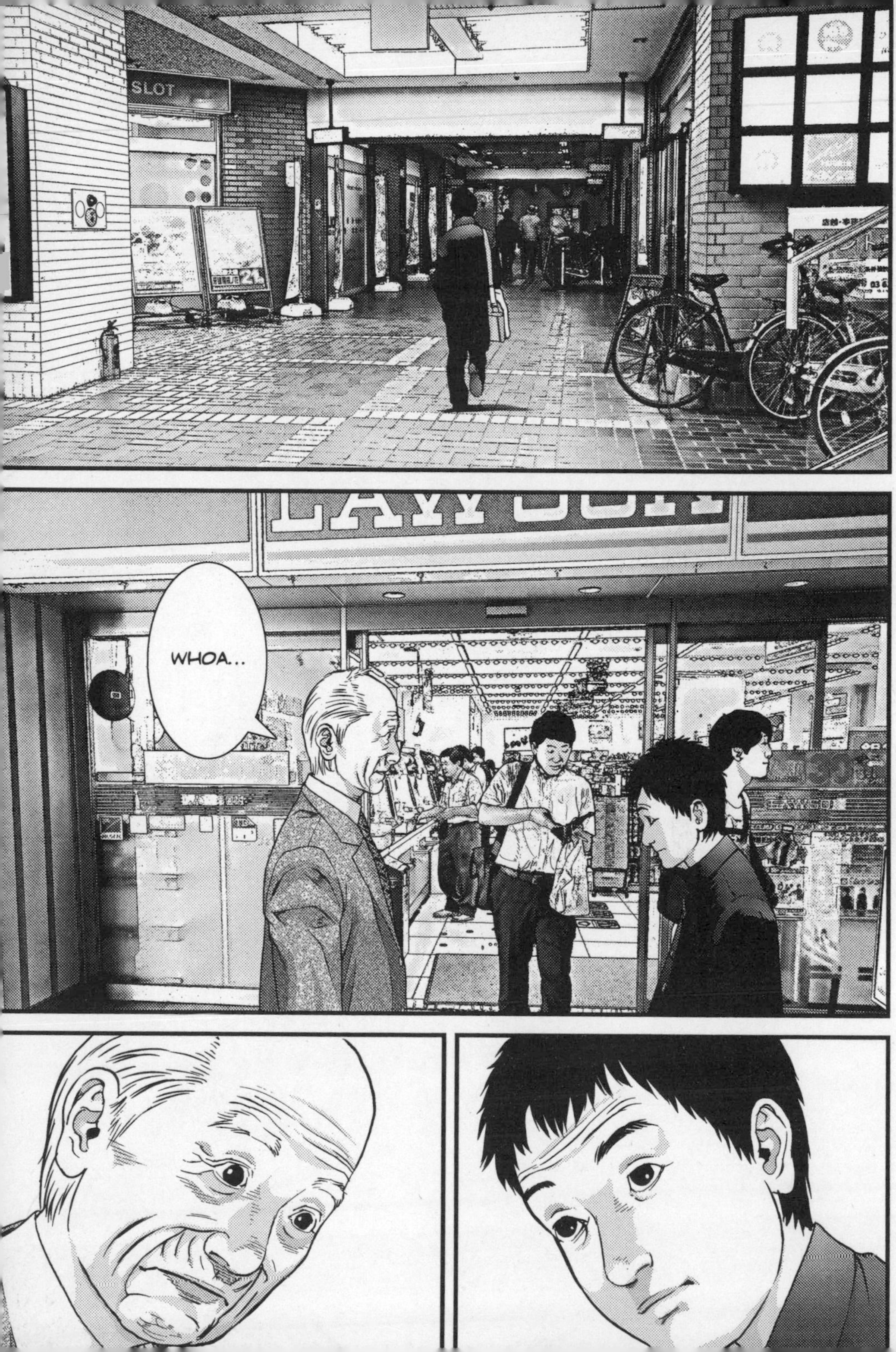
SLOT
LAWSON
WHOA...

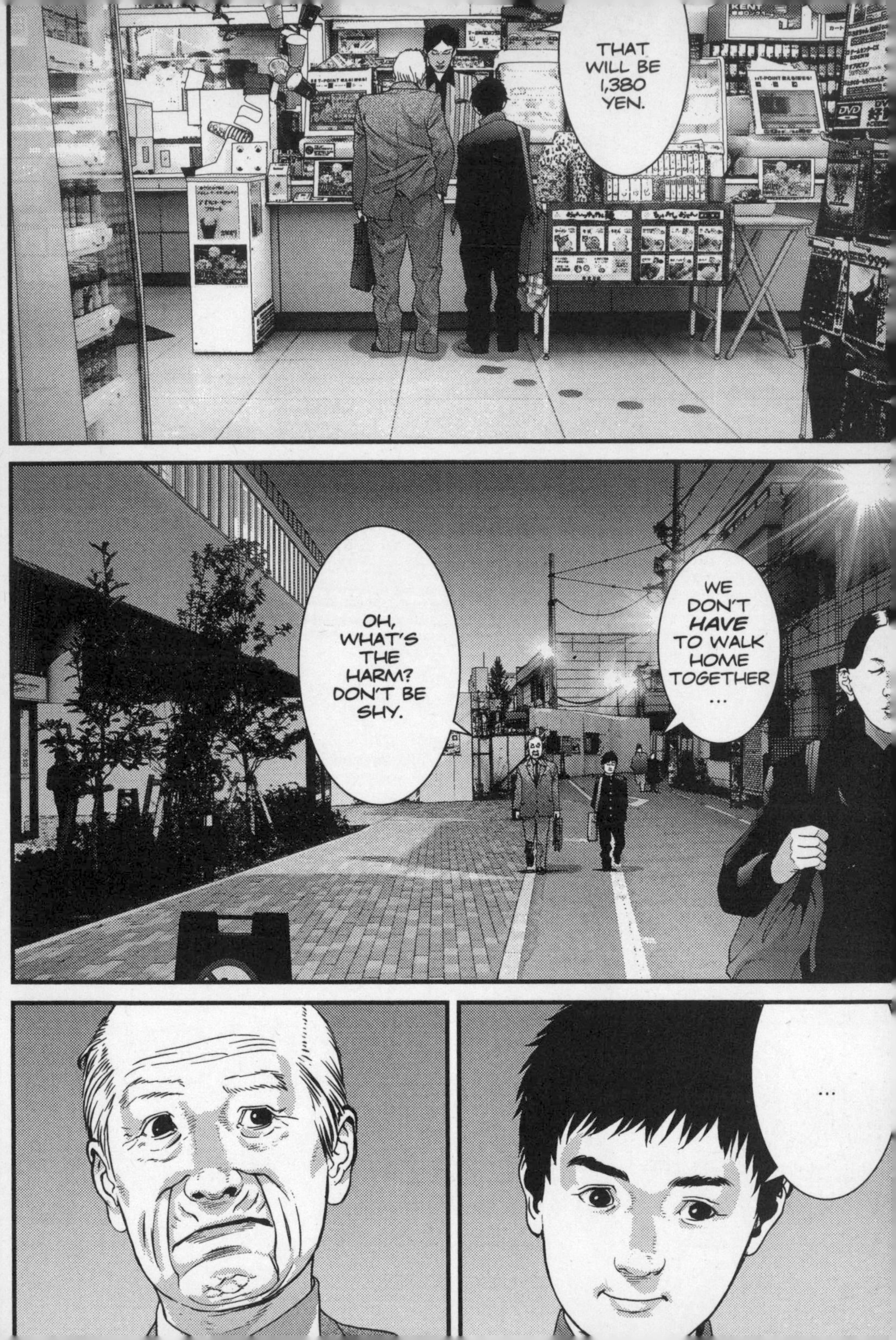
THAT WILL BE 1,380 YEN.
WE DON'T HAVE TO WALK HOME TOGETHER ...
OH, WHAT'S THE HARM? DON'T BE SHY.
...

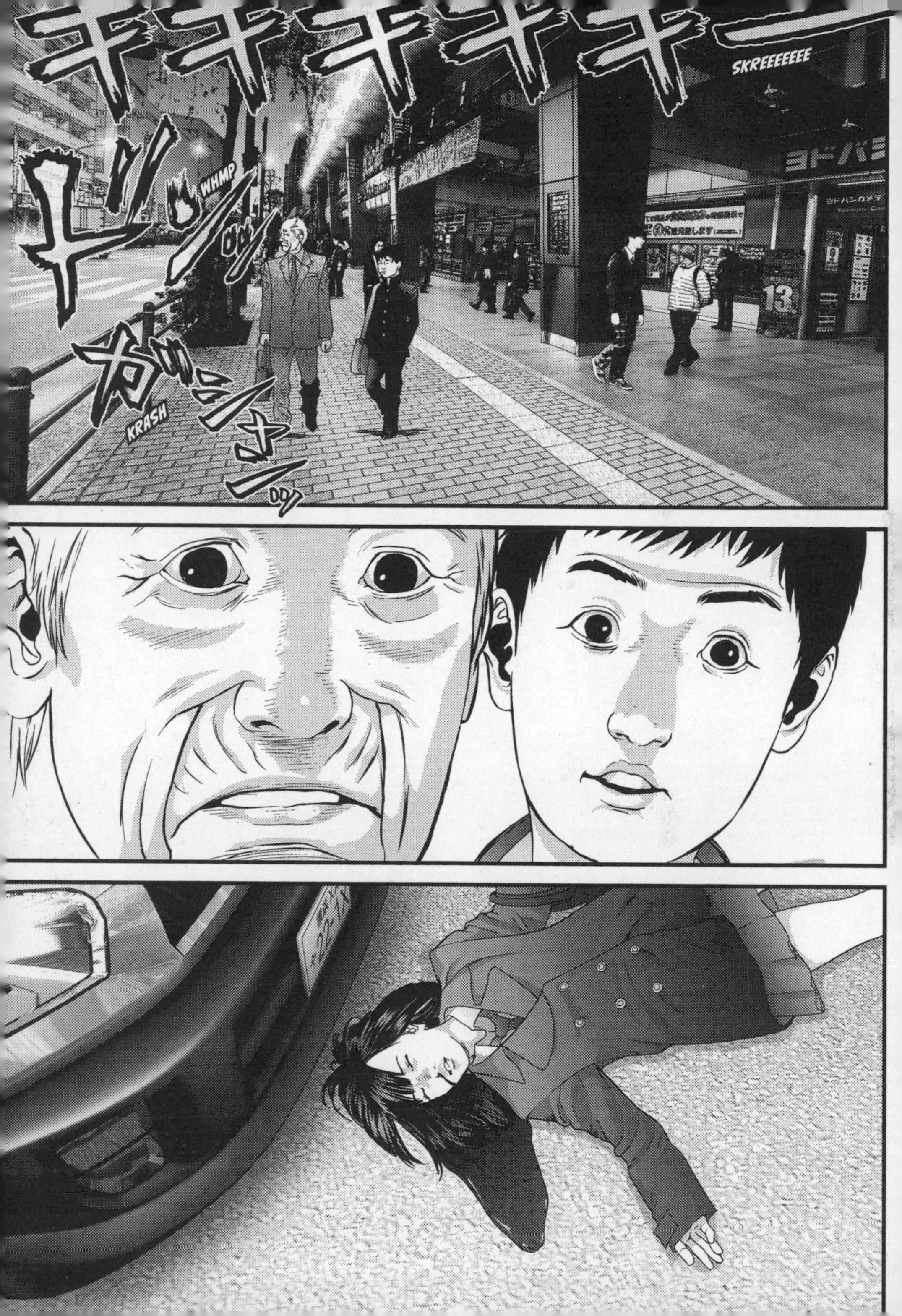
SKREEEEEEE
WHMP
KRASH

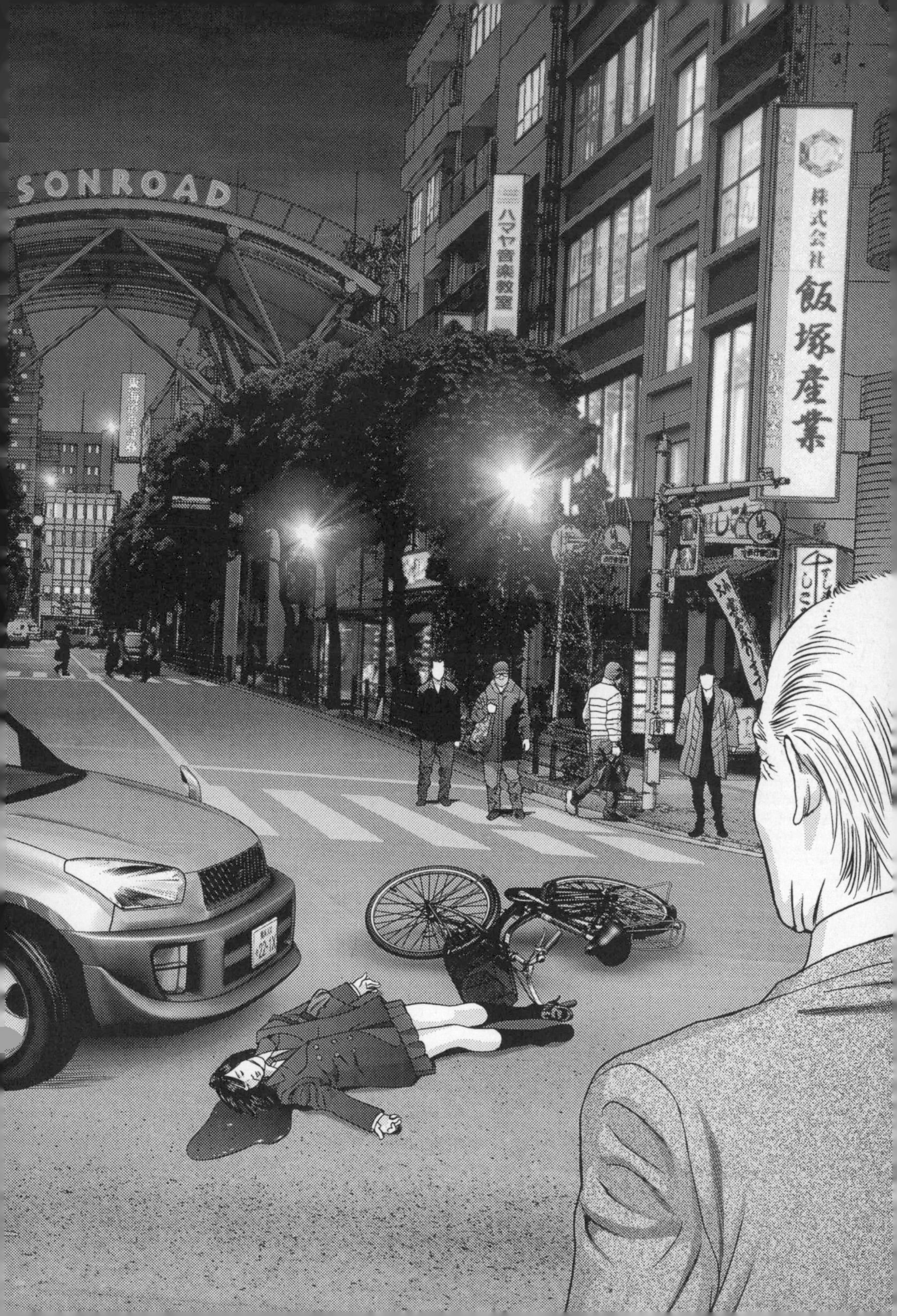
SONROAD
株式会社
飯塚產業

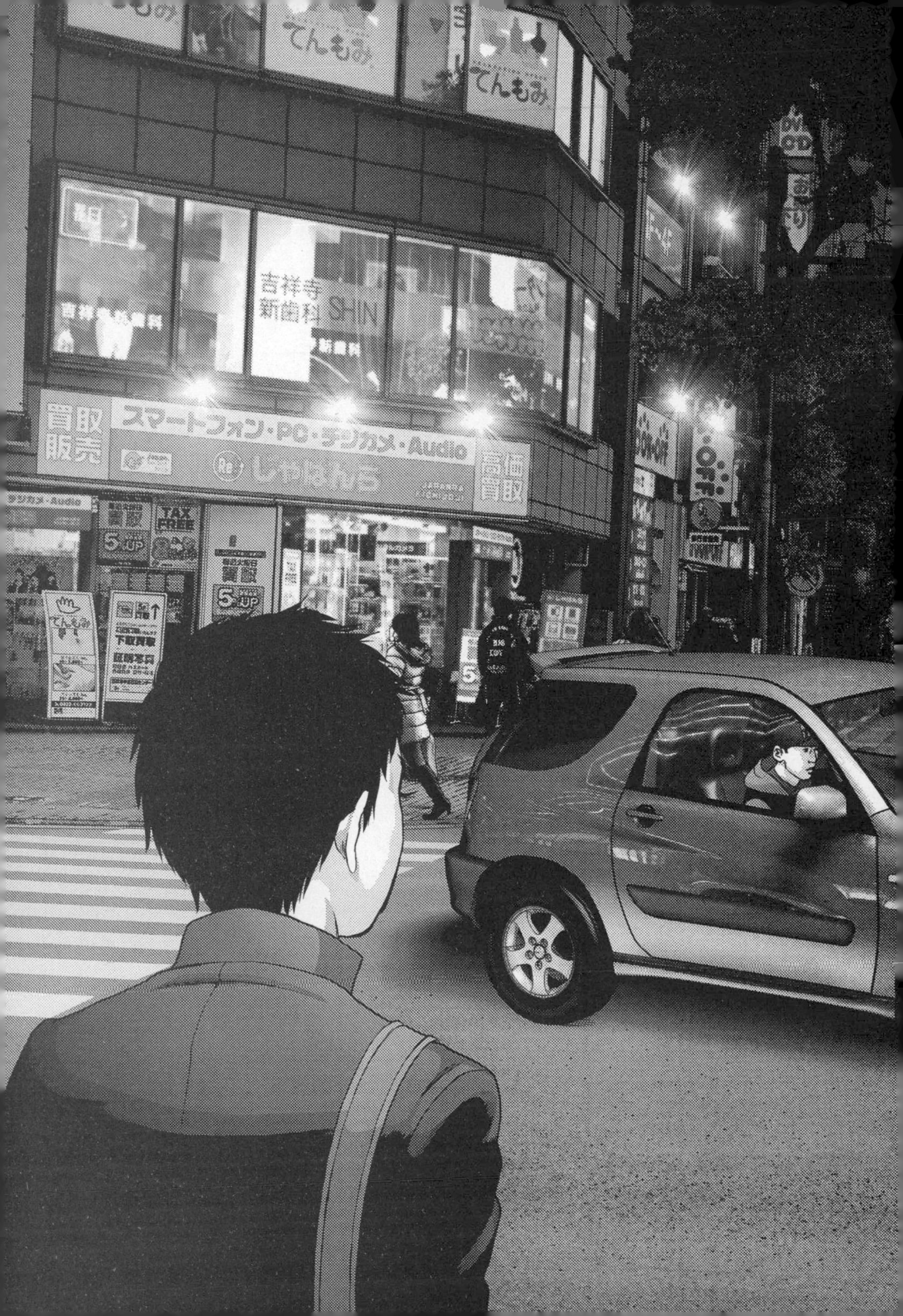

てんもみ
てんもみ
吉祥寺
新歯科
SHIN
買取
販売
スマートフォン・PC・デジカメ・Audio
じゃぱんる
高価
買取
TAX FREE

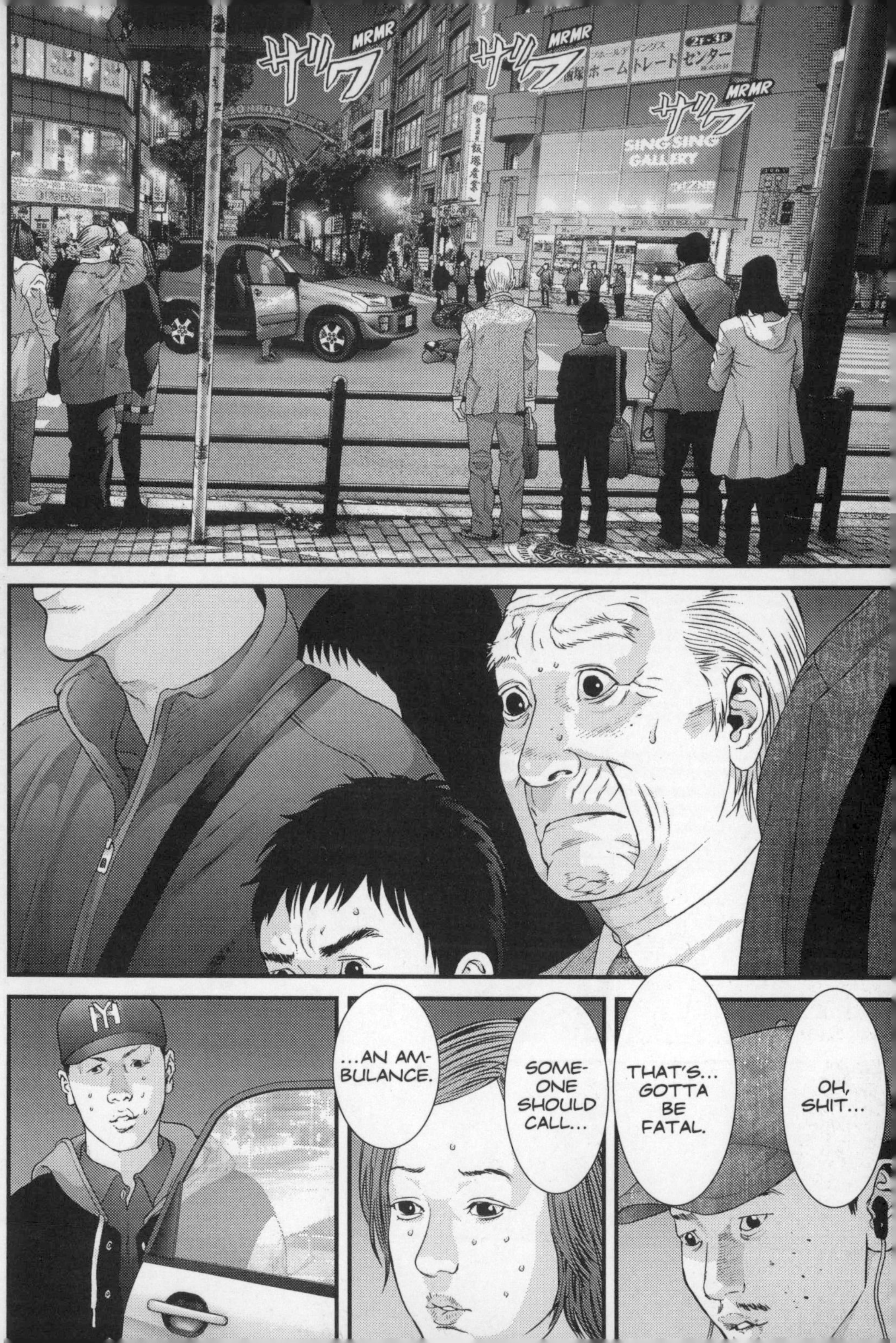
MRMR
MRMR
MRMR
SING SING GALLERY
OH, SHIT...
THAT'S... GOTTA BE FATAL.
SOME-ONE SHOULD CALL...
...AN AM-BULANCE.

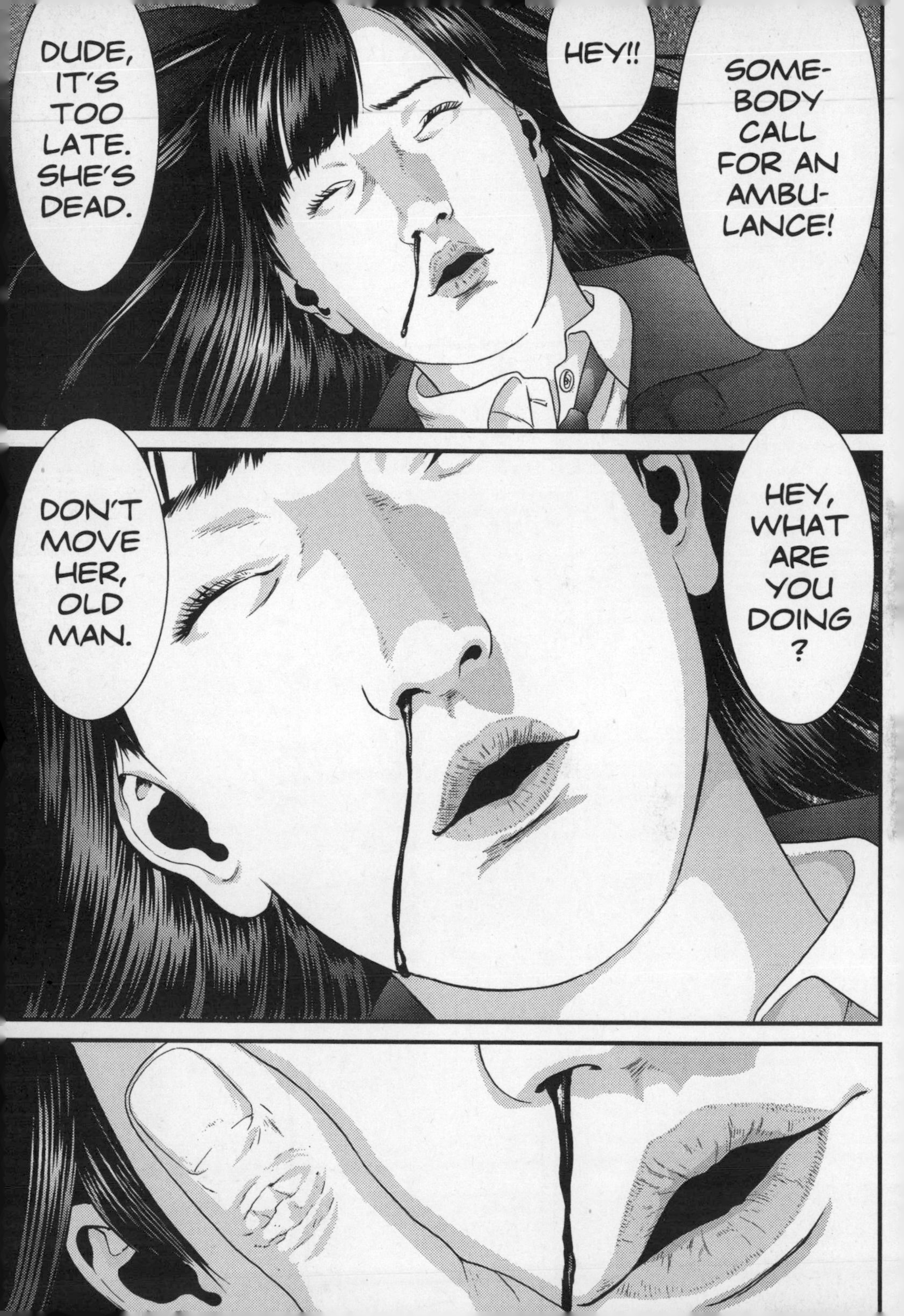
SOME-BODY CALL FOR AN AMBU-LANCE!
HEY!!
DUDE, IT'S TOO LATE. SHE'S DEAD.
HEY, WHAT ARE YOU DOING?
DON'T MOVE HER, OLD MAN.

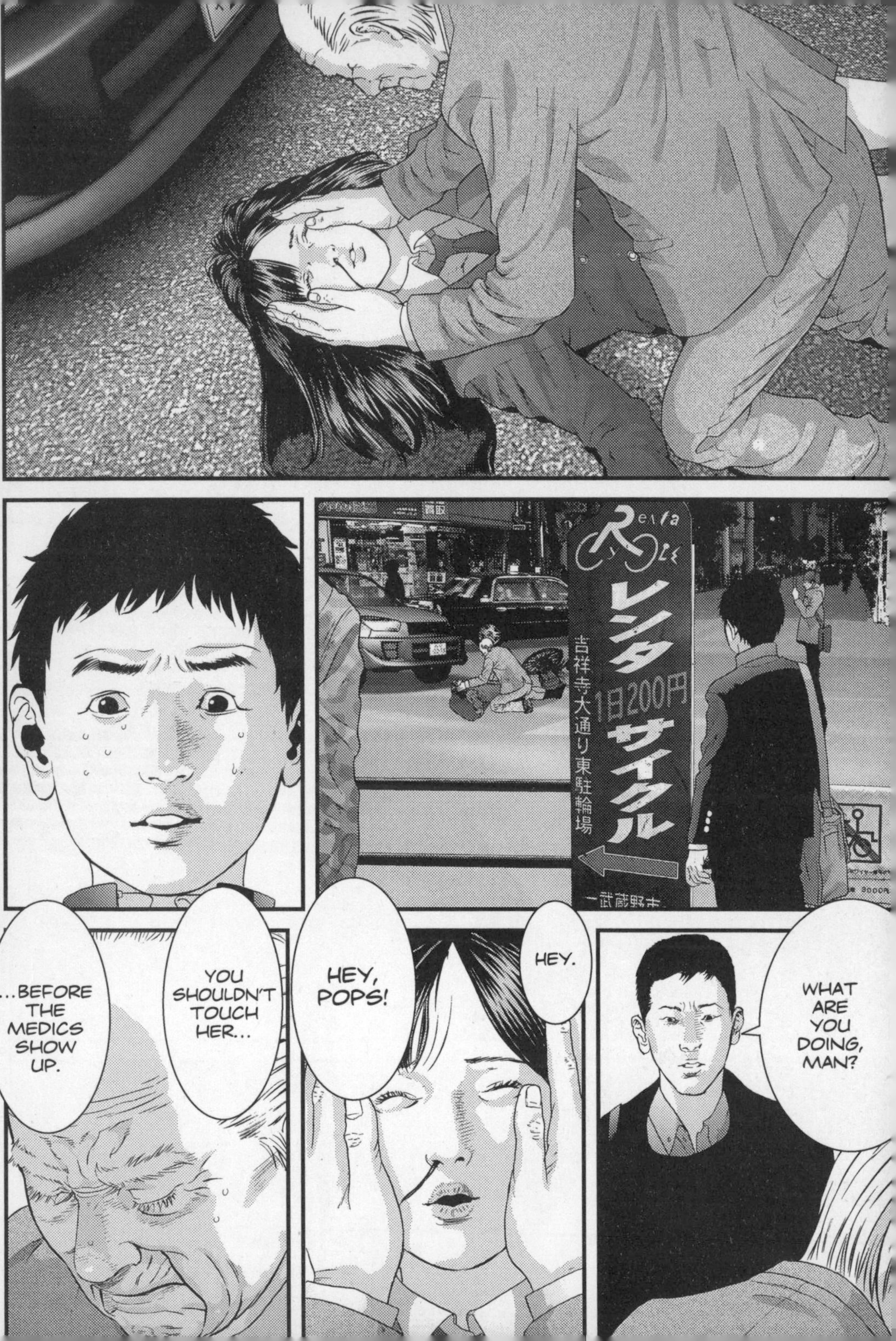
レンタサイクル
1日200円
吉祥寺大通り東駐輪場
WHAT ARE YOU DOING, MAN?
HEY.
HEY, POPS!
YOU SHOULDN'T TOUCH HER...
...BEFORE THE MEDICS SHOW UP.

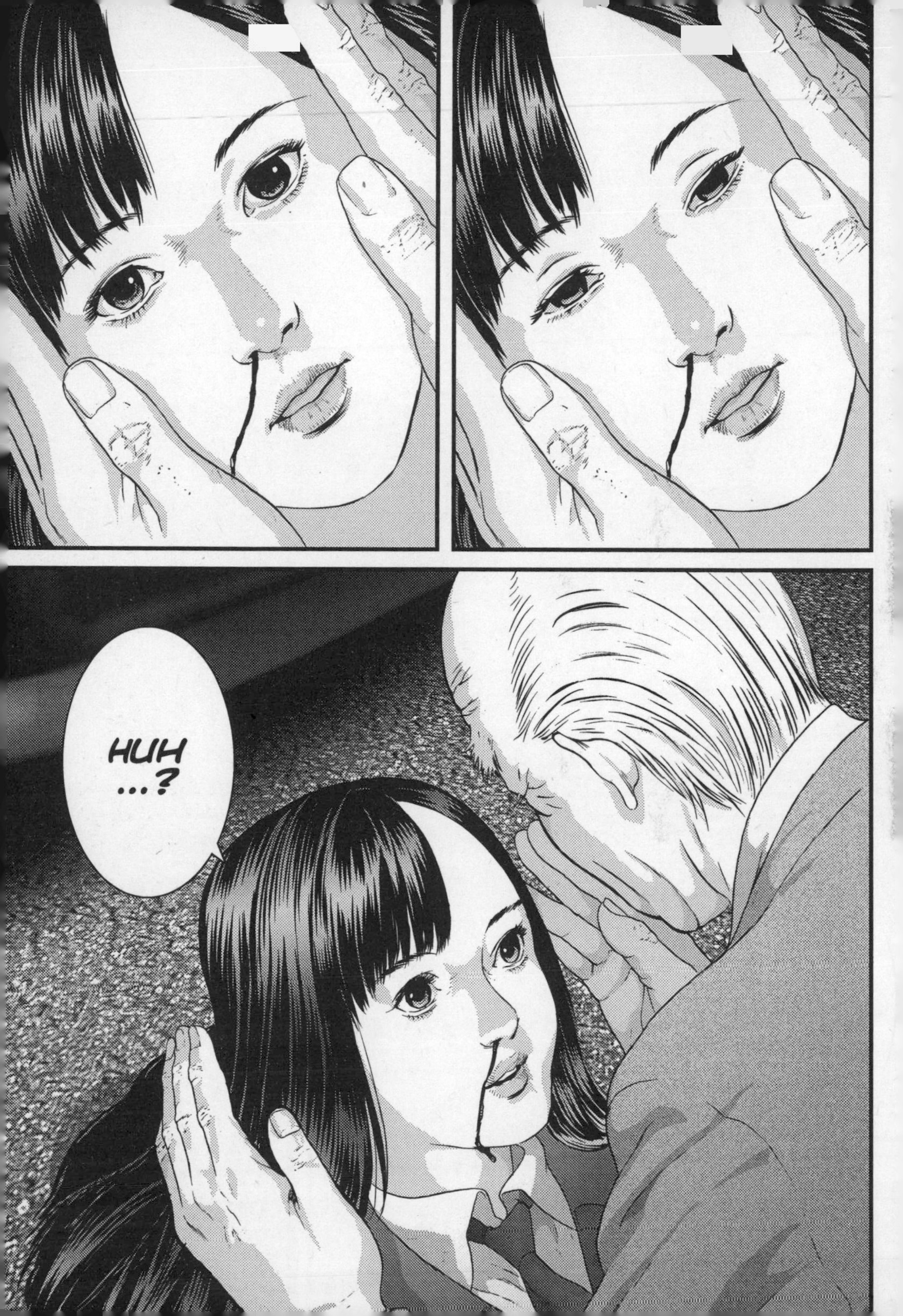
HUH ...?

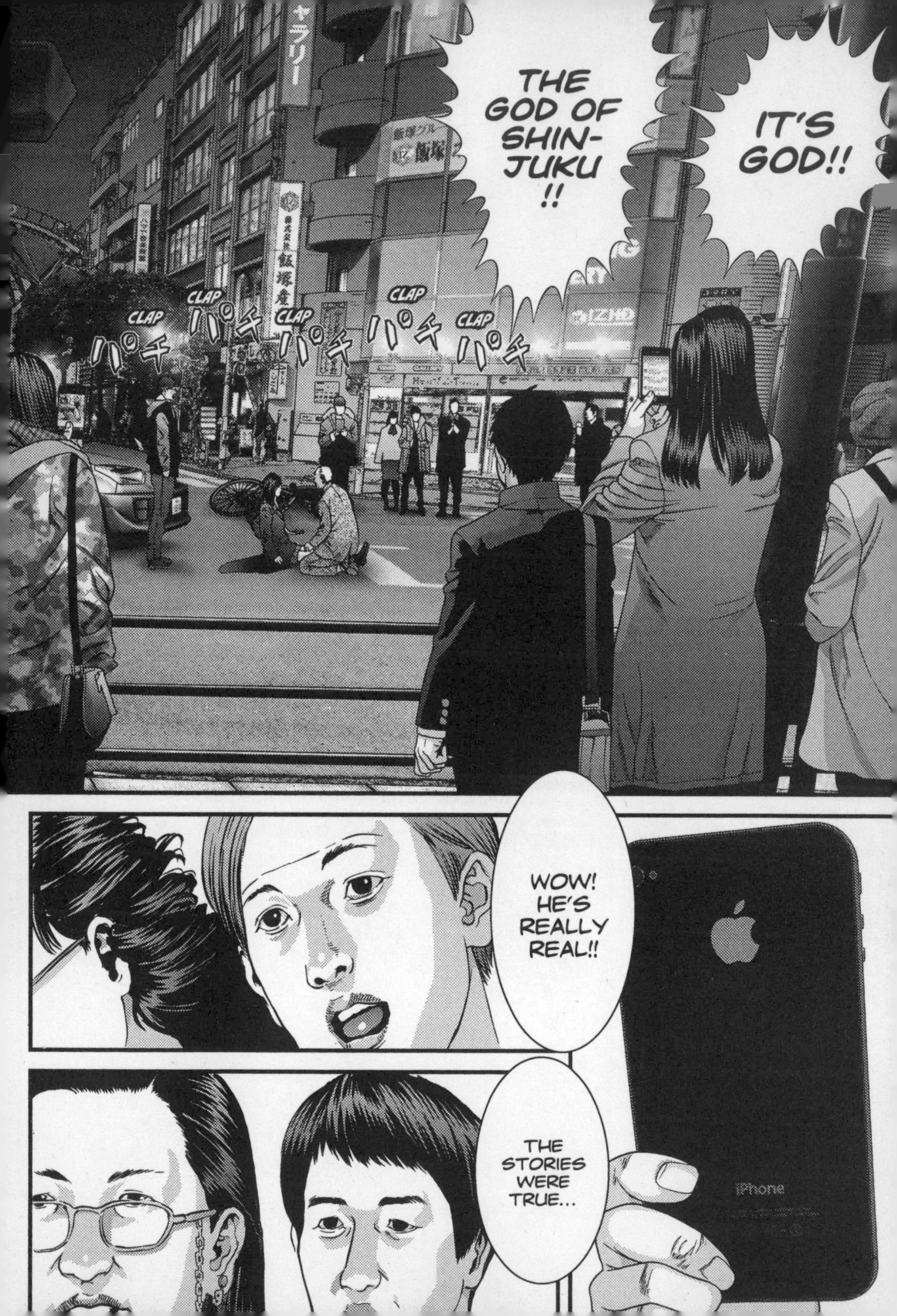
IT'S GOD!!
THE GOD OF SHIN-JUKU !!
CLAP パチ
CLAP パチ
CLAP パチ
CLAP パチ
CLAP パチ
WOW! HE'S REALLY REAL!!
THE STORIES WERE TRUE...
iPhone

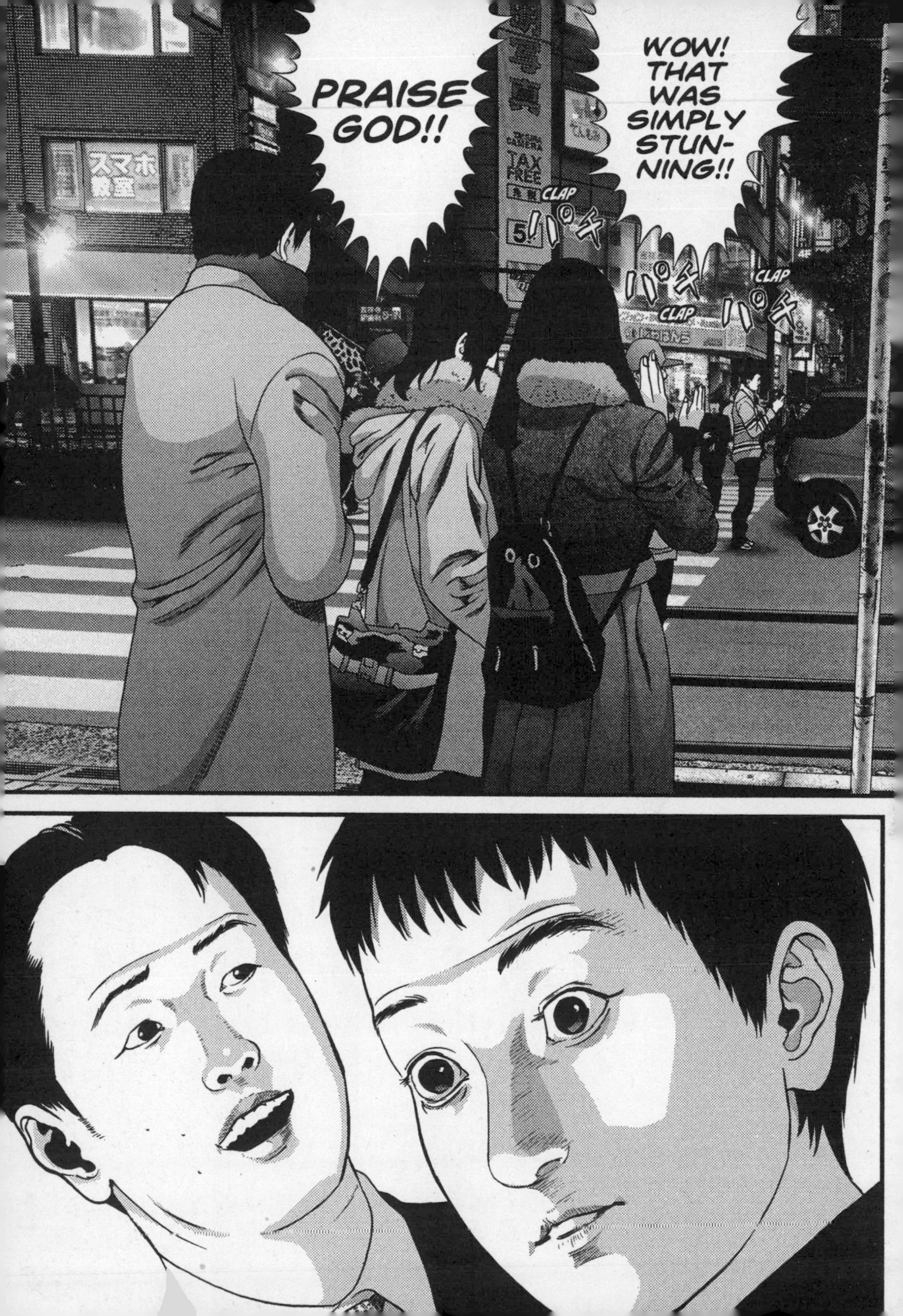
WOW! THAT WAS SIMPLY STUN-NING!!
PRAISE GOD!!
CLAP
CLAP
CLAP

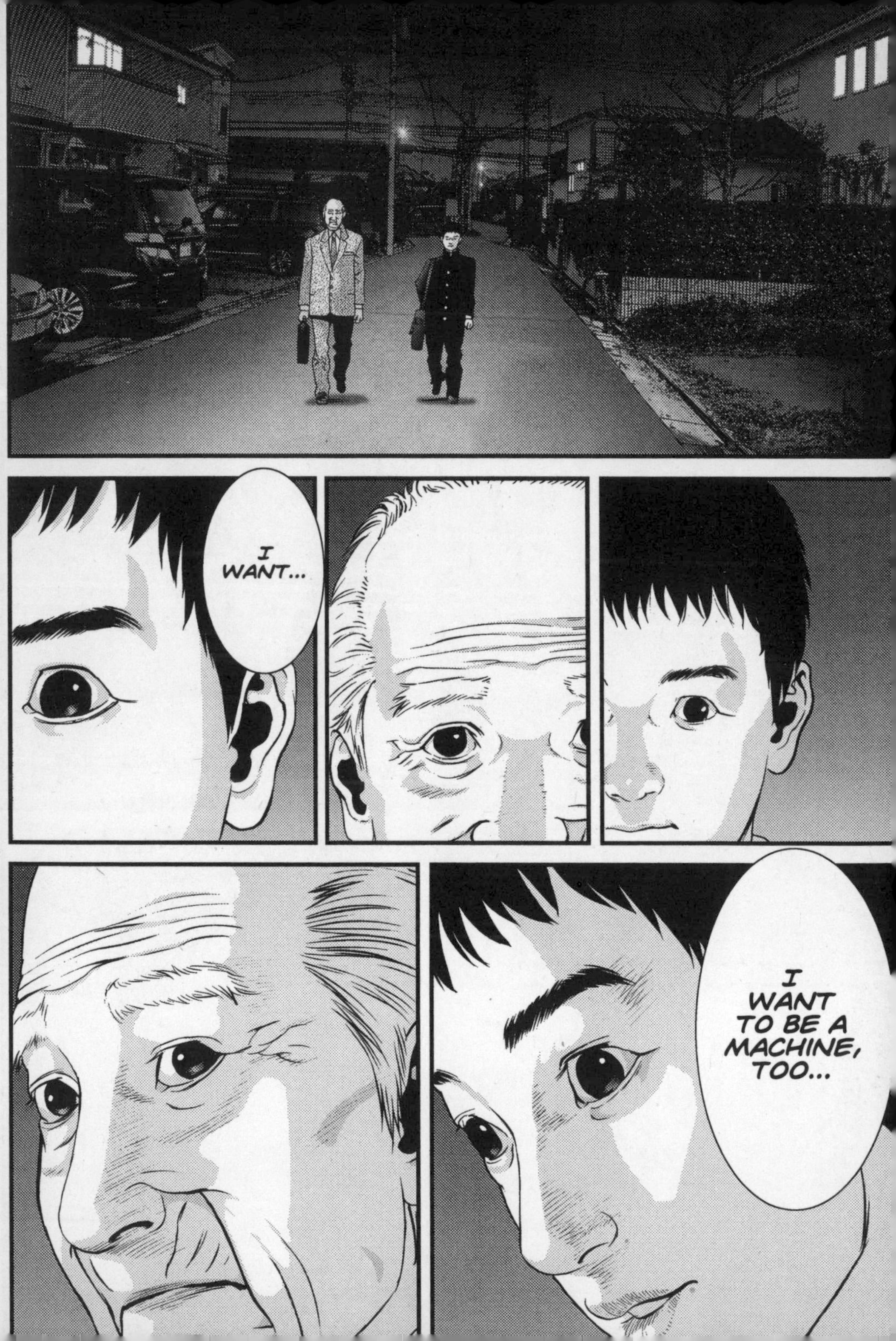
I WANT...
I WANT TO BE A MACHINE, TOO...

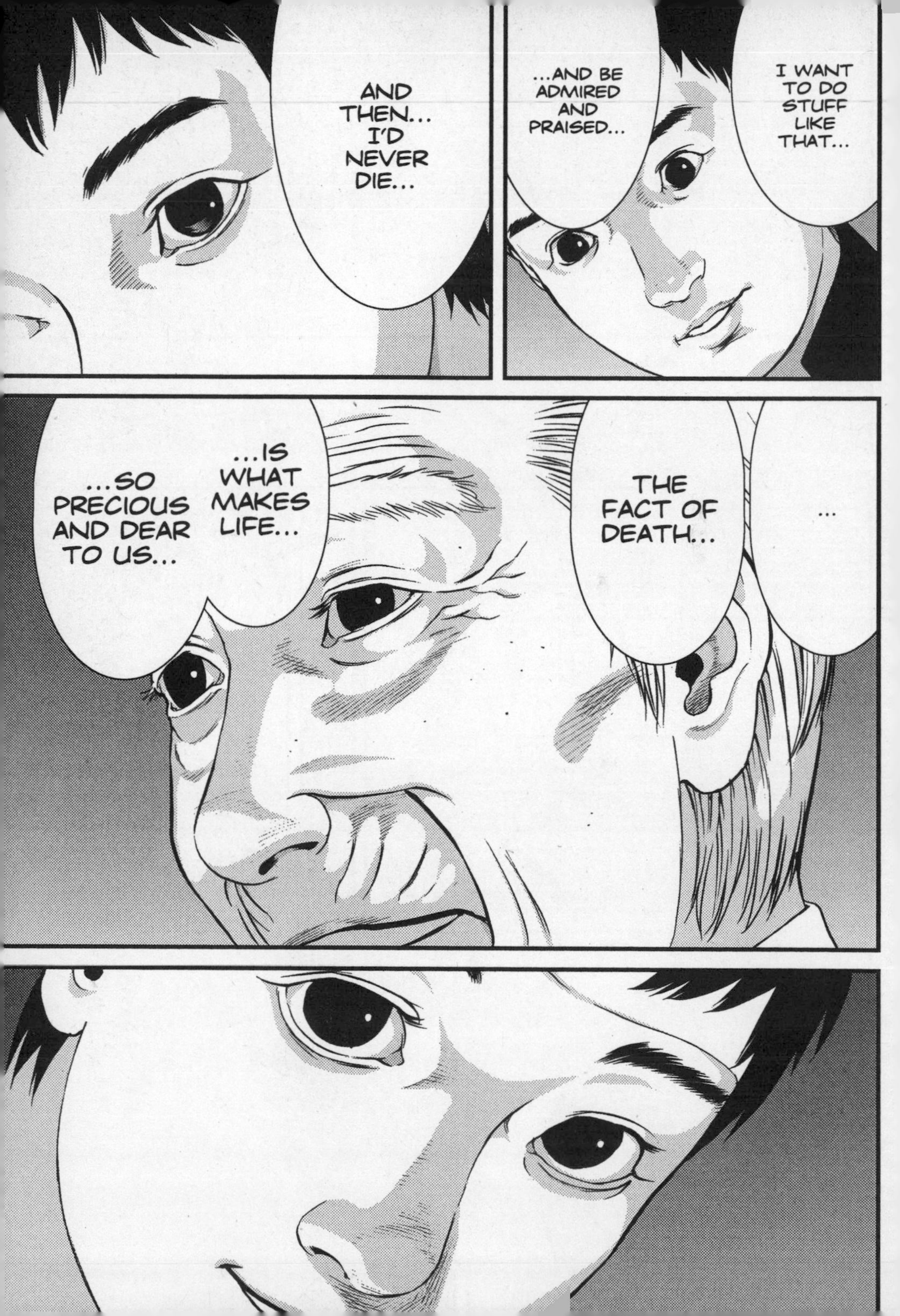
I WANT TO DO STUFF LIKE THAT...
...AND BE ADMIRED AND PRAISED...
AND THEN... I'D NEVER DIE...
...
THE FACT OF DEATH...
...IS WHAT MAKES LIFE...
...SO PRECIOUS AND DEAR TO US...

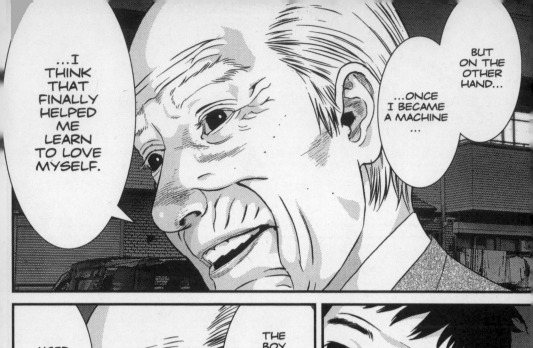

BUT ON THE OTHER HAND...
...ONCE I BECAME A MACHINE ...
...I THINK THAT FINALLY HELPED ME LEARN TO LOVE MYSELF.
...
THE BOY WHO WAS MECH-ANIZED ALONG WITH ME...
...USED HIS NEW BODY TO KILL.
BUT... I CHOSE...
...TO SAVE HUMAN LIVES.

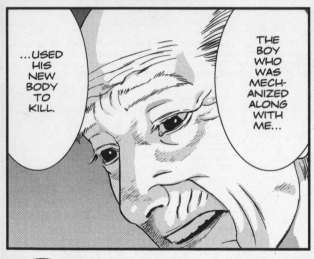

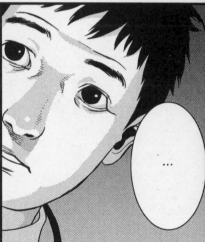

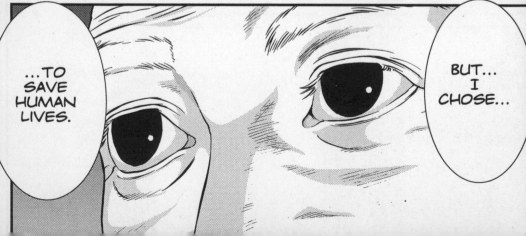

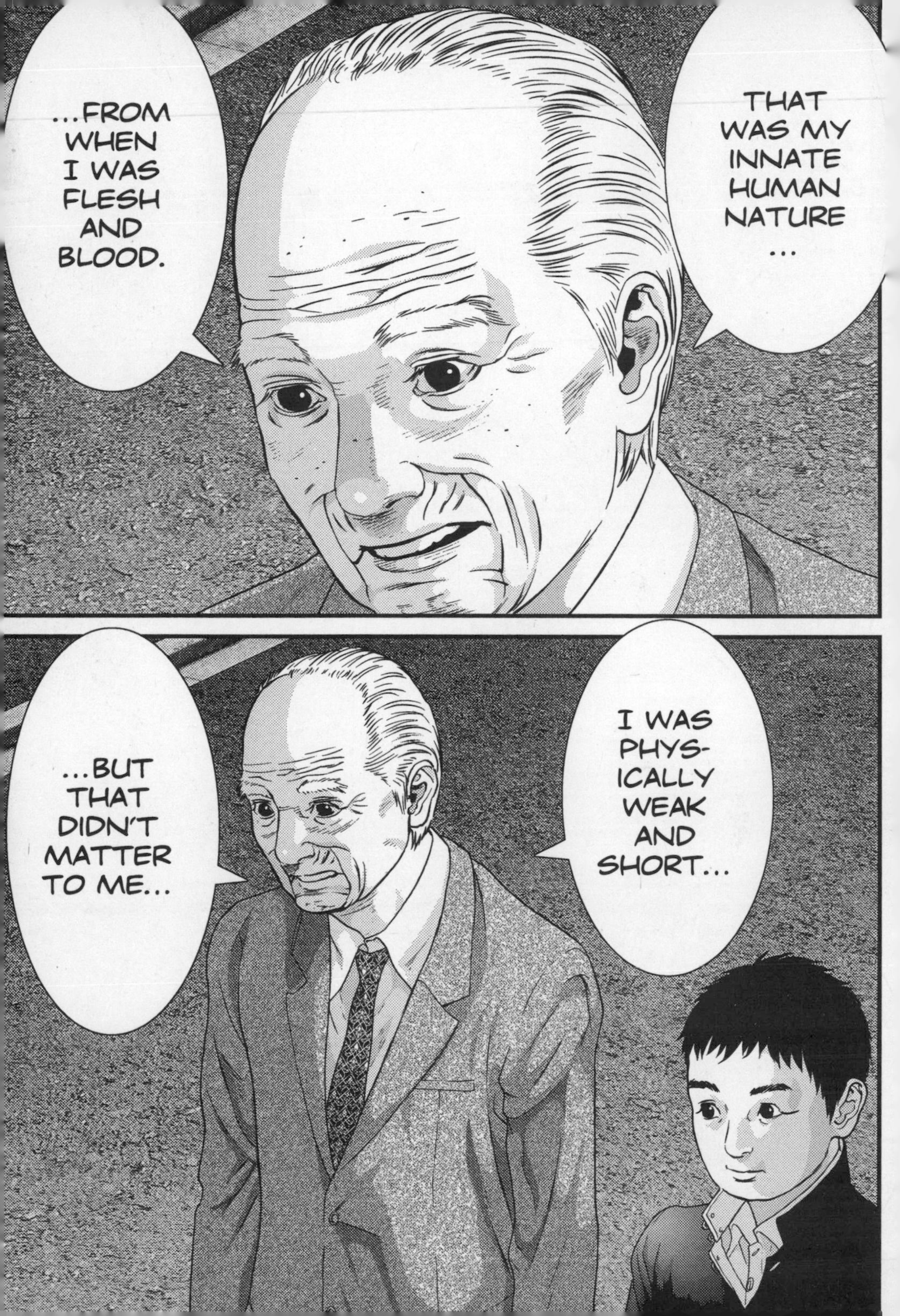
THAT WAS MY INNATE HUMAN NATURE ...
...FROM WHEN I WAS FLESH AND BLOOD.
I WAS PHYS-ICALLY WEAK AND SHORT...
...BUT THAT DIDN'T MATTER TO ME...

...CAN LOVE HIM-SELF...

EVEN A HOBBIT...

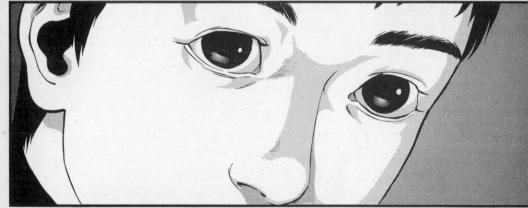

CHAPTER 75 - END

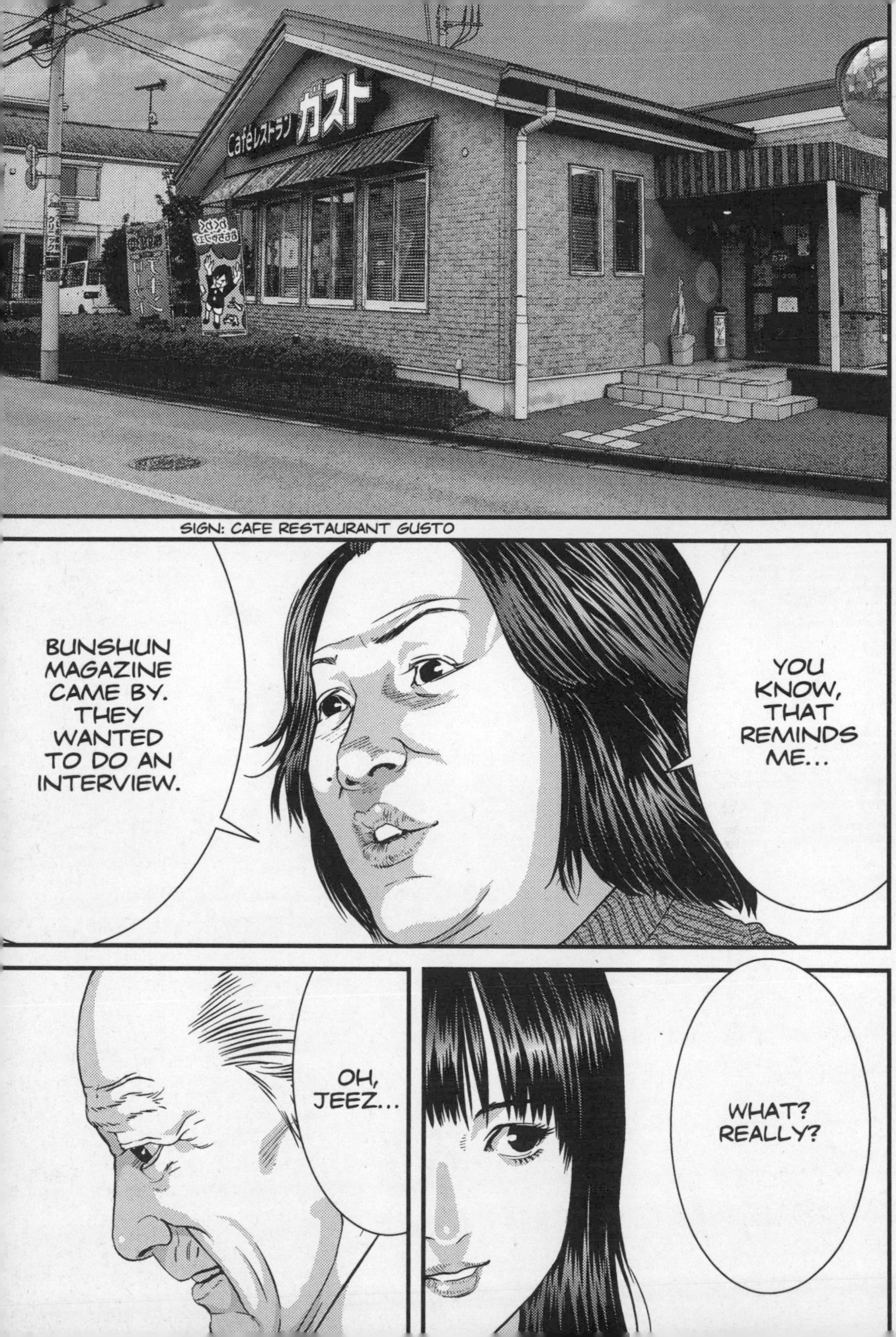

Cafeレストラン ガスト
SIGN: CAFE RESTAURANT GUSTO
YOU KNOW, THAT REMINDS ME...
BUNSHUN MAGAZINE CAME BY. THEY WANTED TO DO AN INTERVIEW.
WHAT? REALLY?
OH, JEEZ...

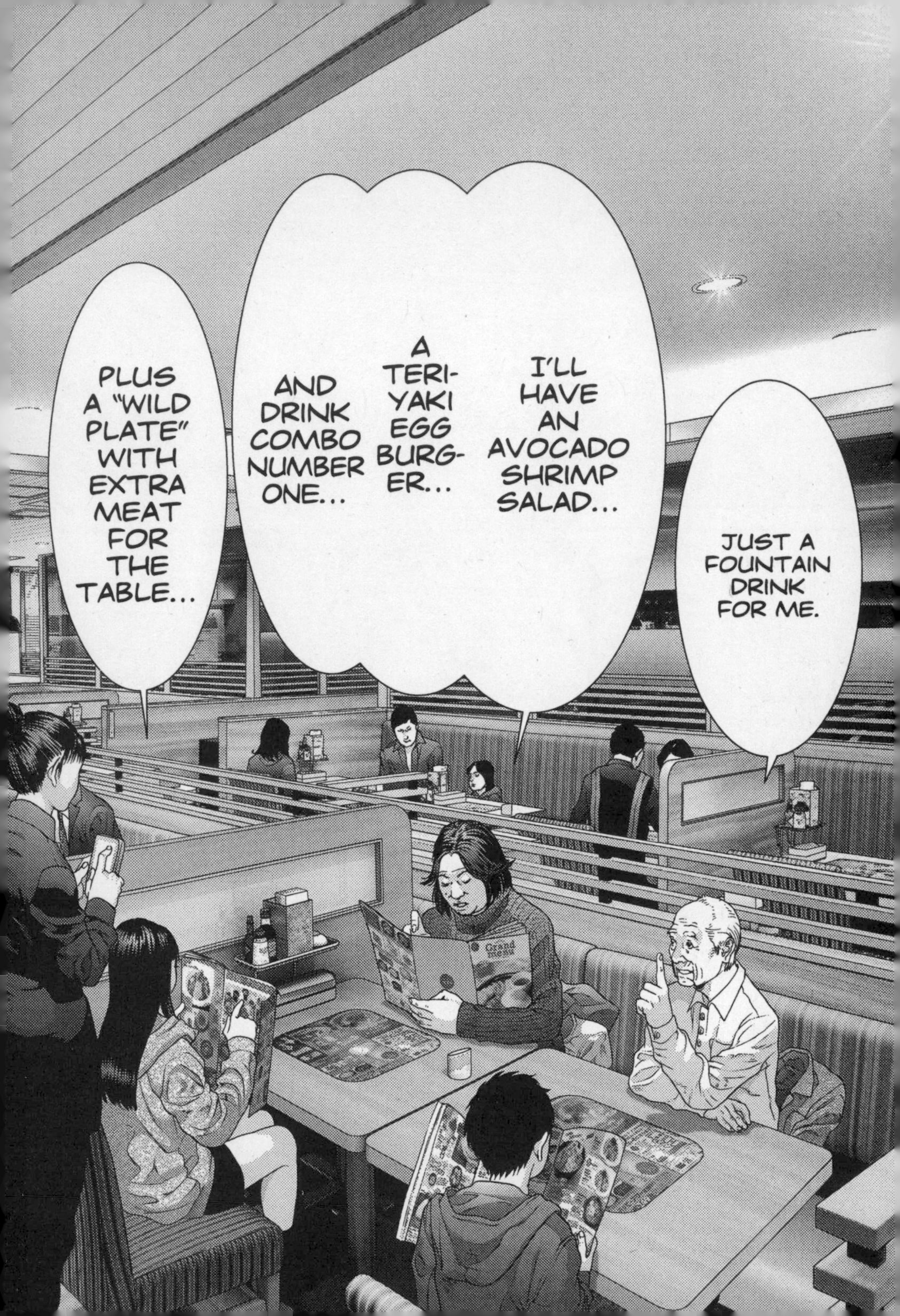
JUST A FOUNTAIN DRINK FOR ME.
I'LL HAVE AN AVOCADO SHRIMP SALAD...
A TERI-YAKI EGG BURG-ER...
AND DRINK COMBO NUMBER ONE...
PLUS A "WILD PLATE" WITH EXTRA MEAT FOR THE TABLE...

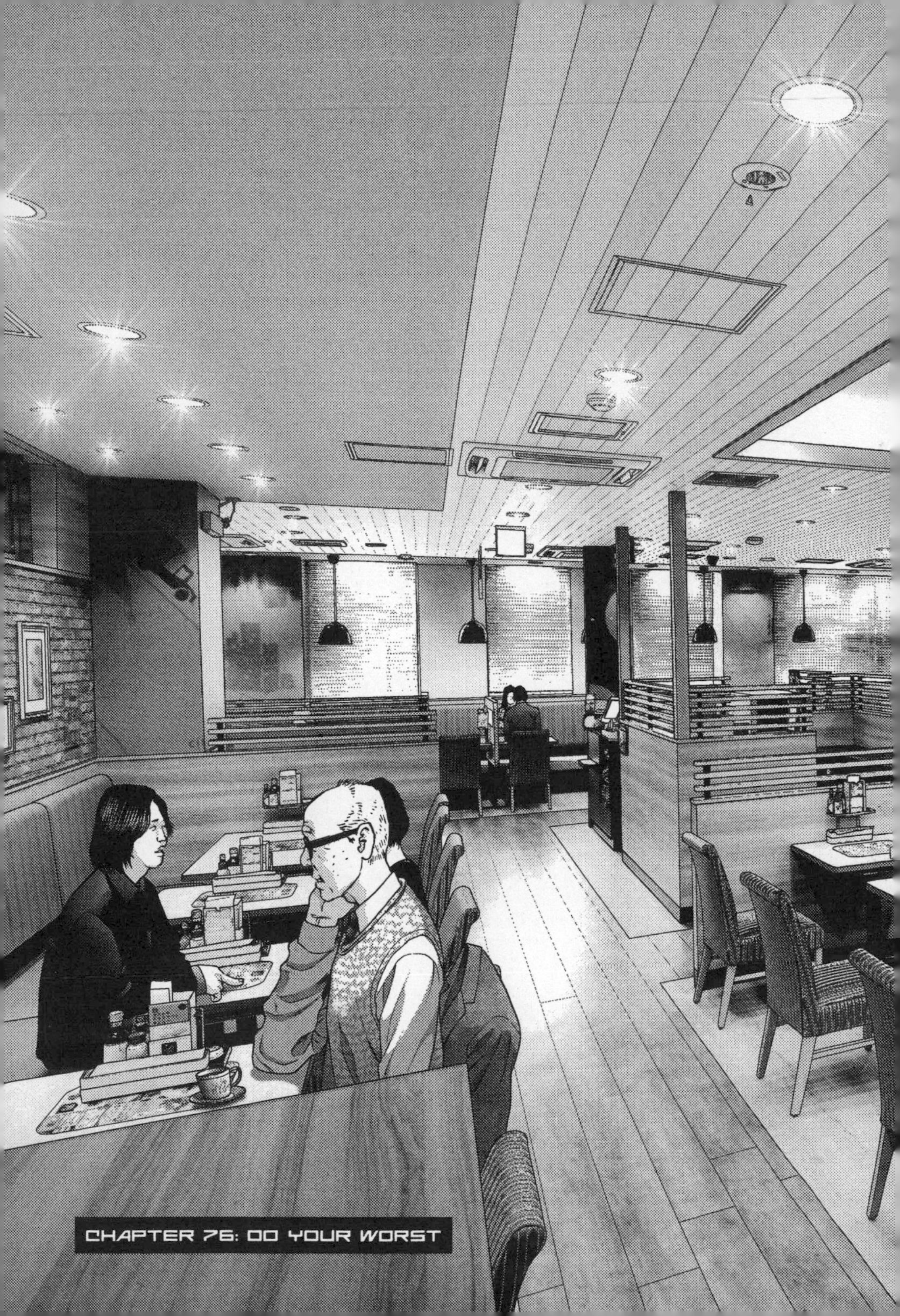
CHAPTER 76: DO YOUR WORST

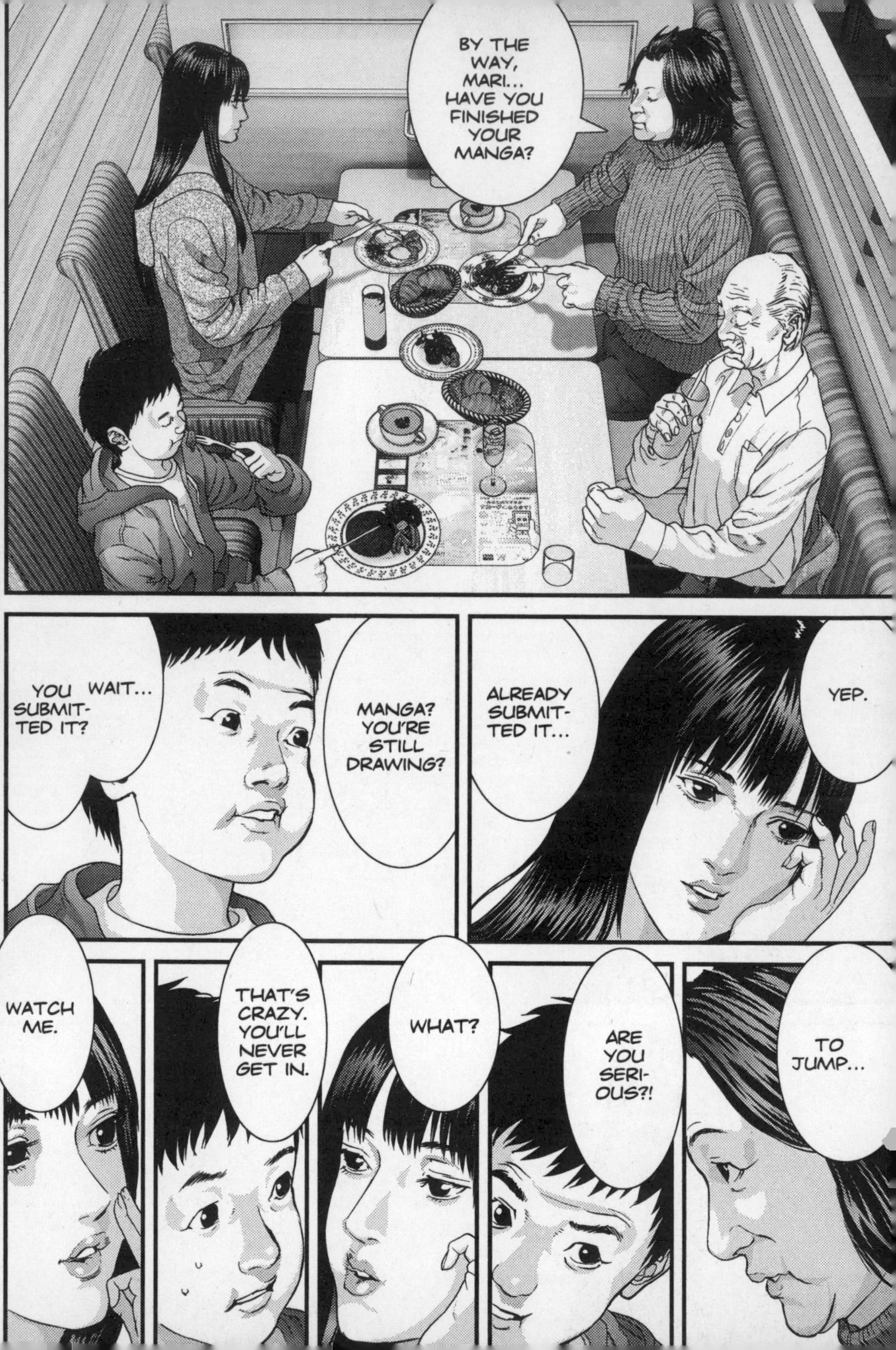
BY THE WAY, MARI... HAVE YOU FINISHED YOUR MANGA?
YEP.
ALREADY SUBMIT-TED IT...
MANGA? YOU'RE STILL DRAWING?
WAIT...
YOU SUBMIT-TED IT?
TO JUMP...
ARE YOU SERI-OUS?!
WHAT?
THAT'S CRAZY. YOU'LL NEVER GET IN.
WATCH ME.

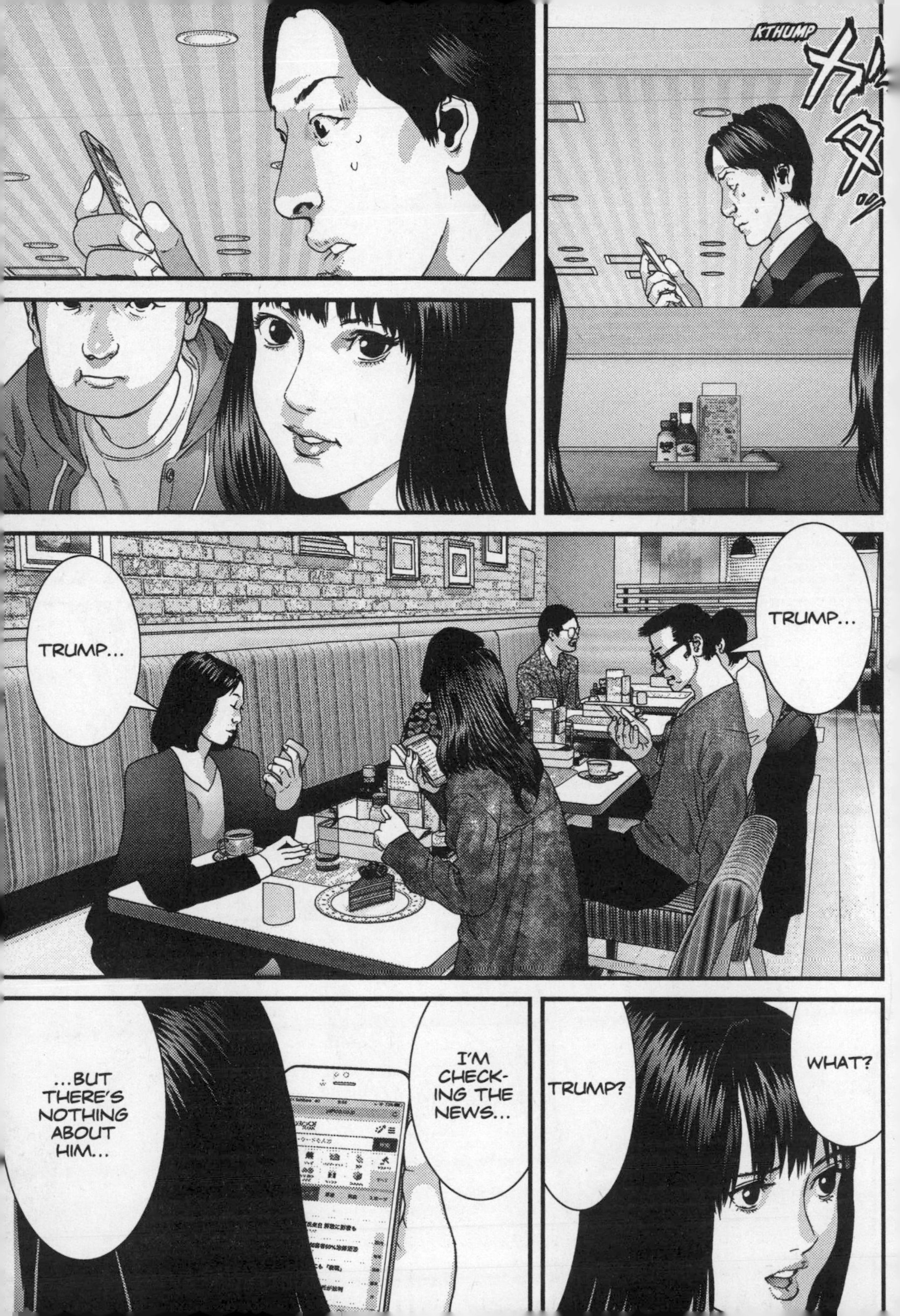
KTHUMP
カタッ
TRUMP...
TRUMP...
WHAT?
TRUMP?
I'M CHECKING THE NEWS...
...BUT THERE'S NOTHING ABOUT HIM...

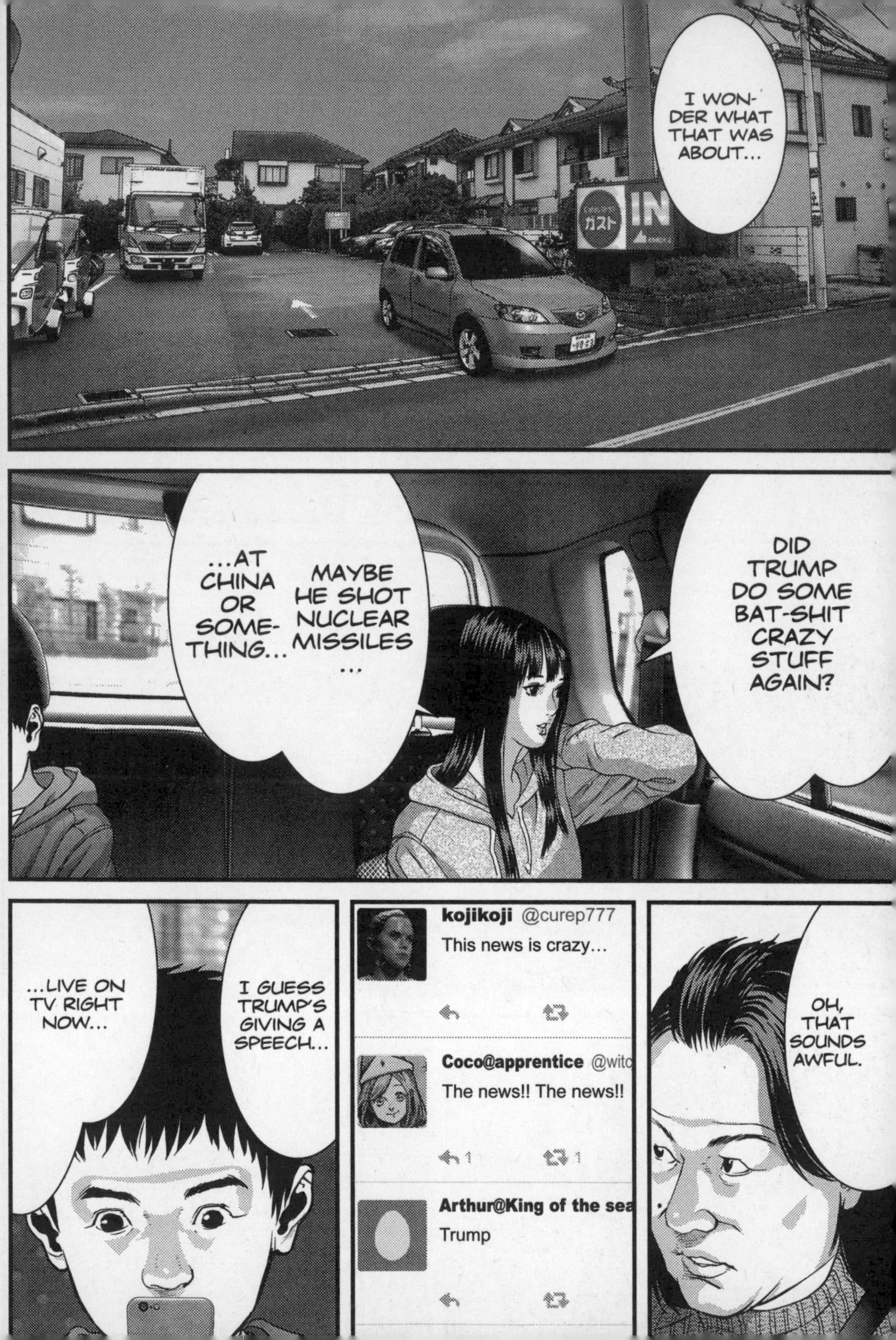
I WON-DER WHAT THAT WAS ABOUT...
DID TRUMP DO SOME BAT-SHIT CRAZY STUFF AGAIN?
MAYBE HE SHOT NUCLEAR MISSILES ...
...AT CHINA OR SOME-THING...
OH, THAT SOUNDS AWFUL.
kojikoji @curep777
This news is crazy...
Coco@apprentice @witc
The news!! The news!!
1
1
Arthur@King of the sea
Trump
I GUESS TRUMP'S GIVING A SPEECH...
...LIVE ON TV RIGHT NOW...

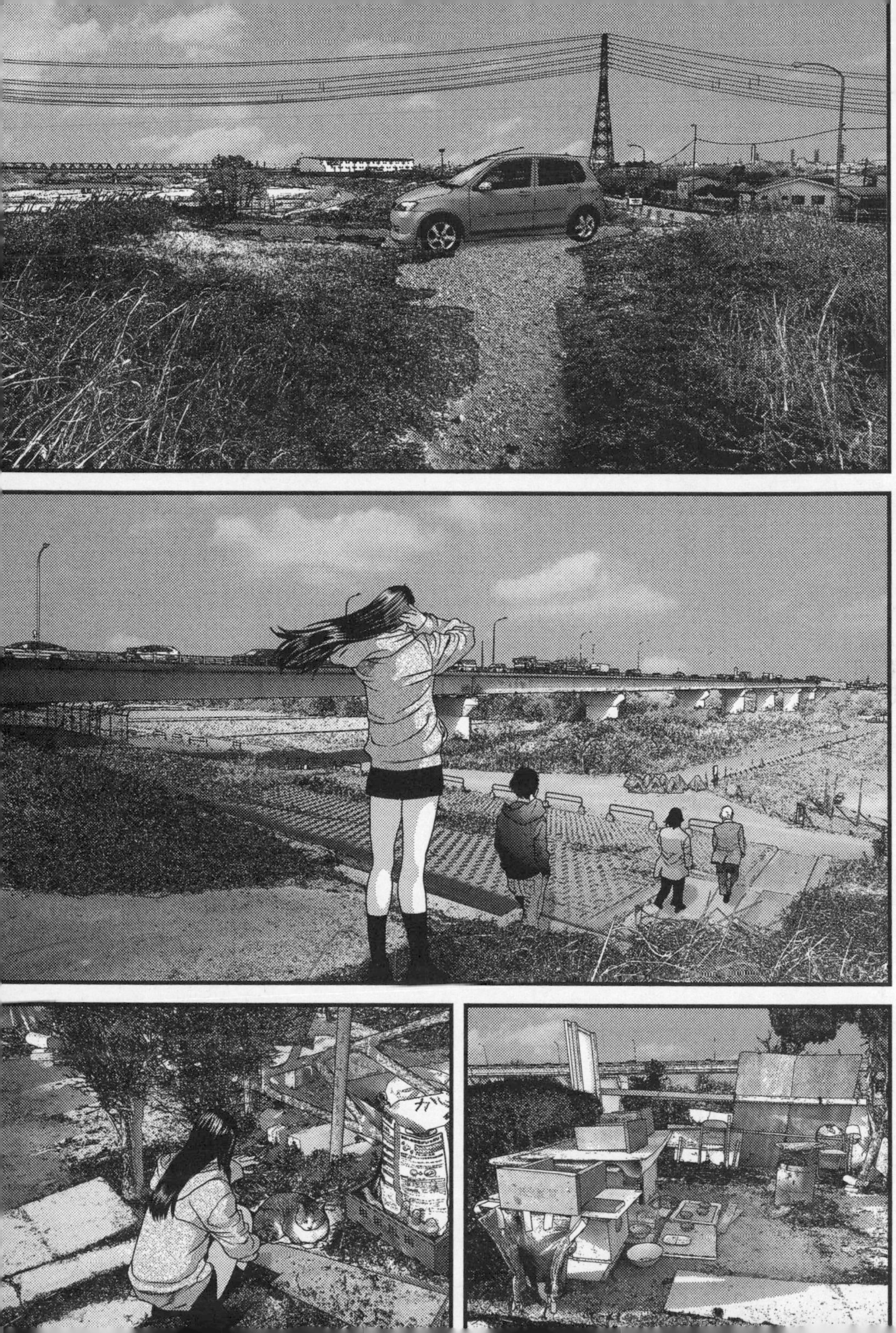

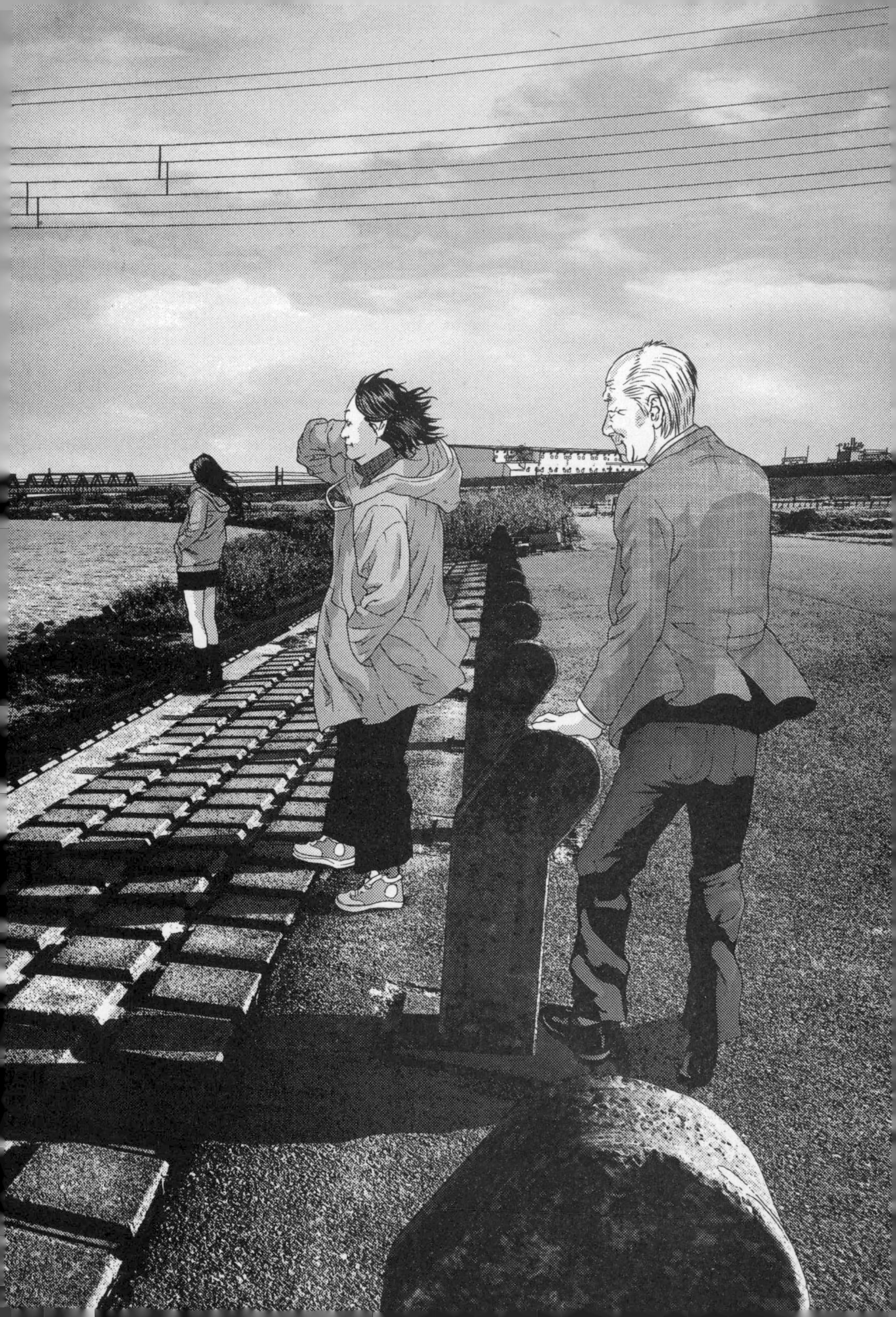

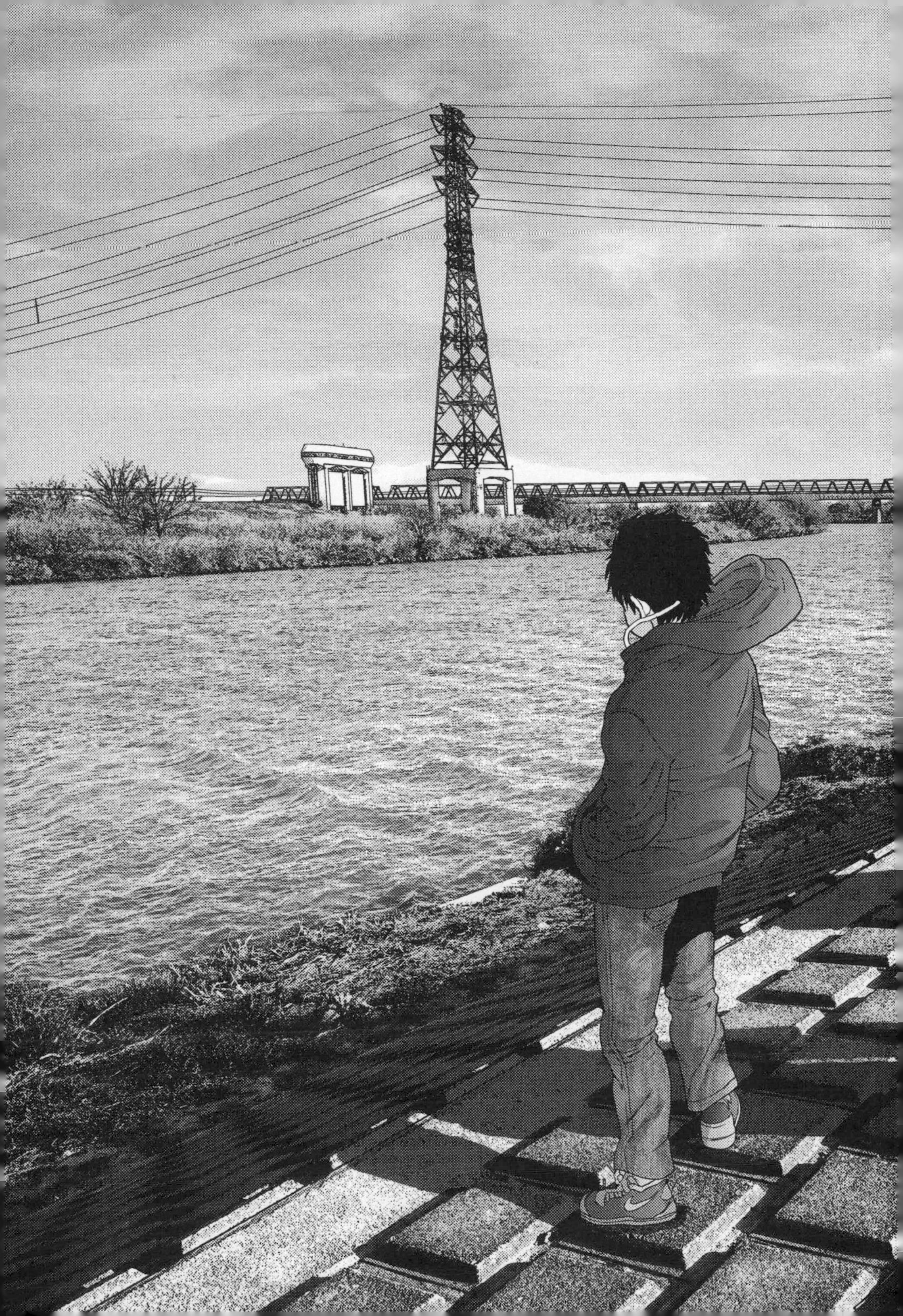

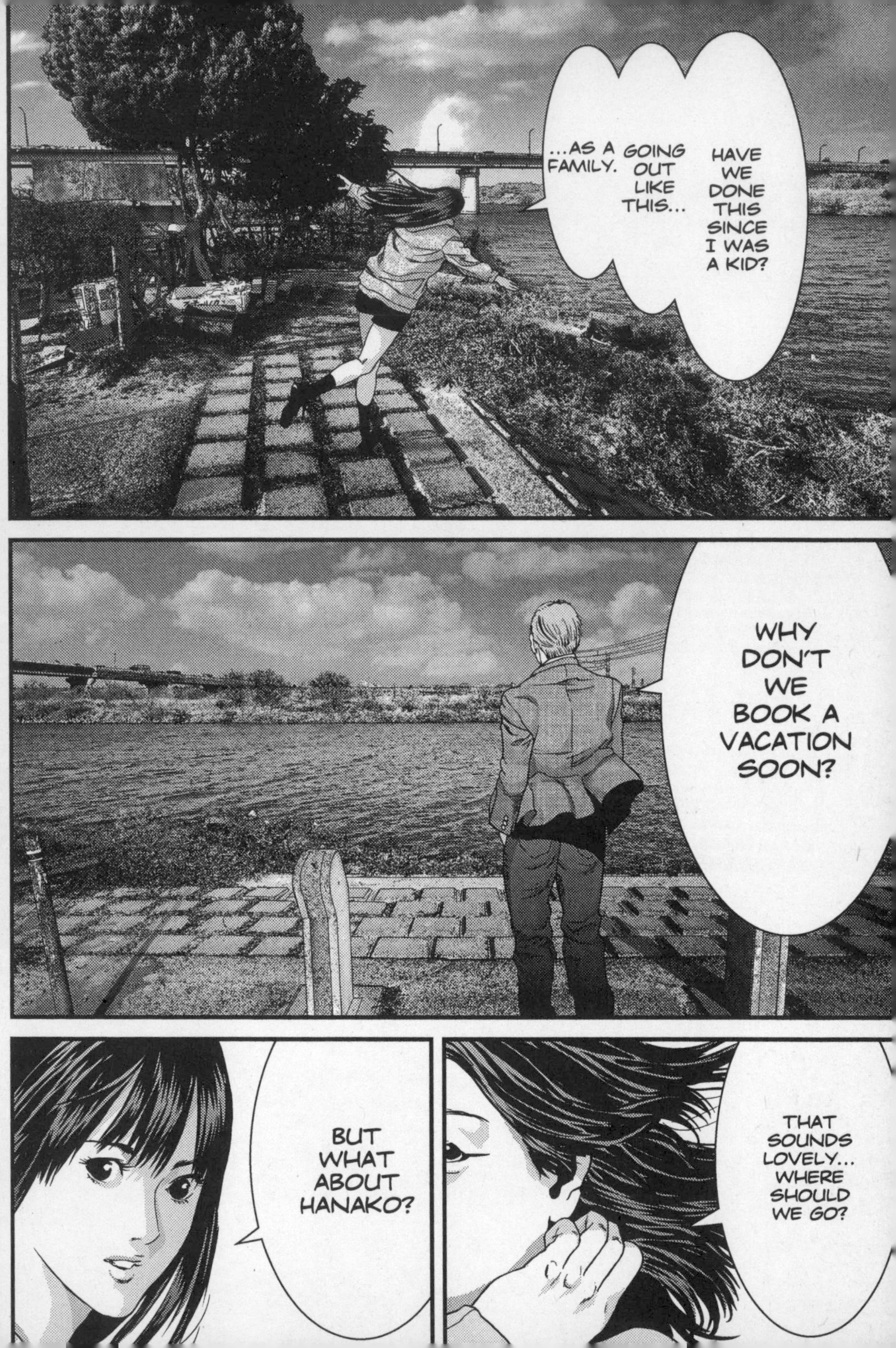
HAVE WE DONE THIS SINCE I WAS A KID?
GOING OUT LIKE THIS...
...AS A FAMILY.
WHY DON'T WE BOOK A VACATION SOON?
THAT SOUNDS LOVELY... WHERE SHOULD WE GO?
BUT WHAT ABOUT HANAKO?

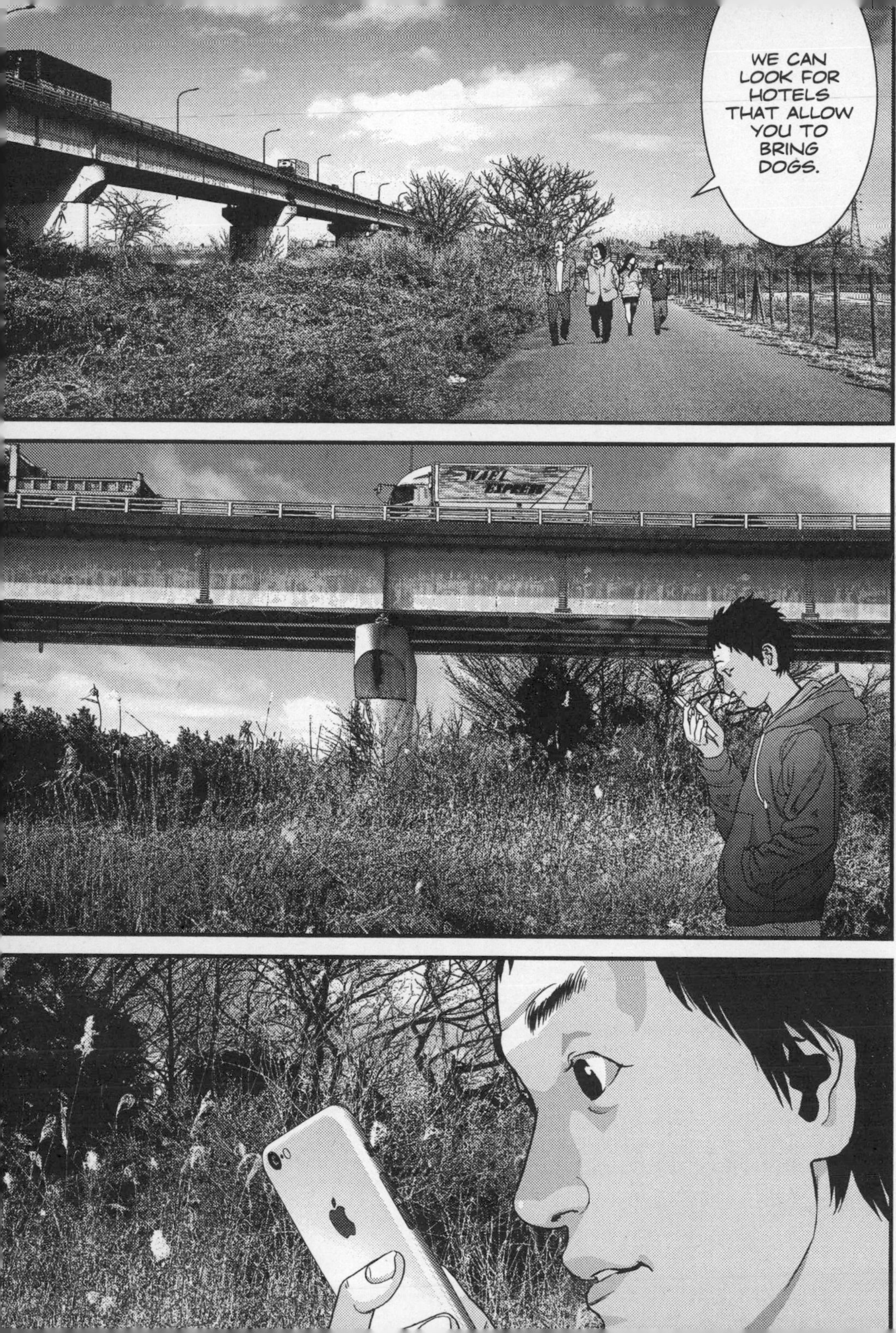
WE CAN LOOK FOR HOTELS THAT ALLOW YOU TO BRING DOGS.

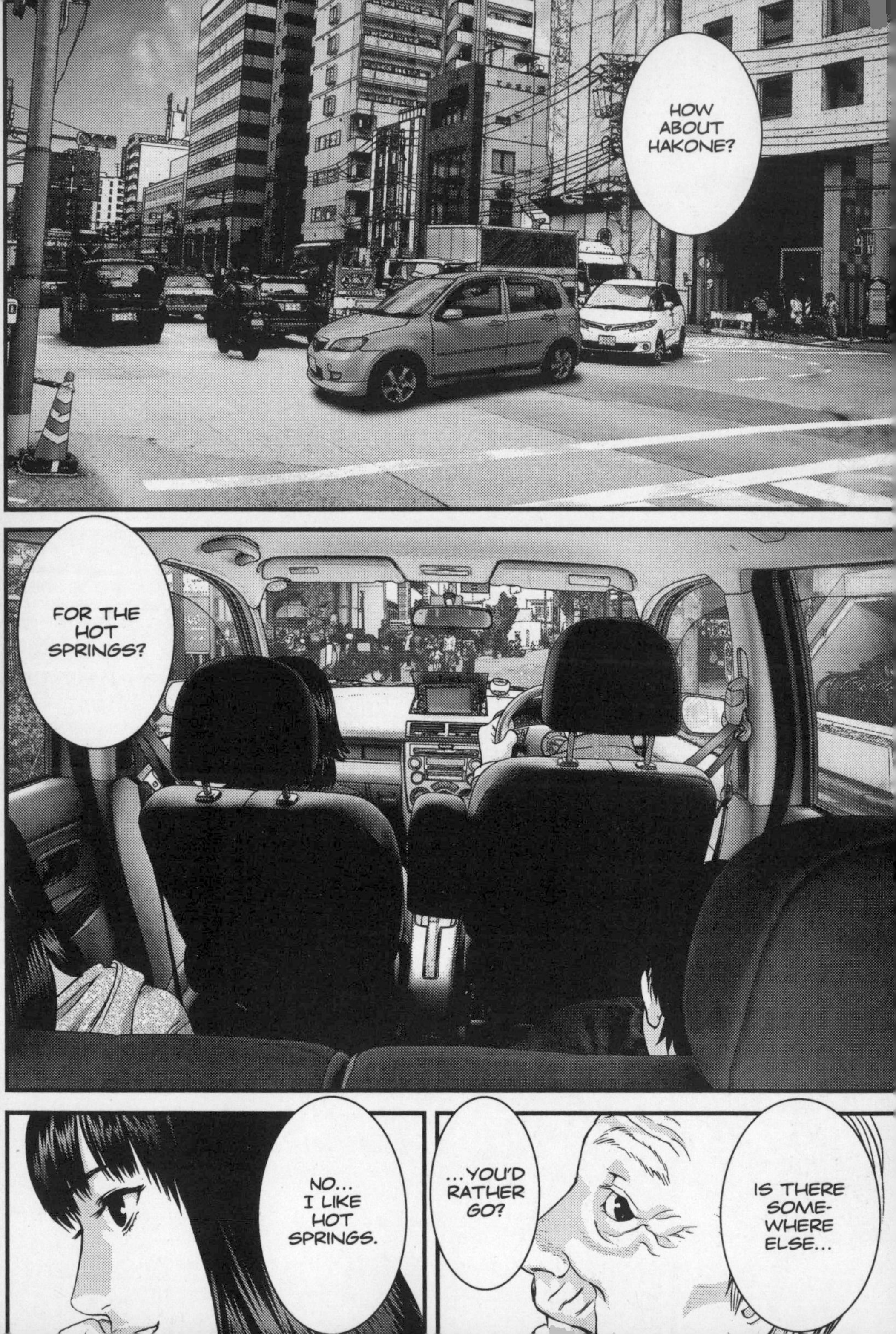
HOW ABOUT HAKONE?
FOR THE HOT SPRINGS?
IS THERE SOME-WHERE ELSE...
...YOU'D RATHER GO?
NO... I LIKE HOT SPRINGS.

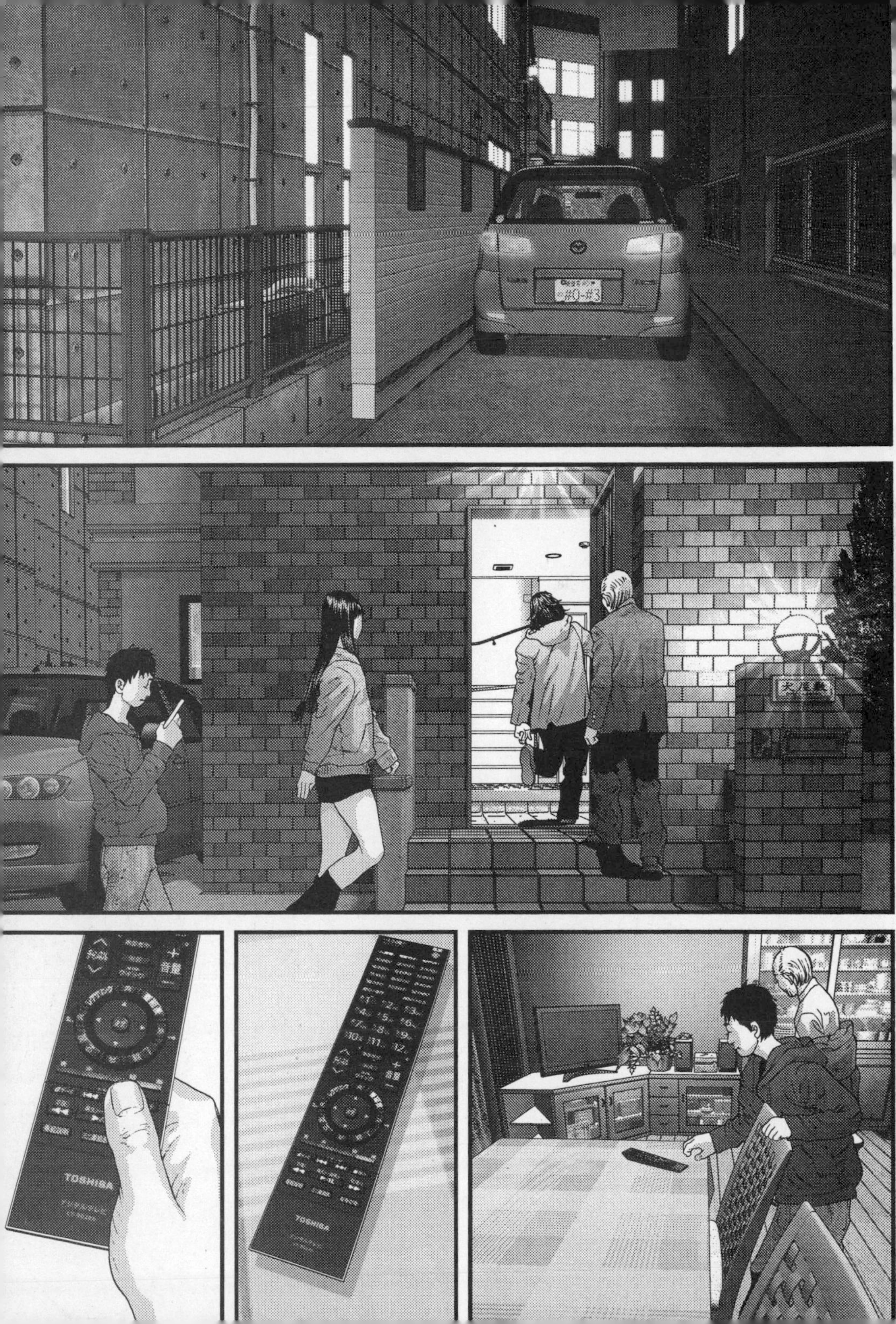
音量
TOSHIBA
音量
TOSHIBA

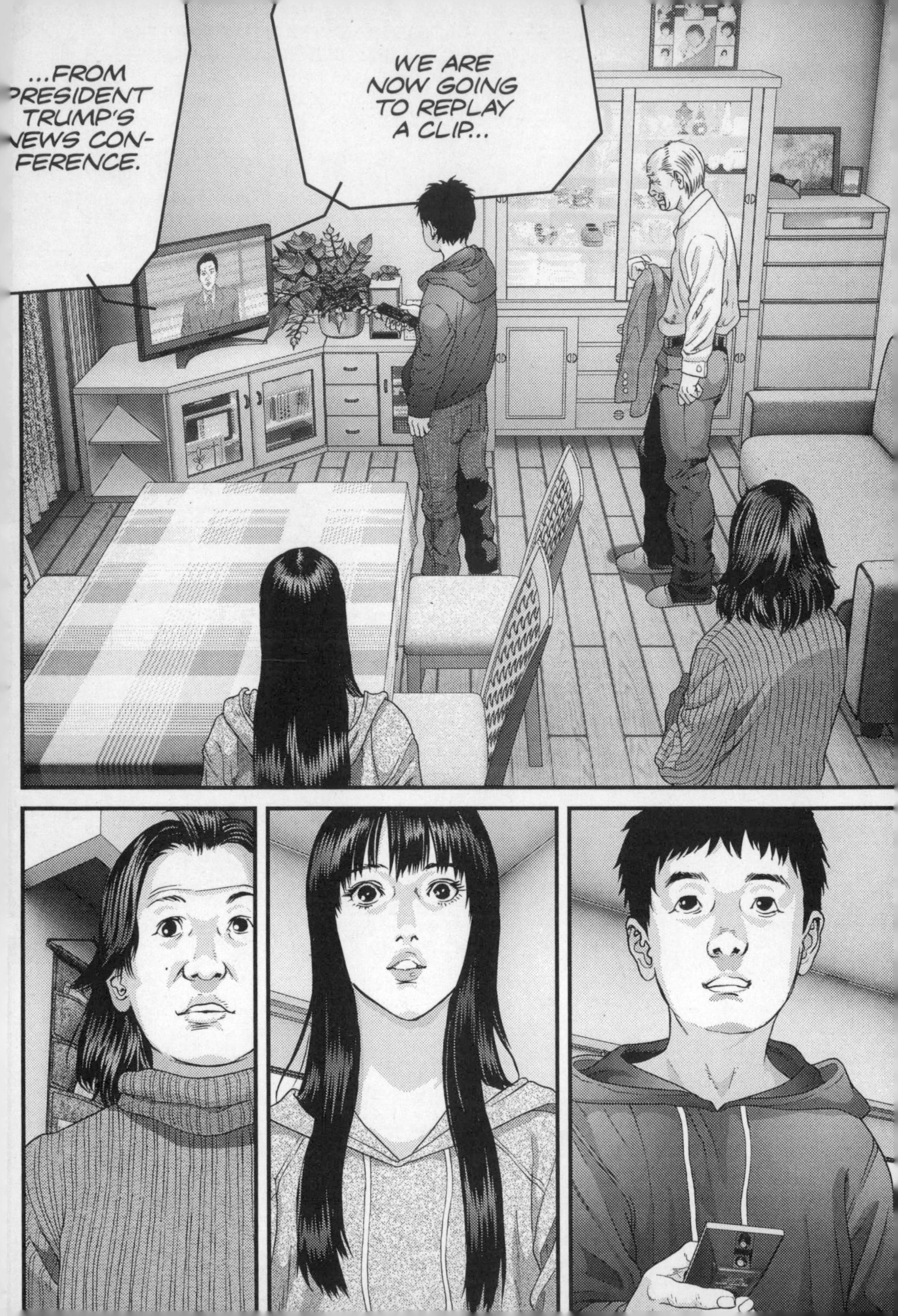
WE ARE NOW GOING TO REPLAY A CLIP...
...FROM PRESIDENT TRUMP'S NEWS CON-FERENCE.

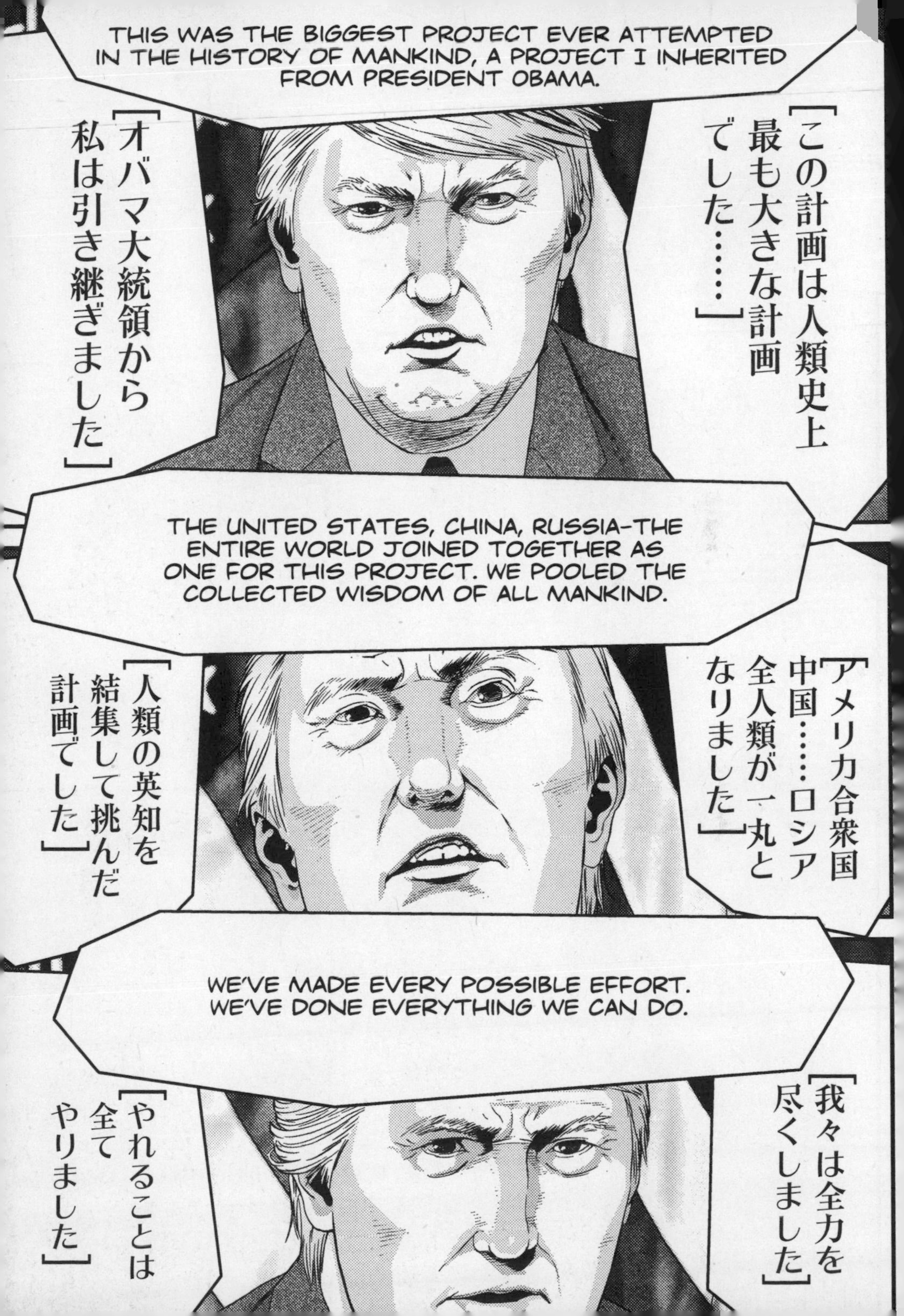
THIS WAS THE BIGGEST PROJECT EVER ATTEMPTED IN THE HISTORY OF MANKIND, A PROJECT I INHERITED FROM PRESIDENT OBAMA.
「この計画は人類史上最も大きな計画でした……」
「オバマ大統領から私は引き継ぎました」
THE UNITED STATES, CHINA, RUSSIA–THE ENTIRE WORLD JOINED TOGETHER AS ONE FOR THIS PROJECT. WE POOLED THE COLLECTED WISDOM OF ALL MANKIND.
「アメリカ合衆国中国……ロシア全人類が一丸となりました」
「人類の英知を結集して挑んだ計画でした」
WE'VE MADE EVERY POSSIBLE EFFORT. WE'VE DONE EVERYTHING WE CAN DO.
「我々は全力を尽くしました」
「やれることは全てやりました」

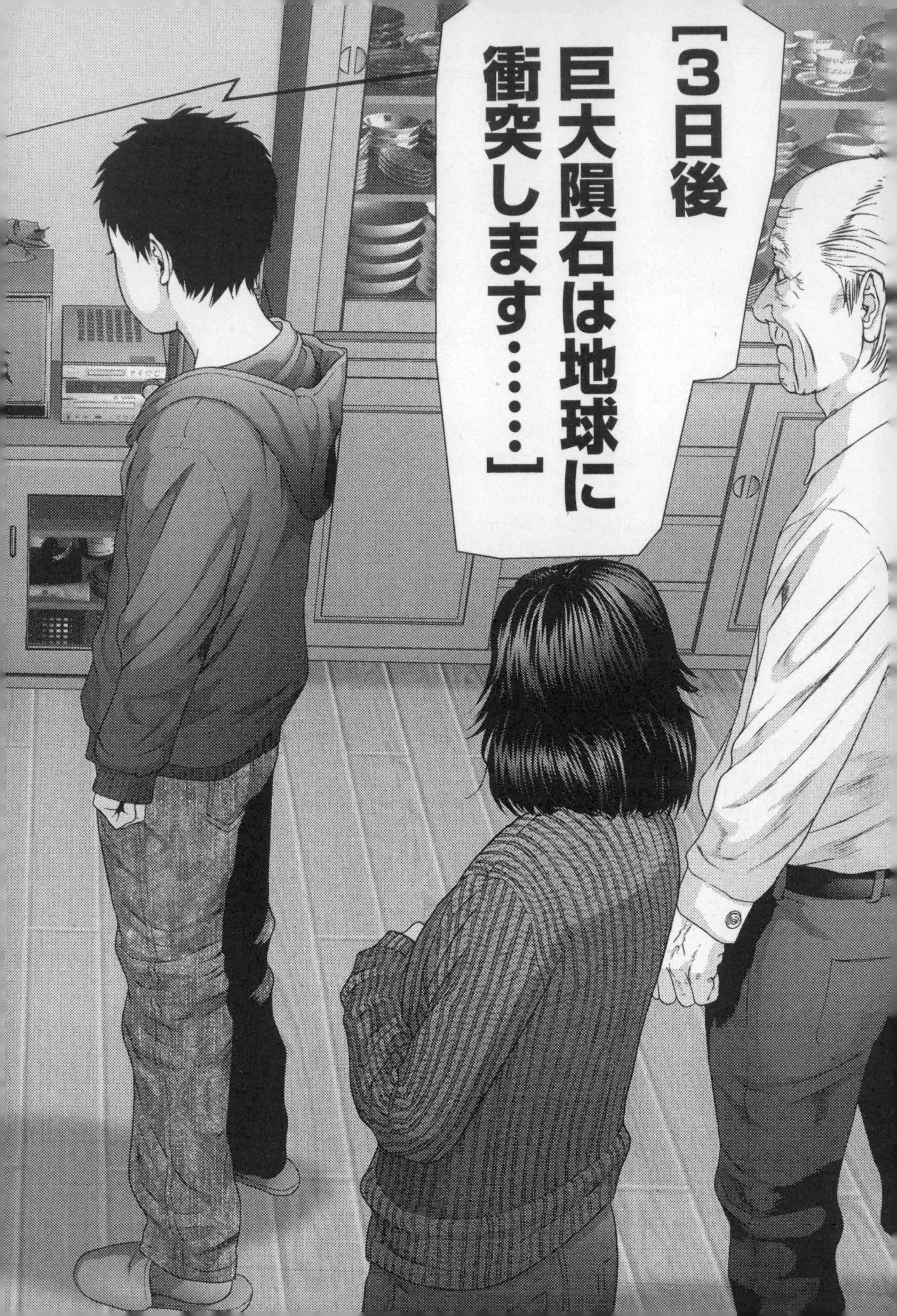
「3日後巨大隕石は地球に衝突します……」

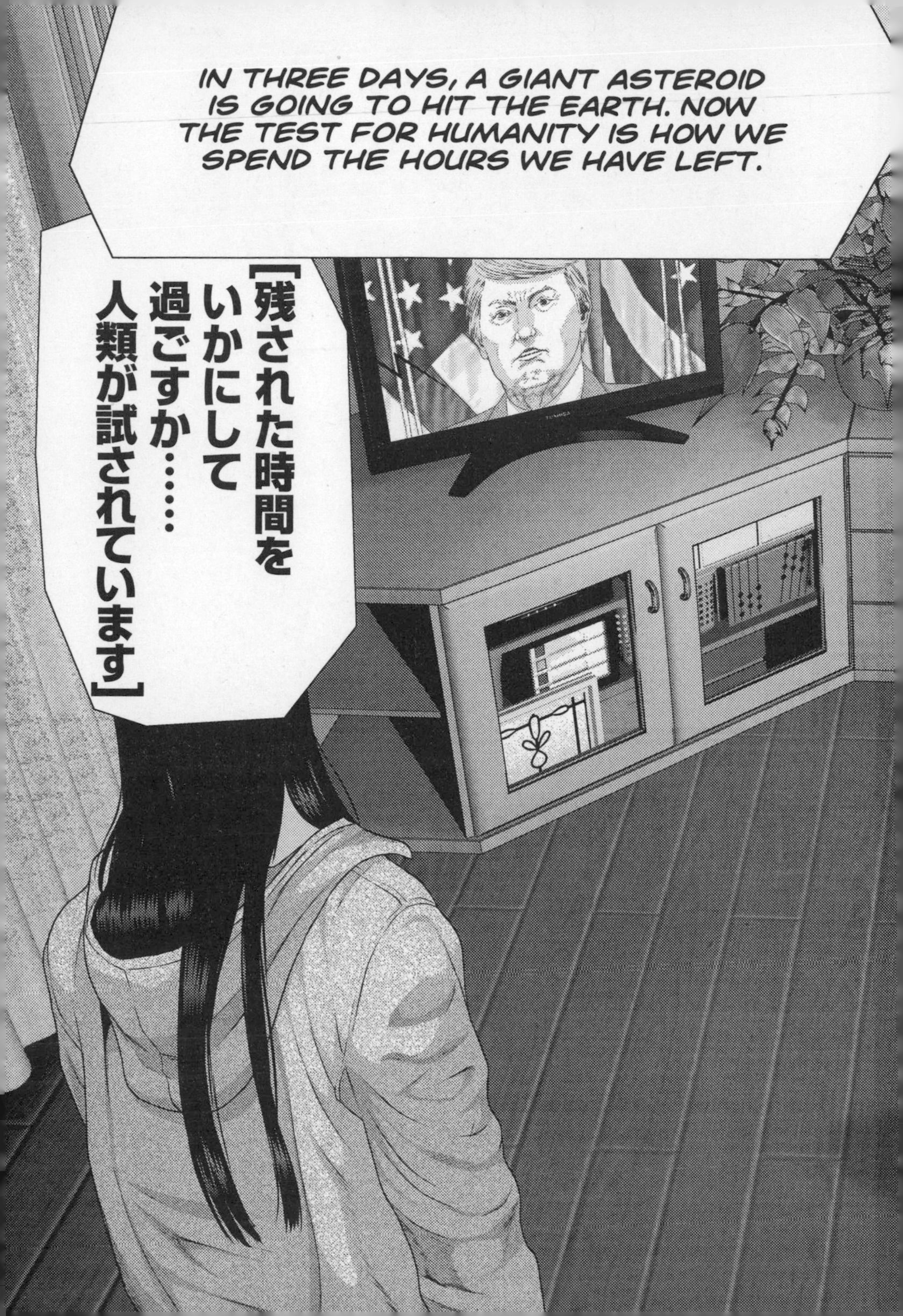
IN THREE DAYS, A GIANT ASTEROID IS GOING TO HIT THE EARTH. NOW THE TEST FOR HUMANITY IS HOW WE SPEND THE HOURS WE HAVE LEFT.
「残された時間をいかにして過ごすか……人類が試されています」

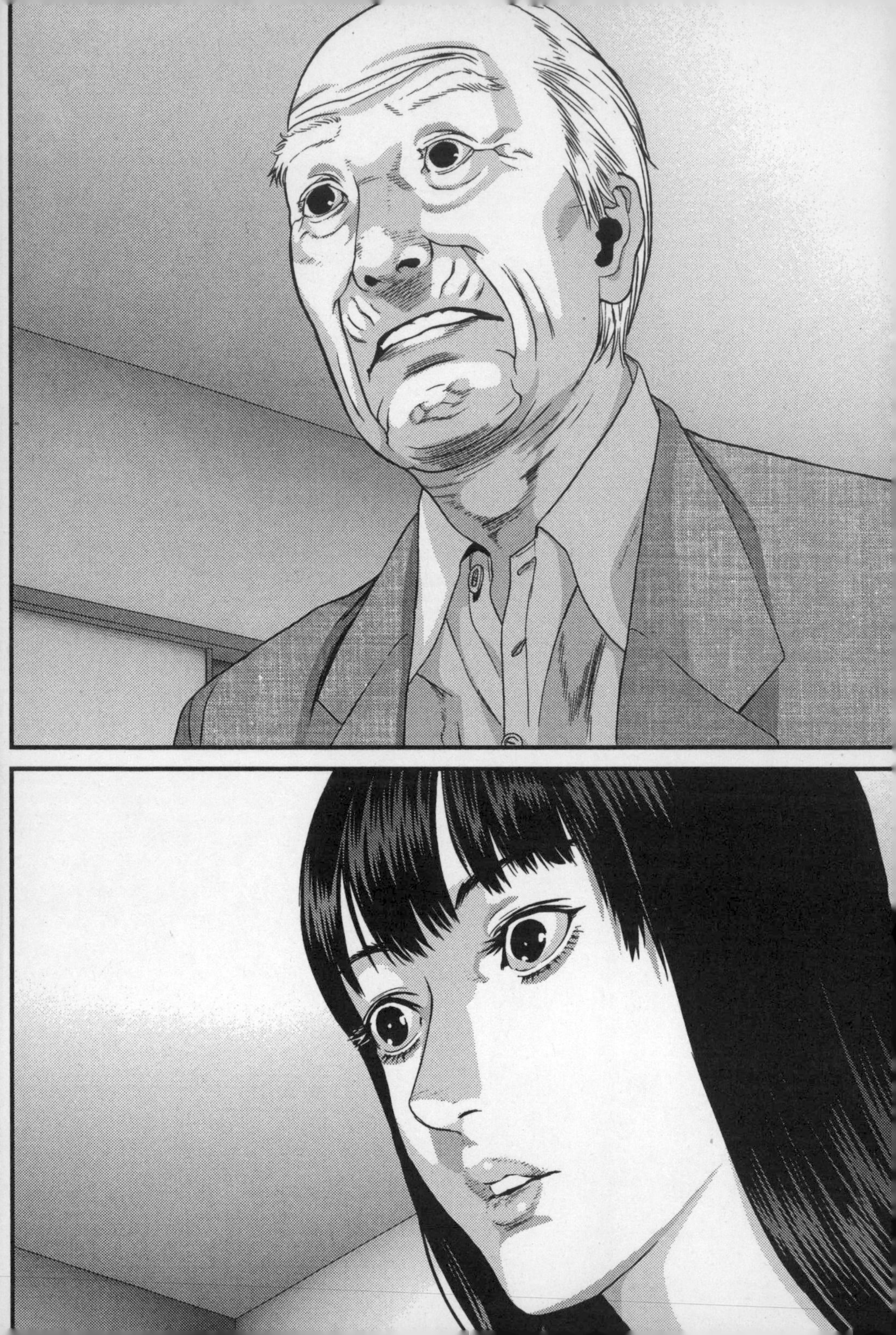

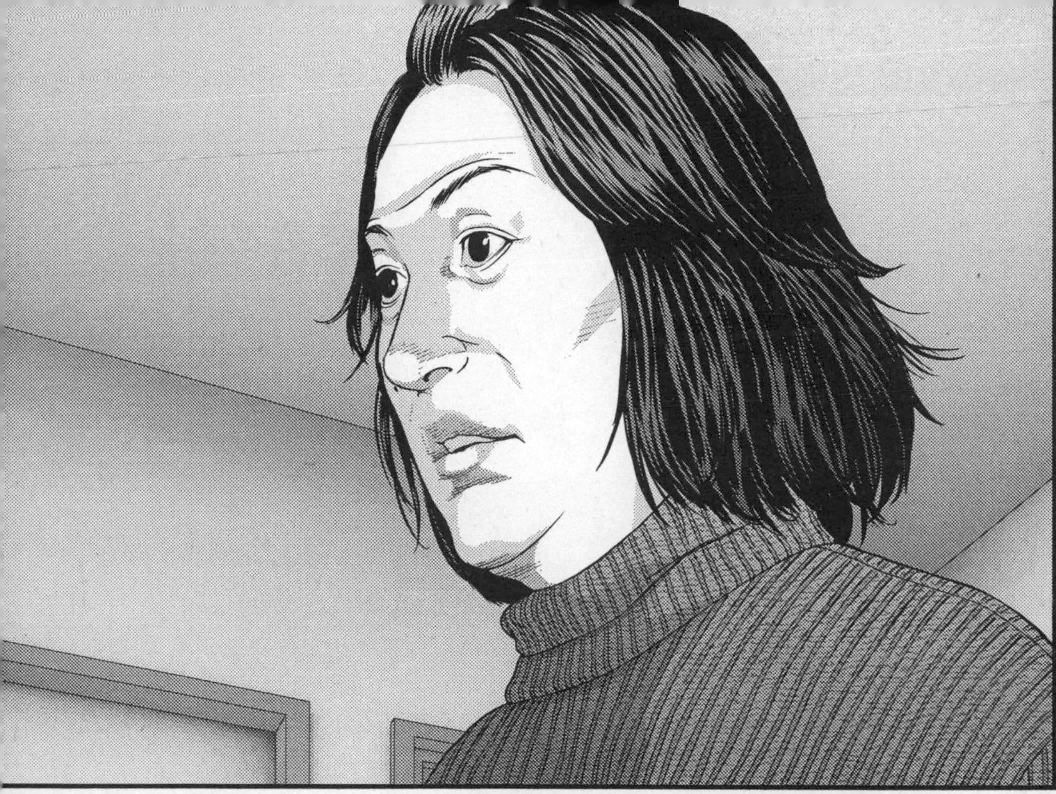
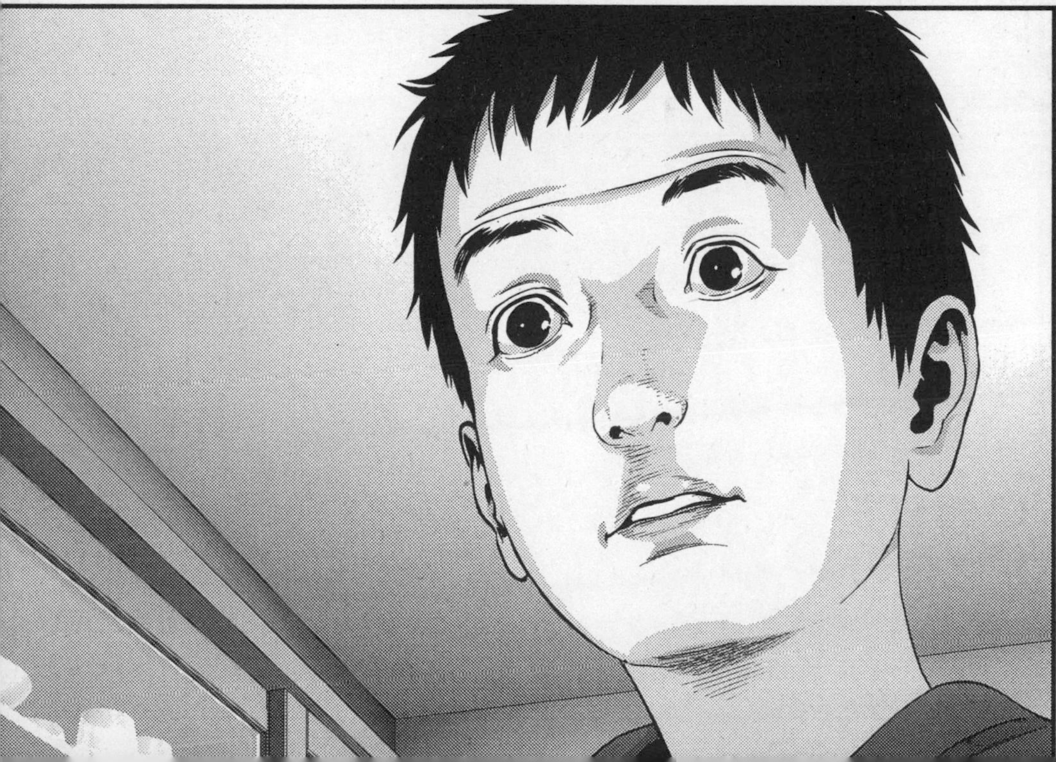

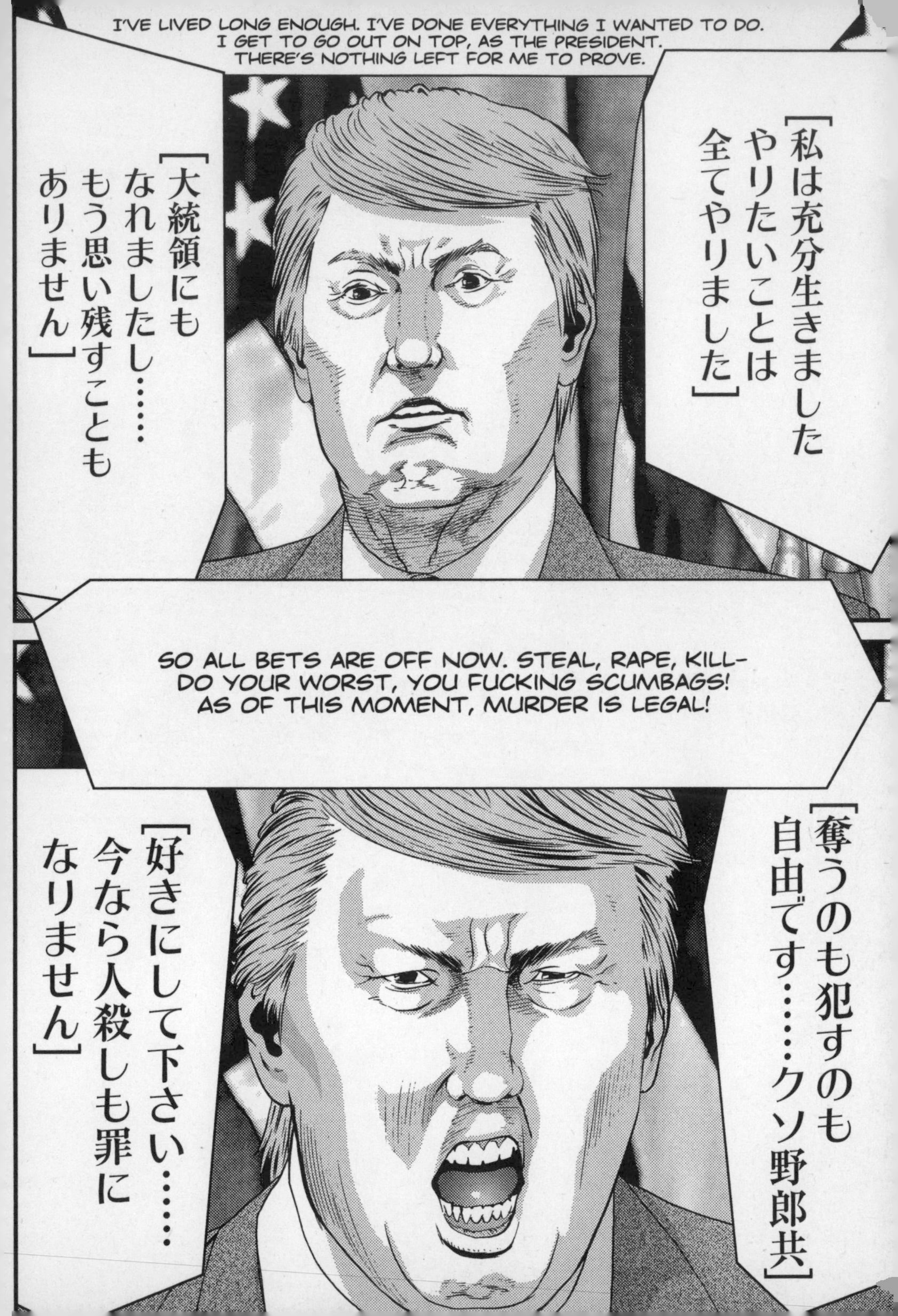
I'VE LIVED LONG ENOUGH. I'VE DONE EVERYTHING I WANTED TO DO. I GET TO GO OUT ON TOP, AS THE PRESIDENT. THERE'S NOTHING LEFT FOR ME TO PROVE.
「私は充分生きました やりたいことは 全てやりました」
「大統領にも なれましたし…… もう思い残すことも ありません」
SO ALL BETS ARE OFF NOW. STEAL, RAPE, KILL- DO YOUR WORST, YOU FUCKING SCUMBAGS! AS OF THIS MOMENT, MURDER IS LEGAL!
「奪うのも犯すのも 自由です……クソ野郎共」
「好きにして下さい…… 今なら人殺しも罪に なりません」

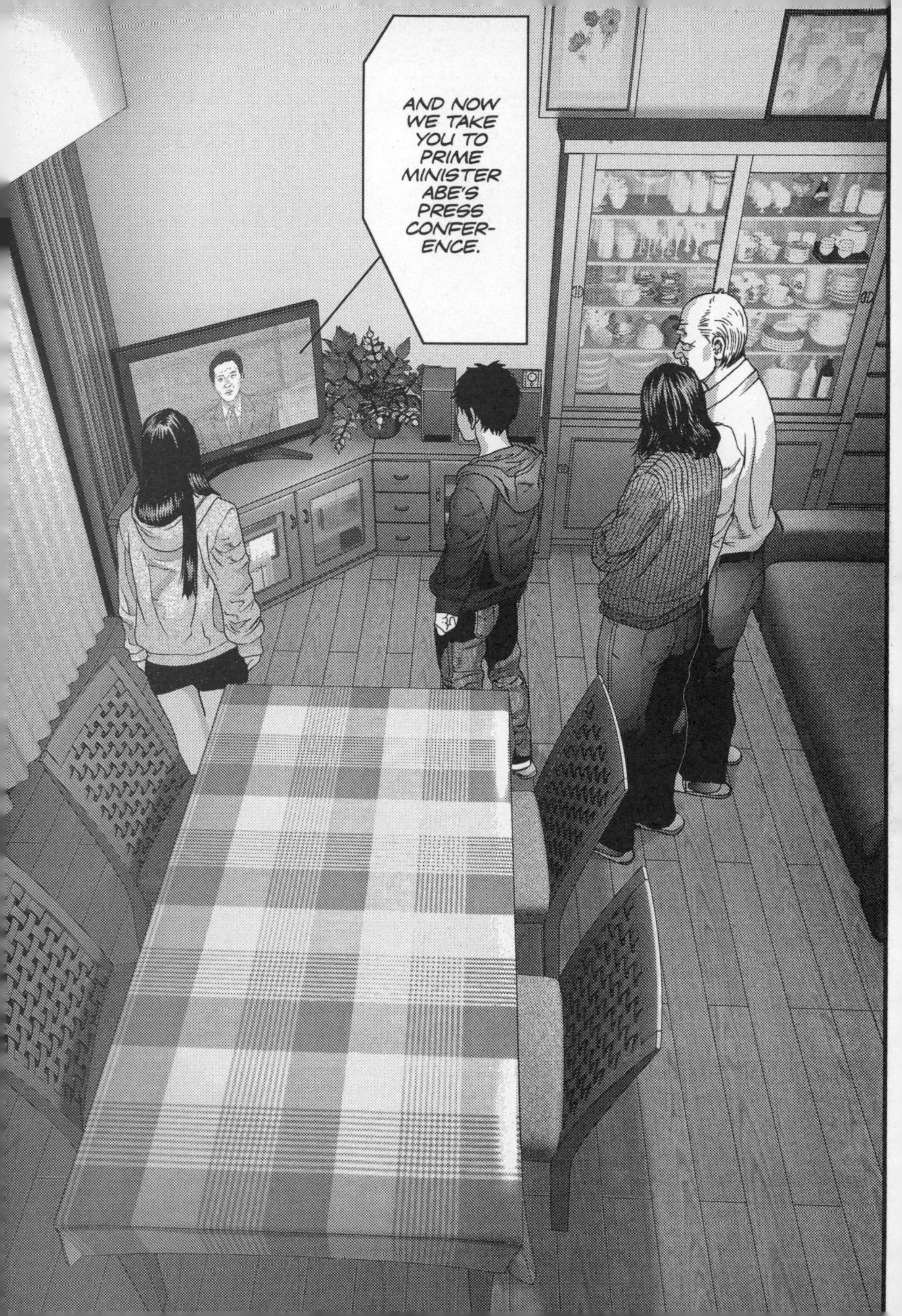
AND NOW WE TAKE YOU TO PRIME MINISTER ABE'S PRESS CONFERENCE.

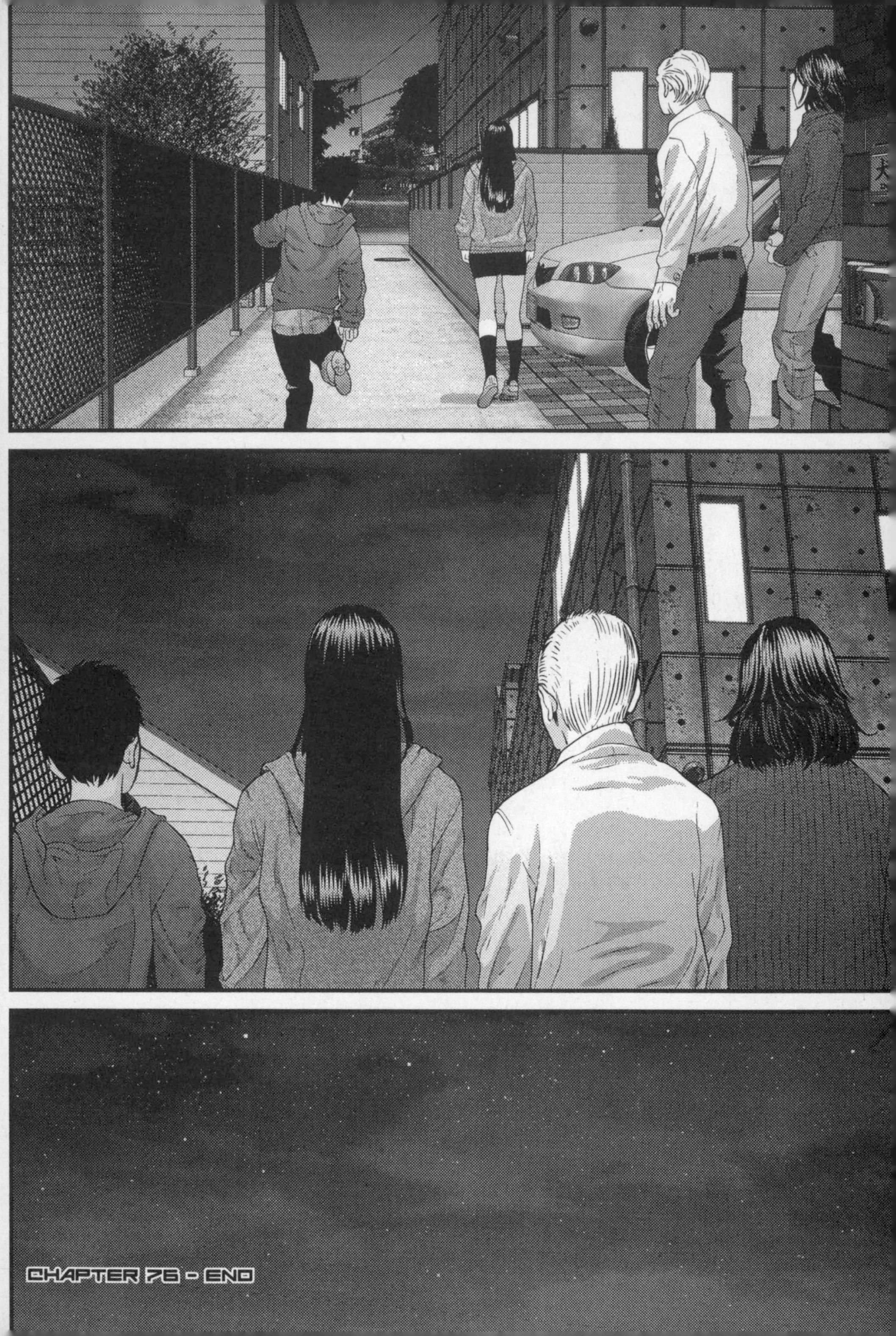
大
CHAPTER 76 - END

INUYASHIKI

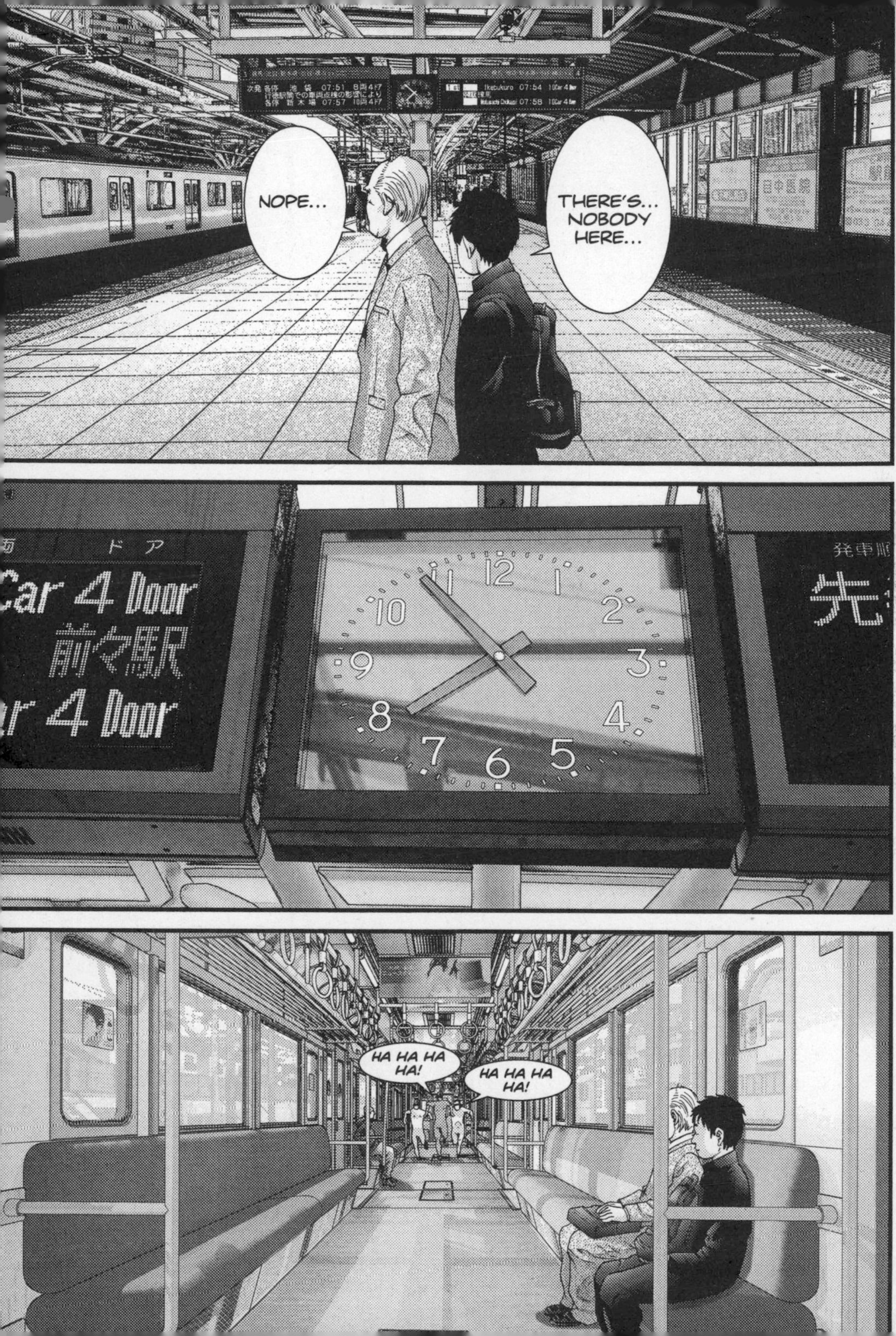
THERE'S... NOBODY HERE...
NOPE...
ドア
Car 4 Door
前々駅
HA HA HA HA!
HA HA HA HA!

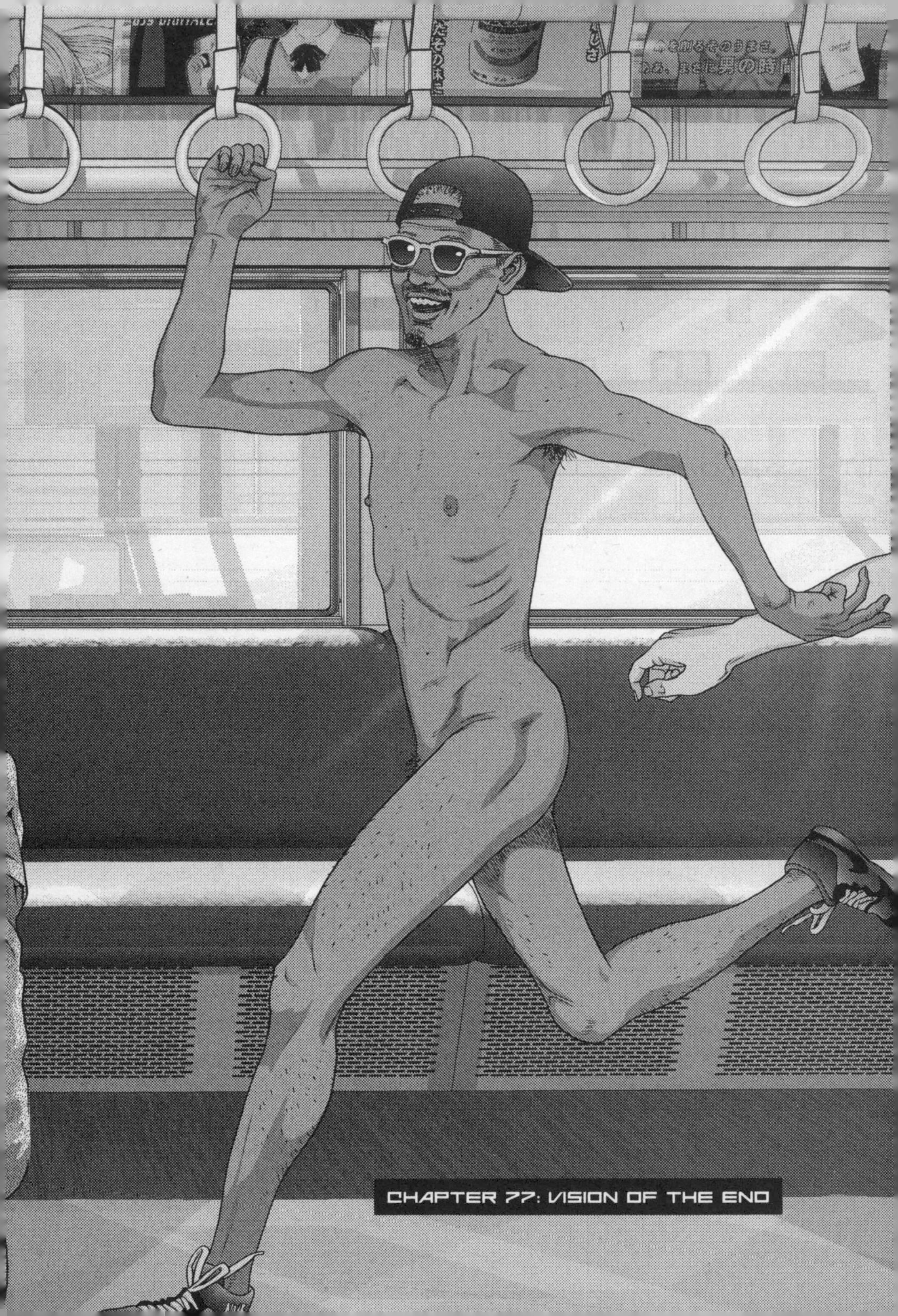
CHAPTER 77: VISION OF THE END

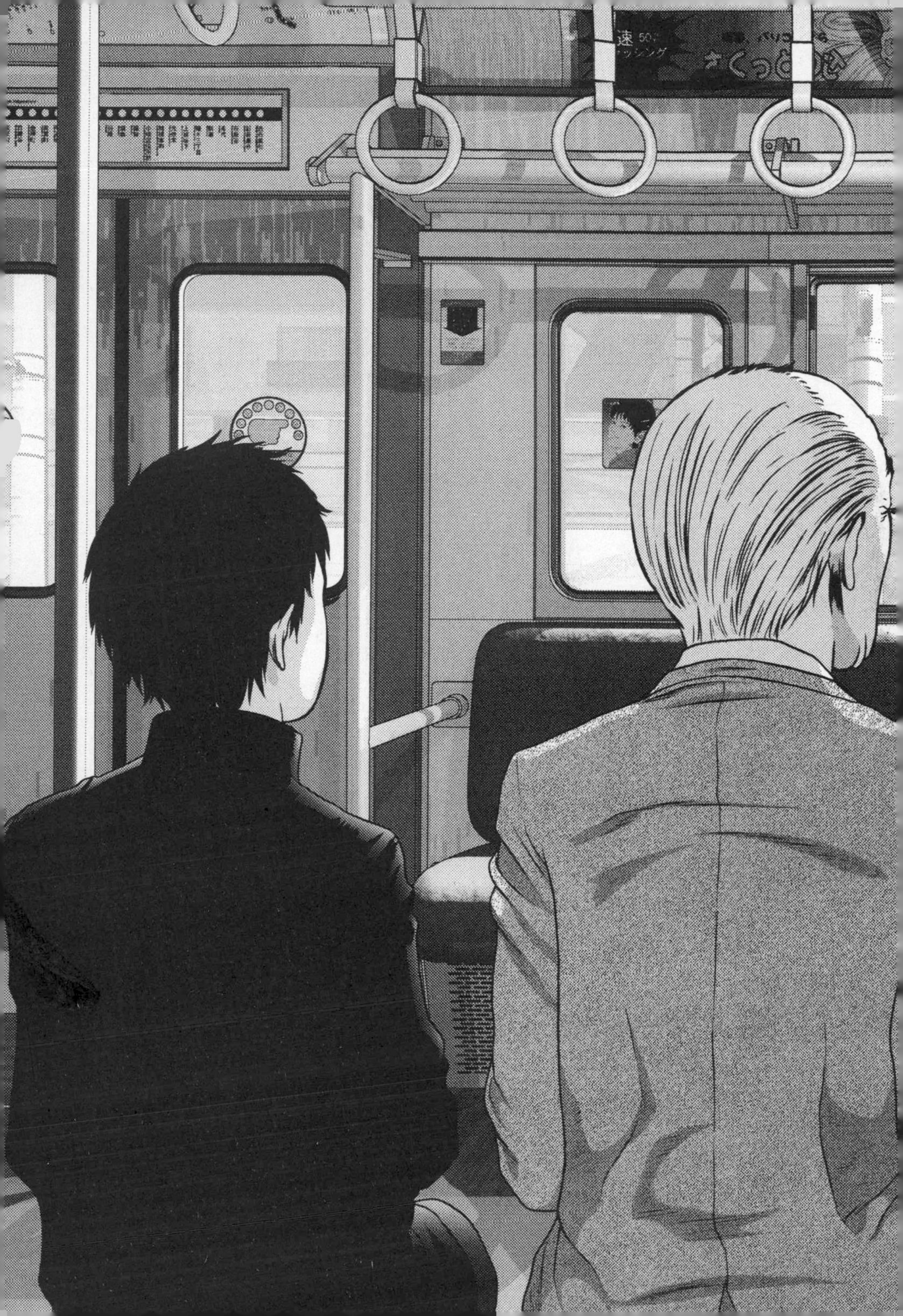

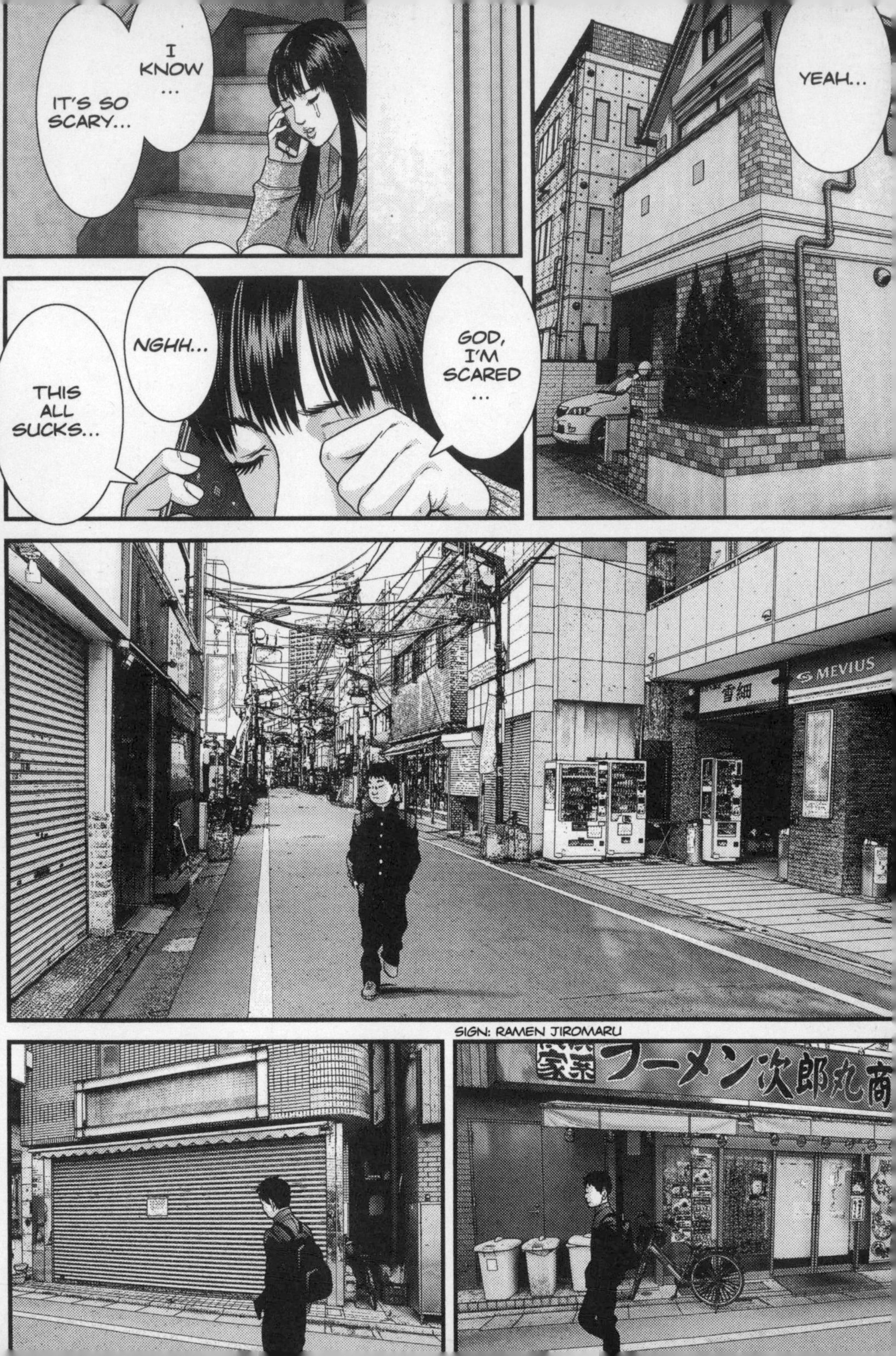
YEAH...
I KNOW ...
IT'S SO SCARY...
GOD, I'M SCARED ...
NGHH...
THIS ALL SUCKS...
MEVIUS
SIGN: RAMEN JIROMARU

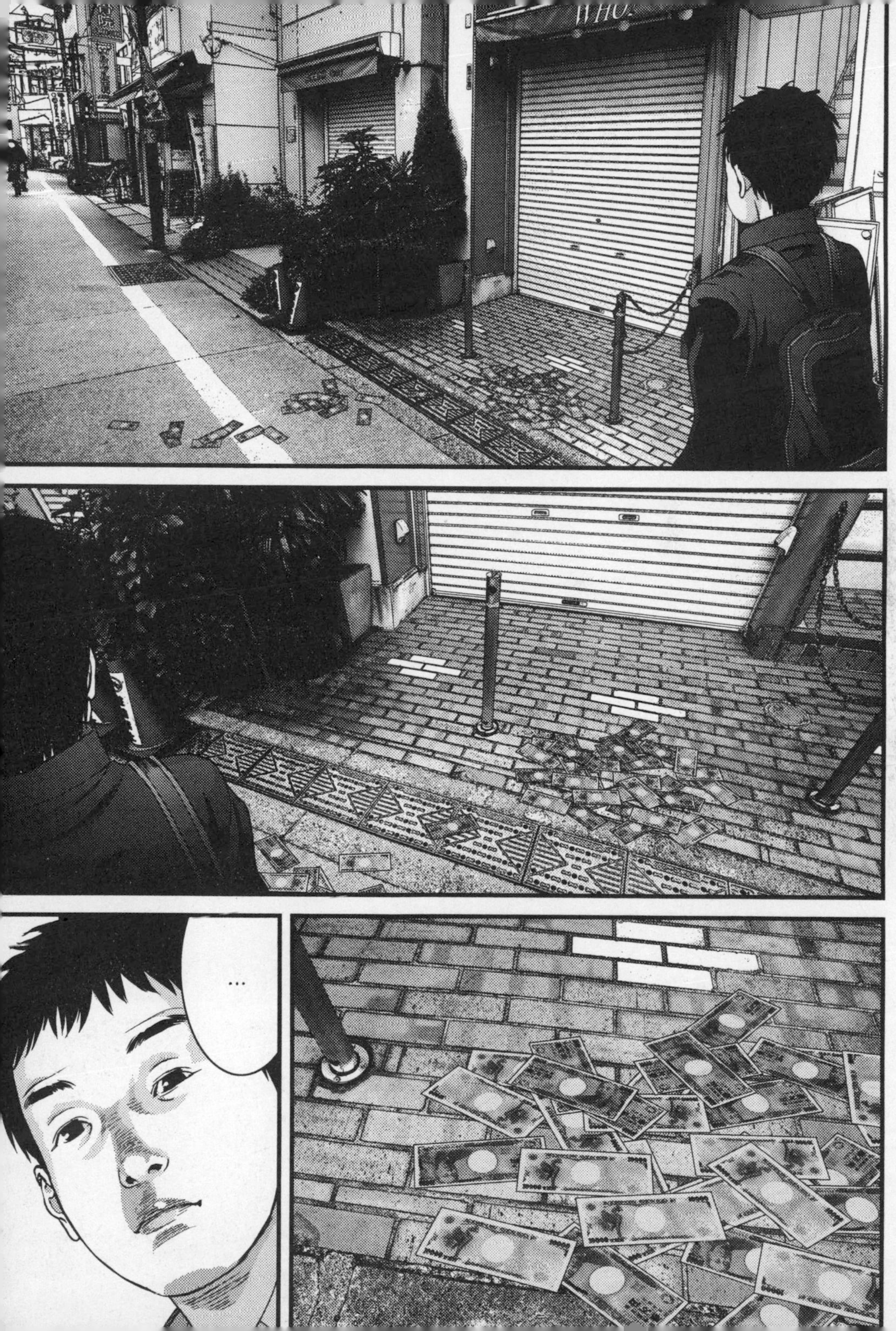
…

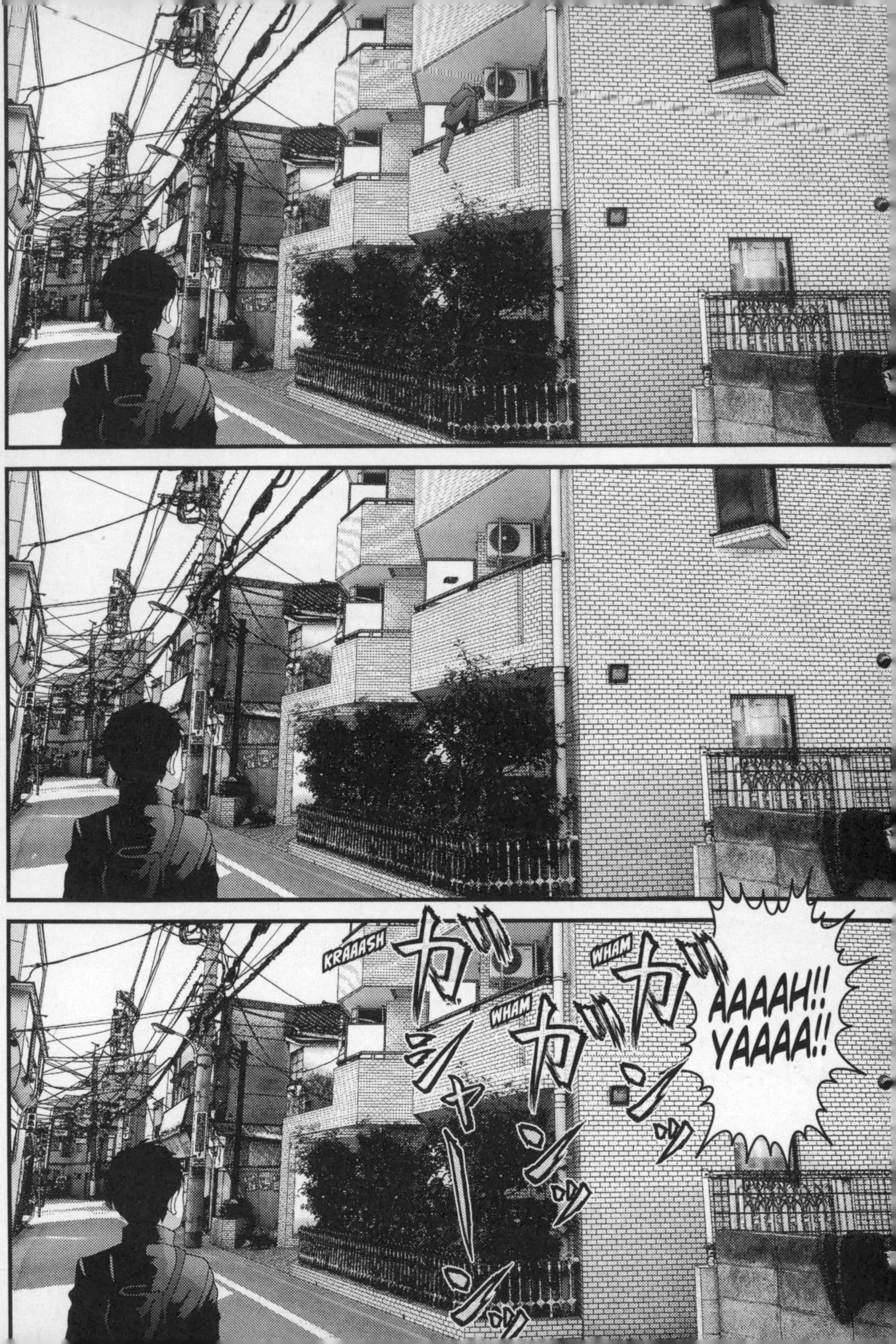
AAAAH!! YAAAA!!
ガンッ
WHAM
ガンッ
WHAM
ガシャーン
KRAAASH

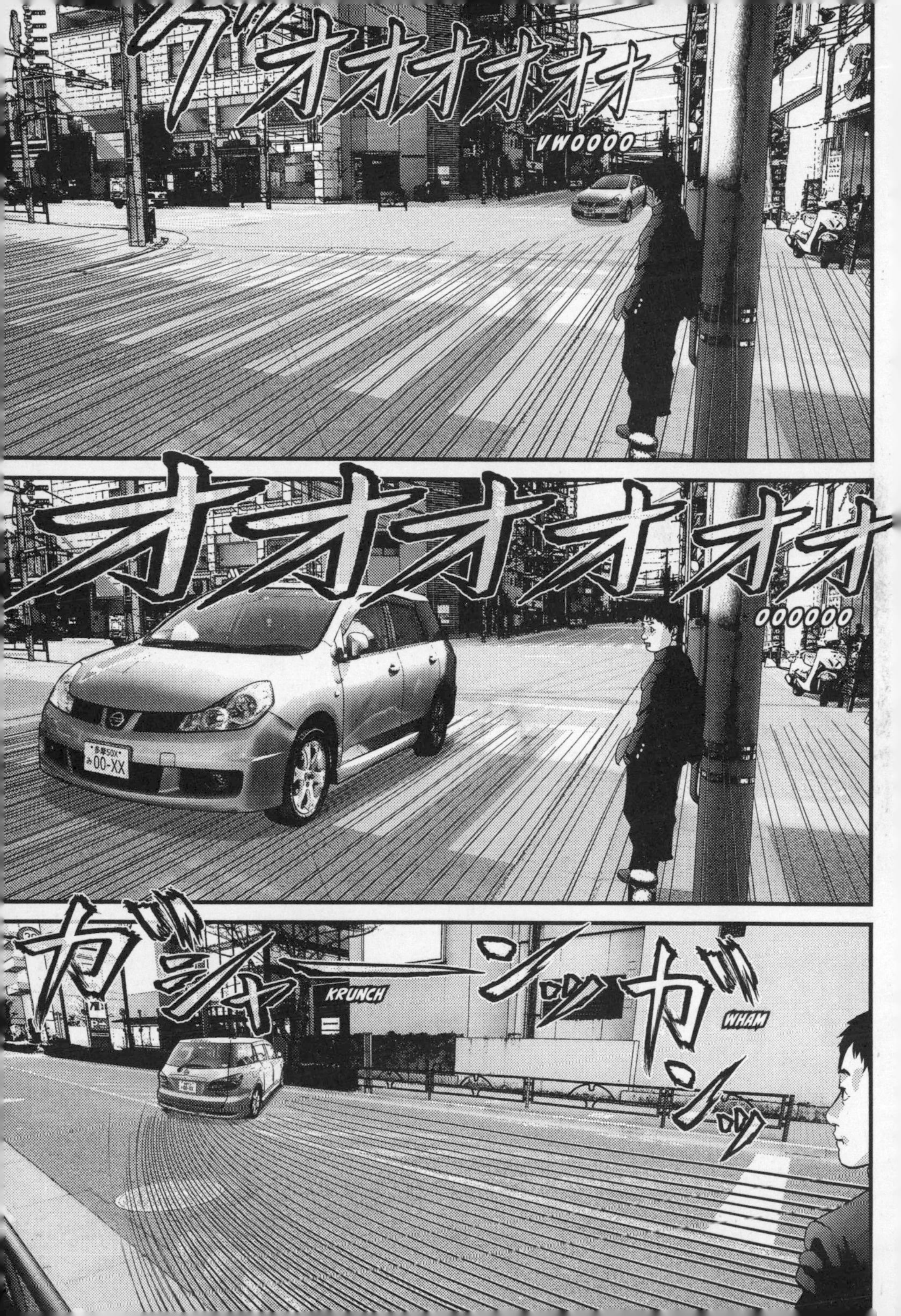
グオオオオオオ
VWOOOO
オオオオオオ
OOOOOO
多摩50X
み00-XX
ガンッ
WHAM
ガシャーンッ
KRUNCH

AHH!
AH!
AH!
AH!
AH!
AH!
AHHHH!

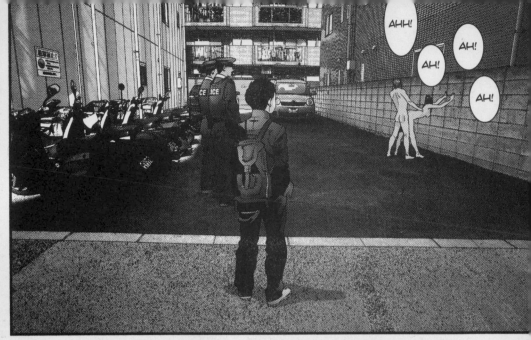

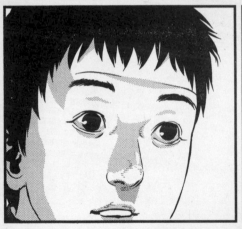

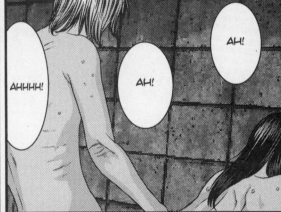

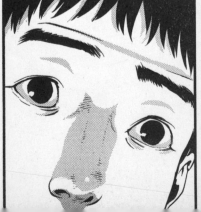

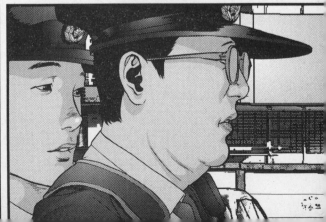

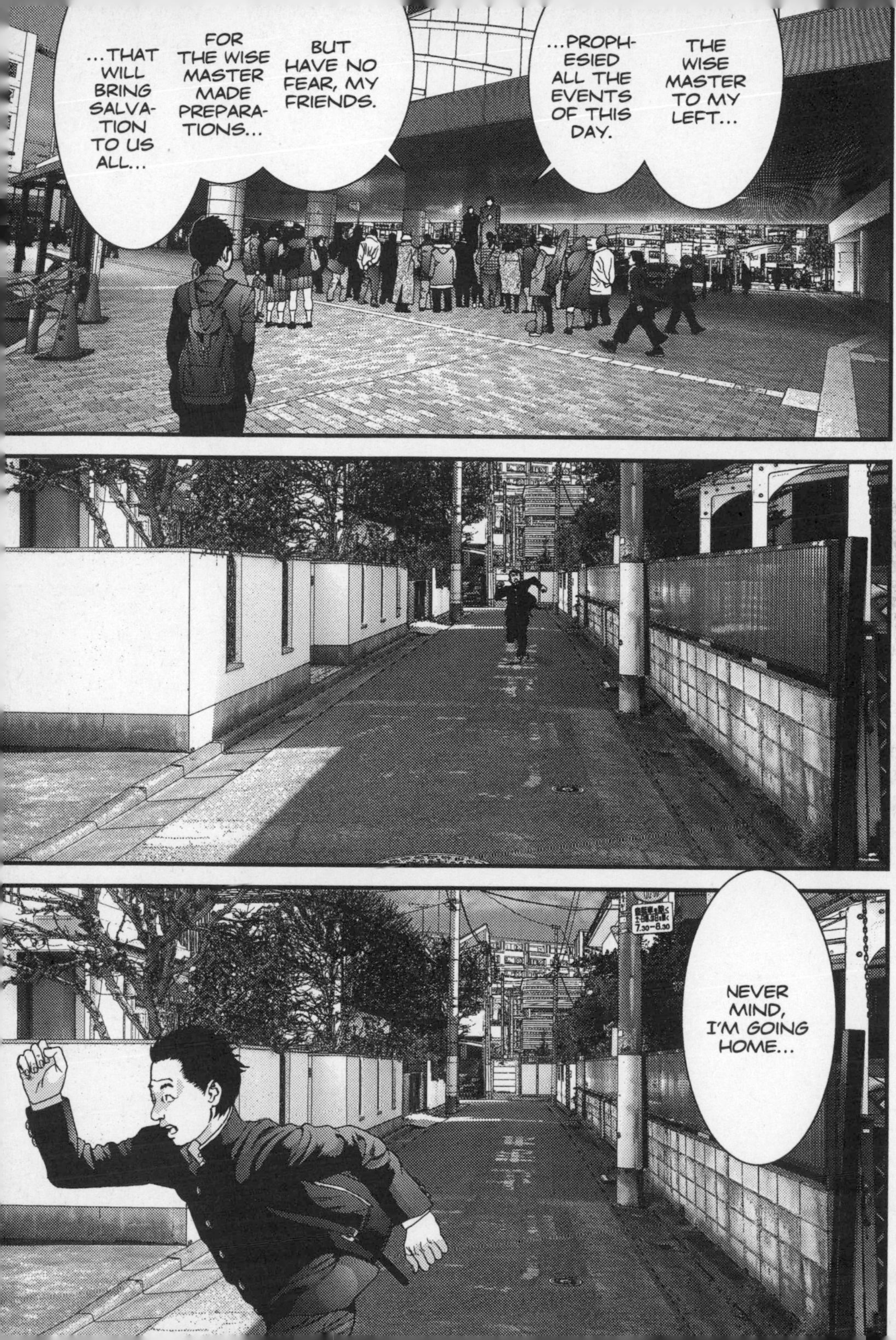
THE WISE MASTER TO MY LEFT...
...PROPHESIED ALL THE EVENTS OF THIS DAY.
BUT HAVE NO FEAR, MY FRIENDS.
FOR THE WISE MASTER MADE PREPARATIONS...
...THAT WILL BRING SALVATION TO US ALL...
NEVER MIND, I'M GOING HOME...

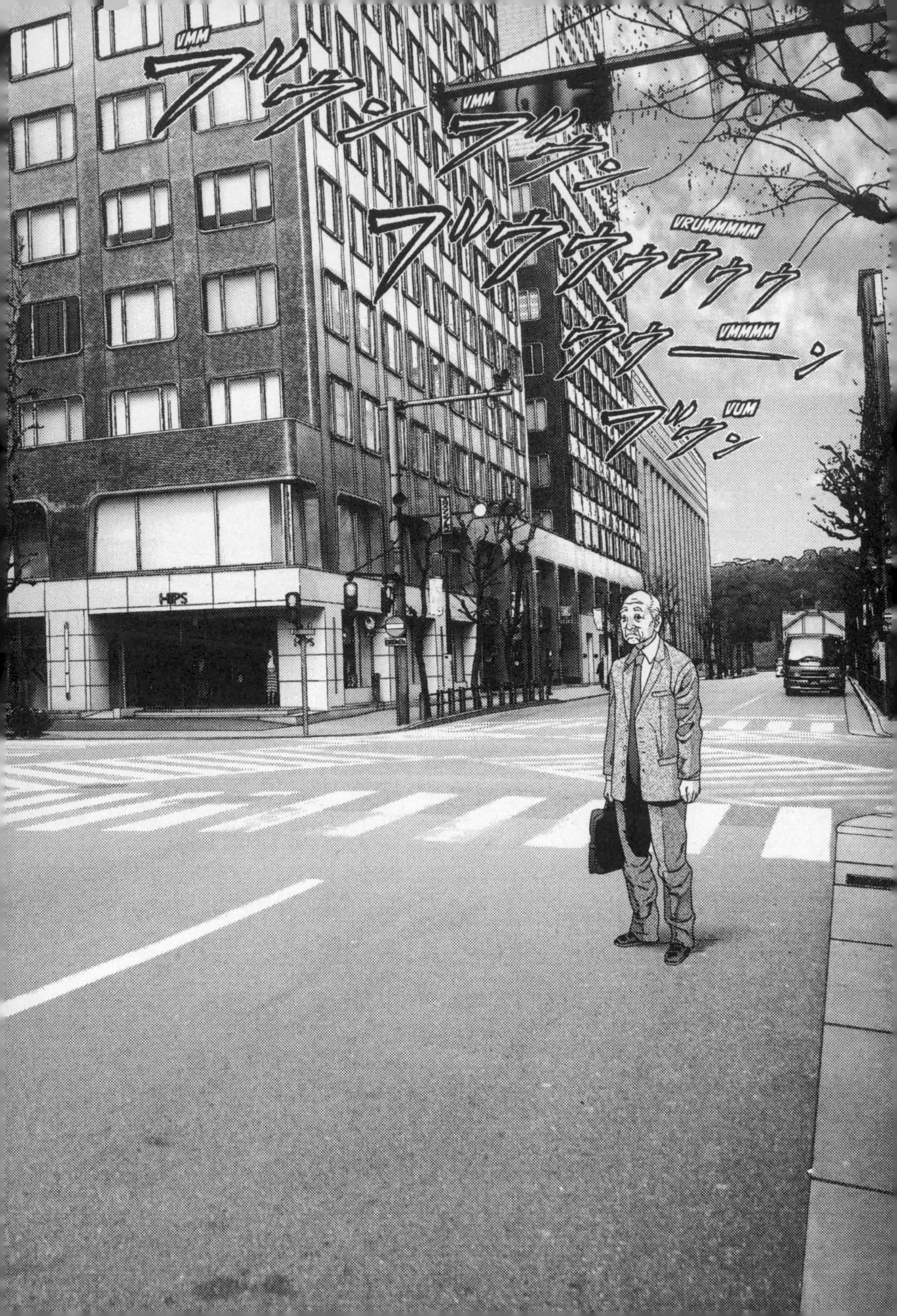
VMM
ブゥン
VMM
ブゥン
VRUMMMMM
ブルウウウウウウウ
VMMMM
ウウーン
VUM
ブゥン
HIPS

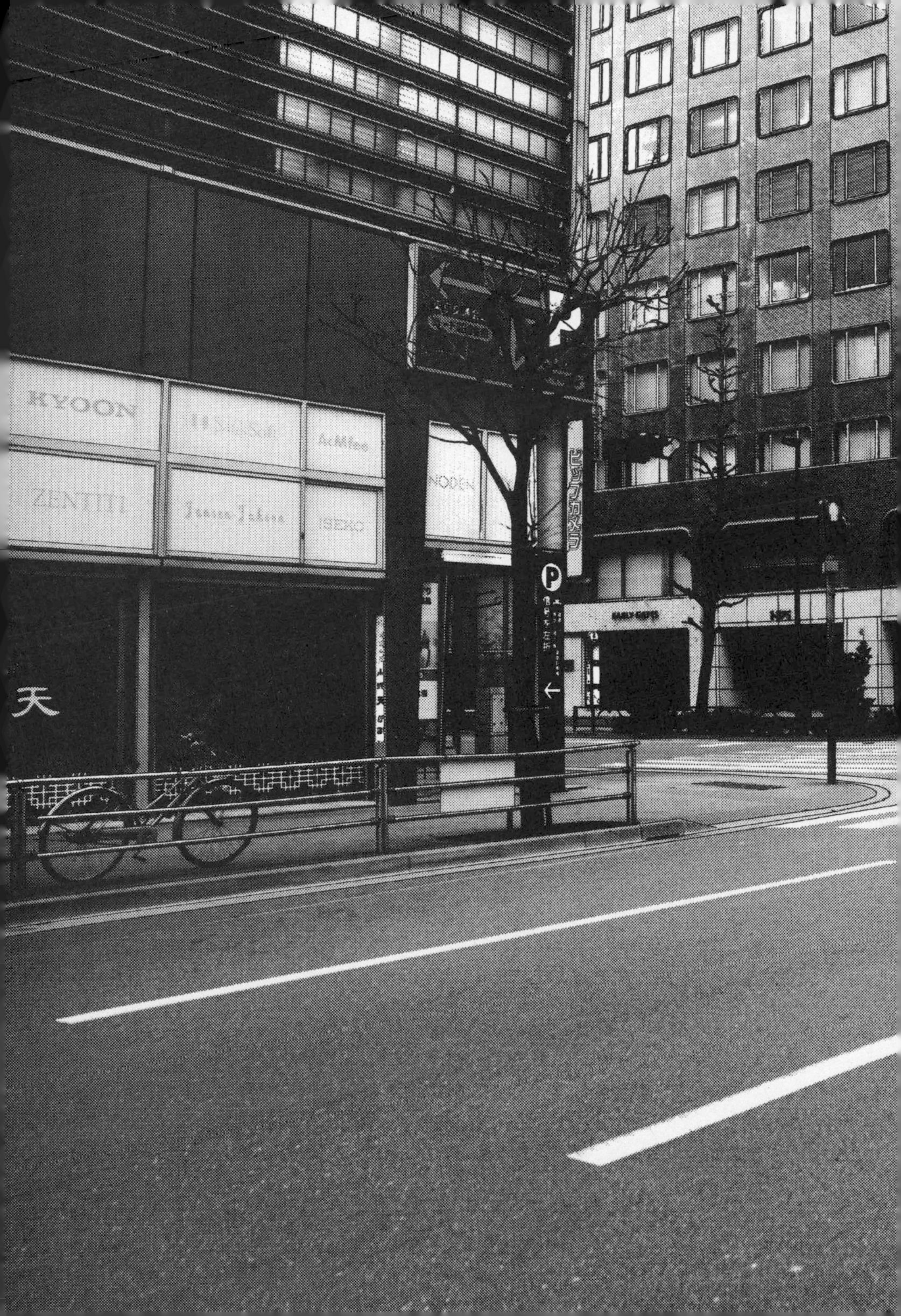
KYOON
ZENTITI
ISEKO
NODEN
ビックカメラ
P
天

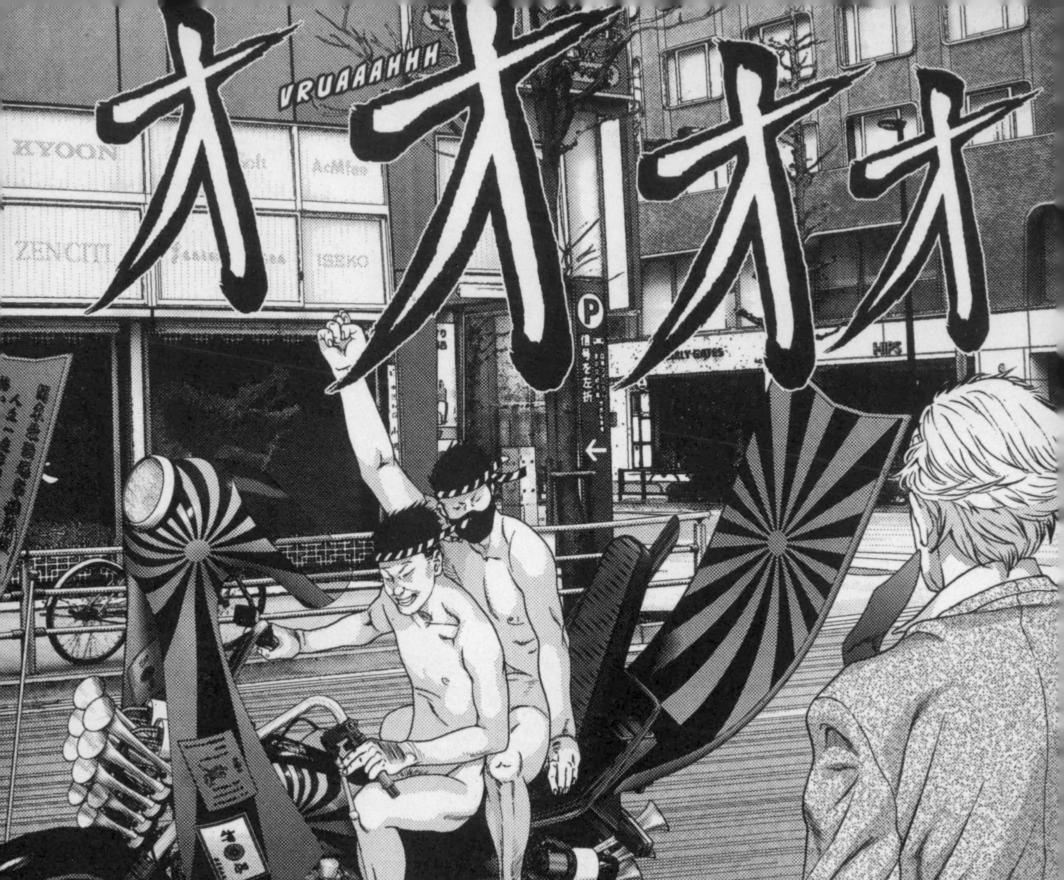
オオオオ
VRUAAAHHH
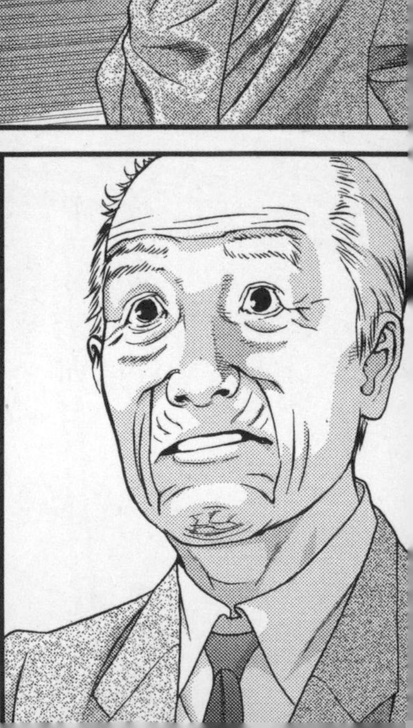
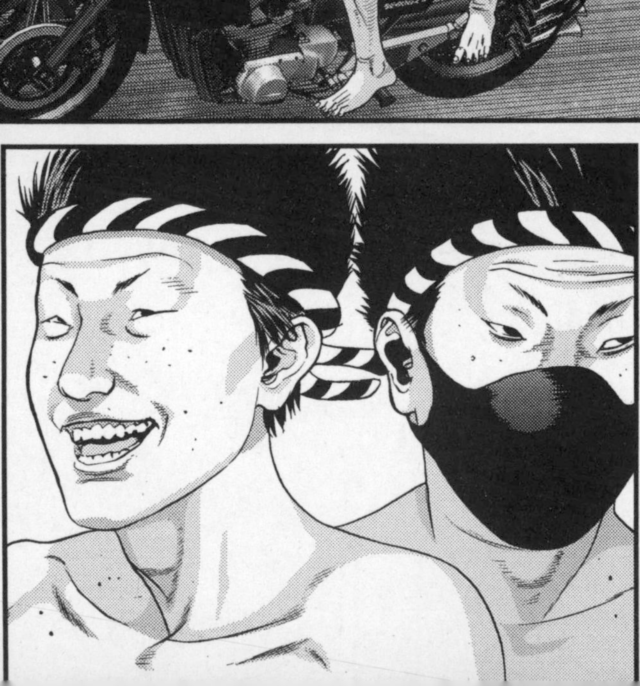

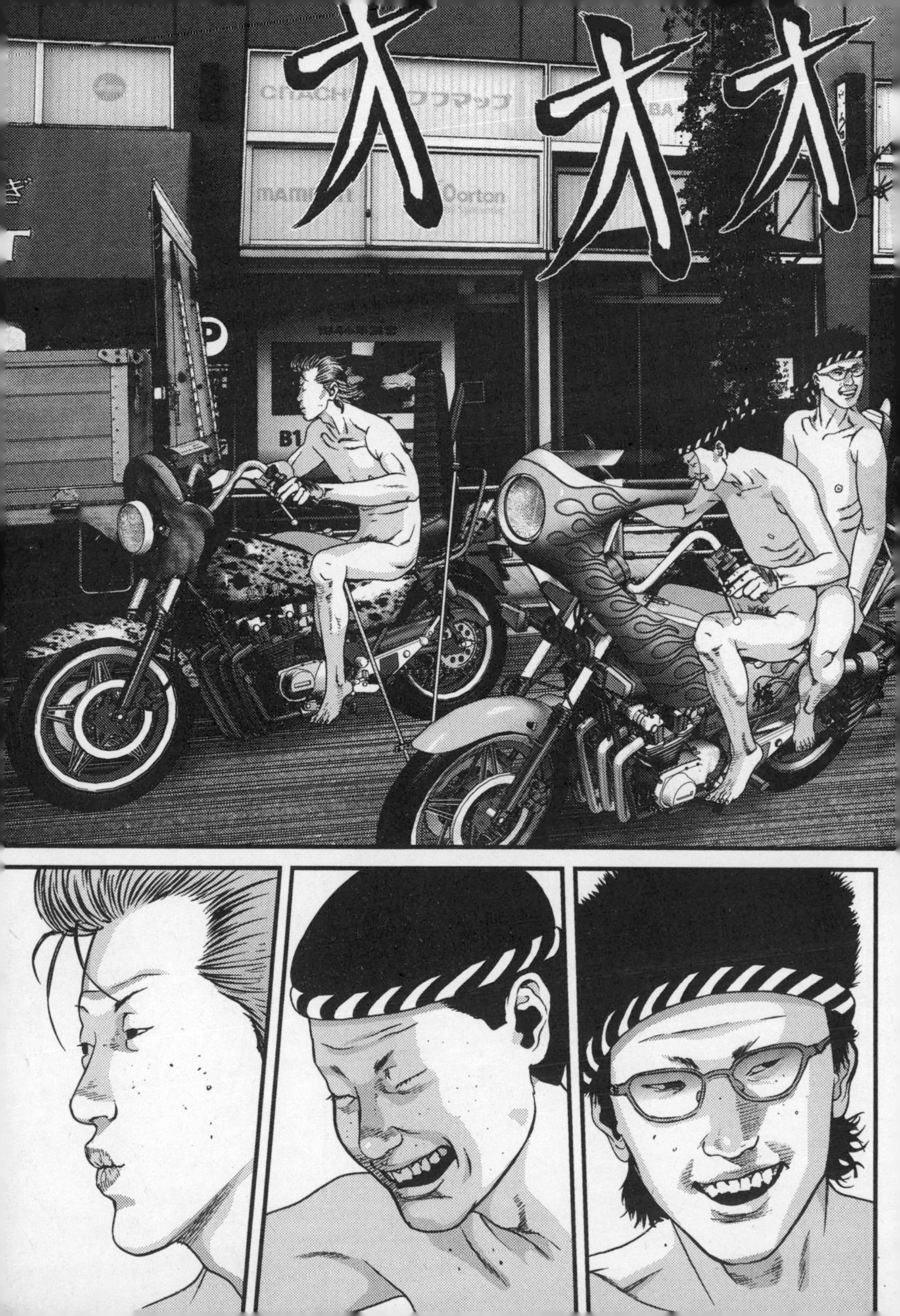
オオオ
B1

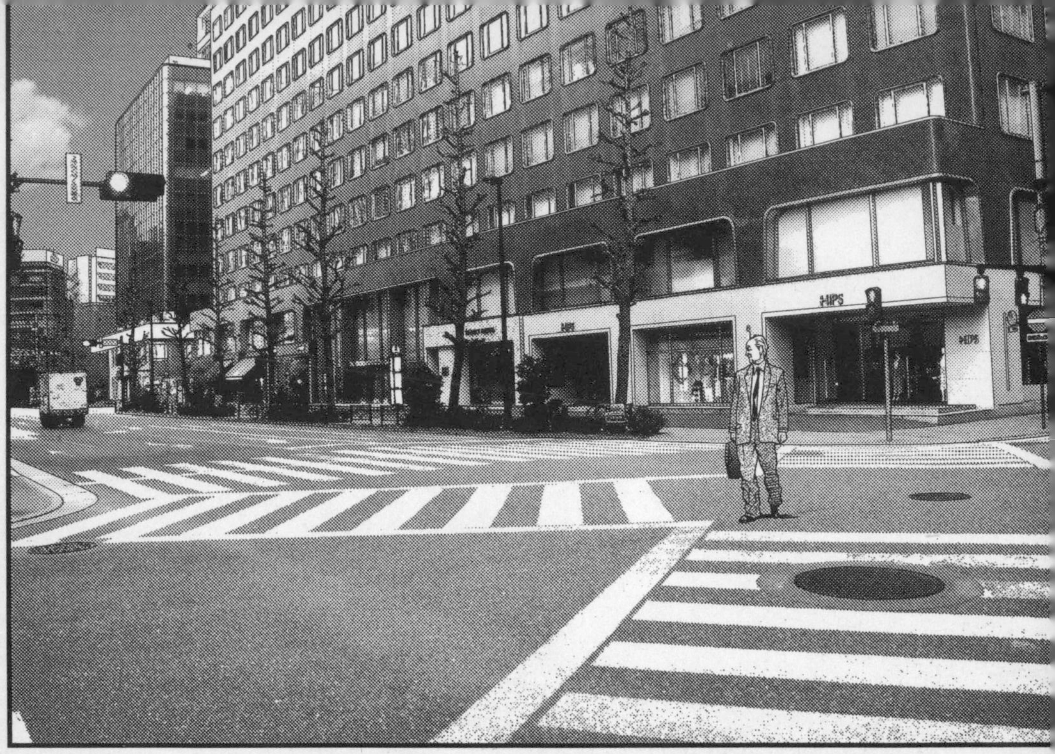

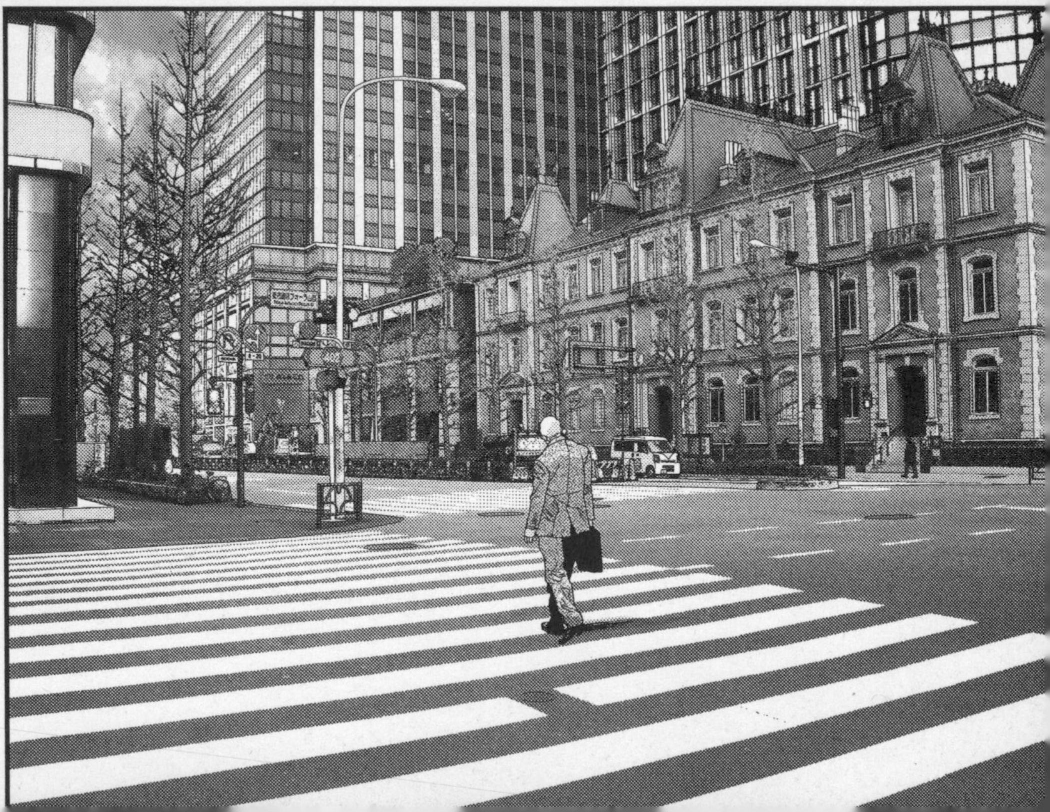

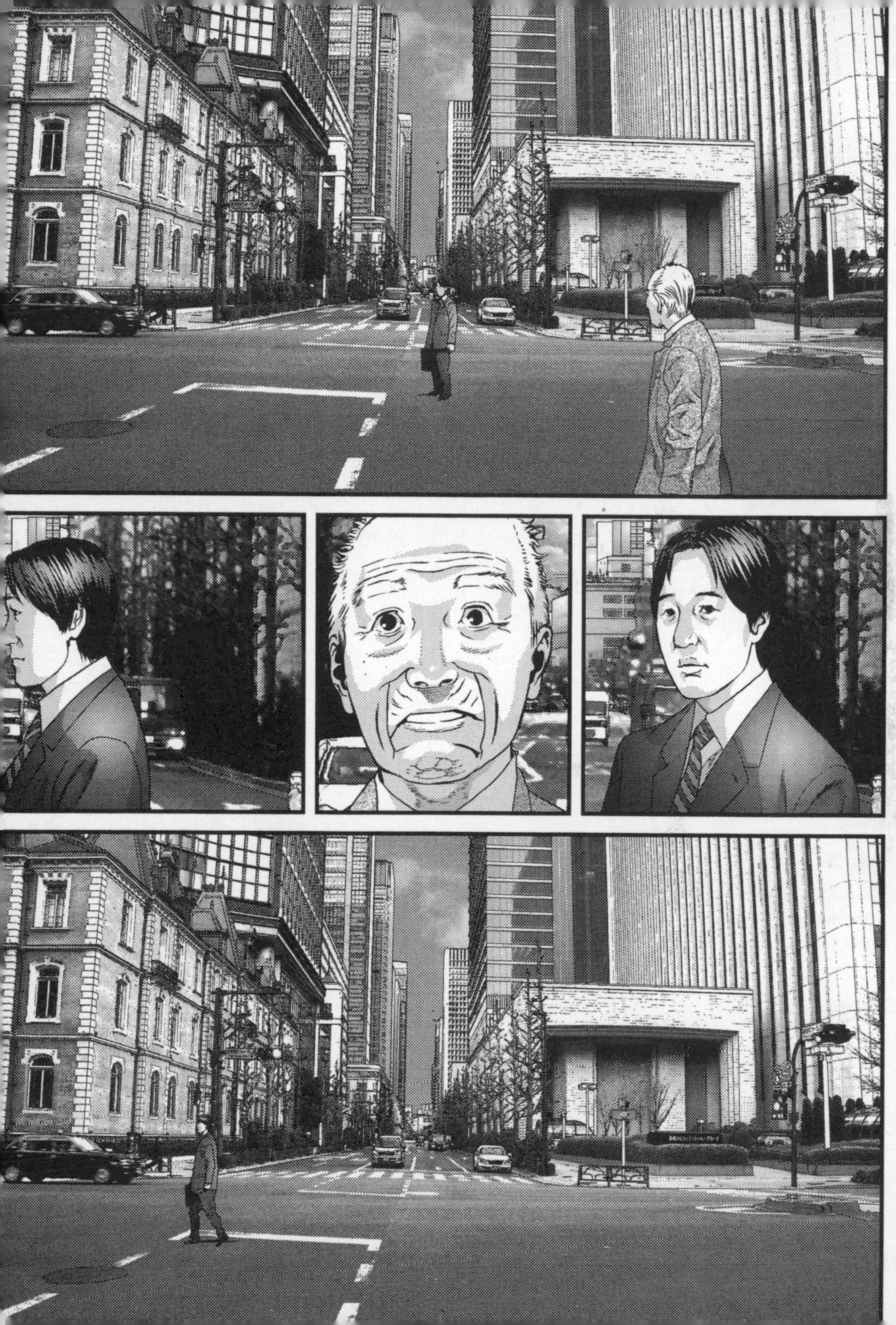

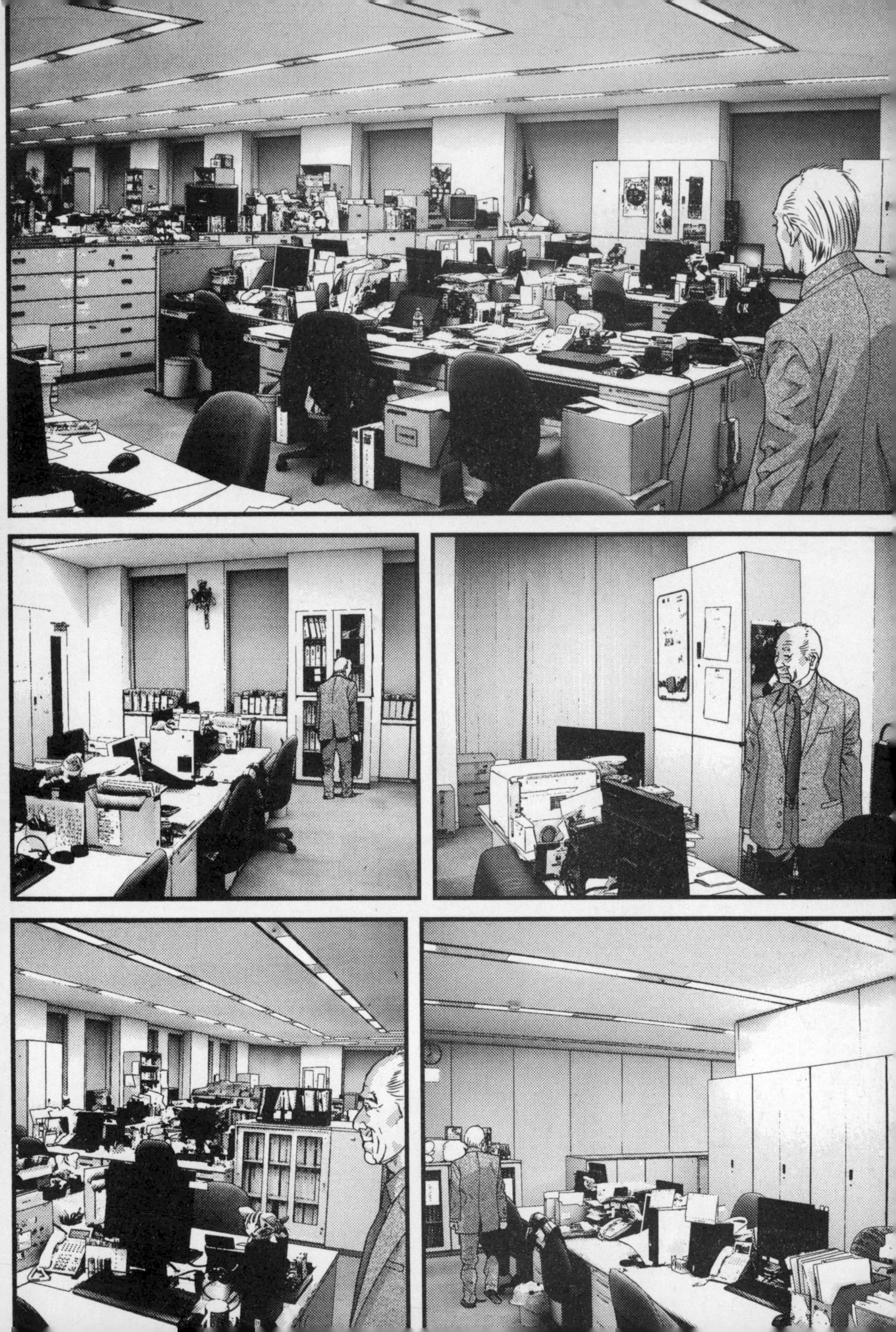

OH!
...?!
...

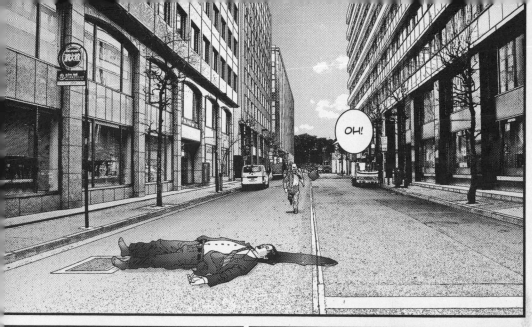

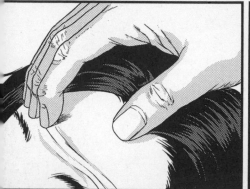

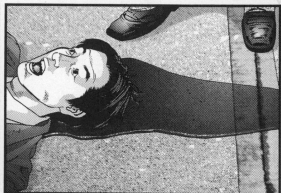

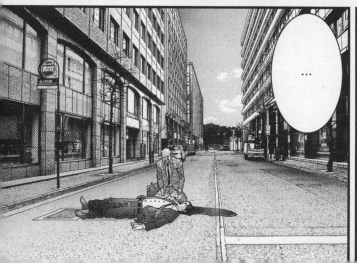

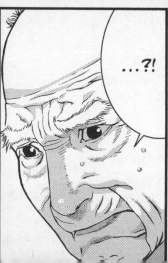

I'M TIRED OF ALL THE ADS BEING FOR THE ADVERTISING COUNCIL...

A~C~!

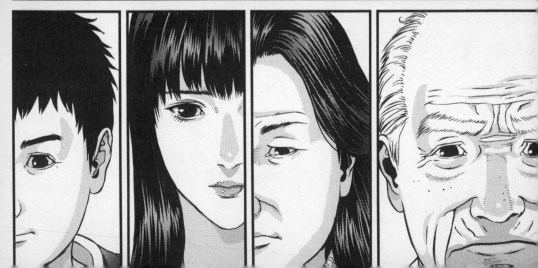

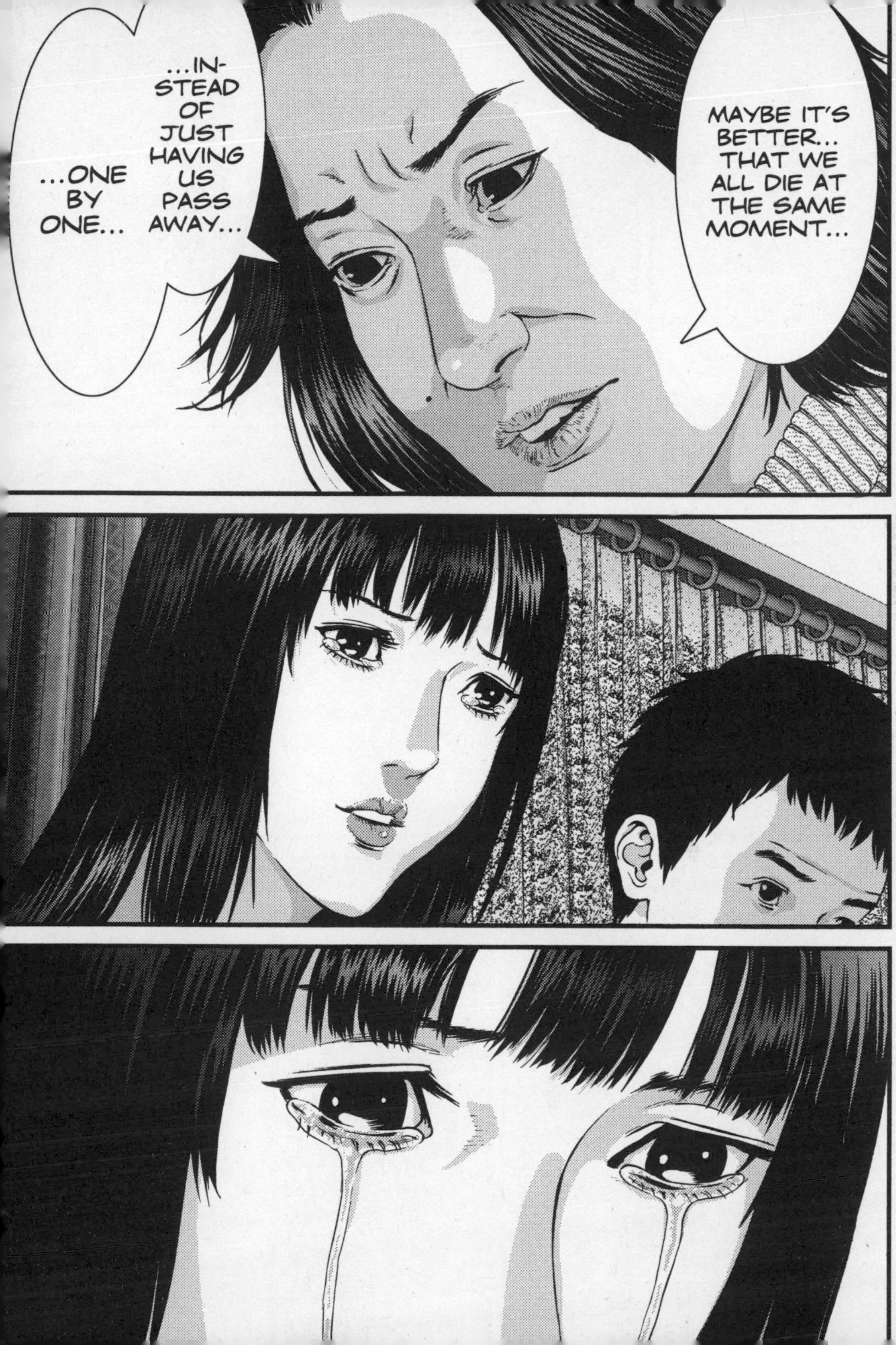
MAYBE IT'S BETTER... THAT WE ALL DIE AT THE SAME MOMENT...
...INSTEAD OF JUST HAVING US PASS AWAY...
...ONE BY ONE...

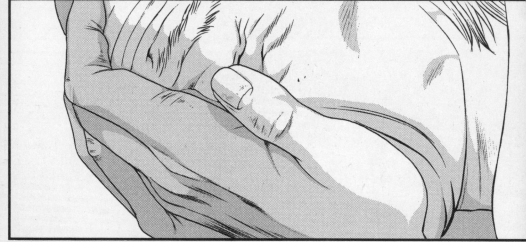

IT'S ANDO-KUN...

...OH...

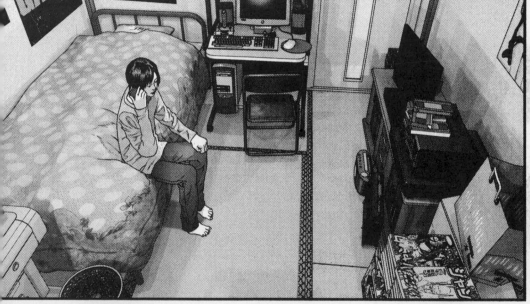

I'M SO SCARED...

I'M SCARED...

WHO WOULD THINK THAT IT'D COME TO THIS...?

IT'S CRAZY...

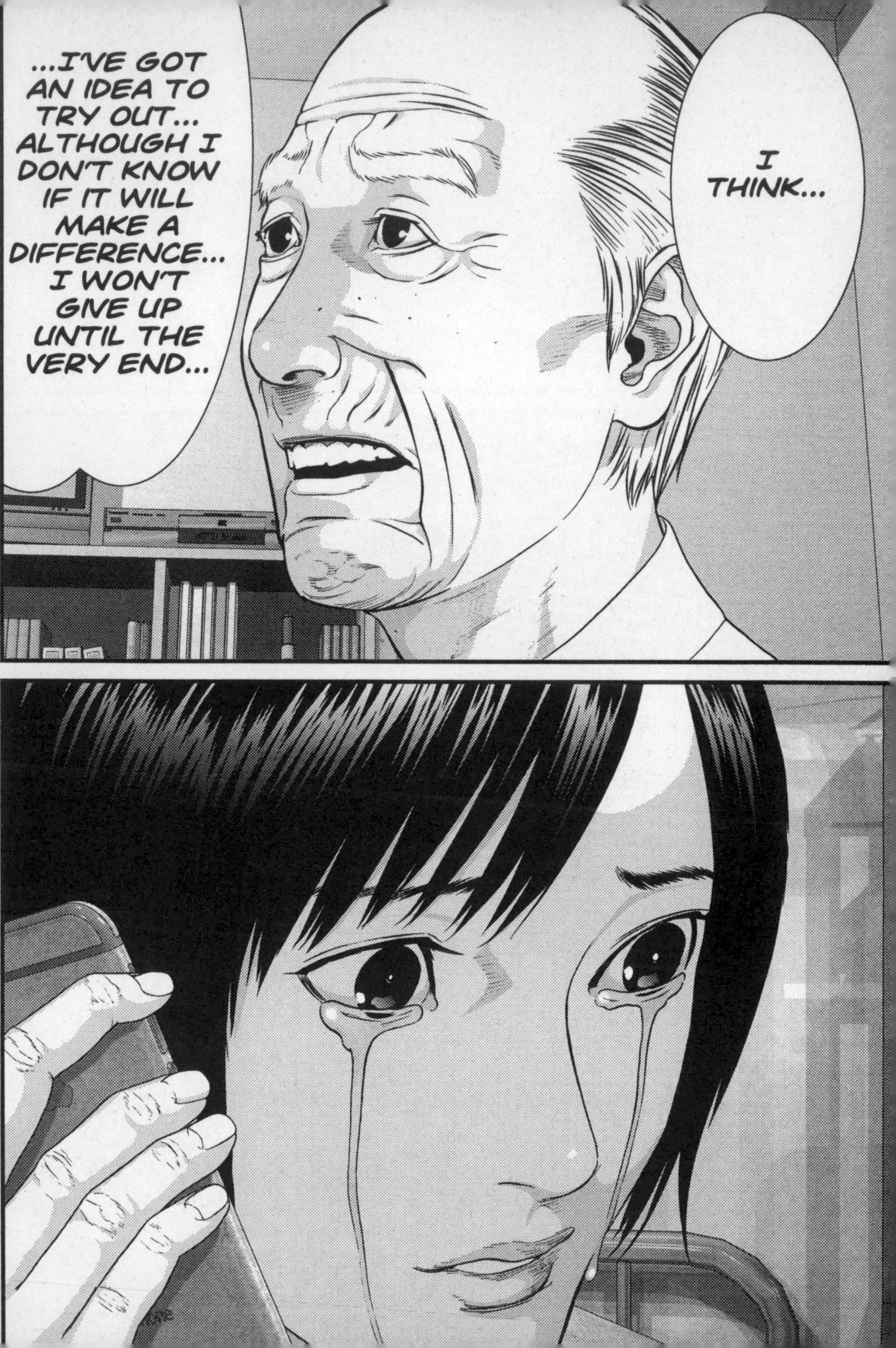
I THINK...
...I'VE GOT AN IDEA TO TRY OUT... ALTHOUGH I DON'T KNOW IF IT WILL MAKE A DIFFERENCE... I WON'T GIVE UP UNTIL THE VERY END...

INUYASHIKI 9 - END

Translation Notes

Atami, page 42

Atami is a coastal city in Shizuoka, relatively close to the west of Tokyo and Yokohama, that is known as a resort area for its ample natural hot springs. The name Atami literally means "hot sea," and due to its close proximity to the capital, is often considered a cheaper and more convenient vacation destination than Okinawa or Hawaii.

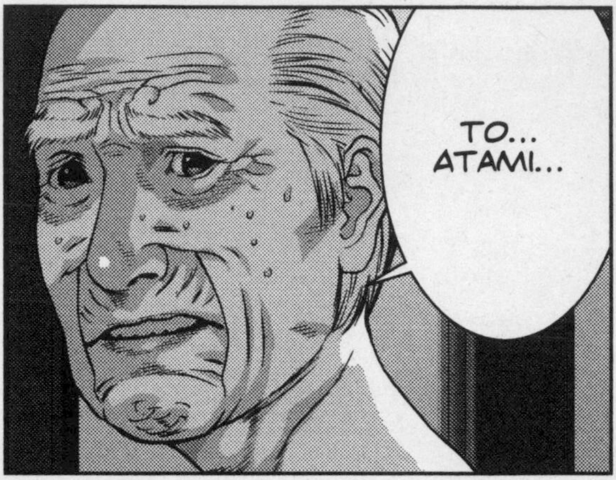
TO... ATAMI...

Forerunner, page 98

The name of a bipedal, humanoid robot (Xianxingzhe) developed in China and completed in 2000. It was quickly picked up on by the Japanese Internet and mocked for its primitive appearance and certain features, such as a cannon-like protrusion on the robot's crotch that resembled an erection.

982: No-Rehosting Anonymous (Laf3-lyrS): 2017/0X/14 (Th) 01:32:27.172 ID:a+9u
Is Hiro NASA-made?

983: No-Rehosting Anonymous (wf1a-kkJf): 2017/0X/14 (Th) 01:32:35.370 ID:0Hy
It's the new model of the Forerunner

The Black Museum The Ghost and the Lady

By Kazuhiro Fujita

Deep in Scotland Yard in London sits an evidence room dedicated to the greatest mysteries of British history. In this "Black Museum" sits a misshapen hunk of lead—two bullets fused together—the key to a wartime encounter between Florence Nightingale, the mother of modern nursing, and a supernatural Man in Grey. This story is unknown to most scholars of history, but a special guest of the museum will tell the tale of The Ghost and the Lady...

Praise for Kazuhiro Fujita's *Ushio and Tora*

"A charming revival that combines a classic look with modern depth and pacing... **Essential viewing both for curmudgeons and new fans alike.**" — Anime News Network

"**GREAT!** The first episode of Ushio and Tora captures the essence of '90s anime." — IGN

"An emotional and artistic tour de force! We see incredible triumph, and crushing defeat... each panel [is] a thrill!"
—Anitay

"A journey that's instantly compelling."
—Anime News Network

WELCOME TO THE BALLROOM

By Tomo Takeuchi

Feckless high school student Tatara Fujita wants to be good at something—anything. Unfortunately, he's about as average as a slouchy teen can be. The local bullies know this, and make it a habit to hit him up for cash, but all that changes when the debonair Kaname Sengoku sends them packing. Sengoku's not the neighborhood watch, though. He's a professional ballroom dancer. And once Tatara Fujita gets pulled into the world of ballroom, his life will never be the same.

KC
KODANSHA COMICS

Having lost his wife, high school teacher Kōhei Inuzuka is doing his best to raise his young daughter Tsumugi as a single father. He's pretty bad at cooking and doesn't have a huge appetite to begin with, but chance brings his little family together with one of his students, the lonely Kotori. The three of them are anything but comfortable in the kitchen, but the healing power of home cooking might just work on their grieving hearts.

"This season's number-one feel-good anime!" —Anime News Network

"A beautifully-drawn story about comfort food and family and grief. Recommended." —Otaku USA Magazine

sweetness & lightning

By Gido Amagakure

"I'm pleasantly surprised to find modern shojo using cross-dressing as a dramatic device to deliver social commentary... Recommended."

-Otaku USA Magazine

The prince in his dark days

By **Hico Yamanaka**

A drunkard for a father, a household of poverty... For 17-year-old Atsuko, misfortune is all she knows and believes in. Until one day, a chance encounter with Itaru–the wealthy heir of a huge corporation–changes everything. The two look identical, uncannily so. When Itaru curiously goes missing, Atsuko is roped into being his stand-in. There, in his shoes, Atsuko must parade like a prince in a palace. She encounters many new experiences, but at what cost...?

Based on the critically acclaimed classic horror manga

The first new *Parasyte* manga in over 20 years!

NEO PARASYTE f

BY ASUMIKO NAKAMURA, EMA TOYAMA, MIKI RINNO, LALAKO KOJIMA, KAORI YUKI, BANKO KUZE, YUUKI OBATA, KASHIO, YUI KUROE, ASIA WATANABE, MIKIMAKI, HIKARU SURUGA, HAJIME SHINJO, RENJURO KINDAICHI, AND YURI NARUSHIMA

A collection of chilling new *Parasyte* stories from Japan's top shojo artists!

Parasites: shape-shifting aliens whose only purpose is to assimilate with and consume the human race... but do these monsters have a different side? A parasite becomes a prince to save his romance-obsessed female host from a dangerous stalker. Another hosts a cooking show, in which the real monsters are revealed. These and 13 more stories, from some of the greatest shojo manga artists alive today, together make up a chilling, funny, and entertaining tribute to one of manga's horror classics!

KC
KODANSHA
COMICS

*New action series from Hiroyuki Takei, creator of
the classic shonen franchise Shaman King!*

In medieval Japan, a bell hanging on the collar is a sign that a cat
has a master. Norachiyo's bell hangs from his katana sheath, but he is
nonetheless a stray — a ronin. This one-eyed cat samurai travels across a
dishonest world, cutting through pretense and deception with his blade.

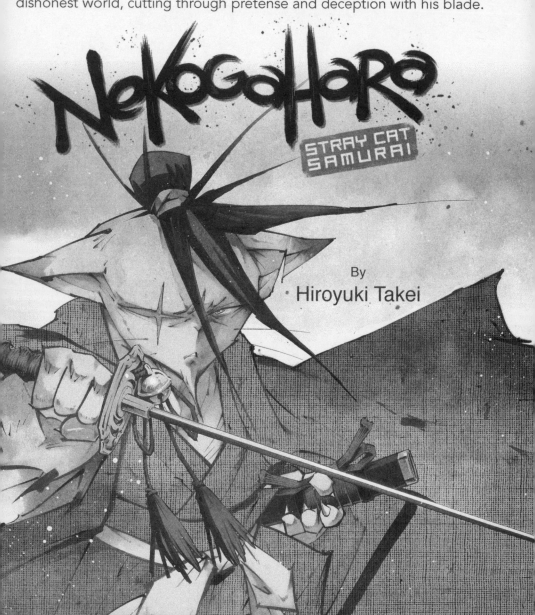

Nekogahara

STRAY CAT SAMURAI

By

Hiroyuki Takei

KC
KODANSHA
COMICS

Japan's most powerful spirit medium delves into the ghost world's greatest mysteries!

Story by Kyo Shirodaira, famed author of mystery fiction and creator of *Spiral*, *Blast of Tempest*, and *The Record of a Fallen Vampire*.

Both touched by spirits called yôkai, Kotoko and Kurô have gained unique superhuman powers. But to gain her powers Kotoko has given up an eye and a leg, and Kurô's personal life is in shambles. So when Kotoko suggests they team up to deal with renegades from the spirit world, Kurô doesn't have many other choices, but Kotoko might just have a few ulterior motives...

IN/SPECTRE

STORY BY KYO SHIRODAIRA
ART BY CHASHIBA KATASE

HAPPINESS

—ハピネス—

By Shuzo Oshimi

From the creator of *The Flowers of Evil*

Nothing interesting is happening in Makoto Ozaki's first year of high school. His life is a series of quiet humiliations: low-grade bullies, unreliable friends, and the constant frustration of his adolescent lust. But one night, a pale, thin girl knocks him to the ground in an alley and offers him a choice. Now everything is different. Daylight is searingly bright. Food tastes awful. And worse than anything is the terrible, consuming thirst...

Praise for Shuzo Oshimi's *The Flowers of Evil*

"A shockingly readable story that vividly—one might even say queasily—evokes the fear and confusion of discovering one's own sexuality. Recommended." —The Manga Critic

"A page-turning tale of sordid middle school blackmail." —Otaku USA Magazine

"A stunning new horror manga." —Third Eye Comics

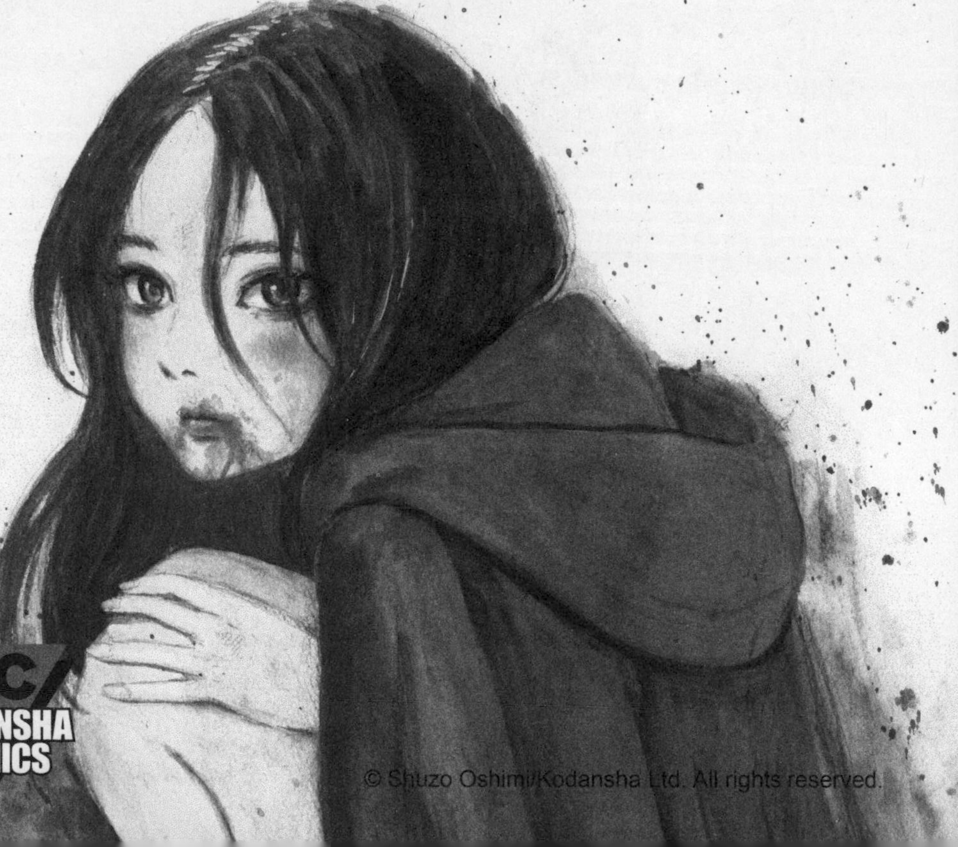

KC KODANSHA COMICS

A Kodansha Comics Trade Paperback Original.

Published in the United States by Kodansha Comics, an imprint of Kodansha USA Publishing, LLC, New York.

Publication rights for this English edition arranged through Kodansha Ltd., Tokyo.

First published in Japan in 2017 by Kodansha Ltd., Tokyo, as *Inuyashiki* volume 9.

ISBN 978-1-63236-554-5

Printed in the United States of America.

www.kodanshacomics.com

9 8 7 6 5 4 3 2 1

Translation: Stephen Paul
Lettering: Scott O. Brown
Editing: Ajani Oloye
Kodansha Comics edition cover design: Phil Balsman